The Villain

A PORTRAIT OF DON WHILLANS

The Villain

A PORTRAIT OF DON WHILLANS

Jim Perrin

THE MOUNTAINEERS BOOKS

THE MOUNTAINEERS BOOKS
*is the nonprofit publishing arm of The Mountaineers Club, an organization
founded in 1906 and dedicated to the exploration, preservation, and
enjoyment of outdoor and wilderness areas.*

1001 SW Klickitat Way, Suite 201, Seattle, WA 98134

Published simultaneously in Great Britain by Cordee, 3a DeMontfort Street,
Leicester, England, LE1 7HD

Manufactured in the United States of America

Cover photograph: © Ken Wilson

*A Cataloging-in-Publication record for this book is available from the
Library of Congress.*

♻ Printed on recycled paper

For Will Perrin

1980–2004

As gracious in his life
as he was graceful on the rock

Contents

Illustrations

Annapurna South Face, 1970 – Don belays Dougal Haston (© *Chris Bonington Picture Library*)

Don and Mike Thompson arrive at Camp Two on Annapurna (© *F. Jack Jackson*)

Torre Egger (© *Leo Dickinson*)

Mick Coffey on Torre Egger (© *Leo Dickinson*)

Making the headlines again, 1975 (© *Daily Mail*)

Don in the Red Sea (© *F. Jack Jackson*)

Gangotri 1981 – Don meets a yogi

Doug Scott's 1983 Karakoram ensemble

Don and Bill Peascod – Great Slab, Clogwyn Du'r Arddu, May 1985 (© *F. Jack Jackson*)

Martin Crook and Ed Douglas on Matinée at the Roaches (© *Ray Wood*)

Unless otherwise attributed, all photos are from the Audrey Whillans collection.

Preface

. . . your past . . . naturally has its share in all you are now meeting. But that part of the errors, desires and longings of your boyhood which is working in you is not what you remember and condemn. The unusual conditions of a lonely and helpless childhood are so difficult, so complicated, open to so many influences and at the same time so disengaged from all real connections with life that, where a vice enters into it, one may not without more ado simply call it vice. One must be so careful with names anyway; it is so often on the name of a misdeed that a life goes to pieces, not the nameless and personal action itself, which was perhaps a perfectly definite necessity of that life and would have been absorbed by it without effort. And the expenditure of energy seems to you so great only because you overvalue victory; it is not the victory that is the 'great thing' you think to have done . . . that great thing is that there was already something there which you could put in the place of that delusion, something true and real.

Rainer Maria Rilke, *Letters to a Young Poet*

What follows is an account of the life of Don Whillans, who was one of the greatest of British mountaineers, and one of the most characterful and controversial members of the British mountaineering community – in the words of Sid Cross, 'the hardest man that was ever on the fells'. It is written from the perspective and understanding of one who has spent his own life within that community, and witnessed its changing nature. That Whillans, twenty years after his death, remains an enduring figure in climbing legendry is testimony both to the power of his personality and to his extraordinary ability. Both aspects here present problems. To bear witness to the ability has demanded that some of the writing in this book is of a technical nature, with which I hope any more general readers it may attract, who may not necessarily be interested in the detail of extreme rock-climbs, will have patience. The myths and legends that have come to surround the subject have been more difficult to contend with, and whilst recognising the value of story-telling in our lives, I have erred on the side of caution and a desire to establish their factual source in choosing from and relating them. I should make clear from the outset that this is no saint's life, and that no part of my purpose has been hagiographical. Whillans the man, with all his flaws and shortcomings as well as his remarkable gifts, is what has interested me. This is a tale of squandered talent and a life that was to far too great an extent soured by resentment and circumscribed by the more negative values of his background. It is also one of exceptional accomplishment, and of a need and an occasional gift for friendship that were out of the ordinary. In order to body forth the context accurately, the language has needed at times to be strongly vernacular, and accounts of some events that took place, however neutrally related, can make disturbing reading. Again, I hope the reader will bear with me here and understand the necessity.

Don's legacy of rock-climbs, in my own prime in that sport, I found impressive but not ultimately to my taste – their essential quality often centring more around affront than appeal. Many have asked me in the course of this book's genesis how I rate the relative contributions to climbing of Don and of Joe Brown, with whom his name is indissociably connected. I think they were very differently gifted, and vastly different in character – which expresses itself singularly through a person's climbs. Joe, to my mind, is the greatest of all British climbers. Don's flawed genius rivals Joe's in a couple of spheres of mountain activity – alpinism, and in a handful of British rock-climbs from his great pioneering days in the decade following 1951. What Don brought to his rocks and mountains, it seems to me, was an approach more narrow and constrained, focused more nearly on reward than delight, and in that lies his individual tragedy, if we wish to see it as such. It is inevitable in this book that Joe's character and achievements cast a long shadow across the story of Don's life – and one with which the latter, I believe, never truly came to terms.

I first took on this book nearly twenty years ago, shortly after Don's death and at the urging of various of his close friends. Don himself was someone I had then known – and known of – for over twenty years. During his life I found him at times difficult, at times extraordinarily helpful and generous, but I had no wish either to be camp-follower or close associate of his. After his death, in the course of researching for this biography certain scruples led me to the conclusion that it should not be published during the lifetime of Audrey Whillans, Don's widow, who was a good-natured, long-suffering woman of whom I became very fond. Her wish at the outset was that the story of Don's life should be told 'warts and all', and I have tried to do that, with kindness. I have been helped in its writing by a very large number of people – in a sense, this book has been written not by me but by the community of British climbers.

The assistance given me by some has been outstanding, and I would like to give my particular thanks here to the following: the guidance and encouragement of Val Randall during the writing of the first half was astute and invaluable; after the production of a first draft, the commentary and amplification from three good old friends, Joe Brown, Chris Bonington and Derek Walker, have ensured that an inadequate account has become more rounded, judicious and complete. They have, on frequent occasions, saved me from myself, and I thank them for that and for their contributions. If this book possesses any merit, much of it is due to them. The factional nature of British climbing being as it is, this has been an extremely difficult book to write, one that I have often regretted taking on and viewed as a poisoned chalice. These last few months in particular have given me the sense of a book that did not want to be written. My son's death has made its completion very painful and arduous, but this has been balanced by the brave support of my wife, and the warmth and generosity that have flowed from the community of climbing, to which I give my heartfelt thanks. I need to thank also two other people whose roles have been crucial in this time. Keith Robertson, an old climbing partner and friend of mine, has kept me sane and solved all technical problems as computer after computer bizarrely burnt out in the process of writing; and my editor at Random House, Tony Whittome – himself an ardent mountaineer – has been a model of forbearance, exemplary in his editorial skills, and a bringer of enthusiasm and wise perspectives when both were sorely needed.

To thank everyone else who has contributed to the book I can only do by a list, from which significant names will surely be absent as the result of my forgetfulness, for which I apologise in advance: the late Nat Allen; Sylvia Allison; Pat Ament; Jacky Anthoine; the late Giles Barker; John Barry; Malcolm Baxter; John Beatty; Martyn Berry; Vin Betts; Eddie Birch; Polly Biven; Maggie Body; Sir Chris Bonington for extracts from _I Chose to Climb_, _The Next Horizon_, _The Everest Years_ and _Annapurna South Face_; Martin and Maggie Boysen; Derek and Julie Bromhall; Joe Brown for extracts from _The Hard Years_; Val Brown; Greg Child for correspondence and extracts from _Thin Air_; John Cleare; Frank Cochrane; 'Tiger Mick' Coffey; Jeff Connor for extracts from _Creagh Dhu Climber_ and _Dougal Haston: The Philosophy of Risk_; the late Dave Cook; Ingrid Cranfield; Dave Crill; Ken Crocket for extracts from _Ben Nevis_; Leo Dickinson; Ed Douglas; the late Ronnie Dutton; the late Sir Charles Evans; Eric Flint; Bruce Goodwin; Dennis Gray for long years of friendship and stimulating company, for keeping us all amused with his tales, and for extracts from _Rope Boy_, _Mountain Lover_, _Tight Rope_ and _Slack!_; Ray Greenall; Tony Greenbank; Pete Greenwood; Tony Howard; Roger Hubank; Jack and Babs Jackson; Hamish MacInnes for extracts from _Climb to the Lost World_; Robert Macfarlane; Colin Mortlock; Bernard Newman; Ian Parnell; Edna and Alan Parr; the late Sir Anthony Rawlinson; Steve Read; Royal Robbins; Don and Barbara Roscoe; Paul Ross; Doug Scott; Tony Shaw for the invaluable resource of Shaw Library Services; Morty and Sylvia Smith; the late John Streetly; the late Geoff Sutton; Ian Thompson; Mike Thompson; Walt Unsworth; Doug and Ann Verity; Tom Waghorn for extracts from 'Confessions of a Yo-Yo'; Patsy Walsh; the late Ronnie Wathen for perpetual good humour and support, and a stanza from 'Don's Ode'; the late Audrey Whillans for support throughout and extracts from _Portrait of a Mountaineer_; Robert Wilkinson; Ken Wilson; Ben and Marion Wintringham; Eric Worthington.

Finally, a technical note: I have used footnoting extensively at times to contextualise without interrupting narrative flow. I hope this device does not annoy, and that on occasion it might amuse, the book's readers.

Jim Perrin
Hiraethog, October 2004

1

The Summit

At five o'clock, with relief, Dougal realises that the thinning of darkness he's been desiring and imagining for restless hours is now real, that grey dawn's seeping into the tent. He carefully disengages two months' growth of beard from the ice around the breathing space in his tightly closed sleeping bag and struggles into a sitting position. Ice-crystals which rime the tent's interior shower down on him, and on Don, who's cocooned in a corner, wilfully quiet, no doubt aware of every move being made. But there's no sense in two of them stirring, and Dougal feels small resentment at his companion's prolonged rest. He eases as little of himself out of the sleeping bag as is compatible with cramming a billy full of snow, lighting the Gaz stove and setting it on, then settles back into his bag to await its boiling.

After a few minutes he drops in another block of frozen snow; it dips below the surface, melts with agonising slowness. A little sally of wind jets a swirl of spindrift in through the gap at the top of the entrance zip, and it homes on Dougal's face, making him blink. At last the water steams and bubbles, though it's still barely warm. He takes the handle, pours it on to powder in the plastic mugs. It's not tea, but it's liquid, and that's all that matters as they begin their ninth day at 24,000 feet. He directs a dry-throated grunt at Don, who, right on cue, rolls over, perfectly conscious of the stove's position, and thrusts a huge forearm out of his sleeping bag for the proffered drink as Dougal goes back to packing the billy with snow.

The two of them are a team, and the front-runners of a much larger one which is now scattered among the other camps down the South Face of Annapurna. Their vaulting through to this position on top of the pile has aroused a degree of animosity among the other members of a highly motivated and ambitious group of climbers.

Tom Frost, the only American on this prestigious expedition that's ushering in a new era of British Himalayan climbing, acted as spokesman and voiced the objections of several of the other climbers when he argued against Chris Bonington's plan to send Don and Dougal into the lead. In his view the team spirit and camaraderie of the expedition was diminished or even destroyed by choosing two from the team and sending them ahead out of turn for the summit bid. Nor was his criticism simply reserved for the choices Bonington, as leader, had made. The comments he directed against Don and Dougal were particularly sharp, and rooted in mutually supportive values that had traditionally held sway in mountaineering:

> . . . is this teamwork? Up to now we've kept roughly in turn, though Don and Dougal have done less carrying than anyone else and have definitely nursed themselves for the summit. I'd rather risk failure and yet have everyone feeling that they had had a fair share of the leading.

Whatever the opinions of other members of the team, it was Bonington's view, as leader of the expedition, that its best chance of success in the final stages of the climb, as the monsoon approached and time ran out, lay with putting Whillans and Haston in the lead. He sums it up thus in the expedition book:

> Don and Dougal had a single-minded drive to get to the summit. They had done comparatively little load-carrying, but at the same time they seemed to have a greater corporate drive than any other pair. Dougal felt, and I think he was right, that he and Don made a very well-balanced team, that could not be replaced by any other pairing. Although very different in character, interests and outlook on life, in their single-minded determination to climb the mountain and their mutual respect for each other's ability they had an extraordinary unity – almost like an old married couple.

Bonington's language here – note that 'corporate drive' – reveals the hard-edged approach that can brush aside Frost's romantic idealism. His team is here to succeed, and Haston's view of Whillans reinforces the faith Bonington puts in their climbing partnership:

I've learnt a great deal from Don – simple things that I had never really thought of, but which are of vital importance in this kind of climbing. He sites a camp like a real craftsman: thinks very carefully of just where to put the box,[1] taking every possible factor, of avalanche potential, drifting snow, exposure to wind, into consideration. When he digs the platform or erects the box, the same thoroughness goes into it.

Whillans and Haston are very different characters, not men you can readily imagine socialising together. It's hard on superficial impressions to discern much common ground between them. Haston, a 30-year-old former Edinburgh philosophy student, is intense, lean and wild-eyed. An apparently contradictory blend of ascetic and playboy, his life has been haunted by tragedy. A gaol sentence served for killing a pedestrian in a drink-driving incident in Glencoe has galvanised him into modelling his life on some Nietzschean ideal. Whillans is seven years older than Haston. His great days as a climber are receding fast, his last significant achievements almost a decade old. There are mutterings among the younger team members that he's 'past it'. But he's a pragmatic pocket Hercules with a dismissive wit and a no-nonsense, get-the-job-done approach, behind which are concealed the skills of a master of his own craft. What matters is that the combination of characters works. They complement each other, the respect between them is palpable: '. . . we just untied our belays and carried on climbing,' said Haston. 'This is where mutual confidence in ability shows. I was leading but Don was only about ten feet behind. One bad move and I would have taken us both to oblivion.' Don's wryly respectful view of Dougal, expressed with typical economy and graphic Lancashire imagery to Martin Boysen, ran thus: 'When we get up there, I'll slip the leash and let the greyhound off!'

The intensity of expectation from both without and within that is operating on these two men is extraordinary. The status of the climb on which they have been engaged unremittingly for the last eight weeks is radical. It has been proclaimed throughout the outdoor and national press as the most difficult venture yet undertaken

---

[1] The Whillans Box – a very sturdy-framed square tent, easy to erect and redesigned by Don for this expedition. Made by Karrimor, it was to prove very useful on all the major British Himalayan expeditions of the 1970s.

in the Himalaya: a two-mile-high face of a steepness never before attempted at this altitude, leading to the summit of one of the world's highest mountains. All the great peaks of the high Himalaya have been climbed by this date. This is a new departure, and one that will usher in the next era of high-altitude mountaineering objectives. The fact, too, that expeditions to the Himalaya have only latterly become possible again after a hiatus of several years due to border tensions and skirmishings gives this climb added prominence and importance to British national pride. If Don and Dougal succeed in their ambition – and they have manoeuvred very carefully, or cynically, depending on your point of view, for the past few weeks to place themselves in the most advantageous position to do so – the effect on their careers will be incalculable. And they are both career mountaineers.

So what stages were those careers at?

Haston's was still in the steep phase of the learning curves. There had been his apprenticeship of early climbs in Scotland with Jimmy Marshall and with Robin Smith, the great young Scottish climber who had died in a fall whilst roped to the accident-prone Wilfrid Noyce in the Pamirs in 1962. The North Wall of the Eiger in 1963 and the epic ascent of its direct route, the John Harlin Climb, in 1966 were all behind him. So too was his 1967/8 failure on Cerro Torre in Patagonia – reputedly the world's most inaccessible summit – with Boysen, Mick Burke and Peter Crew. Annapurna South Face was his first Himalayan climb, Boysen and Burke were here with him. In terms of Himalayan experience, by contrast with Whillans, he was a beginner. He was also, in terms of human dynamics, a passive character who tended to sit back and allow situations to evolve to his advantage. He knew that Bonington was, in the words of another member of the expedition, 'in love with him – Dougal was his blue-eyed boy and he could do no wrong'.[2]

But he also knew, having climbed with him on the crucial ice-ridge between Camps Four and Five on Annapurna South Face, that

---

[2] Rather mischievous, this, on the part of its source. Dougal welcomed the pairing with Don, and Bonington concurred in it because, in his own words, 'they were by far the strongest pair'. He went on to comment that 'the thing the others couldn't come to terms with, understandably, was that Don and Dougal were in a different league. They had the extra drive of genius and motivation that were very complementary. Mick and Tom were very competent, as shown by their ascent of the rock-band, but still hadn't got that extra push. Martin and Nick were

Chris Bonington, despite his wealth of previous successful experience in the Himalayas at the beginning of the 1960s, was simply not as strong as Don; and perhaps Haston sensed too that Bonington's route-finding ability was less finely honed and instinctual than that of Whillans, the 'Deputy Leader, Climbing Leader, and Designer of Specialised Equipment'. He recognised Don's superior strength and mountain sense, realised that with him lay the best chance of success, and in consequence quietly positioned himself alongside him, colluded with him in tactical resting and retreats, and when the time came, had calculated himself into the right place with the right companion. It is pointless to take moral stances on this. The simple fact – as anyone who has witnessed them will vouchsafe – is that the personal manoeuvrings on Himalayan expeditions are seldom a pretty sight.

As for Don, this climb for him had an element about it of all-or-nothing. His previous Himalayan trips had been a catalogue of illness, tragedy and failure. His great days in the Alps and on British rock were dimming down into history. Some of his most memorable achievements – the Freney Pillar, the Central Tower of Paine – had been accomplished in company with the slightly younger, and less obviously and naturally talented Bonington, who had beaten him to the first British ascent of the Eiger North Wall; who had surpassed him in the perception of the newspaper-reading masses; and to whom he was now deputy. Putting aside the need for a result to reward the teamwork and effort of the entire expedition, for Don himself the psychological situation was acute, the necessity for success over-riding

But now, it is dawn on 27 May. Whatever criticism may be levelled at their tactics, Don and Dougal's acclimatisation programme has been well-nigh perfect. Bouts of activity and ascent have been interspersed with rest at altitude, with descents to base camp to recover. Bonington's ruthlessly unsentimental judgement is absolutely sound. In the right place at the right time,

---

tired from the amount of carrying they had done, and also had not got the push of Don and Dougal. I was going as well as anyone else in the team, and as leader had to take on the bigger picture and quite often filled fire-fighting roles to keep things going. This was particularly the case at the end, when I supported Don and Dougal from Camp Five, first with Nick and then with Ian, ferrying up the loads they needed to sit it out. Without that support they would have been unable to make their bid for the summit.' More on the politics of the expedition in Chapter Sixteen.

they are the right men for the job. For the last week their diary has run thus:

> May 20: Rest day at Camp 6 (24,000 feet).
> May 21: Climbed halfway up 1000-foot gully leading to top
>   of rock-band, returned to camp.
> May 22: Climbed to top of gully, returned to camp.
> May 23: Rest day at Camp 6.
> May 24: Climbed to top of gully and down again.
> May 25: Rest day.
> May 26: Rest day.

As a training schedule for a summit bid on an 8000-metre peak, that could not have been more perfectly devised. Now the time has come to put it to the test. Dougal, fully clothed even down to his overboots against the corrosive cold, sloughs off his sleeping bag and peers out of the tent-flap: 'The weather was by no means perfect. Spindrift and cloud were still making their presence felt. But compared to the other days in the gully it seemed relatively mild.'

The understatement in that should be acknowledged. Haston is not talking about the mere confusion of mist on a Cumbrian fell, or the discomfort of hissing powder-snow rivulets as you hack up the final stages of a Ben Nevis gully. His words conceal more than they admit. They disguise the bite of each frozen crystal at that altitude, the searing numbness it inflicts on exposed flesh. They own nothing of the cloud's disorientations, the shelving treacheries of its blank perspectives. Up there, success and failure hang in the wind's whim.

Already, below them, the monsoon has arrived, is pasting a uniform featurelessness of snow across the cloud-obscured face. Below the cloud, and invisible to them, their fellow team-members are anxious, concerned for them, aware that things have become critical and that the strength of most of the team has slipped away. Time is running out as surely as the incessant avalanches of powder-snow down the hour glass gully up which lies the first stage of their climb today. Five days before, Dougal had described the conditions thus: 'Going round into the gully was like entering a special kind of refrigerated hell. Don had never felt it so cold in the Himalayas and I had never experienced anything like it in the hardest Alpine winters.'

There is no question but that today is the last chance they will have. Ostensibly, as they leave the tent at seven o'clock, they are setting out to establish Camp Seven. In practice, both men share the unstated knowledge that this is the summit bid, that they are going out to balance along the fine thread tensioned between conditions, ambition and survival. 'Don said, "I think we should press on and find a campsite as close to the final wall as possible." I was in complete agreement but we were both obviously thinking of greater things.'

The 1000-foot gully takes them four hours – in itself a good Himalayan day. Above, there are 1500 feet to go to the summit – an ice-field, a sharp snow-ridge, a steeper, broken face of rock and ice. They are already at 25,000 feet, do not have rope to fix, carry only a single 150-foot length. This is soloing, finding the route as they go, on new and difficult ground that leads into the 8000-metre realm where life is only briefly sustainable. If the weather closes around them, if cloud and storm from below wipe every recognisable feature from the face of the mountain, then lost and without stoves, sleeping bags, food, oxygen, at this altitude their situation would be desperate.

They press on, Don leading, Dougal weighed down with tent and rope. Don pieces together an intricate line towards the summit ridge. Then he disappears over the crest, is hidden from Dougal's view, leaves the latter briefly alone. Dougal follows. The last 50 feet to the ridge are surprisingly difficult. Dougal moves carefully, brushing the snow from flat, loose holds. Beyond the crest, sheltered suddenly from the freezing wind, he rejoins Don, who is already fixing a piton from which to abseil back down the last rock wall. No words are exchanged, there is no feeling of triumph, exaltation, conquest – all those wearisome imperial abstracts that the uninitiated imagine to be the province of the mountaineer. Instead, they have to contend with the climber's usual summit reaction: 'The mind was still too wound up to allow such feelings to enter . . . the greatest moment of our climbing careers, and there was only a kind of numbness.'

They had achieved the most momentous ascent to that date in the history of mountaineering. From Annapurna's summit, it only remained to go down.

2

Railings, Ramparts and a River Stack

Walk down Salford's Blackburn Street to cross the Irwell by the Adelphi footbridge today, and you enter a world significantly changed from that of Don Whillans's childhood. In the crossing of the Irwell's water – no longer quite so black and noisome as it was in the 1930s – there is a challenge to your imagination. It is to take yourself back to the times and social conditions into which he was born – to reconstruct something of them from the traces which lie around and ponder how, anyway, they might bear upon a man's life.

Forget for the moment the tenement tower blocks along Silk Street which loom in the mist or cast their 15-storey-high shadows across Adelphi in the morning sun. Ignore the rotting posts, a scatter of crushed lager cans around them, of an abandoned children's adventure playground – a gesture of 1960s social hope – and the jerry-built contemporaneous maisonettes. These are not the clues to the time we seek. For those, you must look instead at the derelict street-corner pub, its gimcrack stucco steeped for decades in an industrial marinade of soot and sulphurous smogs. Or you must catch at the sharp sourness, the damp reek which clings to the piles of rubble lining the bridge approach. In their demolition, as in their life, that is the defining smell of poor housing, of the slums. Crumbled brick, failed mortar, sodden plaster, rotted timber – this rubble is all that remains, or deserves to remain, of the old Adelphi.

How the area ever came to be called Adelphi is an unfathomable mystery and a dreadful cosmic joke. Its social history over two centuries was a denial of the Greek fraternal ideal which the name so boldly proclaims. Physically, Adelphi is defined within a great meander, a horseshoe bend of the Irwell, low-lying, looked down on by the Georgian elegance of The Crescent, bounded on the river's west bank by Peel Park, from which on fine days you can look out over the rooftops of northern Manchester to the Pennine moors – 'the ramparts of paradise', Robert Roberts called them, describing in his autobiographical classic, *A Ragged Schooling*, how his mother brought him to view them from this exact spot. But as for the old Adelphi, from wherever you glimpse it in space or time, it is down there – physically, and socially too.

These days, if you saunter between the spiked parapets of the footbridge into the Meadow Road estate, the only signs of the old landscape are a few stained walls, left jaded and pragmatic among those of new industrial developments. There are bright new council homes of clean, warm brick. A well-dressed young woman with none of the weariness of the slums upon her crosses the bridge and balances a Sainsbury's bag on her knee as she leans over to unlatch her garden gate. An old man comes out of another door and idles along the pavement. I ask him where Nora Street was.

'Nora Street? Nora Street, d'you say? That was a street from the old time,' he corrects me. 'It would be just about where you're standing now, but it was no sort of a place. No sort of a place at all . . .'

His voice tails off. There's a look of pained remembrance on his face. The tones are those of the west of Ireland, County Mayo maybe, or Connemara or Roscommon I hazard, and he endorses the last. We look across the river together. The squat fins and black towers of Strangeways-of-the-riot fill the skyline. What memories my question raised for him I don't know, and don't question. But for me, the resonance is of the thousands of his fellow countrymen who fled the imposed, certain starvation of Ireland's famines only to die here in the Manchester and Salford slums in epidemic upon epidemic of typhus and cholera. Adelphi in the 1830s was Salford's worst slum and one of the worst of all slums of the industrial north.

Not that the Adelphi of Don Whillans's childhood was the pestilential sink about which Engels wrote in *The Condition of the Working Class in England*. Things did change in the hundred years between. By the 1930s and the time of the Great Depression, narrow cobbled streets and hastily built terraces had been standing here for half a century, had replaced the reeking scandal of the Irish immigrant workers' shanty town. Engels's working class had climbed a step up the ladder of social condition and become the inhabitants of Robert Roberts's *The Classic Slum*. Salford was now the 'Dirty Old Town' of Ewan MacColl's song – filthy, narrow, constraining, but with a bitter sort of romance about it too: 'Smelt the spring on a Salford wind/Kissed my love by the factory wall'. It was the social milieu of Walter Greenwood's *Love on the Dole*, strong in community, sentimental in its aspiring, but knowing in its appraisal, impoverished, supportive.

This, then, was the district and its history into which Mary – formerly Mary Burrows – and Tom Whillans moved, after their marriage in August 1932, to set up home at 105 Nora Street. Mary was 23, and came from a family with a tradition of soldiering. Her father was a regular army soldier who served in India before the Great War. A family photograph shows her as a small child in his arms outside a tent, with the foothills of the Himalaya in the background. Tom Whillans was 26 at the time of their marriage. Both families were local to Salford – Mary's mother lived in Earl Street, 200 yards away across the Lower Broughton Road. In the two-up, two-down, outside-toileted house on Nora Street on 18 May 1933, Mary gave birth to her honeymoon baby – a son, who was christened Donald Desbrow Whillans. (The 'Desbrow' was after a member of Mary's family who had been press-ganged into the navy but who had ended up being decorated for gallantry at the Battle of Trafalgar. His medal is still preserved as a family heirloom.) The birth was without complications, the baby healthy but even for those days notably small.

As parents go, Don could be thought particularly lucky in his. The balances and bargains of matrimony, according to the testimony of those who knew them, were struck sound and early between them. Mary was a warm, outgoing, engaging woman with a bright sense of humour and fine timing in the delivery of a story or a joke. She was physically powerful, too, and in appearance Don took after her. Tom Whillans was a perfect foil to Mary, laconic in style, an embodiment of the old-fashioned virtues of straight-forwardness and uprightness, a believer in the tried and true, in maxims such as 'having the courage of your convictions', 'sticking up for the underdog', and 'staying with a job – once started – for as long as it takes to finish it'. Study a photograph taken of him in his mid-thirties, in soldier's uniform, and the physical characteristics passed on to the son start out at you – the small stature, the broad, high forehead, the glittering, piercing eyes, the unwavering firmness around jaw and mouth. It's a strong and characterful face, that of a man not to be trifled with. But there is a reticence and a hovering kindness about it too. This was the man to whom Don was closest. Between father and son throughout their lives there flowed a reciprocal fierce loyalty and pride.

Tom's job was in John Allen's, Grocers. It was the type of establishment which awarded itself the epithet 'high-class' – an old-fashioned emporium with sawdust on the floor and a composite aroma of coffee, bacon and salt ham. The shop was by The Shambles – the row of medieval half-timbered buildings that miraculously survives to the present day in the centre of Manchester. Tom spent his working life there, apart from the break taken by most men of his generation during the 1939–45 war. He rode motorbikes and was reputed a good sportsman in his youth. Both parents, in the way of northern people from what is now termed the 'inner city', loved and yearned for the weekend release of the outdoors, for the breadth and spaciousness of the surrounding moors. That was the way out, the escape, the future, at a time when the present, to a child, looked like this: 'My world was the backyard and the entry and a set of railings where the river flowed past and I could see the footbridge that crossed the river and was forbidden.'

Across the bridge – the same spike-railed Adelphi footbridge of today – was Don's first school, St Matthias's Infants. It's gone now, cleared. Over 30 years later, he was to recall his first impressions of it thus: 'I couldn't grasp the fact that I had to stay in one place all day. I can remember looking through the railings of the playground and feeling like some animal in a cage. I thought: "Well, what they got me blocked up in here for?"' Railings, spikes, barbed wire, walls topped with broken glass – these are the ever-present obstacles which contain or debar the street kids of the city, and which spring out at you from their perception of every adventurous situation. In a more physical time, before video security equipment and rapid-response professional guards, a simple physical response was enough to break through the barriers into the forbidden environments. The initiative and independence of action required for this was evident in Don's character from a very early age:

My mother used to come and collect me from St Matthias's. I remember thinking, 'I can make it home on my own', so one day I tried it. I hung about for a bit waiting for my mother, half-hoping she wouldn't come, but I knew she would so I buggered off early and wound my way through all these streets – my first bit of route-finding – and I was really pleased and relieved when I got to the Adelphi footbridge and could see the house.

Don would have been barely five at this time. His mother's response was understandably less than enthusiastic: 'She was very upset about it. She lectured me and gave me a clout or two and I couldn't work this lot out at all. I thought it was a real big effort on my part.'

It was not the only big effort towards independence that Don made at this age. Mary's sister-in-law Dolly remembers being in the kitchen at Nora Street one afternoon when Don returned from school. His shoes were muddy so his mother asked him why he hadn't come by the road and footbridge. He calmly told her that he'd come by the river-bank because it was more adventurous. At about the same time she was called to Manchester's Exchange Station to collect him after he had presented himself at the ticket office with sevenpence in old money and asked the booking clerk how far that would take him and back again.

In 1935 Mary gave birth to her second and last child, a girl who was christened Edna. With the family growing and Tom's job at the respectable grocers more secure as the country came out of recession, a move to a better area was obviously desirable. An application was made to be put on the council's housing waiting list. In 1938, when Don was five, the offer came through of a first-floor maisonette on a newly built council estate in Lower Kersal. Less than two miles away up-river to the north-west, it was set in a different, cleaner, freer world than the one Don had known throughout his infancy.

> We went on a bus – a number 13 it would be – and there were rows of houses with gardens. I kept running on and stopping outside each one: 'Is this ours, Mam? Is this ours?' There were trees in some of the gardens, big trees not bushes, and when we came to our house it had a grass patch in front of it. The door was at the side as we only had the top part of the house. I always wanted the door at the front . . .

The 'cottage flat' had a garden, the address was 26 Stanton

Avenue, and the Whillans family seized the chance and tenancy with alacrity. One of Edna's earliest memories gives a graphic illustration of the newness of it all. She and her mother were in the sitting room of the flat when Don came racing up the stairs with an enormous worm in his hand, shouting, 'Mam, Mam, I've found a snake in the garden!'

Even today, Lower Kersal estate is compact, tidy and surprisingly green in its surroundings. Built on the west bank of the next great Irwell meander upstream from Adelphi, on three sides there is open ground. Littleton Road playing fields and on their far side the Northern Cemetery lie to the west. To the north, in succession came Brand's Fields, where shabby, empty tower blocks from the sixties now await demolition, then the wide spaces of Old Manchester and Prestwich golf courses, with Kersal Moor between and Carr Clough leading out beyond unhindered into rural east Lancashire. To the east, within the loop of the river as it curved under the wooded slope, above which the large, expensive houses of Higher Broughton stand, was Manchester Racecourse. In the 1980s, Groundwork Trust schemes and urban fringe renewal projects cleaned up the detail, planted trees, cleared eyesores away to produce a tidier, almost picturesque landscape. Today there are wild duck along the banks, spiky yellow gorse, and the river runs almost clear, a suggestion of gravelly bed beneath the filmy water. But even in the late 1930s, when Don was growing up here, it was a marvellous adventure playground, and one of which the young Whillans made full use.

Don's new school had only been open nine years when he started there in September 1938. Lower Kersal Council School is a light and spacious building in large grounds, their boundary defined by substantial green railings on the other side of which runs the Irwell. Moving into the area just before the start of term, Don had not had the chance to make friends, and his first memory of the place was a painful and unsettling one:

> You've no mates. You know you're on your own, and then the standard stuff for a new kid, first thing you get is 'D'you want a fight?' Then they gave us the old diphtheria jab [a numbing blow with the knuckles to the top of the arm], and I thought, 'Well, if this is a sample of what they're doing here, I don't want to know.'

Don was very small for his age – even as an adult he measured less than five feet four inches – and it's easy to imagine the bigger children picking on the little newcomer, bullying him on this first day at a new school. In the course of time, they would not find it quite so easy. His physical courage soon became obvious. Edna remembers him going to the local baths in Broughton, climbing on to the high diving board, holding his nose, jumping off into the deep end and relying on necessity to do the rest in teaching him to swim.

As he grew in confidence, the river became the focus of activity. At first his explorations were tentative. There was a point on a bend at which the water broke over shallows and could be waded to the racecourse bank when the flow was weak. One of Don's friends once dropped a shoe in here and Don, though he could not swim at that time, went after it. But downstream the river deepens and he was soon in over his head and struggling to the bank, where he stripped off and the boys made a fire to dry his clothes.

Eventually, even though it was then as polluted as any river in the country, an open gutter of effluent and industrial waste, black and oily, and even though, as Edna remembers, 'It was a well-known fact that if you swallowed Irwell water you'd be poisoned', the local boys, Don included, took to swimming there:

> We used to go in five or six times a day in the holidays and at weekends. No towels, no trunks. I just sort of walked out of my depth and then had to swim. I did some daft things there. I used to come out with my feet cut by broken bottles and there were hundreds of bloody black leeches that stuck on you. We used to have some good fun diving into great lumps of foam that came drifting down from the weir above Littleton Bridge. 'Here's a big 'un,' we'd shout, and we'd dive right into it.

There were problems, of course, about playing by the river, and one of the main ones was parental concern, which would naturally manifest itself as ferocious disapproval:

> There was a big log just off the bank and when the river was high it was covered. We played for hours on it at 'King of the Castle', jumping on and off, scrapping, getting filthy wet. You couldn't see the street from around the log and suddenly some

kid would shout, 'Hey, your mam's coming,' and there'd be a panic, charging round after your shoes and socks. If my mother had found out that I swam in the Irwell, she'd have killed me.

Even had she known, and even though this could never have been explained to her, she needn't have worried. The prudence which was to keep him alive as a mountaineer throughout a career in which so many of his peers were killed was evident in him, alongside the derring-do, right from the outset:

Up the river from Littleton Bridge was a weir, and that was a place that frightened the hell out of me because here was a lot of water coming over and the river was wide at that point and you couldn't hear yourself speak. The water was churned up white and the kids said there were knives under it. I was scared stiff of the place. Later there was one kid drowned there.

Another challenge which Don's discretion forbade him from accepting was the ascent of the 'Roman Bridge'. This is the pier which is all that's left, marooned mid-river, of an old industrial railway. You can still find it, a few hundred yards downstream from Littleton Bridge and the Racecourse Hotel. Twenty feet high and built of smooth red Ruabon brick, the water runs fast and deep around it. The invitation of the silky grass on top is alluring, but to reach it would involve climbing at least of Very Severe standard, and the same route would have to serve both for ascent and descent. 'I'd think. "Can I do this?" And if I thought I could – even going all out – I'd do it. But there were certain things I just wouldn't attempt, and swimming out and trying to climb that buttress was one of them.'

It was a wise decision. There is an insistent mutter of danger about the place. But encounters with features like this at any age implant their images in the mind. The consummation of which, perhaps, is in that fearful desire to climb.

3

Hang Around the Inkwell

An urban landscape through which a large river flows is a landscape informed by the forces of nature. As they cross high above it in its culvert below the approach to Exchange Station, Manchester people might dismiss the Irwell, along with its tributary rivers the Medlock and the Irk, with a disrespectful jingle about the Inkwell, the Mudlark and the Murk, and an involuntary shudder at the blackness down there. But for the young Don Whillans, who grew up in its intimate acquaintance, its presence was a power to be respected. When rains fell on the Rossendale moors, it flexed its muscles, gathered speed, the roar of the weir could then be heard from playground and house-door, the rats swarmed up out of their holes in the river-bank and into the schoolyard and Brand's Fields. To live with this moody changeling was to know elemental power and your own size and opportunity within that scheme of things. For the boy who was to become a mountaineer, the lessons so learnt were more than useful – they were invaluable.

The river filled Don's childhood imagination. When one of his teachers told him that there used to be fish in it, he queried why there shouldn't be still, and set out to find them for himself. And he did – sticklebacks and minnows in pools around little gravelly islands just upstream from Littleton Bridge. His first direct experience of climbing, too, centred on the river. Downstream from the Roman Bridge and on the opposite bank to the racecourse stretches The Cliff. For most of its half-mile length this is little more than a steep wooded slope. But at one point a buttress of bright red sandstone thrusts out into the river, 30 feet high and crossed by a thin ledge which the riverside path struggles to reach. This is the Red Rock: 'I did my first bit of climbing here, a traverse high over deep black sludge.' It isn't high, not to an adult eye. But Whillans is speaking here from the memory of a child to whom it would have seemed so. And the feelings which places like the Red Rock evoke in a child can insist on reawakening in the adult.

Respect for natural power and a proper response to the feelings it inspires are one matter, but sorting out your position with regard to human authority is quite another. The river-bank was exciting and adventurous not only because of the opportunities for natural play which it provided. It also raised the challenge of official prohibitions: 'An expedition along the river-bank was a risky undertaking. If the guards patrolling the War Department dump on Brand's Fields didn't get you, there were the golfers on the course which backed right on to the river edge.'

Ian Thompson, who lived on Northallerton Road opposite the school and was one of Don's closest childhood friends, gives an interesting perspective on their attitude, as seven- or eight-year-old boys, to these two sets of opponents:

> From 1939 on, they stored war effort boxes in Brand's Fields. There were piles of big packing cases higher than a building. We used to break them open and steal ball-bearings from them for our catapults. Don used to leap around on top of them quite fearlessly, and the idea was to let the guards see you so they'd give chase. It was a great game, really.
>
> On the golf course, there was one hole which was uphill to the green, which was in a hollow and out of sight of the tee. We used to hide in the trees and the golfers would drive 200 yards on to the green, then we'd whip out, pinch the ball and get back in the trees again. After they'd given up looking for the balls and gone on, we'd go round to the start of the course and sell them for a penny a time. We made a lot of money that way.

The catapults were an essential item in their armoury, and Don, with the same eye for detail he applied to the design of climbing equipment in later life, described how they were made:

> We'd walk down some of the streets that had privet hedges in the gardens and look for good forked branches. Mine had to be a perfect 'Y', and when I found one I'd go back when it was dark and hack some poor bloke's hedge to bits to get at it. These catapults were lethal weapons. We pinched the rubber

from a garage that had a pile of inner tubes dumped in the yard. It had to be red rubber, black was no good. We made the slings out of bits of leather and bound the whole thing up with shiny copper wire.

There were several uses to which the catapults were put. Smashing the glass in street lamps well off home terrain was in the usual unhallowed tradition of boyhood vandalism. Hitting the starting bells on Manchester Racecourse was more inventive, though it seems that facing out the chaos which would have resulted from doing so whilst a race meeting was in progress was too much even for Don and his mates. The elementary test of skill with a catapult was to break milk bottles which people had left standing on their window-ledges without breaking the windows. This was something which Don could accomplish quite easily.

Their main application, however, was in rat-hunting. The racecourse bank of the river, all along from the Roman Bridge past Red Rock and the golf course to Cromwell Bridge, was, and still is, honeycombed with rat-holes. Don, Ian Thompson, and the rest of his close friends of the time – Bill Holland, Arthur Crofts, Eric Hodgkiss and Jacky Wedge – used to stalk along the bank, imagining themselves big-game hunters, letting fly with the steel bearings at any sign of movement and cheering as the mud and sand spurted up. Don's recollection was that they never killed any rats by this method, though he himself had an impressive tally of rat-kills by another means. The Irwell shallows were littered with barrels swept down by the river, and rats lived in them. He would sit on top of a barrel, bang on it with a hammer, and knap the rats as they rushed out. Ian Thompson remembers with surprise the rapidity of his reflexes in this.

The other necessary part of their armoury for these forays along the Irwell was a quick pair of fists, and this Don certainly possessed:

The thing was, that you were on new territory once you left the street, and there were always marauding gangs of other kids. I remember once being stopped by a gang. I was dead small and very scared.

'What d'you think you're doing?' a big lad said.

'Why?' I asked, right back in his teeth.

'Because I want to know,' he said.

I thought, 'Well, I'm going to get clobbered anyway so I might as well get in first,' and I cracked the lad and laid him flat. That did it. I was in with that gang then because the lad I'd flattened was their chief tough.

Ian Thompson was involved in a similar incident at much the same time which gives a less innocent flavour to Don's native aggression. The two of them were walking along the river-bank on The Cliff side near the Red Rock when two lads appeared on the same path walking towards them:

'D'you think we can fight them, Ian?' Don asked.
I thought, 'Oh, no!' But Don went straight up to the biggest one – and I was twice his size at the time so I should have taken him on – and cracked him and down he went so I had to set to with the other.

Ian went on to comment generally about Don's behaviour at this time:

His attitude was terrible. but then you can understand that in a way. Because he was so small, everyone picked on him, and the result of that was that he came to hate authority, because it was always doing him down. He was always in trouble, regularly fighting, and he always had to prove things. There was another kid in the school very like Don, Jimmy MacDonald he was called, and a showdown between them was inevitable. When it finally came, on Littleton Road fields, it lasted an hour. There was a great circle of kids round, and they just went at each other. Neither of them would give way to the other, and it was the mother of one or other of them who finally broke it up, otherwise I'm sure they'd be there to this day.

It was probably Don's mother who broke it up. The only memory Don ever recorded of Jimmy MacDonald runs like this:

There was a mate of mine called Jimmy. I remember calling for him once. I was just going to knock at the door when it flew open and Jim came hurtling out. Right behind him, winging through the air as if it had come from a gun, came an axe. They were a hard lot, that family!

Another occasion on which Don's mother was called to drag him out of a fight sounds a different note, and one in keeping with an aspect of Don's character. His sister Edna tells the story:

There had been a period when Don had been in trouble more than usual, so when a neighbour knocked on the door and said that Don was fighting again, Mother pulled on her coat and dashed out ready to apply all sorts of punishment. When she arrived at the scene of the fight, she found Don laying into two lads, both much older and bigger than he was. She pulled him off one of them by the scruff of the neck and told him to stop or he'd get a wallop.

'But Mam, they were pulling the legs off frogs!' he protested.

'Oh were they now,' said Mam, putting him down. 'Well then, you'd better get on with it.'

And off she went and left him to it.

These interventions aside, lack of parental control was an inevitable side effect of the war. Tom Whillans, Don's father and the only person whose bidding Don would willingly and unquestioningly undertake, was called up in 1941 and sent for basic training to Wolverhampton. Don's allegiance to his father is clear from Bill Holland's recollection that whenever they played football, Don would always 'be' Wolverhampton Wanderers rather than the usually favoured and local Manchester United. After training, Tom Whillans was posted halfway across the world to Ceylon (Sri Lanka), where he remained for most of the war. The absence of his adored father for those four years – from when Don was eight to when he was twelve – was perhaps one of the most crucial factors in Don's formative years. It may well have affected his attitude towards authority, and in its ensuing sense of betrayal and loss have had a significant role to play in the disappointment and bitterness Don felt about the course of the most significant friendship of his early climbing career, that with Joe Brown.

Don's mother was put on war work as a sewing machinist in a factory making gas capes, and worked from seven in the morning to six at night. So Don and Edna, along with most other children from the estate, went to school for their breakfasts. 'Very good they were, consisting of porridge, bacon, fried bread and tea,' is how Bill Holland describes them. 'One morning Don tried to eat a long string of bacon rind, got most of it down, got into difficulties and pulled it back, bringing most of what had gone before on to his plate, which was not a pretty sight.'

By late 1940, before Tom Whillans was called up, German bombing of industrial areas had begun in earnest. Lower Kersal was barely a mile away from Manchester docks, which the German planes were targeting with particular vigour. So each night, when the sirens went off, the families would file down into the Anderson shelters in their back gardens. Tom Whillans had made two bunks in their shelter for Don and Edna, and Mary slept in a deckchair. Don recalled lying awake and watching the condensation run down the walls, or standing in the doorway and seeing the tracer bullets from the anti-aircraft batteries arcing up into the sky and the searchlights swaying across the darkness and the flashes as bombs exploded, until his mother woke and roused herself and ushered him back with a slap and a worried scold that he would get hit by shrapnel if he didn't stay inside. 'People said you could be killed, but it never bothered me,' Don recalled. 'As far as I was concerned as a seven-year-old, it was just good fun.'

The blitz on Manchester continued for weeks, Heinkels and Junkers and Dorniers loosing their strings of bombs on docks, factories, even civilian dwellings. The little terraced house on Nora Street which had been Don's birthplace was wiped clean away by one direct hit. The children collected shrapnel as souvenirs, traded particularly interesting pieces for comics, stamps or severely rationed sweets. One night a landmine dropped near Stanton Avenue and blew out the front door of the Whillans's home.

The authorities decided it was time for the children to move to safer regions. In Don and Edna's case, they were evacuated to Crawshawbooth, a factory hamlet on the moorland ridge between Rawtenstall and Burnley, 20 miles to the north. Their clothes and few childish possessions were packed into a pillowcase apiece, and away they went:

> My mother came with me. I'd no idea where we were going or in what direction. I remember meeting a woman in her house. I'd never seen her before.

'I've been expecting you,' she said, 'and I've got some of your favourite lemon cheese for you.'

'How do you know I like lemon cheese?' I asked her.

'A little bird told me,' she replied.

'A little bird?' I thought. 'This is a real set-up, this! How could a little bird have told her?'

My mother went, and that was that. I thought she'd gone for good.

The emotional shock of a parting like this should not be underestimated, nor the pain implicit in that last line ignored. At first, in fact, Don's mother and sister were billeted only a few streets away, but Don's father, who had not yet been called up, fell ill and Mary went back to Lower Kersal with Edna to look after him. Don's separation from her lasted six months, after which – the worst of the blitz over – it was deemed safe enough for children to return to Salford. Almost as soon as he arrived back, his father's call-up papers arrived, instructing him to report to the Royal Pioneer Corps.

Mary Whillans continued at her war work, and Don was left not only with lots of time on his hands, but also with the responsibility of looking after his little sister. Since his favourite activities were swimming in the Irwell, scrumping apples from the orchards in the gardens of the big houses along Oaklands Road, and playing on the 'death slide' on the firemen's training ground at Moor Lane, Edna was found to have her uses. 'Having been told that he had to look after me while Mam was at work, he soon had me trained as a look-out. I had big blue eyes, blonde hair done up in a big pink bow, and the most piercing whistle you ever heard, so as a look-out I was the best in the business and they never got caught.' Edna goes on to describe what it was like to have a big brother as physically audacious as Don. 'I used to trail him around like a shadow. Even his friends found his exploits difficult to keep up with. I was two years his junior and a girl to boot, but I was determined not to be left out.'

If you meet Edna today, you notice immediately the breadth of her shoulders and her good humour in recalling these times, and conclude that this would have been a girl who would have been as good as her word. One story she tells, which reflects on the growing reputation of Don in the district, is of walking back home along Moor Lane with a girlfriend one night when a boy accosted them.

Matters became tense. Edna describes taking a swing at him and feeling his nose crunch beneath her fist. He landed in the gutter, scrambled furiously to his feet, and was about to launch himself upon her when his companion warned him that it was Whillans's sister he was fighting, at which the attacker ran off into the night, blood streaming from his face.

Don and Edna grew up, then, in wartime as 'latch-key kids' – except that, in Edna's account, the latch-key was superfluous:

> It was the custom during wartime for people to leave the door-key hanging inside the letterbox on a piece of string. But that method of entry was too tame for a budding mountaineer. When he came home from school, Don used to climb up the drainpipe and go in through the bathroom window. Of course, being his shadow I had to follow. I drew the line, however, at using the bedroom window as an emergency exit. The long reach to a shaky drainpipe and the drop to the path below – I never had a head for heights – were too much for me. To Don's disgust I used to use the front door. I would have been eight at this time, and I won back Don's respect when I became one of the few girls to go down the Devil's Sledge Run on the golf links, and to go on the boy's slide in the playground.
>
> Another thing I remember was the way Don had of getting out of the garden. He'd climb the plane tree, crawl out along a branch till he could reach the cross-bar of the street lamp, and swing on that till he had the momentum to clear the privet hedge and land in the middle of the road. One more promise of his future climbing came when we were both supposed to be confined to bed with measles and he swung and jumped round the bedroom by the furniture and the picture rail, for the challenge and to get some exercise.
>
> I believe that in those days Don was fearless. In fact, I think he was always fearless, but as he grew older and more experienced, he learnt to assess risk with an unerring instinct, and invariably he was right. But it was still hair-raising to watch. We used to have to go to visit our grandparents on Earl Street on Sundays, and had to cross two bridges – one with a stone parapet and one with iron girders – to get there. It was a point of honour with Don that he crossed only by the

parapet and the girders. I used to keep my fingers crossed until he was safely across each one, going and coming back. The Irwell wasn't a river you'd want to fall into from those heights.

Bill Holland backs up Edna's view with the recollection of seeing Don race Jimmy MacDonald across the top of the Irwell bridge by the Albion dog-track and win at a tremendous speed. The stone parapet of this bridge, 30 feet above the water, is sharply ridged. To cross it at any speed would be a feat of balance; to run across is one of great gymnastic skill.

Whilst Don's reputation along the river-bank was established, official perception of him in school was radically different. Ian Thompson notes, with devastating logic, that 'He hated authority, authority was invested in schoolteachers, therefore he hated schoolteachers too.' This apparently insoluble situation was further exacerbated by the arrival at Lower Kersal Council School when Don was eight of a new headmaster. His name was Arthur Gale. In his youth – something which might have recommended him as a hero to many schoolboys – he had played professional football for West Bromwich Albion, and when they won the FA Cup he was reputed to have scored a goal in every round. Any popularity he might have gained from that was militated against by the fact that, as a schoolmaster, he was of the Wackford Squeers persuasion. Ian Thompson again:

> He was some disciplinarian! He used to give you a crack round the ear soon as look at you, and he'd been a professional footballer, mind, so he was a powerful bloke and they used to hurt. He wore a hearing aid, and I think quite often misheard what the kids said, assumed it was cheeky, and hit them for it anyway. I'm sure Don came by a lot of cracks that way. There was no love lost between them.

Edna adds her view of Arthur Gale to this:

> The headmaster at Kersal didn't help. He knew Don had no fear of him and tried to break his spirit by caning him on the slightest excuse. If he had had the foresight to channel some of Don's obvious sporting ability, as the head of Don's

secondary school did, perhaps Don wouldn't have been so impatient and dismissive of authority and red tape.

Don's own memory of the man was crystal clear:

> Shortly after I moved up to the Junior Department at school, a new headmaster arrived. He proceeded to behave like a new broom. He'd been a professional footballer and he could hit all right. Jimmy MacDonald was the first to get it. He came out like he'd had the third degree. I was next, and I was nearly dying of fright. Swish! My eyes nearly came out of my head. I shot off to the toilet, flushed it and stuck my hands in the water – that was supposed to be the magic cure. He really hurt me . . .

It's interesting that in Don's accounts the admission of fear occurs frequently and naturally, which is often the best defence against it. To some extent, to own your fear is to exorcise it. From personal experience, I remember one climbing trip to the Himalayas where the member of our party whose posturing was the most persistently macho had what should have been the experience of a lifetime ruined for him by the incapacitating effects of unacknowledged terror. Don's fears, however openly he owned them to himself, were never so evident to others, as Ian Thompson recalls:

> I don't remember him ever being afraid of anything, apart from being late home when his dad was there. When they were building a new canteen at Kersal School and the scaffolding was up, we challenged Don to climb it and jump from the top. It looked very high and no one thought he would do it. Certainly none of us would have done. But he shinned up there without any hesitation and jumped straight off the top. He wouldn't have been more than 10, and it can't have been much less than 20 feet.

Musing on his own psychological make-up 30 years after these childhood days, Don gave the following tentative analysis of his mental processes:

I did have to depend on myself a lot because my mother was so busy that I couldn't run to her at every situation which arose. Maybe this having to make decisions when I was young and sticking by them made me aggressive and stubborn, which a lot of people accuse me of being. And they're quite right too. I can be so bloody stubborn that nothing'll shift me. I tend to look at a lot of things on both sides and then suddenly I make up my mind and I just won't budge.

I was just the same when I was young. I'd say to a kid – a big lad, because I never fought anybody my size, working on the principle that they were too little to hit – 'Yeah. I'll fight you.' Then later on in the afternoon I'd wish I hadn't said it, but I wouldn't back out. Once I'd said it, it stood.

An account of character like this raises as many questions as it answers, gives you a sense of the weight of separation and responsibility that was settling on his young shoulders. Where are the outlets for the expression of weakness and especially loss? What are the chances for journeying when everything resolves into confrontation and opposition?

Maybe we have to go back to Peel Park, above the old, now-bombed-out Adelphi, to find the answers to some of this on that high esplanade from which Robert Roberts's mother pointed out to her son the 'mountains' of the Derbyshire Peak District which he perceived as the 'ramparts of paradise'. Or perhaps we need to take, as the Whillans family often did, the olive-green number 96 Salford bus which ran from the bus station at the end of Chapel Street down Plymouth Grove, through Longsight and Stockport and out to Hazel Grove. And if we had alighted there any fine Sunday in the late 1930s, we would more than likely have found ourselves in company with the Whillans family, setting out on their Sunday ramble through Middlewood to Lyme Park, or past the Roman Lakes to Marple, Rowarth and Glossop.

Most Sundays, even after Tom Whillans had been posted off to Wolverhampton and then Ceylon, this is what they did. In 1940 Tom's two sisters Winnie and Dolly moved to Hayfield, and the foothills and approaches to Kinder Scout became even more strongly the magnet for Sunday hiking. Here is a story from Edna to end this chapter of a mountaineer's childhood:

One time when Dad was in the army and Don would be about 10, Mam took us, along with my friend, also called Edna, rambling, and we ended up by the river in Hayfield to finish our sandwiches. Whilst we were eating, a group of men, obviously very excited, came along the opposite bank, pointing into the water and following something rapidly downstream.

We got up to see what all the fuss was about, and were told that they were following an enormous trout that had been in the river for ages, and that no one had been able to catch.

As we spoke, the fish left the bank where the men were and came to rest under a rocky ledge on our side. The men started to give Don instructions. He was to slide his hand slowly into the water, curl his fingers under the trout's belly, stroke it gently, and when his fingers were right underneath, in one movement he was to scoop the fish out and on to the bank.

Don followed the instructions to the letter, and no one was more amazed than he was when the trout landed on the grass by his side. The men were delirious. One waded across the stream, shoes and all, grabbed the trout, and they all disappeared in the direction of the village. It was only after they'd gone that we realised the colossal cheek of it. After Don had caught the fish, they'd made off with it!

However, he'd got the taste for tickling trout[1], and with his terrific reflexes, it wasn't long before we had four or five other big ones to take home with us for supper, and with rationing well in force, that was a real treat.

Even in this idyllic environment of Sunday escape, the story hammers home, through the men's behaviour, the necessity for guardedness and self-reliance and the impossibility of easy trust. Lessons like this in the careful marshalling of self-interest, achieving expression in his adult life, were to exact a high price as Don's greater mountaineering career peaked in the early 1970s, and he came into conflict with the larger egos of the climbing world.

---

[1] In his later life, Don developed an interest in tropical fish, had a huge tank in his house in Penmaenmawr, and for his reading matter on Everest in 1972, whilst Dougal Haston was flitting through *Lord of the Rings* ('Fucking fairies!' was Don's considered verdict on Tolkien's ersatz medievalism), Don's reading matter was the *Observer's Book of Tropical Fish* – which choice gave him a definite weight advantage.

4

Escapee

Attitude – contemporary youth-focused culture uses the word with guarded approval. For those of Don's generation, running hard against the ossified values of an apparently secure social order, the word was more pejorative. It was a branding, was used to express a rebellious nature which demanded stern response. Inevitably, that was what Don received when, in the autumn of 1944, he moved on to Broughton Secondary Modern School.

All the accounts of his contemporaries, as well as his own recollections, suggest that he was aggressively uninterested in school work, and both surly and uncooperative in his relationships with teachers. He was made to sit at the front of the class, and girls were put alongside him in the belief that they were a civilising influence. The arrangement appears for the most part to have been mutually distasteful. In Ian Thompson's account, which strikes rather an odd note given the small age difference between Don and his sister, 'Don was frightened of girls as a kid, and because he had this reputation of being more than a bit wild, they didn't like him much either.' One of his classmates appeared to win his respect, however:

> She was very bright. She came from a scruffy home but she was always top of the class. She helped me a lot. On the other hand, I once had to put up with a girl who was even thicker than I was. What made it worse was that she had a crush on me. I used to pray for a change round because I wasn't making any progress in my lessons at all sitting next to her.

Not only was he poor at schoolwork, he was also poor at games, with all the social stigma that implied. Ian Thompson again:

He had absolutely no hand–eye co-ordination, and because he was so much one on his own, he had no sense of the team either. So in consequence, he was completely useless at the football and cricket from which most of us got our social standing among our peers. At cricket, if you didn't bowl Don out in two or three deliveries, then you just couldn't bowl straight. And when you did, he wasn't exactly sporting about it. He'd throw the bat down in a temper, and then he'd refuse to field. He could box, mind you, and every twelve months Broughton Secondary would have matches against other schools. But the thing was, Don was always disqualified. You see, he didn't realise that boxing wasn't fighting – so some kid would come along and plant one on his nose and when that happened Don would just go wild and hit them anywhere and with anything he could lay his hands on. He'd have used the corner posts if he could have done. So obviously it was the same every match – the teacher or the trainer or whoever yanking this flailing little wildcat out by his pants and holding him at arm's length while the other lad, having picked himself up off the canvas, was given the bout.[1]

He was in trouble continually. Every Friday he turned up in the 'other activities', the school's punishment zone, where the genteel pursuits of chess or gardening were intended to inculcate a little mildness in the miscreants' savage breasts. Part of Don's difficulty was a near-total inability to submit to what he saw as unjust authority. There was one master, a Mr Burke, with whom he got on particularly badly. One lunchtime Don was accused by Burke of causing some petty piece of trouble of which he was quite innocent. He was ordered to stand out at the front of the class. He refused. Five times the order was repeated and Don remained seated until the master, rather than he, had either to escalate matters or back down. Burke did the latter, and despite the subsequent Friday punishment, Don had proved his point and undermined the teacher's authority.

None of this endeared him to the headmaster, Mr Quinn – a short, fat man who was pompous in manner and disinclined to

---

[1] Ian Thompson does omit to mention that Don later played rugby for the school XV.

praise. Don was often up in front of him to be punished corporally for things he had not done. Even more cutting were the public denunciations – the humiliation of having his sins read out after Christian prayers in morning assembly. Most days, some misdemeanour or other was attributed to him in this manner. It would have been unsurprising if all this pressure of disapproval had pushed Don in the direction of juvenile crime, and there were others in the school who did follow that path. Ian Thompson remembers 'one lad in Broughton who you knew would end up in gaol. He broke into the pencil works once and was at school giving them out next day, but no one split on him.' Don's case was different. Yes, there was truculence and resistance in him, but there was also a fair-mindedness, a sense of morality deriving from the old-fashioned, straight-seeing father against whom there is no suggestion from any of his childhood friends that Don ever seemed significantly to rebel. The verdict of all his early friends is unanimous: if Tom Whillans said do it, throughout his life, without question, Don did it. His father was the only one who had control.

There are two anecdotes from his early teens which illustrate the parameters of fairness and morality within which Don operated. Ian Thompson tells the first:

> A gang of local kids – girls and boys – used to hang around in the evenings outside Miss Hawkins's laundry on Ayrshire Road. Miss Bagwash we used to call her. She hated kids, was always out moving us on, confiscating balls, things like that. One evening I'd been to the Cromwell Road picture house and walked back along Littleton Road to Ayrshire Road, where there was a watchman's hut and a brazier at that time. I'd been expecting to meet up with some of the others, but there was no one there so I carried on walking back home when Miss Bagwash collars me from behind and marches me along demanding to know where I lived. Well, I was dumbfounded by this, but I gathered from her ravings that something had gone off which had annoyed her, and that I was going to cop for the blame. But just at that moment Don runs along and screams at her to let me go. He told her I'd been to the pictures and it wasn't me had done it – they had. He just came from nowhere, by himself, and none of the others who'd been involved in whatever it was were anywhere to be seen. But

Don was like that – he was always very protective of his mates, of Edna, of people he liked, and he stayed so right through his life.

The second – and more brutal – anecdote reveals a different side both of Don's character and of the activities of the neighbourhood children. Down the side of the school on Cromwell Road was an area of waste ground on which Don and some friends were playing after school when he was about 13 or 14. A girl came up to one of the group of boys and asked him to go with her into a shed on the croft. They had sexual intercourse, and when the boy had finished she sent him out to summon another member of the group. So it went on. All took their turn with the exception of Don, who was extremely reluctant to join in, and who eventually walked off without doing so, to the accompaniment of ribald barracking.

All this is to emphasise the negative aspects of Don's adolescence. Had it been entirely thus, the outcome of his life might have been unremittingly bleak. As it was, there were redeeming features, outlets, chances for distinction and of escape – though even with some of these, the initial promise was ultimately betrayed:

I couldn't wait for gym lessons, but of course there were only about three a week. It would have suited me if there'd only been three other lessons and we'd had all the rest of the time in the gym. Funnily enough, the gym teacher in the first year was a woman, Miss Yates. She was a good gymnast herself, and she really encouraged me. Then she left and her replacement was a chap who wasn't interested in gymnastics. He was mad keen on ball games, and I wasn't, so I started skipping his lessons. After he'd been there about a year, he stopped me one day in the corridor.

'What's your name?' he asked.

'Whillans.'

'What form are you in?'

'2A.'

He thought for a minute. '2A? Well, I take them and I've never seen you.'

'No, you haven't,' I said.

He appeared slightly puzzled by this and asked me if I was excused PE. I told him I didn't go to any of his lessons because

he didn't get any of the apparatus out. He was taken aback
and wasn't sure what to do. After a short pause he said that
he'd get the stuff out next time, so I replied that I'd go along
in that case. I went for a week or two but he showed no
interest so I just stopped going again and that was it. He never
bothered me and I never bothered him.

The self-possession is extraordinary for a 13-year-old, the
teacher's waste of an educational opportunity lamentable. But there
was some recompense in that the school ran a gymnastics club, and
through that, Don found himself for once the object of the
headmaster's approval, the recipient of his encouragement at the
time, and his praise at a later date as the best gymnast Broughton
School ever produced. So at last there was something to balance out
the morning denunciations.

It was outside school, however, that his main avenues of escape
from orthodoxy and authority lay. The entry to them, oddly, was
through joining one of the most traditionally and formally
authoritarian of all boys' groups, the Boy Scouts. At the age of 12,
Don and Bill Holland joined the First Broughton Scouts, the 'Oates
Troop', and it provided a focus – lessening in intensity as time went
by – for the next four years. Don recalled much later how he viewed
admiringly the rows of badges down the other boys' arms and
wondered how anyone could possess the intelligence to pass them
all, reflecting ruefully that in all the time he spent in the Scouts he
never passed more than his Tenderfoot badge. Despite being once
again a failure at the formal side of things, he did gain an understanding ally in the short, stout, middle-aged figure of 'Pop' Travis,
the Scoutmaster. And also through the Scouts came his induction
into the camping and walking among the Peak District moors and
dales which led ultimately to his beginning to climb.

He joined before a week's summer camp, which was held in
Ennerdale in the Lake District. The Scout system definitely hadn't
managed to suppress his independence of thought:

I remember one day when most of the boys had gone off
somewhere and there was just Bill Holland and myself left in
the camp. I suggested that we nip off and go up one of the
fells. We knew that we'd get in bother if the rest got back
before us and found that we'd left camp, but anyway, off we

went. We set out for a nearby crag and climbed the stream bed
. . . we found a little bone dice right at the top of the stream
and I couldn't fathom how it had got there because I was so
sure no other human being had ever been up there.

On his return he could talk of nothing else for weeks, and because
his two aunts, Dolly and Winnie, had moved to Hayfield, at the foot
of the Peak District's highest hill, Kinder Scout, that became his
base for operations, in which, sooner or later, he managed to
involve most of his friends. Ian Thompson was one of the first to
suffer:

We went off camping to Hayfield. It was supposed to be for a
week, but that didn't work out. We got the bus from Mosley
Street and staggered up towards Kinder, rucksacks laden with
tins – Don's father, remember, worked at Allen's the grocers
– and it never stopped raining. Anyway we crawled into this
wood, got into our waterproofs, set the primus stove going,
ate, and then decided we'd better stay there and get the tent
up. That was when we discovered we'd left the tent-pegs at
home. It was going dark and the rain was blasting down from
the moors, so we wrapped the guy-lines round boulders and
lay all night with this sagging tent flapping away above us.
Next morning we ate all the food and came back home, and I
think that was our first time away.

Don's memory doesn't seem to have served him much better on
another occasion, remembered by his aunt Winnie:

My husband and myself had been out for the night and it was
about midnight when we arrived home. There were two boys
sitting on the garden wall. It was Don and another boy. He
said they'd missed the Manchester bus, so I gave them supper
and fixed them up for the night. Don started to unpack his
rucksack, and suddenly burst out, 'I've left my compass up on
Kinder Scout. I know where I've left it. I'll go and get it now.'
I said, 'You can't go now, it's one o'clock in the morning,' so
he says, 'OK then, I'll get it tomorrow.' Next morning I gave
them breakfast and then took the two of them into the back
garden to show them a short cut back to Kinder. I went back

inside and waited for them to come back and say good morning, but I didn't see him again. That was how he was. He'd have been about 12 at the time.

By the Easter of the next year, 1946, when he was still only 12, Don's endurance and route-finding abilities were well established, as Bill Holland recalls:

Don asked me if I fancied a walk in the Peak District during the Easter holiday. I borrowed Eric Hodgkiss's huge rucksack and we set off by bus on the Friday evening to Hayfield, and from there over the moors and through the dales to Ashbourne – a distance of 40 miles in two days over rough country. On the journey we never walked along a road, only crossed them. Whenever I asked Don where we were, he'd squat down, unfold his map, point, say 'There!', and we'd be off again. He always seemed to know where we were. On the way we met two other boys and Don invited them to join us. This meant four of us sleeping in an American army bivouac tent intended, I think, for one man. It wasn't that comfortable. But one thing I remember is that it was always tidy. The first thing you'd notice about Don was his personal neatness. Where I'd throw things in a sack, he'd stow them properly. We didn't have sleeping bags, only blankets, and Don's was always immaculately rolled. It was the same later when he started as a plumber – his job was always safe because his work was so neat.

The pace of these excursions, the distances covered, was stepping up. Holland recalls a Sunday walk in 1946 when four of them circumnavigated Kinder from Hayfield to Bamford and back to Glossop – 25 rough moorland miles of tussock and peat hag. On another day and another walk of similar length with two companions, after 20 miles or so Don ended up carrying all three packs. 'I thought nothing of 30 miles a day when I'd been at it a bit. I knew the moors like the back of my hand; I knew every funny-shaped tuft of grass, I knew every stretch of peat, I knew every grough, every feature in a radius of 20 miles from Hayfield.'

On one occasion, on a wintry day on Kinder Scout, the opportunity came his way to turn the tables on those by whose systems of assessment he had been found wanting:

It was blowing a blizzard, snow lay on the ground and it was coming down thickly. I was walking up a gully, head down, battling away, when I came across a bloke sitting on a rock. I couldn't believe my eyes, he had shorts on. Shorts in that weather! He was a Scoutmaster and he'd got lost. He looked at me – a little nipper – and I said: 'Where d'you want to go?' So he told me and I said: 'OK. Follow me.' We set off across Kinder. He must have been desperate, to follow a kid. Anyhow, I got him there. I'll bet he never told anybody what happened.

A rambling club was formed at Broughton School, but Don quickly came to view its Sunday-afternoon-strolls-round-Heaton-Park activities as beneath his dignity. In his autobiography, he mentions one companion with whom he did form a partnership for a time, and in his description of its breakdown there sounds for the first time the note of disappointment or even betrayal which is to recur as a motif in the stories of other significant friendships and partnerships of his life – though it is tempered here by humour in looking back on his own naivety:

I suppose he'd be in his forties. He was just an ordinary bloke to look at, nothing special. He told me he was an ex-army officer, I remember. We just sort of met one Sunday and walked together. From then on, I used to meet him at Mosley Street bus station and we'd be together all day. We used to go to places that had nice names – Ashbourne, Hartington, Bull i'th' Thorn, Wimberry Rocks. We never talked much except about the particular walk. I suppose this went on every week for nearly a couple of years, and then one Sunday he said: 'I won't be coming next week, I'm getting married.' This was a big shock to me. I looked at him and said, 'When? Next Sunday?' And he said: 'No, Saturday.' So I said: 'Can you not come out Sunday then?' I didn't understand what all this was about. I couldn't imagine the partnership breaking up. He said he didn't think he could and so I asked him about the week after and he said he probably wouldn't be able to make it. I only saw him once after that and that was a while later when I was climbing. He was on the bus going back to the city. I said, 'Howdo,' and he asked me if I was climbing now and I said I was. That fella pushed me pretty hard on those walks. There were many times when I'd really to work at the last eight or nine miles. Funnily enough, I never knew his name.

Nor have I, in writing this biography, been able to find it out. But in a sense, his very anonymity is the more telling, letting him stand as representative of all the people who, from the time of the Industrial Revolution onwards, poured out of the northern cities to the moors on their margins to spend their brief hours of leisure in the pursuit of some form of freedom in natural surroundings.

For those adventurous and unconventional spirits who found themselves ill-at-ease, wanting and restless in the impoverished streets, this was the sole and the natural outlet. It brought to their lives self-reliance, meaning, physical challenge, escape from workday monotony, contact with the seasons and a discovery of the beauty of the world. It deepened friendships, sustained character, helped them grow. And it was surely inevitable that this was the path Don would take.

5

Work and Play

Both in what he said and what he wrote, the word 'job' was one of
the most significant and recurrent in Don's vocabulary. At times
this jars on the leisure-fixated or romantic ear. It can sound
reductive or dismissive when he talks about great climbs in terms of
'getting on with the job'.[1] But this is to disregard the craftsman's
pride invested in the term. To Don's father, raising a family in the
great depression of the thirties, a job was a source of dignity, to be
kept for life. Whilst the latter in conventional terms never held in
Don's case, the idea of work as value never left him. But at the
outset, as Don left school in 1948 (the statutory school leaving age
had been raised from 14 to 15 for the first time for his year), the
question to be answered was what sort of job he might take. He had
neither the qualifications nor the inclination for academic or
professional work. Shop work he ruled out as being indoors. His
choice was thus narrowed down to labouring or learning a trade. A
friend of his father's mentioned that Emett & Smith, plumbers and
heating engineers, of Knott Mill, Manchester, were looking to take
on an apprentice. Don went along to their office and workshop
under the railway arches at the end of Deansgate – fashionable now,
but dingy and smoke-blackened in those days – where it crosses the
Rochdale Canal and runs into Hulme. Mr Emett interviewed him,
thought him handy, tidy and quick on the uptake, and he landed the
job.

The hours were eight till five, Monday to Friday, eight till two-
thirty on Saturday, and the wages were 29 shillings and three

---

[1] Derek Walker, who climbed with him in the 1960s, remembers how he would
never want to climb later than five o'clock: 'Knocking-off time,' he would
proclaim.

farthings[2] a week before deductions. 'When I started work, I was earning just £70 a year,' Don recalled. The work was physically gruelling. The 15-year-old Don would leave the house at quarter past seven to get the bus down Broughton and Blackfriars Roads to Salford bus station, run down Deansgate and be set straight to work loading the hand-cart with materials for the day's contracts.

> The firm used to do really big jobs – central heating systems, hot and cold water supply right through new schools – and the only transport they had was this old hand-cart. I remember once when another apprentice and myself were pushing it loaded up Whitworth Street. We just got in the middle of a set of traffic lights when we heard a sound like somebody running a stick along some railings. Before we had a chance to wonder what it was, the old hand-cart lurched over. Every single spoke in the wheel had come out. It dumped the whole lot of the junk right in the centre of the lights.

His diaries of the time record the work he did with terse economy:

> Newton Heath tech. with Fred, working in prefab putting in central heating.

> Collecting sections of drainpipe all day – got soaked.

> Working at Thorneycrofts, fastening lead gutters. Went to night school.

> St Malachi's with Bill Smith, getting new boiler down cellar steps. Buggered – didn't go to night school.

He was supposed to attend night school every Tuesday, Wednesday and Friday at Salford Technical College to study for his City & Guilds examinations in plumbing – there was no day-release from the firm of Emett & Smith – but there were occasions when he

---

[2] A farthing was a tiny copper coin bearing a wren motif and worth one quarter of an old penny. Even in the Manchester of the 1940s, the most it might have bought would have been a smallish gobstopper.

was too tired to do so. The men he worked with were much older than him – Bill Smith, his usual partner, was in his seventies – so much of the physical work fell to Don, and to manhandle sections of boilers weighing up to half a ton up and down narrow basement stairways, to carry cast-iron radiators to upper storeys and lead guttering across roofs was exhausting labour: 'I never realised until I left that firm, when I was about 20, that the only reason I couldn't get up in the mornings was that I was absolutely buggered.'

The extent to which the work was developing his strength and stamina is obvious, and Don was lucky as well, during this time of rationing, in a home diet that helped it to build. His father still worked at Allen's the grocers, and Don's friends of the time remember that the food he took away with him at weekends was better than any to which they had access. Allied to the agility and aggression he already possessed, the physical basis for his mountaineering career was being soundly laid. And that career would soon begin.

It came about through a chance meeting with a friend Don had known for most of his life. His name throughout his school years at Cromwell Road – which he had left a year before Don – had been Eric Hodgkiss. The boy had been orphaned at a very early age, his three sisters had been placed in an orphanage in Tunbridge Wells, and he had been brought up by an aunt in whose name he was registered. But on leaving school he had reverted to his own name of Eric Worthington. He was calm and friendly in character, tall and powerful in build, and he and Don had shared many childhood escapades.

One which Worthington particularly remembers is of following Don one lunchtime to the Frederick Road bridge near the school. The bridge crosses the Irwell between the gasworks and Pendleton bus depot. Don squirmed across underneath it on the steel lattice-work between its box girders and then climbed over the flange without any problem. When Worthington got to the same position, 30 feet above the foul waters of the river and with the flange at chest level pushing him off balance, he found there was nothing but the domed heads of rivets sticking up from the flat surface to pull himself over on.

'I'm falling off!' he shouted to Don.

'Don't be a silly bugger,' the reply came back. 'You'd better not!'

'I should have realised then,' Worthington commented later, 'that

Don and not myself was the one who was going to be the climber. It was the same when we started climbing. When a thing got beyond the point of balance, I just didn't have the strength or technique, whereas Don came into his own.'

After Worthington had left school in 1947, he and Don lost contact for a while. Worthington joined the local church youth club, and his activities centred round that. One Sunday, its leader had taken them on a ramble from Glossop to Hayfield, in the course of which the youth club group had stopped to buy tea and eat their sandwiches at the Snake Inn, on the A57 road between Manchester and Sheffield. Don turned up, in company with Bill Holland and Peter Owen, and they chatted for a while before heading off in their separate directions.

Later that evening, back in Salford, Worthington was standing on Littleton Road talking with a group from the youth club when Don and Bill Holland walked past and the conversation was taken up again:

'I didn't know you were interested in going out hiking,' Don said.

He hadn't been, but he wanted to have another try at it. They made arrangements to go out the next weekend, caught the Sunday morning bus to Glossop, and Don introduced his old friend and new companion to the delights of the Dark Peak with a 20-mile moorland round over Bleaklow to the Grinah Stones, down the Alport by Grains-in-the-Water, and back by way of Doctor's Gate to Glossop. Worthington wasn't put off, and the shared weekend activities became a regular fixture. Tom Whillans was particularly pleased at his son's new friendship, and thought Worthington a steadying influence on him. Worthington himself returned the appreciation: 'His mother and father were super people, and no matter how early Don was away at weekends, his dad was always up to cook him breakfast and see him off. They were just good people, and there was a real warmth about the house.'

Weekend after weekend they ranged over the wide moors, with their subtle features, their winds, mists and distances, their deep heather and chirring grouse, their stamina-sucking black groughs of slippery peat and their demand for an acute sense of whereabouts and direction. The walks became longer and longer, and with 10 shillings spending money a week now that Don was working, their geographical range increased too. Worthington remembers walks from Crowden to Ashbourne; he recalls walking back from the

Ladybower reservoir to Glossop in the dark: 'It wasn't dangerous, there were no cars about in those days. You tend to forget with all this talk about safety these days that we rarely finished in daylight anyway in the winter. Sometimes we'd have torches, but not always, and even when we did have them, we'd use them sparingly.'

He goes on to explain the almost imperceptible drift from rambling and hiking into rock-climbing:

> I think the notion about climbing came from me. I'd been reading Smythe's *Spirit of the Hills* and Whymper's *Scrambles in the Alps* and had a head full of romantic notions, and Don would bring me back to earth. 'This is just crazy,' he'd say, when we'd see climbers out on Laddow or those places. 'Look, you can get up easy round the side and get the same view, so why d'you want to go risking your neck?'

But the point was, the excitement and adventure of walking out into Derbyshire was diminishing. It was known country. They no longer even bothered to take maps, so well did they know it. There were other directions of interest they could have taken – girls, for example. At Christmas 1949, in Langdale, Don met Frieda Kenworthy from Ashton-under-Lyne and a brief romance developed. His diary for the first few weeks of 1950 is full of references to her:

> January 3: Rang Frieda and received letter and sent one also. Received receipt for Ramblers' Association subscription for 1950.

> January 7: Frieda rang.

> January 8: Hike with Frieda from Greenfield up to Chew reservoir, over moors to Ogden Brook and then to Mottram cutting. Home 10 p.m.

Eric Worthington remembers that he began to 'feel like a gooseberry', and he stopped going out for a few weeks until Don asked him why, and he explained.

'Oh, bugger that,' said Don, 'you're my mate. I'm not worried about her.'

The truth of that was borne out by his diary entry for 21 February: 'Went to night school. Packed Frieda in.'

Next Sunday, the two mates from Salford were back in their weekend routine, catching a 'Ramblers' Special' train organised by the Ramblers' Association from Manchester's Exchange Station to Llangollen. These trains were a feature of northern outdoor life in the 20 years after the Second World War, and until the extensive access to cars of the 1960s. I remember from my own experience the value of the open and friendly interchange of information and debate which took place upon them, the making of friends, the enthusiasms expressed for areas and walks.[3] At the very least, excursions like this can be viewed as setting a context for Don's future life in climbing. How close he was to the threshold of that life is apparent in his diary entry for the following Sunday: 'March 5: Hike from Hayfield to the Downfall and back. Did a bit of rock-climbing.'

It's generally thought that Don's first climb was a route called The Atherton Brothers on the Bleaklow crag of Shining Clough, which he did in April 1950, when he was still 16. Don himself, in his autobiography, refers to it as 'the first climb I did'. In the kind of apprenticeship to the outdoors to which he was committed, it is perhaps misleading to insist on a firm date for a first climb. Whilst you can recall the first time you tie on to a rope and climb in that formal and defined manner, it was usually the case within the tradition in which Don grew up that that event would be preceded by a period of experimentation: scrambling around in chimneys on the less exposed side of buttresses on Curbar Edge, perhaps, or scrabbling up corners in the quarry at Windgather Rocks. In his diary throughout March there are several references to climbing, of which the following is typical: 'March 19: Hike from Hayfield to Downfall. Met Gordon Williams climbing, joined him, arrived home 10 o'clock.'

These references are backed up by other indicators of his growing interest. His walks were taking him increasingly among climbing venues in the Peak District: 'Hike from Hathersage, return over Burbage Rocks.' There were preparations being made:

---

[3] See my essay, 'Trains, cafés, conversations' in *On & Off the Rocks* (Gollancz, 1986).

March 18: Bought six shillings' worth of clinkers.

March 23: Stayed in and clinkered hiking boots.

(The received wisdom of the time, expressed in books like J.E.Q. Barford's Pelican paperback, *Climbing in Britain*, of which Eric Worthington had a copy, was that clinkers – a broad climbing nail made of mild steel, soft enough for rugosities in the rock to bite into – rather than the hardened steel edge-nails, called tricounis, were the appropriate equipment both for general climbing and – except in dry weather when rubbers were preferable – for the sort of friction climbing which predominated on the gritstone outcrops of the Peak.)

Don was already planning his summer holiday, and that the anticipation was building up shows:

March 25: Bought map of SKYE!

March 30: Went to Johnny's – gave me map of Inverness and SKYE!

There was a more immediate excitement at hand, however, and it seems best to give the outline of it, and a sense of Don's meticulous preparation, from his diary entries. Again, these are minimal to the point of banality, but their significance is in selection of detail, clues to outlook and priority. They are the only contemporary indices of an evolving interest and approach:

April 1: Waterproofed tent, rucksack, sleeping bag.

April 2: Hike from Hayfield. Came back early. Packed rucksack. Stayed in.

April 5: Repacked rucksack.

April 6: Beginning of holiday today. Going to North Wales tonight with Eric. 5.35 train from Exchange Station, change at Chester, taxi from Bangor.

Their itinerary for the next four days was, in traditional Welsh fashion, dictated to them by the weather. On the first day they

walked up from Llyn Idwal, where they had spent the night, by way
of the Devil's Kitchen on to the Glyders and thence to Glaslyn,
beneath Snowdon, where they camped. It rained all night and all of
the next day, so they walked along the road, miserably and buffeted
by rain and wind, to Capel Curig, where they were in bed in a barn
full of hay by 5.30. The following morning they decided to abandon
the mountains and their continuing rain, and crossed the low pass
to Crafnant, walking down the side of the valley's exquisite lake to
Trefriw and Llanrwst, where they slept in a hut at the station, were
woken at 5 a.m., and spent four hours in a transport canteen before
catching the first bus to Y Rhyl and the train home.

On the surface of it, this was an averagely wet and enterprising
first excursion to Snowdonia by a couple of 16-year-olds. That
there was more going on – that foundations were being laid here –
is made clear in Eric Worthington's recollection of the Easter trip:

> When we came down off the Glyders on the Good Friday, we
> walked along to camp by Glaslyn, under Snowdon there. It
> was drizzling a bit – quite good weather for this holiday,
> because most of the time we had gales – and after we'd had a
> meal, we skirted round to the far side of the lake and set off
> scrambling up Lliwedd. We'd got up a fair way, and there was
> a big drop opening up beneath us when Don turns to me and
> says, 'This is stupid! If we're going to get into this climbing
> lark, let's do it properly with ropes and that.'

The prudence and mountaineering sense which was to keep him
alive throughout a mountaineering career in which so many of his
companions and friends died is clearly evident here. The following
Saturday Don and Eric, having pooled their money, went to an
industrial chandlers in the basement of a warehouse off Shudehill in
Manchester, laid out eight shillings on the counter – all the cash they
could spare, having kept back their bus fares for the following day
– and in return for it received 80 feet of five-eighths-of-an-inch-
diameter Italian hemp rope:

> It said in Barford's book that Italian hemp was the stuff
> because the fibres were that much longer, making it a stronger
> rope. So that's what we asked for and that's what we got.
> Nowadays, they'd think you wanted to smoke it and you'd get

arrested. Of course, I erred on the side of caution and got it thick, so it was probably more use for towing barges than climbing. Anyway, I hid it in the garden shed so that my dad wouldn't see it, we read up a bit that night about laybacks and mantelshelves, and the next day I stuffed it in the rucksack and off we went on the bus to give it a try. We'd have been all right if the bus had broken down with that bloody thing with us. It weighed a ton . . .

It was Sunday 16 April 1950, the first day of British Summer Time and little over a month short of Don's seventeenth birthday. They took the bus to Glossop, walked up by Mossy Lea and Yellowslacks Brook to the cairn on Bleaklow Head, headed north across the quagmires of Shining Clough Moss, and dropped down from the edge of the plateau into Longdendale to arrive at the foot of one of the finest and most imposing rock buttresses in Derbyshire. They put down their rucksacks at the foot of the crag and craned their necks at the 80 feet of gritstone above them. What they had arrived beneath was a route which is still acknowledged as one of the finest Severes in the Peak District. Severe, in those days, was not a grade at which beginners were recommended to lead too quickly. The serving of an apprenticeship on easier climbs was deemed desirable. Nor was this a crag considered most suitable for novices. Don's account of their adventure on the Atherton Brothers climb runs thus:

This pal of mine, Eric, had been pushing for us to do it for some time, and we'd seen a couple of lads climbing at Shining Clough when we'd been out walking, so that's where we went. I didn't mind so long as we got in a bit of a walk as well.

I looked up a crack in the rock and I said to Eric, 'I wonder if anybody climbs up there?' It looked a bit frightening. I asked him if he wanted a go and he said OK. As it was Eric who wanted to climb, I tied him on first and off he went. One thing worried me – I couldn't fathom what use the rope was tied round his waist. Anyhow, he got on a big ledge about halfway up. It seemed a hell of a way and he'd had a real struggle to get there. I thought, 'Well, this isn't much cop. There's no fun in this.' After he'd got up, I went up after him and we both stood there on the ledge.

I looked round and said, 'Where are we supposed to go from here?'

I gave the wall a good going-over and saw some good holds but it looked overhanging to me. I was thinking we couldn't chicken out of the first climb we'd ever done, so I thought I'd have a go. I set off up a slightly overhanging wall. The holds were good but they rattled a bit. I figured out that they were slotted together like a jigsaw, so I bashed on. I can remember getting to the top and thinking, 'Thank Christ for that!' That was the first climb I did and I never did another quite like it. I said to Eric afterwards, 'Look, the next time we do one, one of us will go to the top and chuck the rope down and the other one'll tie on it. Then we'll do anything you want.'

The flaky holds on Atherton Brothers still rattle a bit. It's still steep and exposed. What is not so sure is whether the two aspiring mountaineers put Don's suggested strategy to the test on the climbs they did at Laddow the same afternoon, before they made their way over Black Chew Head, across the heather and down the Chew Valley – a rough, 16-mile moorland round in addition to their first climbs – to catch the evening bus back home from Greenfield.

6

Young Climber

It has become difficult to appreciate, from the fragmented perspectives and specialisms current in outdoor activities at the beginning of the twenty-first century, just how integrated was the view of mountaineering which obtained mid-twentieth century, as Don was starting out in the sport. There was deemed to be an ideal and proper progression from easy rambles through more arduous hill-walking to scrambling in the mountains. When that had been achieved, the next step was into rock-climbing, the training for which aspect of the sport began on the practice outcrops, whether they be of Wealden or Northumbrian sandstone, granite, whin sill or – best and most arcane of them all – Pennine gritstone. Beyond the outcrops lay mountain rock-climbs, the Alps and the Greater Ranges. Whilst the participant could step off at any point in this continuum, what was regarded as eccentric and limiting was the pursuit particularly of outcrop climbing as an end in itself.

'I was amazed,' Don reflected years later, 'that the Greenfield lads I used to see around in the first year I was climbing set themselves this boundary. They didn't ever envisage going on a big mountain[1], and for me that was the whole point of it. Even when we were doing

---

[1] Eric Flint, who was, as we shall see, a significant influence on Don's early climbing, thinks this comment of Don's to be less than fair and accurate: 'At that time some of the "Greenfield Lads" had already been to the Alps, and probably all had been to the Lakes, Wales and Scotland. I don't think it's true that these climbers had set any boundaries. Most of them had been inspired by reading books from local libraries – Winthrop Young, Mummery, Eric Shipton, etc.'

As one of a later generation of 'Greenfield Lads' from the end of the 1950s and beginning of the 1960s, I can vouch for the truth of Flint's testimony, but the limiting socio-economic factors bearing upon climbers from less advantaged backgrounds than those of most pre-war mountaineers still need to be borne in mind – available time and money acted as a definite curb on their ambition.

those first climbs on grit, I was always thinking in terms of training for when we went to Skye in the summer.'

A curious facet of Don's character is that whilst his attitude towards formal authority throughout his life was ambivalent or even hostile, his acceptance of the conventions of mountaineering – which, despite being the norms of a community of the social margins, tended to mirror those of the wider society – was, with one important proviso, unquestioning.

The proviso concerned progression through the grades. As mentioned in the last chapter, it was not the done thing for beginners to choose as their first climb, without supervision, a steep and exposed Severe. But then, Don simply did not know that Atherton Brothers was a Severe. There was no current guidebook to tell him that it was. He had almost certainly read in *Climbing in Britain* about grades, but he had no way of correlating that with what was in front of him. In fact, he never had much patience with guidebooks throughout his climbing career. 'I don't bother with guidebooks, me – I just walk along and I might think, "Oh, that looks good! We'll have a crack at that." That was how it was on the first day, and that's how it's been ever since.'

With an approach like that, despite his obvious natural ability, given the rudimentary protection techniques of the day he could have come to grief very early on. But he and Eric Worthington, as they made their way over to Laddow from Shining Clough, having survived their first roped climb, were fortunate again. On Laddow they met Eric Flint. Flint was a local climber from Oldham. He was a couple of years older than them, and for some time had been one of the outstanding performers on the local outcrops. His route on Dovestones Edge from 1947, The Stint – an exposed and delicate arete – was one of the hardest climbs of its type and time on the Chew Valley outcrops.[2] Flint was not only a good climber, he was also a friendly, helpful and encouraging character who was willing to demonstrate practically to the two youngsters what they had so far only read in their instructional manual, and also to tell them where else in the area there was good climbing to be found. The information he imparted was quickly put to good use:

---

[2] Flint later said: 'It was done while people were packing up to go, and they hadn't noticed, so I had to do it again to prove it. It was definitely easier second time around.'

April 23: Hike to Ravens Rocks, climbing all day with Eric.

April 30: Went to Greenfield – Dove Stones – did Cooper's Crack and a few Severes.

The contrast between these two minimal entries is telling. In the week between them the focus has shifted. The 'Hike to Ravens Rocks' (in fact this is Ravenstones, and the mistake indicative of his newness to the sport), where they met Flint again, is the last time that term 'hike' takes precedence in the diaries. In an unpublished interview from 1984, Don reminisced: 'I didn't mind climbing at first, in fact I quite enjoyed it and we were out again the next week. So you see, we went very quickly from walking to doing it, but only so long as a walk was included. I used to insist on that.' Perhaps so, but in his diary it is notable how quickly the object becomes the crag and the climbs upon it, which now begin to have names and grades: 'Cooper's Crack and a few Severes'. The choice of route, too, is significant. Cooper's Crack may only be Severe and 35 feet long, but it is hard for its grade, and imposing, with a difficult initial bulge which would merit a higher grade on a mountain crag. That the boy with attitude was becoming a climber with attitude was made even more apparent the following weekend, when he and Worthington returned to Shining Clough.

There is an anecdote in Don's autobiography[3] which is at the same time both puzzling and revealing. It runs like this:

We were walking along the bottom of the edge when Reg [Gray] pointed to a crack in the rock.
'They'd climb things like that in the Lake District,' he said.
I looked at him and then I looked at this crack.
'Get away, would they hell as like. They can't climb things like that,' I said.
'Oh yes,' he said, 'that'd be Very Severe.'
'Aye, I don't doubt it,' I said sarcastically.
Two weeks later I came back and led the thing. It's called Phoenix.

[3] *Don Whillans: Portrait of a Mountaineer*, by Don Whillans and Alick Ormerod (Heinemann, 1971).

The relevant diary entry runs thus: 'May 7: Went to Greenfield on 9 o'clock bus with Eric. Went to Laddow, led North Wall. Went to Shining Clough. Led Phoenix. Led Stable Cracks.'

The small discrepancy here, and there are many such in the autobiography, is not important ('It all tends to get muddled up together when I look back,' he said, in one late interview, and Don's widow Audrey also remembered that, like most of us, Don, particularly as he got older, had trouble distinguishing even between years in which things took place). The diary, being contemporary, is obviously the more reliable testimony, but the meeting with Reg Gray no doubt took place, and most probably on the day they did the Atherton Brothers climb. What is striking is the rapidity with which Don has gone from ignorance and incredulity to a grasp of the concepts involved, and a willingness and ability to take on the challenges and to overcome them.

Phoenix, the pure and striking crack which splits the blank wall left of the groove taken by the Atherton Brothers, had first been climbed three years previously by the great cragsman of the 1940s, Peter Harding. It's 85 feet high – long for a gritstone climb – and demands a degree of skill in the use of quite awkward techniques of jamming up wide cracks. In 1950 it was a completely unprotected lead, and it still rates as a three-star classic towards the upper limit of its VS (Very Severe) grade. The other two climbs Don and Eric Worthington did on the same day are graded Hard Severe (North Wall), and VS (Stable Cracks). Beginners, with the benefit of sticky rubber boots, chalk, harnesses, perlon ropes, climbing-wall training, sophisticated protection techniques, a different culture and a vastly higher plateau of average performance, are taken up routes like these as a matter of course even on their first day's climbing nowadays. In 1950, for a 16-year-old beginner on his fourth day out to lead them in clinker-nailed boots and trailing something resembling a ship's hawser behind him was entirely exceptional. The anecdote from the autobiography gives the general stance. Eyebrows would have been raised, the myth-making machine would have ground into gear. The character of Don Whillans within the climbing community was in the process of creation:

We'd seen these blokes around the place with anoraks and karabiners and stuff, and we didn't have a clue at the time. But I pretty soon came to realise that it didn't matter, having the gear, because you could still do the moves even if you hadn't got it, and it wasn't long before I found out that I was as good as them.

One of the first times he came to realise that simple truth was probably the following weekend, when he caught the Greenfield bus again: 'May 13: Went to Thorneycroft's with Tom. Went to Greenfield, arrived at campsite 8.15.' The old Chew campsite (strictly unofficial but tolerated for years until the advent of new reservoirs, parking lots, traffic wardens, bailiffs, countryside warders[4] and others with sub-degrees in public exclusion and control ended the tradition in the mid-1970s) was close to the Scout hut and Chew Piece plantation, around the eastern side of which is a collection of huge rocks fallen from the edge of the moor above. The largest of these are 25 feet in height, they have individual names like The Matterhorn, Sloping Top, The Tank, Shell Shot, The Sugar Loaf and The Whale, and collectively they are one of the best bouldering areas of The Peak. Chris Hardy and Carl Dawson, in their current guidebook to the Chew Valley crags,[5] give a clue to their significance throughout generations of climbing:

> Regular guidebook readers will have noticed that boulders are at last receiving rightful recognition. And quite rightly so, for they provide more pleasure than many of the more formally recognised 'routes'. Is this because bouldering epitomises the central dynamic of climbing – competition – in its healthy, most taintless form?

The answer to that artful question is surely affirmative, and as much so in relation to a sunny Saturday evening in May over half a century ago as it is today. No record exists of who Don and Eric met at the campsite on this weekend, but there is one thing of which I would be quite certain – that they met other climbers here. From my own infancy as a climber, 10 years after Don's, coming weekend after weekend on the bus from Stephenson Square to the Clarence Hotel, walking up past the papermill and along by the peat-brown water to this same worn patch of grass by the stream, among the

---

[4] My editor suggests that this should be 'wardens'.
[5] *Moorland Gritstone: Chew Valley* (British Mountaineering Council, 1988).

boulders, with its charred remains of campfires and its sheltering trees, I can testify that there was never a spring or summer weekend when it was without its quota of climbers, brewing up, fooling around, wrestling, bouldering, competing, sitting by the fire arguing, gossiping, boasting, imparting information. Your arrival in scenes like this was your induction into the community and practice of the sport – though Don would surely have corrected the use of that last word:

> I suppose I went sliding into it in a natural way, what with meeting up with the Oldham lads at the campsite after we'd learnt where that was, and doing the problems on the Sugar Loaf and the Matterhorn, which I pretty soon found I could do as well as most even though I didn't have the reach. I got to know as much as I needed in them early days just from talking to the other lads. They might say on the bus or at the camp, 'Oh, we're going to so-and-so, like, this weekend or next – see you there,' and that's how you knew what was going on and how you heard about things, because there were no guidebooks that we knew of then. It wasn't really a sport, see – I've never looked at it as that. To me, it very soon became a way of life.

Vic, Fred, Leo, Stan, Spike, Ted, Dick, Eric, Jack: from this weekend onwards their names, some with surnames, some without, are the threads which weave through the sparse tapestry of Don's diary and other recollections. In my own early days, some of them were still there on the Chew Valley crags, edging slowly away from climbing into respectability and responsibility, reminiscing, elaborating on the myths, drawing on the credit which accrued from association and experience ('When you talk about an experienced climber, what you actually mean is someone who's old and buggered,' was Don's commentary on that term). Don may later have disparaged their commitment to the mountains or their appreciation of the whole scene:

> I could never understand these lads who'd just go up to the crag and fiddle about on something or other without ever seeming to be aware of the scenery, which to me was a very important part of it. And of course these would be the lads

who later on just faded away. You might meet them here and there afterwards and they'd have become doctors and things.

But his own appreciation of the community into which he had been accepted was steadfast and lifelong:

> I got a lot of enjoyment just from being with lads of a similar kind, from the camping and the mateyness. It might have been harder to get around in them days, and the money was tight for sure, but all that actually made it more of an adventure, less of a snack and more the meal itself. It was the whole atmosphere of the thing that drew me in.

Ultimately, and in rather subtle ways, Don became a part of that atmosphere – innate quality of place reflecting his own mature quality of character. It is perhaps no accident, therefore, that this Pennine landscape was the one which drew him strongly at the outset of his climbing career and with which, 40 years on from his greatest exploits within it, his name is most clearly associated. He is one of a handful of climbers whose names form the legendry of gritstone: Frank Elliott, Peter Harding, Joe Brown, Malcolm Baxter, John Allen, Ron Fawcett, Jonny Dawes. But his name, more perhaps than any other, has come to express something of the nature of the rock on which his career began. We need, before we proceed with the chronology of Don's life, to attempt to define the character of the rock which was one of its determinants.

Millstone grit is the geological name for the rock-type known to climbers and celebrated by them worldwide as gritstone. A late-comer in the geological time-scale, it was laid down in delta deposits 300 million years ago, lifted up as the capping strata of the Pennine anticline, eroded away, and now asserts its presence chiefly in the moor-rimming outcrops of Derbyshire and Yorkshire. It occurs in several geological series, but the one predominant in the Chew Valley, where most of Don's early climbing took place, is the Kinder Grit, which is the thing itself, possessing all the characteristics of the entire rock-type in their most exaggerated form. In its outward show it is the unkindest of rocks, brutally steep, abrasive, studded all over with razor crystals of quartz and feldspar, smoke-blackened, wind-eroded into jutting nebs, standing proud of the sour peat and shelving rubble beneath. The crags in which it outcrops may only be short – its average height range is from 30 to 60 feet, and its natural buttresses never reach beyond 100 feet – but those who arrive at an estimate of its character and qualities on those grounds alone are committing an error similar to that made by Don's childhood and later adversaries. Size is not everything. Look up 'grit' in the dictionary and you will find one of the subsidiary meanings written thus: 'Firmness or solidity of character; indomitable pluck or spirit; stamina.' Even in the softer climate of today's sport, you still need something of these qualities to climb on it successfully and with style.[6] It is not as other rocks are. Its holds for the most part are sloping and indefinite, its bulging cracks lacerate your hands. It demands a style based on confidence and agility, on both sophistication of technique and aggression in approach, on ingenuity and faith in friction.

There is a cultist – and it might also be said a northern chauvinist, though northern chauvinists would inevitably dispute that – aspect to gritstone climbing. People love it with a religious fervour or leave it strictly alone. It is not rock for dabblers; it demands effort and commitment of its devotees, and was renowned at one time for the outlandish underassessment of its route-grades. But for all this, it has its aesthetic side, its emotional colouring, its sentiment. The mill-town terraces were built of rock from its quarries, its crags were up there above them, signifying release and wider horizons, and from their crests the sky's vivid palette of sunsets made more brilliant by air pollution above the moors' fading pastels, the shadowy valleys with the strings of street lamps at twilight, the Northern Lights, the flickering stars . . .

For Don, I am quite sure from snatches of conversation I had with him, quiet moments when I observed him leaning against one of the weird rock-shapes and looking out west from the Bridestones after an evening's bouldering and before the pub, that gritstone in general and the Chew Valley in particular were special venues, unique in the blend they offered of pragmatic effort and beauty of landscape.

'May 14: Went to Ravenstones with Vic and Fred. Did Wedgwood Crack Direct.' More significant than the climb – awkward and gymnastic though it is – in Don's first day out from

---

[6] Significantly, leading gritstone routes has become something of a minority fashion in recent decades. I put this down to climbers' balls having shrunk because of hormones in their recycled drinking water. The gifted and brave minority, however, still performs . . .

the camp is the company he kept. The 'Fred' who led the route was an intriguing character by the name of Fred Ashton, who was renowned for three things: his extreme youth, his hardihood, and the vigour of his language. A couple of years before, at the age of 12, in biting cold weather he had provoked Joe Brown into leading Freddie's Finale on Wimberry Rocks – the hardest of the early routes on what many consider the finest of all gritstone edges. Eric Worthington recalls that 'He'd try anything with anyone and struggle away on it for hours. He always used to wear a Jaeger cap, and he seemed more concerned about that falling off than himself coming to grief.' Ray Greenall adds that 'Fred would climb in any conditions whatsoever. He had this army jacket he always wore, and as he grew, so the jacket shrunk, and I remember him at about the age of 14 with big, bony wrists red from the cold and the jacket sleeves halfway up his arm, but he never once complained.'

As to his language, even among a group which was happy with the usual street vernacular, it was renowned for its vehemence. Ray Greenall again:

> He was the dirtiest swearer of any of us. There was one occasion when Slim Sorrell brought along his girlfriend for the first time, and as he came in he said to Fred, 'Now then, young Fred, watch your language,' because of course swearing in front of the ladies was not the done thing in those days, but Fred, without thinking, just came out with his natural response: 'I 'aven't fucking spoke yet!' He ended up as a university lecturer.

Through Fred, Don came to hear, albeit in terms which lacked in precision what they possessed in emphasis, about the exploits of the man with whom he was to form perhaps the most significant partnership in climbing history. And Don's accomplishment was rising steeply towards the level at which that might begin. The following weekend, having celebrated his seventeenth birthday in the week, he went with Vic, one of the Oldham lads, to the Bleaklow crag of Yellowslacks, where he led another of Peter Harding's recent gritstone benchmark climbs, the overhanging and insecure corner of Qui Mal y Pense: 'Did Qui Mal y Pense – led it!' his diary gleefully notes. It was his sixth day's climbing, and he was closing in fast on leading at the top standard of the day.

Whit Week was coming. It was time to relax and consolidate. Don and Eric Worthington took the Saturday afternoon bus from Lower Mosley Street up to Ambleside and on to the Dungeon Ghyll Hotel in Langdale, walking up the steep path by the side of Rossett Gill in the twilight to camp at Angle Tarn. The following day they crossed Sty Head and climbed Great Gable, descending by Windy Gap and over Base Brown to Seathwaite, where Fred Ashton turned up ('Young Fred, 'e used to arrive in the most unexpected places, just turn up out of the blue, like. Mind you, 'is language was always blue, so maybe that explains it') to camp with them for the night and walk down Borrowdale on Whit Monday to catch the bus home from Keswick. Coming after such an intense bout of outcrop activity, it feels like a reassertion of basic values.

After three days back at work, Don and Eric balanced that by hitch-hiking to Wales for the weekend and climbing, in perfect, sunny weather, their first VS on a mountain crag – Ted Hicks's classic and exposed route of 1929, Heather Wall. Afterwards they lazed down to the lake and spent the rest of the day – Idwal being less crowded in 1950 than it is now – swimming naked and sunbathing on the rocks, before returning from Wales next morning refreshed and ready to resume the quest for gritstone difficulty.

In the few weeks that followed, Don went out every weekend to the moorland outcrops, camping, sleeping in the gamekeeper's hut at Torside Clough on Bleaklow or the barn above Mossy Lea Farm on Saturday nights, and climbing, wandering around, talking with new friends, learning more about the world of which he was now an initiate throughout the course of the long, hot summer Sundays with the bracken, cloudberry and bilberry brilliant green against the brown moor, the grouse calling and the peat crumbling to dust under their feet. He led Gremlin Groove and Monkey Puzzle on Shining Clough, and took his first fall off the steep finishing move with its long reach on Yellowslacks' technical and insecure Grey Wall.

His action in running down the rock and landing on his feet and unharmed between boulders at the bottom of this route gained currency among the climbing gossips of the day, and was soon being widely reported as a fall from the top of Twin Eliminate on Laddow, with Whillans leaping down into the Twin Chimney climb on the left to escape injury: right impulse and outcome, wrong crag and route.[7] In fact, Don fell off very few times in his climbing career. A year or so before his death, looking back on them, he recalled half a dozen times at most, many of them short and on gritstone. Eric Worthington, too, confirms that 'he was a very safe climber. Of course, none of us were safe in those days in the way you can be today, but Don in particular made up for that by a pretty strict adherence to the traditional dictum that "the leader never falls". Or at least, in his case almost never . . .'

The fall off Grey Wall seems to have had no physical or mental ill effects, for he was out on Laddow a week later and led Cave Crack (HVS, 5a), Priscilla (HVS, 5a), and Twin Eliminate (E1,5b). (E1 is the shorthand version of the lowest subdivision within the 'Extremely Severe' grade. The second sets of numbers and letters – '5b', etc – denote the supposed difficulty of actual moves, as divorced from factors of exposure, strenuosity, looseness and lack of protection which bear upon the overall difficulty – as assessed in the adjectival, E-grade – of a climb.) Those who are tempted to comment that by the most rigorous modern standards this is still a fairly modest level of achievement might modify that view when reminded that essentially all these routes were soloed, trailing a heavy hemp rope and wearing clinker-nailed hiking boots.[8] It would be interesting to see how today's climbers might perform with that equipment.

In the next couple of weekends Don led two more climbs – the Trinnacle Face West on Ravenstones and Ferdie's Folly on Dovestones – which now merit a grade of E1, 5b (at the time, to give an insight into the harshness of contemporary grading, they were considered VS). But as June gave way to July his attention was focusing more on his forthcoming trip with Eric Worthington and Leo – one of the Oldham lads – to Skye. He had bought the Scottish

---

[7] E.g., 'A story was told that this exceptionally powerful lad had fallen from the top of Twin Eliminate at Laddow Rocks. He had jumped from wall to wall in springboard style, landing at the bottom, fifty feet below, in an upright position without a mark on him.' Joe Brown, *The Hard Years* (Gollancz, 1967). Don Roscoe recalls stories current in 1951 about a walker coming out and starting to lead Severes instantly.

[8] 'It wasn't until about a year after I started that I caught on to wearing black rubber pumps for climbing on grit. Before then we did everything in our boots, and quite often after that as well, if the weather was at all bad.' Don Whillans, unpublished interview, 1984. The effect of this in neat and deliberate footwork was obvious to anyone who saw Don climb, even in his declining years.

Mountaineering Club guidebook to the island from Ellis Brigham's shop[9] and – in defiance of his usual practice – spent evenings on end poring over the complex detail of the Cuillin Ridge.

The auguries for the trip were not good. On St Swithin's Day, which Don and Eric spent in the Torside Clough cabin, the rain poured down incessantly – though they still ventured out to repeat Phoenix and Green Crack at Shining Clough. A week later, Don – in capital letters to denote his excitement – records in his diary his departure for SKYE! It took him 30 hours to hitch-hike from Cleveleys, near Blackpool, where he was then working, to Glenbrittle. He arrived at the campsite above the beach on a Saturday evening to the traditional Glenbrittle welcome of downpour, midges, and a dreich mist enveloping all the hills. The weather on Sunday was no improvement. Undeterred, they squelched across the boggy shoulder of Sgurr Dearg into Coire Lagan and up to the base of Skye's finest cliff, the 1000-foot-high Sron na Ciche: 'The first thing we did was a Very Difficult route on Sron na Ciche and it nearly put an end to us all.'

What they had embarked on was the Cioch Gully, a 500-foot-long climb which ends on the terrace crossing the cliff at half-height. A natural drainage channel, it was perhaps as bad a choice of route as they could have made under the conditions:

> The climb finishes up an open gully and we were just about in this when a tremendous cloudburst turned it into a waterfall. We bashed on quick as we could to the top. On the last pitch I got completely stuck. I unfastened myself from the rope and shouted down to Eric to try further to my right. Then that silly bugger got himself stuck too. This only left Leo, who thought it was all a great joke. He came off his belay and climbed straight up through the torrent of water to the top. Then he dropped a rope to Eric and got him up and then he did the same for me. It wasn't a very good start to the holiday and in fact it wasn't a very good holiday for climbing.

---

[9] Ellis Brigham's was the original climbing shop in Manchester. It had begun as a small cobbler's establishment in Upper Conran Street, Harpurhey, came to specialise in nailing boots for the luminaries of the city's Rucksack Club, and expanded to selling then-difficult-to-obtain climbing equipment and literature before branching out still further in the 1960s under the management of Ellis's sons to become one of the major chains of climbing shops in the country.

Don's final reflection will strike a chord with many who have experienced the bleak misery of Skye in the rain. A necessary and traditional part of every mountaineer's apprenticeship, it comprises wet clothes for a fortnight,[10] swirling mist, slippery basalt where you expected frictional gabbro, topographical confusion, searing drops, anxious descents, endless clammy hours spent swatting midges and avoiding contact with the tent fabric as you gaze out at the waves soughing in from a grey sea on to the grey shingle of a Hebridean beach. Not, under those conditions, one of life's more pleasurable passages, it is one of humanity's interesting and perverse psychological quirks that from the enduring and overcoming of these difficulties and discomforts, some considerable quota of the appeal of mountaineering derives.

The only other recollection Don left of this first serious mountain holiday (and the Black Cuillin of Skye are serious mountains, quite different in character from any other British hills) gives another early glimpse into the prudence which was to ensure his survival and perhaps moderate his record as a mountaineer:

My first big rappel was off the top of the Inaccessible Pinnacle. There was a big fat bloke sat on top when I got up and I said, 'Hey, how d'you get down off here?' He said, 'Oh, you rappel down.' I looked round and I said, 'What off?' You didn't use pitons then, it was a big crime. He said, 'Off that block there.' I saw that it was a fair-sized block but there was no crack at the back of it. I said, 'What? Off that bloody thing? Is it safe?' He laughed and said, ''Course it's safe. I'll hold it on for you.' I wasn't too sure about this, it looked risky to me, so I said, 'Have other people gone off this?' 'What?' he said. 'Ten thousand people have rappelled off that!' Anyhow, I took his word for it because I thought he had superior knowledge and I didn't want to appear a coward. I know now that people like that who think they're a bit of an authority on things can cause really nasty accidents.'[11]

---

[10] Cheap and effective waterproof outdoor clothing was unavailable in Britain before the mid-1960s. Before then, if you went out in the rain, you just got wet. Some – sceptical of the claims of gear manufacturers and the endorsements of sponsored outdoor celebrities – might claim that you still do, the only difference being that modern outdoor clothing keeps the moisture in long enough for it to warm up.

[11] Nowadays, in recognition of its inherent instability, there is a chain looped round the base of the block for threading the abseil rope through.

The Skye holiday seems for a time to have dampened Don's enthusiasm. On his return he made a couple of desultory excursions to Laddow and to Black Rocks at Cromford, at neither of which crags he appears to have done any climbing. A young woman from Sutton Coldfield whom he had met on Skye came to visit at his parents' house one weekend, and he went camping with her on the Saturday night to Ravenstones, where he noted without humour that the tent, after the Scottish holiday, was not waterproof. He spent one more weekend with her in early September, walking in Dovedale, after which he doesn't mention her again.

The lack of activity at this time, the demise of his new friendship and the grumpiness about the tent may have an explanation in an event that took place on 15 September. Don had been with Mr Emett, one of the firm's partners, working on a job at Seymour Road in Crumpsall when he blacked out and collapsed. He was rushed by ambulance to Hope Hospital in Salford, where he was kept in for 11 days and signed off work for three weeks thereafter. Initially, he was diagnosed as suffering from stomach ulcers, though examinations failed to confirm that. In retrospect, it is apparent that this was the first time he suffered from as bizarre and distressing an ailment as can affect a mountaineer – vertigo.

In Don's case, the affliction seems to have been caused by labyrinthitis, a condition of the inner ear which causes recurrent bouts of nausea and dizziness and which affected him intermittently throughout his life. This first bout lasted for over a fortnight, and after he came out of hospital, he spent most of his time sleeping, reading, and catching up on the latest westerns – *Rio Grande*, *Copper Canyon*, *Lust for Gold* – at the many picture houses, rejoicing in names like Alhambra, Rialto, Hippodrome, Trocadero and The Picture Palace, with which Salford and Manchester were then endowed. Soon he gravitated back to the crags, walking up to Dovestones ('Got soaking!') two days after his discharge from hospital, and to Ravenstones with Eric Worthington three days later. By the next Sunday, when he and Les Wright visited Yellowslacks, he seems to have forgotten his calamitous last visit to the crag and been well on the way to recovery, managing to lead a VS there, the Bilberry Face, and also Black Wall (HVS, 5b), which was probably its hardest route at the time.

Back in action for the dog-days of the year, he patrolled his familiar outcrops of Dovestones, Ravenstones, Shining Clough and

Yellowslacks, adding to his repertoire of routes on them. Among other feats which suggest that his ability was growing, and not restricted just to strenuous climbs, he climbed down the very delicate and technical balance moves of Ferdie's Folly (E1,5b) on Dovestones ('A climber should be able to reverse any move he makes,' went the traditional dictum). He was extending his geographical range too. He made his first visit to the massively sculpturesque and forbidding outcrop of Wimberry Rocks in November, picking off a clutch of its excellent Severes, and accompanied Fred Ashton on a weekend trip to the Roaches – biggest of all the natural gritstone crags.

In December there were heavy snowfalls. He went to Ellis Brigham's shop and bought a Stubai Aschenbrenner ice-axe. On 22 December, he and Eric Worthington caught the 10.20 p.m. rather than the 5.35 p.m. train for Bangor from Exchange Station, Fred Ashton having told them of the Manchester climbers' routine on trips to Wales. It arrived in the small hours of the morning, its occupants emerging to make a rush for a dirty and dilapidated carriage in a siding of the station. This was the first train to Bethesda,[12] the quarrying village at the foot of the Nant Ffrancon which was the nearest point to the mountains around Llyn Ogwen accessible by regular public transport. Once in the carriage, Don had a near-altercation which shows something of the briskness of his character at the time, and which might even have ended before it began the most important partnership of his climbing life. He and Eric were involved in the general mêlée in the carriage when Don found a compartment with only two people in it:

Suddenly a big bloke leaned out of the window right over me.
'It's full up in here,' he said.
'What are you talking about? There's bags of room,' I replied.
He shoved his face down to mine.
'It's full up,' he said.
I thought, 'Hello, this looks like a good start to the holiday – a punch-up before we've even got there.' Just then, Eric grabbed hold of me and dragged me away to a compartment

---

[12] The branch line to this station, as also the one to Llanberis at the foot of Snowdon, was closed down in 1961, courtesy of Dr Beeching, in one of the Conservative Party's periodic onslaughts on public services.

with plenty of room in it. I spent the rest of the night on the luggage rack and I didn't wake up till we got to Bethesda. It was a long walk up to Williams's Barn where we were going to be based, so Eric and I and a few others got a taxi. We passed two climbers walking up the road.

'Hey, that's Joe Brown and Slim Sorrell,'[13] somebody said.

I looked through the back window of the taxi.

'Which one's Brown?' I asked.

'The little one.'

I remember feeling a bit tickled about this because the big one was the bloke I was going to thump the night before.

Don and Eric's Christmas activity consisted of three long days learning about snow- and ice-climbing, in gullies on the Carneddau and whilst traversing the Snowdon Horseshoe. When they returned home, Eric had only a few days left before he was due to join up in the RAF. They paid a last visit to Dovestones together, did no climbing, but Don records how they 'found some pale ale in the shooting cabin below Charnel Clough', and how they came home with A.Taylor. There are two small but interesting pointers to the future here, negative and positive balancing each other out. As his eighteenth birthday approaches, references to pubs and drinking grow more frequent in Don's diary. And Alan 'Tater' Taylor's girl-friend, Audrey Whittall, whom he was soon to meet, subsequently became Don's wife.

---

[13] One of Joe's earliest climbing partners and the best man at his wedding to Valerie, Slim was originally a Stockport policeman who, on his retirement from the police force, became an instructor at the Outward Bound school, firstly at Ullswater and later at Ashburton in Devon. His wife Dorothy contracted polio in 1956, four years after their marriage, and was wheelchair-bound thereafter. In 1972, Slim's fellow instructor Michael Crook fell to his death whilst he was soloing in Ennerdale. Slim was out with him that day on a map-reading and training exercise, Crook had started climbing an outcrop of rock above where they were having lunch, had traversed round on to a gully wall and fallen to his death. The intense police inquiry into the death and ensuing gossip brought Slim and Crook's widow Susan close, and they later married. Slim's ex-wife Dorothy, from whom he had parted before the accident, had gone to live in a Cheshire home in Windermere where she was befriended by a male nurse, James Nesbitt, who became convinced Slim had murdered Crook. Nesbitt tracked Slim down to a college in Cardiff, and killed him with a sawn-off shotgun as they walked downstairs together past a lecture room where 120 police constables were sitting an examination. At his trial in 1976, Nesbitt was sentenced to be detained in Broadmoor at Her Majesty's pleasure.

With Eric away in the RAF, Don – who was throughout his life reliant on male friendships – needed to find a new regular climbing partner, and over the next few months he was to try several. 'Tater' was one of them, but he was too easy-going and indolent to stand the pace for long with Don. The irrepressible young Fred Ashton was certainly another, and he and Don spent time together, on one occasion doing a new route on the Somersault area at Yellowslacks which may well have been Don's first, though climbers are no longer able to appreciate it: the local farmer blew up the whole buttress in 1963, as protest against and barrier to the crag's increasing popularity. Another weekend saw them climbing at Black Rocks on a frosty January day, and doing most of the existing VS routes on the crag in order to keep warm before catching the 4.40 p.m. bus back from Matlock to Manchester. The weather continued to act as a limiting factor on activities, snow and rain keeping Don and his various companions huddled beneath the overhangs of Wimberry or Dovestones, cowering in cafés, or skulking through the long waterworks tunnel which used to offer the most exciting approach to Ravenstones. The diary entry for Sunday 18 February is typical: 'Went to Wimberry with Spike, Ted, Les, Maureen, Connie, Hilary. Tried the crack under the overhang. No luck. Did first pitch Route 2. Snowing and raining. Did new route on Cave Slab.'

There is no record of the whereabouts of the latter, which may have been on the lower and less impressive tier of rocks. The 'crack under the overhang' is almost certainly Freddie's Finale (HVS, 5b to those who like overhanging fist-jamming in razor-crystalled cracks), on the first ascent of which on an equally miserable day three years before young Fred Ashton had seconded Joe Brown – an event which is part of gritstone folklore. A fortnight later, in more favourable weather, Don came back and did Blue Lights Crack (HVS, 5a – 'hard for its grade', warns the guidebook), a decidedly energetic off-width crack which rises from a sinister crevasse, has a powerful aura, and was first led by Joe Brown in nailed boots in 1948. It was a style of climbing which in later years Don was to make his own, and refine to what are still considerable heights of difficulty, to the extent that subsequent climbers have concluded that Blue Lights Crack must be a Whillans route, in consequence of which he is credited in the current guidebook with its first ascent in 1948 – two years before he started climbing (see Chapter 13).

As the spring progressed, Don climbed more and more with the Oldham lads. He spent a weekend with them in Wales, climbing on the Idwal Slabs in the pouring rain, and on the way back to Williams's Barn at Gwern y Gof Isaf taking a look at Soap Gut, Menlove Edwards's route from 15 years before on the Milestone Buttress, which still retained a reputation for difficulty and which they did not attempt. Back in Greenfield, for a few weekends they used a new base at Wood Cottage youth hostel, on the Isle of Skye road above Holmfirth – reasonably convenient for Ravenstones or for a bracing walk across Black Hill to Laddow. But the welcome at Wood Cottage cooled amidst complaints of late returns from the pub and abuse of the pianola. The diary pub-references, in the run-up to his, Don's, eighteenth birthday, grow ever more frequent – 'Went in the Sugar Loaf', 'Went in The Clarence', 'Went in Bridge Inn, Glossop' – though this early dalliance with drinking ceased once he became involved with the Rock & Ice Club, most of whose members were teetotal. His climbing was drifting rather, as well – same crags, same routes, weekend after weekend. Something was needed to galvanise the undoubted ability he had displayed in his first year into concerted action. That something arrived just over a year from the date of his first climb with Eric Worthington on Shining Clough.

After a morning's work on 21 April 1951, he had taken the Saturday afternoon bus from Lower Mosley Street down to Leek with Jack Gill and Eric Flint, the two best climbers among the Oldham lads. They had walked up to the New Inn and on to the Roaches, where they slept in the small barn with the hayloft at the back of the southern end of the crag. Sunday dawned warm and bright, Don and Flint climbed Via Dolorosa and Valkyrie together – the two routes up either side of the magnificent and statuesque highest buttress of the lower tier which are among the best (and most contrasting) medium-grade climbs on gritstone. Jack Gill, meanwhile, was struggling with the difficult finish to Rotunda Buttress, an awkward VS on the upper tier, so they went across to offer moral support.

Drifting back to the lower tier later in the afternoon, Flint pointed across to the profile of Valkyrie Buttress and a figure poised casually 70 feet up. His rope, unpunctuated by protection, hung straight down from his waist to the ground, where a gaggle of onlookers lazed in the sun:

He was inspecting a wide crack above him which went through two bulges. I knew he was doing something new, so we decided to stick around and watch for a bit. I asked one of the lads who the climber was. 'Joe Brown,' he said, looking at me as if I was crazy.[14] Joe had reached the top of the climb and was on a good ledge. From the foot of the buttress, I could weigh up how he had reached the tip of the overhang. He'd gone by way of a crack running directly up to the bottom of the huge flake. Just then, his second began to climb and I saw it was Slim Sorrell. He went up and then started having trouble near the overhang. Actually, he didn't look like he was trying very hard. He probably just wanted to sunbathe. He made a few half-hearted moves and then he shouted up, 'I'm going down, Joe.'

When he'd got down, a couple of lads asked him if it was hard and he said it was. I thought, 'I wouldn't mind having a try at that.' Before I could have second thoughts, I got to my feet and shouted up to Joe, 'Hey, can I have a go?'

'Aye, if you like,' came the reply.

I tied on and started off. I didn't take long to do the overhang and this made me sure that Slim hadn't been trying. One step to the left and I stood on the tip of the big overhang. I looked up at the wide crack running through the two bulges. Joe's head appeared against the sky. I knew that he hadn't gone up the crack but had found a way round it. We stared at each other.

'Are you coming up there?' he asked.

'Aye,' I replied.

It wasn't too hard, and a few minutes later I was standing with him on the ledge. He looked at me curiously.

'How did you do it?' he asked.

'Fist-jams,' I said, 'and it's a bit tough on the hands.'

Don's account is unclear in its relation to the features of Valkyrie Buttress, and Joe himself has some intriguing points to make around it. His first (and this is supported by Don's diary for the year) is to state that he and Don – of whom he already knew at that time by

---

[14] This comment from Don's autobiography is rather odd, given that Don not only knew of Joe from Fred Ashton and others, but had also seen him on the trip to Wales a few months before.

reputation – only climbed together at the Roaches once in 1951. On that occasion the route they did was Matinee – one of the outright classics of the gritstone crags, and a route which was given its name because of the crowd of onlookers in front of whom the first ascent took place. This climb in some respects fits Don's description more nearly than does the one which it has long been assumed began the Brown–Whillans partnership – the Direct Start to Valkyrie, which is low down on the buttress, rather insignificant, not particularly difficult, and would have been unlikely to have drawn a crowd of spectators. Matinee, on the other hand, has great presence, and takes a striking crack-line leading steeply to the top of the Valkyrie flake before continuing over a notably awkward and difficult bulge above.

The crucial piece of evidence to bring to bear on an inconclusive account not written by Don himself (nor, apparently, checked by him at proof stage of the Ormerod collaborative autobiography) is that in 1984 Joe, Don and Ronnie Dutton went back to the Roaches (Don records the trip in his diary for that year). According to Joe:

> Don's account in his book isn't true. I had climbed the awkward, bulging crack on the Direct when I did that. When Don, Ronnie and I went to the Roaches in 1984, Don was very fat, unfit, and we climbed Valkyrie, which he did very well. I pointed out the bulging crack of the Direct and he had absolutely no recollection of it.

The play Don makes of his 'variation' to Joe's route is an interesting piece of self-assertion, surely to a degree competitive in origin, and comparable to another example we shall come to when we consider his account of the ascent of the West Face of the Dru. The chief points to be considered here are to do with the reliability of Don's ghosted memoirs and the balance of probability about the route done that day. The element of debunking of Joe that recurs here and there throughout the memoirs is highly significant, and the reasons for it will become more apparent as the narrative progresses. As to what the climb was that they did together in April 1951, Joe's recollection is quite clear: the Brown–Whillans partnership begins very worthily not with a trivial link-pitch between two established routes, but with the first ascent of the compelling and powerful Matinee – on which, according to Joe, Don led with ease the difficult and insecure top bulge.

7

New Friends

Don's ascent of Matinee posted a very public notice of the arrival of a new star. In front of a large audience, he had not only followed Joe Brown with ease up a difficult jamming pitch from which Joe's main climbing partner of the time had chosen to retreat; he had also led the route's second and harder pitch, and earned himself a place on the belay ledge alongside a man whose reputation was spreading by word of mouth among the small outdoor community of the day[1] as a figurehead from their own background whose ability on rock bore the hallmark of genius.

The point about background is significant. It would not be true to claim that Joe, Don and their friends comprised the first generation of working-class climbers to be active on British crags. That honour properly belongs to two groups: the Sheffield cragsmen – Frank Elliott, Harry Dover, Gilbert Ellis, Eric Byne and Clifford Moyer most prominent among them – who took to the Derbyshire gritstone edges to alleviate the boredom and frustration engendered by unemployment in the early 1930s, and raised the standard of gritstone climbing significantly in the brief years they were active there before quitting the economic hopelessness and despair of their home town and scattering throughout the country to find work;[2] and

---

[1] E.g., 'Towards the end of the forties, rumours of strange happenings began to circulate through the more active part of the climbing world. A gritstone problem that had baffled the top-rope tigers of three generations had been led on sight by a mere lad, or the same lad, having appeared to experience very little difficulty, would proceed to haul some harassed and hard-breathing immortal behind him up a climb regarded as solely for the very elect.' Geoff Sutton in *Snowdon Biography* (Dent, 1957).

[2] In *High Peak* (Secker & Warburg, 1966), Byne and Sutton's seminal account of walking and climbing in the Peak District, there is an excellent commentary on this, which brings out the importance of a new attitude towards physical training

the Glasgow climbers of the inter-war period who formed into clubs
such as the Ptarmigan, the Lomond and the Creagh Dhu. Clark and
Pyatt, in their history of British climbing,[3] give a picture of the latter
which holds as true for Whillans, the young Salford climber of 1950,
as it did for, say, the Clydesider Jock Nimlin in 1930:

> . . . in the 1930s, increasing numbers of youths and young men,
> poor, tough, and in many cases from the working-class areas of
> the big cities, first took to the sport of mountaineering.
> Glasgow was the centre of the movement, and it is sometimes
> argued that unemployment on Clydeside affected this develop-
> ment. Those who took part in it lived hard, toughly, and
> cheaply, reaching the mountains by exercising the art of hitch-
> hiking – a method of transport only given temporary respect-
> ability some ten years later by the war-time blitzes – and
> sleeping in caves, barns, howffs, and deserted bothies. More-
> over, they climbed extensively and well, providing in following
> years a new generation of climbers who looked at things rather
> differently from their predecessors.[4]

---

in promoting the rise in climbing standards at this period: 'Unemployment was
widespread, and long dole queues lined the gritstone-flagged pavements outside
the labour exchanges. In Sheffield, the steel, cutlery and silver trades were badly
hit by the depression and were constantly standing off men. Apprentices reaching
their time limit after years of existing on a pittance suddenly found themselves
classed financially as men, and were often sacked in consequence. Wages generally
were at a low level throughout the city, and a three-day working week was
common among those who were lucky enough to be employed.

'In those circumstances the energies of young people found an outlet in amateur
gym clubs, which began to spring up here and there. Equipment was bought from
the subscriptions of sixpence or a shilling paid by each of the members. Typical
examples were the Sheffield Weight Lifting and Wrestling Club; Footits Jujitsu
Club; and the Loft Weight Lifting Club at Intake, run by Eric Byne. The popular
paper among members of these clubs was *Health & Strength*, a weekly magazine
to which they were all affiliated, and from which they derived much of their
knowledge about sports and outdoor activities.

'Once people became physically fit in the gymnasium they began to look for
further outlets out of doors. Many who could afford the outlay became cyclists;
others took to fishing; others again took to cross-country running . . . A much
larger number, however, began to wander out into the Peak District each
weekend, and eventually many became bogtrotters, rock-climbers and
mountaineers.'
[3] *Mountaineering in Britain* (Phoenix House, 1957).
[4] It should be stressed that this discussion refers to the *sport* of climbing in relation
to a social movement. That other working people in certain occupations were

These antecedents notwithstanding, the generation spearheaded by Joe Brown and Don Whillans was the first from this background to receive widespread public recognition for its achievements, and one whose activities heralded a countrywide rather than localised spread of activity and involvement in the outdoors.

To come back to the belay ledge at the top of Matinee, a strong sense of Don's own watchfulness and capacity for appraisal comes through in the picture he gives of Joe Brown:

> He was slightly taller than me but of a very similar build. He had long black hair which he pushed back all the time and his face was almost oriental – flattish and oval with wide-set grey-brown eyes which slanted slightly. He had a mouth packed with big white teeth and he grinned a hell of a lot. While he smoked a fag, I looked at his hands and noticed the wide palms and thick fingers covered with hard skin and deep cracks. That's what comes from mucking about with cement and plaster. He was definitely not a bank clerk.

Joe was 20 at the time of this first meeting – two and a half years older than Don – and he had been climbing for four years (though for two of them he had been away on National Service). He and Don in the coming years were often to be lumped together under various reductive and condescending soubriquets along the lines of 'Manchester's pigmy climbing plumbers'. The popular press in particular, and less informed commentary in general, seemed to assume that they were identical and inseparable – two aspects, almost, of one character. In fact, they were dissimilar personalities, with a very different style and approach both in climbing and to life which led perhaps inevitably to the eventual rupture of their relationship.[5]

---

competent rock-climbers is beyond doubt. There is substantial evidence, for example, to support the argument that Slanting Gully on Lliwedd – a 900-foot Severe – was first climbed by Welsh copper-miners in the 1850s, decades before the birth of rock-climbing as an upper-middle-class recreation in the mid-1880s.

[5] When I first went formally to interview Joe, who has been a friend for more than 40 years, for this book, he sat me down in front of his fire, gave me a large whisky, asked why I was writing it, and having had a satisfactory answer, stared at me with the most searching expression in complete silence for fully five minutes, at the end of which he was finally moved to this utterance, delivered in his habitual flat, deliberate tone: 'You do know that he was an absolute bastard, don't you?' Having come out with that indictment, with characteristic generosity he tempered it by saying that, one-to-one, Don was the best climbing partner he ever had.

Some commentators assume a homogeneity about the northern working class from which both Joe and Don sprang. To anyone who is from that background, the falseness of the assumption is manifest. Joe's and Don's upbringings were not the same. Dennis Gray, an early member and the most vivid and amusing recordist of the Rock & Ice Club, within the activities of which Don's first major achievements were contained, rather gets it wrong when, in the course of *Tight Rope*, a very funny and highly imaginative set of memoirs which is required reading for the mood and atmosphere of the period, he writes that:

Don Whillans, unlike most of the other Rock & Ice members, was not from Manchester but Salford. The undiscerning might think of them as the same place, but not those with an intimate knowledge of the area. Lower Broughton was the place where The Villain[6] grew up during and after the last war, and it was at that time . . . matched only by Ardwick in dereliction, for it was also a jumble of grimy brick terraces.

This is a little misleading. Lower Broughton, with its relatively modern council housing, its gardens, its open spaces around the Irwell, was far more salubrious than either Ardwick or Chorlton-on-Medlock, the inner-city areas of Salford's larger neighbour in which Brown grew up, and out of which he was bombed during the blitz. The nearer parallel is with Adelphi, where Don was born and which he left at the age of five. Joe's childhood was spent in circumstances considerably closer to poverty than Don's. The last of seven children of a Catholic family, his father had died of gangrene when Joe was only eight months old, leaving his mother to bring up four girls and three boys on her own. She had supported them by taking in washing, and cleaning offices, and Joe had left school at 14 to work with a jobbing builder for 10 shillings a week. He was still working for him, and not for very much more money, when he and Don first met.[7] By contrast, Don's upbringing – mother a

---

[6] The nickname later bestowed on Don by members of the Rock & Ice Club.

[7] 'At the end of ten years, Archie owed me about £70. He had just had a nervous breakdown and was in a terrible state. I had started doing odd jobs on my own initiative and felt that I could not press him for the money. Finally, I forgot about it. The loss meant much less than the three pounds ten shillings he had given me years before to buy a pair of boots.' Joe Brown, *The Hard Years* (Gollancz, 1967).

machinist and father an assistant in a high-class grocer's shop – was considerably more comfortable and stable. His employment as tradesman-apprentice with a firm of plumbers, studying for City & Guilds qualifications, was more accredited and secure than Joe's. There were contrasts too in their characters and their climbing styles.

Don's character is the implicit content of this book. To sketch in briefly that of Joe, there is an apparently amiable and open front to it. He is very approachable and does, as Don noted, smile a lot. When he does so, it is not with the sort of celebrity's instant rictus which suggests a switch at the side of the head. With Joe, it seems to denote an authentic and warm amusement at the oddity of life which the attentiveness and discernment of his character perceives. His speech is weighed and slow, his responses quite reticent. People pay court to him, he watches them, and keeps his own counsel. When he does present his verbal conclusions, they are gnomic, minimal, and often dance with a teasing wit and badinage. He's a funny and relaxing companion, robustly playful in a physical manner at times. He loves wrestling bouts – on the first ascent of a climb on a Pembrokeshire sea-cliff once, into which I had inveigled him, of which he had led the top pitch and which was the loosest and most dangerous either of us had ever done, I emerged over the edge to find him sitting without a belay and with his feet down two rabbit-holes, from which position he pulled me down on top of him and battered me round the ears to relieve his feelings about the climb. But most marked of all about Joe is the detachment of his character. He is not needy in his friendships as many men are, keeps himself apart within them, and for those who see friendship as bargain rather than appreciation, this frustrates. He is inevitably, through precedent reputation, joint achievement and distinction of personality, the most important male character to appear in relation to the subject of this book. In some ways, too, he is the most enigmatic, difficult, and infuriating one from that subject's perspective.

One of the clearest expressions of the enigma is perhaps in Joe's climbing style. Like conversation with him, it is not straight-forward; it deals in lateral thinking, adjustment, balance. When you watched Joe or climbed with him on a difficult route when he was in his prime, there would be times when what confronted you was an element of mystery, of an ingenuity of thought expressed through exceptional agility and control. He was not an especially powerful climber, more a supremely skilful and relaxed craftsman entirely at home with the material on which he worked, relaxed and economical in the way he dealt with it, not subduing the rock but working with it, turning it to his advantage. Don Roscoe tells how he 'was continually amazed by Joe's ability to relax while he arranged runners in extremely difficult positions where I, as second, would struggle to stay in contact with the rock'. To take an image from a different sport, and one with which rock-climbing in particular has some similarities, Joe was a Muhammad Ali or a Sugar Ray Leonard rather than a Joe Frazier or a Marvin Hagler. Don, on the other hand, was clinically efficient, fast and aggressive, reducing the rock's resistance by sheer force of onslaught – the Mike Tyson of 1950s rock-climbing, brutally and inexorably precise. Where Joe puzzled and surprised, Don awed. It is only rock-climbing that is being described here, the game of mountaineering being far more complex. But these are points and issues to which we will return.

Joe and Don meanwhile, the ritual of introductions over, are on their ledge above Matinee, Joe rolling cigarettes and no doubt fixing Don with his customary levelling gaze as Don tells him of how he and Eric Worthington have arranged to go on Cloggy[8] at Whit Week.

He asks what it's like, and Joe – who is always helpful and straightforward when faced with genuine requests for advice – tells him he'll find the climbs pretty easy by comparison with what he's been doing on gritstone. Don looks askance, doubtful. They drift over to beneath the upper tier and Joe draws Don's attention to a cracked and labiate line of weakness, weeping with moisture and streaked vivid green with lichen, which splits the underside of the biggest overhang, 50 feet up:

'Ever thought of having a try at that?' he asked me.
'I've thought of it, but that's as far as I've got.'

---

[8] Clogwyn Du'r Arddu ('the black cliff of the black height'), a mile to the north-west of Yr Wyddfa (Snowdon summit), is universally referred to thus by climbers. Reaching a height of 600 feet, it is perhaps the most formally beautiful and architectonic of British cliffs, the climbing on it of unique atmosphere and quality. The first significant climbs on the cliff had been made up its obvious lines, which provided routes at the top standard of the day, in the period 1926–33. By the early 1950s standards were rising sufficiently to promise a further phase in its exploration.

Smiles of complicity. They go back to their separate groups of friends, a history having begun. Afterwards, the walk to the road, the 7.30 bus home, the laconic entry in the diary: 'Did Via Dolorosa, Valkyrie, with Flint. Jack did Rotunda Buttress. Did new route with J. Brown.'

It would be nearly two months before Don and Joe would climb together again. Don went back to his weekends with the Oldham lads, frequently teaming with Jack Gill and climbing for the most part on gritstone crags which were new to him: 'April 29: Met Jack at Mosley Street. Went to Widdop. Sunday, did Artificial Wall, Purgatory, went down to pub, got lift to Hebden, went on another small crag near Todmorden. Caught 9.15 bus home.' Or on more familiar ones: 'May 6: Went to Shining Clough with Jack and Vic. Got lift on motorbike and police car, did three-quarters of Central Route.'

The anticipation was surely building up for the trip to Cloggy with Eric Worthington. The latter duly arrived home on leave, they spent a Friday evening packing rucksacks, and on Saturday took the bus out to Altrincham to hitch-hike separately down to Wales – calculating that they would have more luck that way. Don, carrying the tent, arrived first in Llanberis and set off up the path by the mountain railway. At six o'clock he reached Halfway House[9] and went in for a cup of tea. A group of climbers had just come down from the cliff and were talking about the route they'd just done. 'They'd climbed Great Slab on the West Buttress. I was impressed with this, because I'd heard of this climb and I knew it was pretty hard. One of these lads was really quite small, and even younger than I was. I reckoned that if he could climb on Cloggy, then so could I.'

The lad in question was Dennis Gray, who leaves – true Vaudevillian that he is – a more graphic version of the encounter:

_____

[9] A Welsh climbing institution, Halfway House was a corrugated-iron hut sited near the railway a little below the point at which the track to the foot of Cloggy branches off the path up Snowdon from Llanberis. Open at weekends and holidays from Easter to September, and run by the estimable Mrs Williams of Llanberis and her daughter Vember – the latter the object of many climbers' unrequited affections – its tea and home-made lemonade fortified generations who came this way. It blew down in a particularly severe gale in 1992 and the Snowdonia National Park stepped in to forbid, on the grounds that it was an eyesore, its rebuilding in the original style. It languishes now as a particularly unsightly and derelict repository for rubbish and a symbol to local people of the oppressiveness of Park planning officers and regulations towards local enterprise.

I first met him at Whitsuntide in 1951 when he was 17 and I was two years younger. He was walking up to Cloggy on his own as I was walking down and, as he drew level, I got the impression of someone who chewed nails and spat rust. Fairhaired, sporting a small quiff over a boxer's face, he had a wedge-shaped body only as big as mine (then at five feet three) but obviously twice as powerful. He stopped in his tracks and stared hard at me for a moment, and with a withering look came out with an 'Ahh-doo!' as a greeting. I stood transfixed, unable properly to catch this utterance.

'Ahh-doo!' he slowly reiterated.

I could see by his demeanour that his temper was rising and stammered out a 'Hullo', then turned and bolted down the Llanberis track.

'Bleeding stuck up!' I heard him spit out as I took flight.

Whatever the literal version of events might have been, Dennis's story gives an impression which has about it the feel of subjective truth.[10] If the meeting with Dennis did irritate Don, he was soon to be calmed. He walked up to Maen Du'r Arddu, the grassy moraine on the far side of the lake from the cliff. It was seven o'clock, and he sat there looking:

It was a forbidding sight and one that I'll never forget. Everything was still and quiet, the wind had dropped, the sky was in that middle stage between light and dark. Cloggy stood there huge and solid. This was it. I don't know exactly what I thought as I looked at it, but I know that I was impressed – and excited.

It would be strange if his mind had not been running on the

---

[10] My own first meeting with Don, 10 years after his meeting with Dennis, was not dissimilar. I was 14, at an Ogwen Cottage party, felt a tap on my shoulder and heard a voice from behind growl, 'Yer leanin' on me!' I glanced round, saw no one, carried on talking and drinking. Another tap: 'Ah said, yer leanin' on me!' I turned round to see Whillans, astonishingly short, disturbingly broad, slightly drunk, looking at me with intent. 'I'm terribly sorry, I didn't mean to.' 'Aye, but I told you. I think you an' me 'ad better go outside!' I was terror-stricken, said the first thing that came into my head: 'But it's raining outside.' His scowl slowly cracked into a grin, his eyes not leaving mine for an instant. 'Aye, yer look wet enough already.' And with that he stalked off to wind up someone else.

descriptions of first ascents here from Colin Kirkus's book,[11] which he had been reading in the weeks before in preparation for the holiday:

> The traverse was very severe. There was one sloping hold where my rubbers would not grip at all, so at last I took them off and managed to get across in my stockinged feet. I found myself on a tiny grass ledge looking rather hopelessly up at the grim face above . . . The corner was a 20-foot wall of literally vertical grass. I made a mad rush at it. I had to climb up more quickly than the grass fell down. It was nasty and dangerous.

Eric arrived at 7.30, they put up the tent in the cliff's shadow, and next morning they climbed. Eric remembers that they had got rid of the tow-rope by now and for some time had possessed a proper full-weight Italian hemp climbing rope. As they were scouting along the foot of the crag for a suitable line to take, Don shouted across that he recognised from the picture in Kirkus's book the start of Curving Crack – a 30-foot flake leading to a pedestal from which the main crack to the left could be reached. He tied on to the rope, laybacked up the flake, and belayed at its top to bring up Eric, who climbed it by the less strenuous option of jamming. They swung round into the main, rather dirty chimney-crack on the left, and were soon at the top of the route. According to Don, '. . . the climb wasn't too difficult – I'd done things much harder technically – but even though it was a fine day, the rock was a bit greasy and there was a hell of a lot of grass about. Nevertheless, I'd done a famous climb on a famous cliff and I was pleased about it.'

Joe's prediction was proving right. They made their way down the descent by the Eastern Terrace and over the Middle Rock to the bottom of the cliff, where they were joined by Vic, Jack and Stan – three of the Oldham lads with whom Don now joined forces, Eric dropping out to sunbathe. Stan Clough suggested an ascent of Longland's Climb by the rarely done, wet and repulsive original start, in consequence of which, by the time Don got to the Faith and Friction Slab – reckoned at the time to be the crux – his boots

---

[11] *Let's Go Climbing* (Thomas Nelson, 1941), a prelapsarian classic of mountain literature.

and clothing were soaked with water and greased with moss, mud and slime: 'When I got to the Faith and Friction, I thought I'd reached the end of the earth. It was quiet on Cloggy, there was only us on it and I'd lost sight of the other lads below me. It was an impressive moment. I finally made my move up the slab and it was a bit scary but really enjoyable.'

That was the end of their climbing for the holiday, but as Don and Eric slept in the tent again that night with the presence of the great cliff all around them (anyone sleeping here alone, the legend had it, would wake as poet or madman), there would have been the knowledge of another hurdle cleared in the psychological progress that is climbing, and in which the completion of your first routes on Cloggy were an acknowledged step.

Another step to be acknowledged was that the climbing partnership with Eric Worthington was coming to an end:

> Don was a good mate. He pushed harder, was more adventurous than I was, and maybe I slowed him up a bit at the right time. We had a good climbing relationship. But when I went in the RAF and stopped climbing regularly, it was obvious I was holding him back then, so we didn't climb much together after that.

They certainly didn't climb together on the next weekend, that of Don's eighteenth birthday, which found them camping in Langdale. Whilst Eric stayed in the tent on the holiday Friday, Don went up to Gimmer Crag with Ted from Oldham. They didn't climb, but the start of an interesting dynamic between the two locates here. Don climbed the classic VS, Gimmer Crack, on the Saturday with a member of the Yorkshire Mountaineering Club, and as he was doing so, noticed Ted on a nearby Severe:

> There were a couple of hard men from Oldham who were older than us. All the lads were a bit scared of them and you'd almost to ask their permission if you wanted to do a climb . . . I was up in the Lakes at Gimmer Crag and I saw Ted, one of the hard men, performing on the rock. Well, he put the fear of God in me. I thought he was going to fall off any minute, he looked so shaky, but that only made me think the climb was hard; I didn't realise that it was because he was no bloody good.

He met Ted again the following Sunday by chance in the Greenfield café. Jack Gill had stood Don up in an arrangement to meet at the Wimberry boulders, so he had gone there to seek company. Again, he and Ted didn't climb together. Nor did they see each other again for two months, in which time Don's climbing career accelerated away.

In the next couple of weekends, he managed to repeat several of Joe's new climbs: the delicate and exposed Dorothy's Dilemma at the Roaches; The Trident and Coffin Crack, two of his 1948 crack-climbs at Wimberry. By tackling these climbs, which had a terrific reputation because of their originator[12], he was dogging the master's footsteps, deliberately setting out to find out how their abilities compared. The chance to do so more directly was to come very soon.

Joe and Don's next meeting came about through a chance encounter on a wet June Saturday afternoon with Fred Ashton in Ellis Brigham's shop. Fred had regaled Don in colourful terms with the story of a new route up which he, Slim Sorrell and Ray Greenall had followed Joe Brown three weeks previously on Clogwyn y Grochan in the Llanberis Pass. In his autobiography Joe, who found the climb (later named Hangover – it was Joe's first new route in Wales) straightforward, noted that 'the rest of the party was severely pressed to stay in contact with the rock; the difficulties were unusually sustained and everyone resorted to a certain amount of brute force'.

After abusing the route and its progenitor in the usual way, causing considerable elevation to the eyebrows of the old cobbler who was the shop's proprietor, Fred let it slip that he and Ron Moseley, Slim and Joe were to spend the next weekend at Froggatt Edge, on the Sheffield side of the Peak District and an established favourite of the Valkyrie Club[13] to which Joe and his friends belonged.

---

[12] In my own early days as a climber, 10 years after these events, the fact that a climb was 'a Brown route' ensured its infrequent repetition and added at least a psychological grade to its difficulty.

[13] The Valkyrie Mountaineering Club was founded in Derby in September 1947 by a group of climbers, Wilf White, Chuck Cook, Nat Allen and Don Chapman foremost among them, who were leading at the highest outcrop standard of the time. A year later, after a meeting in Wales, Brown and Sorrell joined, and in the autumn before the former was called up, members of the club produced a string of first ascents which now rank as the great medium-grade classics of gritstone climbing.

Don and the two Oldham climbers, Eric Flint and Jack Gill, who had, since Eric Worthington's departure, become his most regular companions, turned up. They camped in a grassy little flat glade below Froggatt Pinnacle, brewing tea, talking, watching the sun set over Sir William Hill, and were up early and active along the deserted edge next morning. Apart from repeating several of Joe's 1948 routes – Tody's Wall and Chequers Crack (which has been misappropriated to the Whillans canon in the current guidebook) among them – Don, climbing in rubbers, led his first significant and still-extant new climb. Called Beech Nut, because it was difficult to crack, it is today regarded as quite a stiff and competitive little problem pitch at its grade of HVS, 5b. Don graded it VS, in line with Joe's routes on the edge.

The effect of this weekend on Don – of the proximity to the man who was, it now seemed apparent, his only peer, and of the success of his pioneering – was galvanising. His first action the next weekend, having had his hemp rope mocked by his new associates, was to return to Brigham's and buy a 100-foot length of full-weight nylon rope.[14] It was put to immediate use on a trip to Stanage with Fred, Jack Gill and Pete Greenall. Two climbs at the time on this longest and most varied of the gritstone edges had reputations for difficulty. Peter Harding's 1946 route Goliath's Groove had been graded Exceptionally Severe, whilst Joe Brown's ascent of the Right Unconquerable crack – a leaning and unprotected layback with a precarious crux to overcome a bulge right at the top – was epochal. Don led them without hesitation and in quick succession. In little over 14 months from the date of his first route, he had arrived as a climber, and he underlined the point a week later when he produced the first of his new routes which bore what came to be seen as the authentic Whillans stamp.

He found it on Gardom's Edge, a little-frequented venue above the village of Baslow, which conceals some of the finest climbs on gritstone among its thickets of birch and rowan and scatter of great, blocky buttresses. One of these was a long-standing top-rope

---

[14] Viking nylon rope, in four thicknesses (line, half-weight, full and extra-full weights), was just becoming available in 1951, although a few climbers – Menlove Edwards among them – had used nylon barrage-balloon mooring cable as climbing rope in the 1930s. Viking rope was hawser-laid, soon became furry and stiff with use, but was vastly superior to the Italian hemp ropes which were still widely available and in use until the early 1960s.

problem known as Moyer's Buttress, after the Sheffield climber of the 1930s, Clifford Moyer. It was entirely unprotectable at the time, at 85 feet was long for gritstone, and its two crux sections both involved extreme stretches in delicate positions for poor holds, with the prospect of an appalling landing on boulders awaiting a falling leader. Its very long reaches without intermediate holds meant that it was not ideally suited either to Joe or Don's physique, and also it was raining, so they top-roped it – and found it very hard, the sloping holds on a climb that had not been repeated since its first top-rope ascent in the 1930s being covered with granular lichen that caused their feet to skate about.

'We could,' Don said at a later date, 'have brushed it, but brushing was regarded as cheating. Brushing and gardening from a rope were not on. You either had a look, decided it would go, and that was that. Or in the case of a few of them, if it was raining, just for a joke we'd top-rope them to see how we'd get on. It was all just fun.' The route was eventually led four years later by Peter Biven – who was well over six feet tall – after extensive brushing and top-rope practice, and with a top-rope trailing close alongside in case he ran into difficulties. Until the advent of modern protection equipment and techniques in the mid- to late 1970s, it ranked as one of the hardest leads on gritstone. Nowadays, it feels stern and magnificent at a grade of E1, 5b.

Joe had recently done two new climbs on the edge, so Don set to work repeating them. The first, Undertakers' Buttress, was a straightforward VS on which he had no trouble. The same held true of the next one, a fine flaky corner known as the Gardoms Unconquerable. So when Don arrived at the easy ground near its top, seeing a break leading out left under a roof and round an arete, without any inspection or demur, he led it to give an intimidating and difficult pitch that became known as Whillans's Blind Variant. It acquired a fearsome reputation, saw some abject failures – competent leaders retreating abjectly from the blind swing on to a steep and greasy wall round the corner – and was infrequently repeated for years. Its modern grade of E1, 5b is realistic, and with a very few exceptions, it was as hard as anything that had been accomplished on gritstone at its time. It actually, because of improved protection equipment, feels to be a harder route these days even than Moyer's Buttress.

Don's annual holiday for 1951 he took in July, and it rained. He

went to Glencoe for two weeks, the first of them in the company of
Eric Flint. There was one fine day – Friday the thirteenth – in the
first week. Don used it to set out to climb, in company with 'this
Robert character . . . an extraordinary bloke, he practically lived on
lentils', one of the test-pieces on the Buachaille Etive Mor. It was a
route called The Gallows[15] which takes a faint line of scoops up the
right-hand side of the east face of North Buttress. First led in
sandshoes and without runners in 1947 by John Cunningham, one
of the two leading climbers in the by-then-notorious Creagh Dhu
Club of Glasgow, despite its short length, which at 80 feet was not
much more than an average gritstone climb, it was – and to some
extent still is – regarded as a considerable test-piece. At its Scottish
grade of 'Very Severe'[16] it had beguiled and then rejected many
gibbering suitors. Cunningham's second had kicked off what was
deemed to be a crucial hold on the first ascent, and the route was
now thought to be impossible:

> I was so pleased to be on good, dry rock that even the
> technical difficulties of the route didn't seem to be too bad. As
> it turned out – maybe he'd eaten too many lentils – Robert
> couldn't manage the traverse to start the climb, so I did it on
> my own. As I was scrambling down, I noticed some lads
> shouting to me from the bottom of the mountainside. We
> went down to see what the fuss was about.
> 'Do you know what you've just done?' one of them asked
> me.
> 'Yeah,' I replied. 'The Gallows.'
> He looked at his companions, and then back at me.
> 'Did ye not find it – a bit hard?' he asked.
> 'Fairly hard – not too bad,' I replied, faintly puzzled by his
> attitude.

---

[15] Eric Flint: 'The whole holiday was wet, wet, wet and Don did Gallows Route
behind my back – I think I was trundling along the Aonach Eagach ridge at the
time, thank goodness!'
[16] This was the highest grade in Scottish climbing until well into the 1970s – a fact
which caused consternation to many more adjectivally pampered climbers from
south of the border and glee to chauvinistic Scots observers in about equal
measure. Unfortunately, the situation has now been regularised. Despite the
mildness of Don's response to Pat Walsh's questioning, he is reputed later to have
asked Cunningham, 'Hey, Jock – where d'you find these bleedin' chop routes!' (A
'chop' route was one on which the consequences of a fall would most likely be
death – 'getting the chop'!)

The questioner was Patsy Walsh, the other leading climber in the Creagh Dhu and a short, powerful Glaswegian straight out of the Whillans mould. He invited Don down – unusual honour for a Sassenach – for a brew of tea in Jacksonville, their idiosyncratic hut at the base of the mountain, and thus began one of the 'hard man' friendships which were a feature of Don's life.[17] For the rest of his time in Glencoe, Eric Flint remembers an ascent – not the most sensible of climbs under those conditions – of Raven's Gully on the Buachaille Etive Mor in heavy rain before he gave up and headed for home. Don's old climbing partner Eric Worthington arrived, the weather became as diabolical as Glencoe can produce, and their activity was limited to a misty day on the Aonach Eagach ridge and an ascent of Stob Dearg by Agag's Groove. Don recalled:

The Groove was obvious, it was well scratched and there was a little stream running down the back of it. I went up all right and reached the crux of the climb. I was standing, working out my moves, when suddenly, without any good reason, I became very apprehensive. The mist had thickened and I could hear the thunder rumbling away over Rannoch Moor. This may have helped, I don't know, but I was certainly scared and I shouted to Eric to watch the rope. He seemed a bit surprised at this, and asked me if it was hard. I replied that the rock was greasy but the holds were big; I didn't mention my feeling of fear. I wanted nothing more than to get off the Wall.

There are many instances in mountaineering of a premonitory instinct, a vague feeling of disaster's imminence. It was something to which, in Don's ventures to the greater ranges, he was

---

[17] Patsy Walsh is now a crofter on Skye with a predilection for telling Whillans stories in a Glasgow accent near impenetrable at times. They involve the dismantling and burying of motorbikes, long drinking sessions, climbing solo after seven or eight pints on the hard routes of the day wearing wellingtons. The memories and the mood are powerful, the detail often vague. 'Where did all this happen, Patsy?' I asked, after one particularly convoluted and outrageous tale over a tumbler of whisky. 'Aye,' he grunted, fixing me with a myopic gaze from behind bottle-bottom glasses, 'up there . . .'

It should be noted that Whillans was by no means universally popular with the Creagh Dhu members, and the pithily expressed opinion of Tommy Paul – 'What a pillock!' – was quite generally held.

particularly sensitive – an area of irrationality to which this supreme pragmatist was wholly in thrall:

> I went like a bat out of hell up the rest of the climb and I began to feel a bit better by the time we were both at the top. We'd heard voices from below and it wasn't long before a lad joined us on top. He was a Scottish student, and he said that he'd done the climb four or five times before. I noticed his boots and stared in disbelief; they were barely hanging on his feet, full of holes and gashes. We talked until his second arrived and then they set off down Curved Ridge.

Don and Eric followed at a distance, the former still feeling inexplicably jittery, and suddenly heard cries for help. 'We looked at each other. I could hardly swallow and Eric had gone white.' Whilst running down the path on the ridge, the boy with the ruined boots had missed his footing and fallen 50 feet over a small cliff. He was lying on a ledge, blood coming out of his ears, his companion shocked. Don went for help. As he was about to return with the rescue party, Eric arrived to tell them that the boy had died.

They returned early from the holiday, and Don returned further to touch the Chew Valley crags which were his talismanic climbing base. But even here, there was trouble in store.

He had gone out by himself on a Sunday (his diary for the previous evening reads: 'Went to Joe's. Not at home. Came back & stayed in all night, reading comics'), to Ravenstones, where he met Eric Flint and Jack Gill, who had been staying at Wood Cottage. Don repeated Arthur Birtwistle's lonely 1938 lead, Pulpit Ridge (HVS), and went on to solo Trinnacle Face West (E1,5b). At this point another climber turned up. For whatever reason, he was out for a showdown. He began needling Don about his new nylon rope, asking him what he'd bought that rubbish for, boasting that he'd had his own hemp rope for 14 years, 14 years he repeated, asking Don if he thought he could climb better just because he had a nylon rope. And then he made his move.

There is a strange rock formation at Ravenstones called the Trinnacle – a 30-foot-high pinnacle composed of three uneven gritstone pillars up which lie several climbs. He challenged Don to a race to the top. He would take the right monolith – which is considerably harder – and Don the left, which is slightly longer.

(*Left*) Every northern child has this selfsame picture – right down to the legless donkey

(*Above left*) Father and son on Blackpool beach, 1935

(*Above*) Don in the garden at Stanton Avenue

(*Left*) In Don's grandmother's backyard on Earl Street – Don and Edna in front, right and centre, with his Aunt Dolly behind

(*Right*) In Ashop Clough, Kinder Scout. Don is fifth from the right on the front row, and very neat and well-equipped

(*Middle*) The Rock & Ice in the Wall End Barn, early 1950s. From left to right, the White brothers, Ray Greenall ('Anderl the Brew'), Jack Gill and Ronnie Moseley.

(*Below*) Sunday family rambles to Marple

(*Below right*) Camping beneath the crags of Stoney Middleton in 1951, with the obvious lines they climbed there that year visible behind.

(*Above left*) Elder Crack, Curbar Edge, 1951 – Whillans repeating a recent Brown classic
(*Above right*) Second ascent of Arthur Dolphin's famous Birdlime Traverse on Almscliffe, 1951
(*Below left*) Llyn Du'r Arddu, 1952 (*Below right*) Everyone knows northerners kept their coal in the bath, so what did they do about personal hygiene? (Note the convenient soap dish.)

(*Top left*) A very early ascent of Suicide Wall, *c.*1952

(*Top right*) Brown's Eliminate, Froggatt Edge, mid–1950s – then a VS, now graded E3,5G

(*Above*) First ascent of Crossover, Stanage Edge – a typically bold Whillans problem. The famous Yorkshire climber beneath is suitably impressed

(*Left*) First ascent of Centurion, Carn Dearg Buttress, Ben Nevis, 1956

Doug Belshaw, Nat Allen and Joe Brown after the first ascent of The Corner on Clogwyn Du'r Arddu, 1952 – the atmosphere of the time is captured to perfection

Nat Allen, Don Chapman and Don Whillans at the Envers des Aiguilles, 1952

(*Facing page*)
Don Whillans on Esso Extra at Stanage Edge. (Don't try it this way – it doesn't work.)

(*Above left*) Capetown, 1957 – Downes, Whillans, Cunningham

(*Above right*) Don and Audrey, Froggatt Edge, 1958

(*Right*) First ascent of Sentinel Crack, 1959, on Chatsworth Edge

Don prudently suggested they use top-ropes if they were to race.

'Oh, get that, he wants top-ropes now,' the climber jeered to the audience. 'Well, go on then, if you're frightened of falling off.'

Eric Flint and Jack Gill were enlisted as belayers. The inevitable happened. In the urgency of his desire to beat Don, he fell off his harder route, the venerable hemp snapped, and he bowled away down the grassy slope beneath where he sustained no bodily injury but terminal damage to his pride. The incident marks a point of departure. Don is moving on, moving away from them, moving into a new group of friends with whom, in the next few months, he will assure himself of a place in climbing history.

8

Joe's Halfpenny, Dennis's Driver:
an Interlude

By comparison with the present-day climbing community, that of 1951 was minute. Other than ancient books and the journals of even more ancient clubs, the only means of disseminating information was by word of mouth. Within a very small group of active people, travelling around a limited number of popular climbing venues, that means was in fact very effective, though it had obvious shortcomings. The oral tradition, when recounting human performance, has never valued the accurate above the imaginative in its reportage. And so myths grow, reflecting as they do something of their community's essential yearnings.

The myth of Don Whillans began to take shape very early in his climbing career. Don Roscoe, an early member of the Rock & Ice Club which was to be, from its foundation in 1951, the major force behind the revolution which took place in British climbing during the 1950s, remembers identifying the mysterious walker who was rumoured to have come out and started to lead Severes as his first climbs with a schoolfriend's uncle who had achieved notoriety as the best fighter in Salford. Curiously, this latter side of Don's character is the one which has always coloured most vividly the two-dimensional view of him within the climbing fraternity as supremely bold climber and instantaneous aggressor – Whillans the Dobber, in the idiom of the day.

Both sides of this shallow popular image in fact need qualifying. Don was not the 'supremely bold climber' the more timid among us require as exemplar. That title properly belongs to any one of a dozen heroes dead on the mountains. Boldness with Don was no more than one quality in the armoury of a mountaineer to whom prudence was second nature. As to the aggression, its celebration could be taken as a disturbing reflection of the violence latent within the predominantly male circle of climbers of the time, the question posed as to why they needed to believe in it, or indeed why the contemporary climbing community continues to need to believe in it.

Alternatively, many of the stories assume the more defensible mantle of little-man-against-authority, or underdog-biting-back. There are, for example, the bus conductor stories. They all follow the same formula: bullying bus conductor meets nemesis in shape of put-upon five-feet-three-inches-tall climber with the weight of natural justice in his fists. Case is taken to higher authority – the Magistrates' Court – by which it is thrown out, natural justice being thereby twice endorsed.

Here's a version of the myth by Joe Brown:

At the age of 15 Whillans was taken before the magistrate to account for punching a bus conductor who had been laid out cold. The court was informed that Whillans had not hit the man with anything but his fist; on that point the magistrate doubted the evidence. Don had been getting off the bus; the conductor had demanded another halfpenny fare; Don had refused, stating that he made the journey to work every day and had paid the correct fare. The conductor got hold of him and tried to prevent him leaving the bus; whereupon the mighty fist of the tiny Whillans shot up from the ground and felled the man.

Leaving aside for the moment the question of whether the story is true or not, it's worth noting that the source is certainly hearsay (Joe didn't know Don when he was 15), that it has the neatness and balance of myth, and that Joe, who witnessed the events which gave rise to some of the myths, issues the following warning about Whillans stories in his own autobiography: 'The stories circulating about Don Whillans over the past 15 years have undergone so many colourful twists that no one can say where fact ends and fiction begins.'

There's another printed source for a bus conductor story. It comes from Dennis Gray's mischievous and irrepressible third volume of memoirs, *Tight Rope*. It's worth noting that in his first book of memoirs, *Rope Boy*, Dennis states his own reservations about Whillans stories:

> . . . his example and his climbing genius have made him the most talked-about climber of his or any other generation. Stories about his exploits abound, some true, some half-true, some mere fabrication. Most of the stories are not mine to tell and would best be recounted by the one person in a position to judge their truth, Don himself.

By the time Dennis reaches volume three, he has cast aside such scruples and gives free rein to his own highly imaginative version. Although long, it's worth quoting at length, and scrutinising closely:

> Shortly after I arrived in Manchester [in 1954], one of the great Whillans confrontations occurred. One Wednesday night, after we had been to the Levenshulme Palais de Danse, he had the first of several run-ins with bus conductors. Why Don and crew members of the Manchester Corporation Transport were such an explosive mix, I cannot now explain. However, on the first such occasion, he was climbing the stairs to go on to the top flight of a 92 Corporation double-decker, when the conductor made some rude remark about Whillans, because he had dived on to the vehicle before it had properly stopped and set off up the stairs immediately, which meant that the conductor had to follow The Villain upstairs to get his fare. On hearing this oath, Don came back down and offered his money, but not without a typically acerbic comment to the effect of 'That's what yer get paid for, mate!'
>
> This was more than the conductor could take, for it later transpired that he and his driver were well-known in their own circles as hard men. In fact, he was the infamous Bully McTeague. This meant nothing to the young Whillans, who took great exception when the Bully, still swearing, suddenly made a grab at him, a manoeuvre which Don anticipated and, lashing out with a fist just as the 92 accelerated, got the added impetus of several tons of metal behind his blow. This had a dramatic effect, which even Don had not anticipated, for the conductor shot off the bus and landed on his bottom in the road. The bus driver had seen what was happening through

his mirror and, slamming on the brakes, jumped down out of his cab, ran round and picked up his battered colleague, who amazingly was unhurt. Meanwhile, Don stood on the bus platform, awaiting their onslaught like Horatio. This not only came at him frontally but also from behind, for as he lashed out at Bully and his mate, some of the passengers came down the stairs and decided to join in.

So far we have the story of an event at which it will later transpire that Dennis was not actually present, but of which the incidental detail he sees fit to include creates the impression that he was: the number 92 bus, for example, did run from Piccadilly along Ardwick Green and down Levenshulme Road to Stockport, though a Mancunian, as opposed to a Yorkshireman like Dennis, would have known that it was far more likely Don would have caught the green number 96 Salford Transport bus, which ran from Hazel Grove along the same route to terminate at Salford's Chapel Street bus station.

Aside from any possible basis in fact, the story's provenance seems to me from two likely sources. Bully McTeague sounds suspiciously like a character from a D.C. Thomson comic strip *circa* 1950. His ability to withstand a punch with the force of several tons which deposited him on the pavement from a moving bus and return unscathed to the fray reinforces the probable *Beano/Dandy* derivation. The punch itself has an even more clearly identifiable source in a famous story, which Dennis has heard many times, from John Barry – incomparably the finest raconteur in mountaineering – entitled 'The 67,000-Ton Punch'.[1] In short, Dennis's tale – of which I've given you about a quarter here, and which carries on

---

[1] In précis, the story runs thus: John Barry, then a captain in the Royal Marines, is on an aircraft carrier in the Indian Ocean on joint exercise with the American fleet and marines. A boxing contest is arranged between the two marine corps. John – a natural middleweight – has to fill in at the last minute for a sick marine in the heavyweight division and finds himself matched with a giant opponent (probably also called Bully McTeague). After several rounds of feinting, running, somersaulting off the ropes, diving between the giant's legs and generally building comic suspense, he eventually has the temerity to commit himself to a shot at the giant's jaw, which has dropped rather in witnessing these antics. At this exact moment a freak wave – the only one in a flat-calm ocean – pitches the carrier's 67,000 tons behind the punch and Bruiser McHuge is summarily vanquished . . .

through ever-greater mayhem to a classic comic-strip conclusion[2] – is not one for the historicity of which I would vouch.

There is, however, a phantom truth behind both of these blood-and-guts myths. Its repository is Don's sister Edna, whose character is vigorously honest and direct. Her memory of the incident which gives rise to the stories is very clear.

Don, having been away on holiday, is on the bus coming back from work. He tenders his fare to the conductor and states his destination – Jubilee Bridge. The conductor asks him for a halfpenny more, Don asks why, the conductor says that the fares have gone up, Don asks to see the book. The conductor refuses to show it him, rings the bell and calls the driver, who stops the bus, comes to see what the trouble's about, makes a grab for Don and is swatted, but not seriously, for his pains. He then asks for the full explanation, it's given, and he tells the conductor that Don, the passenger, is perfectly within his rights to ask to see the fares tables. They're shown, the extra halfpenny's handed over, ruffled feathers all round and the bus continues its journey. No courts, no policemen, no serious violence – just a minor altercation between two very stubborn men, and an interesting study in myth-making, Joe's halfpenny and Dennis's driver giving their stories a tenuous connection back to reality.

This is not to say that none of the stories which have come down through climbing folklore about Don are true. But it is to suggest that many of them are elaborations around a central kernel of truth.[3] I don't wish to dismiss them. Nor, unless they are well authenticated, do I wish to incorporate them into this biography.

There is a crucial point to be made here in relation to the

---

[2] 'When telling the story the next night in the Manchester YMCA, Don, who looked as if he'd been run over by a tractor, declared that he thought he was going to get a real beating when he managed to get a hand free and, reaching down behind him, grabbed the bus driver's testicles. "Bully, he's got me balls!" he screamed, as Don wrenched with all his might and was let go, at which Don managed to fight back and knock McTeague down. But then, once again he felt himself grabbed from behind with both arms pinned to his sides. He was just about to try to repeat his previous manoeuvre, when he heard the unmistakable words, "Hello, hello, what's goin' on in 'ere?"'

[3] Talking with Don's widow Audrey once, the subject of bus conductors came up, she mused awhile, and – with an entirely straight face – told me, 'Of course, there was the bus conductor he thumped, but that was outside Birchfields skating rink and I think he was on the number 47 bus . . .'

character-construct put upon Don by the story-tellers of the climbing world. It is not only an exaggeration of some of his character traits, it is also a double-headed tyranny. The man himself feels constrained at times to play up to it; those who meet him often respond to it rather than the man himself; and those who knew him from the outset of his serious climbing attest to the fact that they very seldom saw him engaged in actual violence.

I have a memory of Don in a pub in Penmaenmawr. He is in his mid-forties, his great days behind him, his girth increasing, standing at the bar. A younger man with the reputation of a street-fighter comes in with a group of Don's friends, walks up to him, and, without any ado, punches him in the solar plexus.

It's a good punch, well delivered. Don, taken by surprise, winded and helpless, assesses the situation as the newcomer turns to the bar and buys a pint. Being in a good humour, and realising that there's no further threat, that the point's been proved, albeit at his own expense, he turns to the rest of us and nods his head.

'Steady lad, that!' is all he says.

No wonder Achilles sulked in his tent. Such is the weight of myth.

9

The Rock & Ice

Whenever a surge in climbing standards takes place, it seems to hinge on a small group of climbers, initially – or indeed, as rock-climbing became more technically refined and independent of mountaineering, even entirely – focused on outcrop-climbing, coming together, competing, bolstering each other's confidence and pooling information and expertise. Usually there will be a pair of outstanding performers,[1] not necessarily climbing together but balancing each other's abilities, spurring each other on – climbing may not be competitive in theory; in practice it is intensely so. In the 1930s it was Colin Kirkus and Menlove Edwards, Liverpool-based and Helsby-trained, who consolidated with their explorations in Wales the highest contemporary standard of climbing achievement. In their activities on Helsby, the great and now sadly unfashionable prow of sandstone near Chester which these days broods over motorway junctions and oil refineries, they may even have advanced it a little.[2] The climbs they produced became in their turn the test-pieces on which the next generation had to prove their prowess, and which they then had to surpass with new ones of their own.

This neat and cyclical view of climbing history obviously ignores the meteoric individual attainments of a few within climbing – Roper, Longland, Streetly – but it holds true generally. Preceding

---

[1] There are numerous examples throughout the history of the sport: Shipton & Tilman, Harding & Moulam, Cunningham & Walsh, Smith & Marshall, Smith & Haston, Crew & Ingle, Livesey & Fawcett, Allen & Bancroft, Moffatt & Moon, etc.

[2] It is worth recording here that – perhaps because of the Alpine Club's opposition towards even the rudimentary protection available on the Continent – British climbing's technical achievements lagged far behind those on German sandstone and Italian limestone until well into the heyday of the Rock & Ice.

chapters have dealt with Don's entry into the sport and – climb by climb, outing by outing – his growing competence and establishing prestige within it. They have also hinted at the significance of the convergence of his career in climbing with that of Joe Brown. If that has seemed to imply the sole importance of these two – Brown and Whillans – in climbing at the start of the 1950s, then the impression is a false one.

The pair were arguably the most gifted climbers of their time – though it should not be forgotten that claims of comparable technical ability in the early 1950s can be sustained for Cunningham and Walsh in Scotland, Greenwood and Dolphin in the Lake District, and the lone genius of John Streetly, from Trinidad & Tobago but briefly based in Cambridge. Nonetheless, in terms of a significant series of new climbs, sustained over a number of years and coincident with the very highest standard of the day, there would be few willing to argue with any conviction against the pre-eminence throughout the decade of members of the Rock & Ice Club. And by the summer of 1951, the conditions for its formation were ripe.

Its predecessor, the Valkyrie Club, after its brief heyday in 1948–49, had become moribund whilst Joe Brown was away on National Service. In his autobiography, Joe makes a slightly barbed comment that 'the disintegration of the Valkyrie was final[3] when Don Whillans joined the Manchester group'. There is a certain amount of evidence to suggest that Don was not an immediately popular newcomer to the small circle of climbing friends who had gathered around Brown in Manchester. Ronnie Dutton, with whom Joe had made his first climbs at Kinder Downfall as a 16-year-old, remembers his own initial reaction:

When he first arrived, I don't know why but I just didn't like him. Every now and then we'd meet and climb, but we never actually got on that well at the time. I was a boxer in them days, a bit older than him, and there were a few times when it nearly came to us squaring up. He was cocky as fuck, wouldn't share or join in that much, combed his hair all the

[3] In fact it wasn't – it staggered on for a few years, holding annual dinners (some of which both Joe and Don attended) and family meets, but its historical moment was over.

time and that. He really thought he was Jack the Lad, just because he could climb a bit. Maybe that was the trouble. Maybe I did too. Anyway, I got to like him later on – you generally do, don't you?

Dutton goes on to tell of how Don set out assiduously to court Joe – finding out where he was climbing at weekends and turning up there, calling round at his house in the week, monopolising his conversation in company. In his account a certain amount of old resentment is apparent.[4] Not everyone's first impressions of Don were so prickly and unfavourable. Don Roscoe states that 'we were a bunch of strong-minded individualists who coped well with each other's idiosyncrasies', whilst Nat Allen, mainstay of the Rock & Ice throughout its history and one of British climbing's enduringly popular characters until his death from cancer in 1995, has the following memory of when he first met Don in the summer of 1951:

I'd been in the Alps at the end of July and beginning of August with Don Cowan, Don Chapman and Eileen Gregory, so I'd not caught up on this courtship of Joe by the young fellow. We'd heard about him, of course – the Greenalls had actually climbed with him – and the way he'd followed Joe up Matinee, which as a route was quite something, was the talk of the town. But I'd not actually seen him. Anyway, I turned up one Saturday at the campsite we used to use under Froggatt Pinnacle. It was about five o'clock in the afternoon, middle of August, and I'd just got myself sorted out and a brew on when Ray [Greenall] and Don walked in. Ray's hands and arm were all burnt to buggery because he'd just held Don as he came tumbling out of The Peapod.[5] Apparently they'd been on that because Ray

---

[4] The dynamic between Don and Ronnie Dutton at this time is probably just a function of Ronnie's not starring at Don's focal activity. As Don grew older, the two did become good friends, though in the face of a continuing superior attitude on Don's part: 'I would never work with Don, even right up to the end. He was just too obstreperous. He had a way of doing things, and that was the right way. There was no arguing with him. You just had to do it his way. Nine times out of ten it could be the wrong way, but that didn't matter . . .'

[5] The Peapod (HVS, 5b) on Curbar Edge had been climbed by Brown in the early summer of 1951. A route of considerable quality and presence up a unique rock feature, it was (and is) quite easy to fall out of the pod where it narrows near its

hadn't been able to find the Deadbay, where there were a couple of lines everyone had their eyes on. So when we'd had a brew we left Ray to get cleaned up and bandaged and I went off with Don to show him where it was. We found it, and I spied out a line which is now Deadbay Climb (HVS, 5a). It crosses over from the right into the groove which the other two routes done later by Joe and Don joined from beneath and finished up.

I uncoiled the rope, tied on and led it,[6] and it was very obvious as Don came up that this was some climber! That night Chuck Cook and Wilf White joined us and next day we went back up on Froggatt. I was climbing with Don again because Ray's out of action, but the roles are now reversed and Don does most of the leading, with me pressed to keep up with him, especially on a couple of new traverses we solo along. One of the things he does is Great Slab (E3, 5b), which Joe had only led himself a few weeks before. He might have fallen out of The Peapod, but the lad was catching up fast. And I will say that, for all his later reputation, he came across as a very nice young fellow, which he always was with me, apart from once, when I had to get him by the throat and shake him.

Popular or not, in a group which couldn't always guarantee to provide Brown with reliable partners, whatever the perception of his character might be among the lesser performers, a climber of Don's ability had a crucial role to fulfil. He was already, from the start of August 1951, becoming a frequent, though not exclusive, climbing partner for Joe. He had spent August Bank Holiday weekend with him in Wales and on the Sunday they had made their first attempt at climbing what was shortly to become Cemetery Gates on Dinas Cromlech, the striking columnar cliff high up in the Llanberis Pass:

---

top, and where the elliptical approach typical of much of Brown's climbing, rather than a direct assault, must be employed to reach good hand-jams in the crack above. Until the advent of jammed nuts in the mid-1960s, like many of the hard climbs on gritstone it was hard and tiring to protect, and demanded a great deal of fiddling around from uncomfortable and exhausting positions to thread line slings behind more-or-less securely jammed chockstones using stiff bent wire. These were pleasures of which a later generation has been entirely deprived.
[6] Another route misattributed to Don by modern guidebook writers.

Joe suggested the crack on the right wall of [Cenotaph] Corner. I didn't understand why he wanted to do the crack when the Corner itself hadn't been done, especially as he'd already almost climbed the Corner not long before.[7] It seemed to me to be doing things the wrong way round. Anyway, I was game because it looked a hell of a route to me. Peter Harding was supposed to have had a look at it and had his doubts. The first time we tried it, we just did the first pitch and left it because it started to rain cats and dogs. But that first pitch was scary enough. Joe led it and he had a really hard time. Eventually he tied on to a holly tree and I climbed up to him.

'About seventy feet, I reckon,' he said.

'Aye.' I wasn't really listening. I was weighing up the chances on the second pitch. That was obviously going to be the crux. We rappelled off from the holly tree and on the way down I pulled a loose block out from just above a small overhang where Joe had had his struggle. That'd make it easier for the next time.'

Joe's version of this attempt differs slightly from Don's:

The right wall of Cenotaph Corner seemed to offer a possible route near its right edge. This edge was gently overhanging for 200 feet. I was not quite ready to try the Corner again but Don Whillans was game to inspect the line of cracks that split the edge of its right wall.

I led the first pitch and took a stance just above a holly tree. I say 'took' because there was no ledge, only a couple of footholds scarcely large enough to accommodate half a boot. I hung on to slings attached to poor spikes sticking out of the rock a few feet higher. This was the first stance in slings, as it is called, that we had taken. The position on the face was very

---

[7] Joe had attempted the climb three years before with Wilf White, controversially using five pitons for protection. In the niche 20 feet below the top, he had dropped his mason's hammer, which had scored a direct hit on White's head, causing Joe to abandon the climb in order to render assistance. Others, notably Peter Harding and Vin Ridgway, had attempted the climb – which had been ascended on a top-rope by Menlove Edwards in the 1930s – in the interim, but none had led past the crucial move at 20 feet. The final section had the reputation of being devoid of holds, and when Brown finally led it, he gave the opinion that it was the hardest of his early climbs in Wales.

sensational and frightening. I brought up Don and he was flabbergasted: 'Christ, this is a gripping place,' he muttered hoarsely. Neither of us seemed able to move. Then it started to rain and we both breathed a sigh of relief. To get down we had to descend on a doubled rope with our hearts pumping. Running down the screes to shelter from the rain we decided that we must return as soon as possible . . . We were now mentally prepared to accept this fly-on-the-wall situation.

There are no significant contradictions between the two accounts, but what does emerge from them both is the sense of an instinctive trust in each other's competence and an ability, present right from the outset, to operate as a team. That Joe recognised this is obvious from the summary comments he makes on Don's character in *The Hard Years*:

He was a born rock-climber. The ascent of rock-faces of every description was completely natural to him; he did not have to learn the craft, he had simply to familiarise himself with it. He could lead VS routes, or harder, virtually as soon as he started climbing.

The spiky side of Don's nature was dormant on the mountain. He was easy-going, and took my advice as readily as I took his on matters of route-finding. Dissension in a party on questions of route-finding has led to many broken friendships. But Don always listened to reason; he was content to accept an opinion that was not entirely consistent with his own and I believe the same was true of me.

The plain fact about climbing with Don was that if you got into difficulties, or couldn't manage to get up at a particular point on a climb, the chances were that he could pull something out of the bag. It followed that climbing with Don was much safer than with anyone else. He is the best rock-climber that I have ever known and he is equally strong on snow and ice on mountain ranges abroad.[8]

---

[8] Don Roscoe, who climbed extensively with both men during the 1950s, comments that 'I liked climbing with Don. It felt safe. It always felt as though we could get out of things, and I never felt quite so safe with Joe. I suppose we were brainwashed by those early climbs into thinking Joe was better than Don, but Don certainly had the edge on strenuous climbs, was determined, bold, and would not give up.'

In terms of friendship rather than the peculiar and calculated interdependence of the climbing relationship, the future for these two is boundaries, distances and rifts. But that Brown could, beyond all those, write summarily about Don thus argues immense respect for the practice of a craft.

It was not only Brown whom Don was courting. He also sought out, no doubt for purposes of comparison as much as for companionship, the other emergent star of the Manchester group, Ronnie Moseley.

Moseley was an erratic, occasionally brilliant, warm and generous character, slightly different in background and occupation – he was a commercial artist – to the others in the climbing circle of the time. In later years he was to become very distanced initially from Don and later from the whole group, viewing his climbing as 10 wasted years in his life. He and Don spent an early September weekend on Stanage together, sleeping in Robin Hood's Cave and homing in on three of the four hardest pre-war climbs on the edge – Wall End Slab Direct, Tower Chimney and the Mississippi Variant – as well as adding the Left Unconquerable to their collection. Despite the success in climbing terms of the weekend, in other ways the chemistry was not right and thereafter they rarely climbed together. In later years, there was a degree of friction between them, and Moseley, according to fellow Rock & Ice Club members, became quite critical of Don's outlook and behaviour.[9] This tension eventually came to a head in competition for the first ascent of what many still consider to be the finest of all Welsh rock-climbs, the White Slab on Clogwyn Du'r Arddu.[10]

---

[9] A response Don returned in full measure. This from 1984: 'We had a friend who was a climber, and he was an intensely competitive person. He was in the same club as me and Joe, but he wouldn't climb with us in case we stole the bloody limelight. That's what he actually said! I thought he was bloody joking, me, because in those days you went for the crack and the camping, and you enjoyed the atmosphere – it was the atmosphere that was great! He gave up climbing quite suddenly.' This isn't entirely true historically – there were occasions when Moseley climbed with both Don and Joe, even several years after the formation of the Rock & Ice. I doubt if it's fair as character-assessment either – Don could be savagely debunking of his fellow-climbers at times.

[10] Some surviving members of the Rock & Ice feel that too much has been made of this as the reason for a rift, though Don Roscoe, Don's second on the first complete ascent of the route, avers that 'Don was livid about White Slab.' A later chapter discusses Moseley's place in the Rock & Ice hierarchy more fully.

The actual formation of the Rock & Ice Club came about from the weekday evenings' social routine of the group of climbers based in Manchester with whom, from August 1951, Don was now spending most of his weekends and holidays. This routine was based on a series of venues: the Birchfields Skating Rink on Anson Road, Rusholme; the Palais on Stockport Road and the King's Cinema (one of Manchester's original and direst flea-pits) on Yew Tree Avenue, Levenshulme; and the YMCA on Peter Street in central Manchester. All of these, with the exception of the YMCA, were within easy walking distance of Joe's home on Dickenson Road, Longsight – a fact which suited Joe's character perfectly, and probably came about because of it. Don first heard of these night-time activities through a chance meeting in Albert Square with Fred Ashton, the latter-day Gossiping Guide to Manchester climbing. Fred alerted him to Wednesday nights at the Rink, and Don went along: 'I used to really enjoy myself there. It wasn't quite the tame sort of thing you might expect. We used to get on the rink and form a big whip – blokes flew off in all directions.'

The standard boys-behaving-badly scenario was not popular with the management and distinctly dangerous to the other clients, so, inevitably, they had to move on. Next stop was the Palais – the Levenshulme Palais de Danse, to give it its full title. The occasional popularity of this lasted well into the rock'n'roll era, by which time most of the group had girlfriends and were taught by them, with varying degrees of success, how to jive. But it did have one serious shortcoming, which was the requirement for a reasonable standard of dress – inspection on the door, exclusion without.

This left the YMCA – the Young Men's Christian Association – hostel, an imposing building of glazed ochre brick on the corner of Peter Street and Mosley Street, where most of the group for several years would gather on Wednesday evenings. There was a membership requirement for use of the hostel's facilities, and an annual subscription to be paid. Dennis Gray comments that:

I don't think any of the club were members, but its position and excellent lounge with a buffet service for the inevitable tea made it the ideal meeting place for the whole club, as some people could not get to other mid-week gatherings. They had been visiting the YMCA for so long [by 1954, when Dennis began to attend] that the staff there thought them God-fearing, paid-up members whom they greeted by their first names as they entered the door.

Don Roscoe slightly dissents from this view in suggesting that 'the staff had a pretty shrewd idea that we were not members, but we were quiet and well-behaved so they never challenged us'.

They played table tennis and billiards, drank tea by the gallon, planned their weekend's climbing, and some time after eleven o'clock most of them trooped off across Albert Square to catch the 93 bus from Princess Street and drink more tea in the hospitable Ronnie Moseley's home on Prout Street, Longsight. Joe Brown remembered:

> Living close to one another about eight of us became inseparable. Every Wednesday evening we went to the YMCA in Manchester to play billiards or table tennis and plan the weekend's climbing. Around midnight we trailed off to Moseley's house and drank tea into the small hours. None of us drank beer and in those days not many of us smoked. (I had started smoking as a youth but contrary to the popular image of a cigarette dangling permanently from his lips Don Whillans did not start smoking until many years later.) If we went to a pub the group ordered a large jug of orange and sipped it from small tumblers, making it last all evening. Rum and orange was indulged in at Christmas to comply with the superstition that one should be merry and gay.
>
> Planning weekend trips in Moseley's front room began with an examination of funds. The average wage of the group was about £7 a week. I had about £4 a week to spend. The biggest expense was travelling to the mountains. We had to budget carefully and keep a reserve for replacing costly equipment. A weekend in Wales was a special occasion, and most of the time we could only afford to go out in Derbyshire. Pre-occupied with this business the meetings frequently broke up at four o'clock in the morning. I lived about 400 yards away but the Greenall brothers and Doug Belshaw had to walk two or three miles home.

Don Roscoe suggests that the main reason for the Rock & Ice choosing Moseley's house as their social hub was his doting mother, who plied them with cake and biscuits, and would always make sure

Ronnie had steak – the family meat ration for a week – to take away at weekends, her son having told her, 'Can't climb on beans, Ma!'

This Wednesday routine at the YMCA suited Don well as it became established. In 1951, he still had three years' study at night school on Tuesday, Thursday and Friday evenings for his City & Guilds qualifications. Central Manchester was only half the distance of Longsight and Levenshulme from his home – if he missed the last bus from Brown's or Moseley's house, it meant an eight-mile walk through the silent city streets. Geographically, and hence socially, he was on the perimeter of a tight-knit group of friends centred around Brown and Moseley and from the same area. This became even more marked as others from Longsight, Levenshulme and Burnage joined the group in future years, and Don must have felt some degree of isolation, exclusion and resentment at this, and at the intense focus on, and admiration for, Joe.

The actual occasion of the formation of the Rock & Ice Club was a trip to the King's Cinema on Wednesday 26 September 1951. Don had called for Joe in the early evening and gone along to meet the others at the picture house. Carol Reed's *The Third Man* was showing, but the lads, sitting in their row, were not paying much attention to it. To the hushings of other filmgoers and the flashing of the usherette's torch, they excitedly discussed the idea that they should become a club – a discussion which continued ever more heatedly as they spilled out on to the pavement and walked the few hundred yards along to the Palais for cups of tea. Why bother with a club? went one side of the argument. Wouldn't it just lead to time being spent on rules and committees and fund-raising and huts and meets, both indoor and outdoor, and commitments? Wasn't it just futile since they already engaged in all the activities of a club without the dubious benefit of a committee telling them what to do? 'I wanted the group to continue the self-initiated policy of sleeping where we found ourselves at nightfall and not become tied down with responsibilities,' Joe, the least enthusiastic, wrote afterwards.

The argument raged backwards and forwards, Joe most stringently opposed to the idea, Moseley and the Greenalls strongly in its favour, Don as a newcomer for the most part just listening. By the end of the evening Joe had been overruled, and the Rock & Ice, with seven members, had come into being. In the next couple of days more were recruited by phone. The original complement was: Joe, Don, and Ron Moseley – the three most gifted climbers; the two eldest Greenall brothers, Pete and Ray; Slim Sorrell, the Stockport policeman who was Joe's long-time climbing companion; Jack Gill from Oldham; Doug Belshaw, another Levenshulme climber friendly with Joe; and a quartet of climbers from the eastern and southern sides of the Peak District who'd been the backbone of the old Valkyrie Club: Wilf White, Don Cowan, Don Chapman and Nat Allen.[11] Joe defined the club as follows:

> The Rock & Ice was a close-knit body, intensely active in the mountains and avoiding the usual relationships with other clubs. We were not represented in any national mountaineering issues or debates and it was not surprising that other climbers viewed us as a secret society. The solitary purpose of the Rock & Ice lasted six years before chinks appeared in the armour of its single-minded members.

The Rock & Ice celebrated its coming-into-being with a meet in Wales the following weekend. Don had managed to arrange a lift down to Wales on the back of a motorbike belonging to Sherwood Wiseman, a Salford climber and founder-member of the soon-to-be-formed Cromlech Club, between which and the Rock & Ice there developed considerable friendly (and occasionally not so friendly) rivalry.[12] Don walked up to Cloggy after being dropped off in Llanberis, found no one there to climb with, so came back down to

---

[11] Other members followed very quickly. Don Roscoe and Eric Price joined later in 1951 after regularly seeing prints of tricouni-nailed boots in the snow on a local croft and catching up one day with their wearers, Ron Moseley and Ray Greenall. Before that, Roscoe, Price and Alan Taylor had been 'The British Tigers Association', membership qualification for which august body was leading Very Severe.

[12] All clubs at this time had their champions, and the Cromlech Club's was 'Black Bob' Hughes – a huge and ferocious character with a penchant for crashing 1000cc Vincent motorcycles. His reputation was such that in one well-documented stand-off between them, Whillans quickly backed down. Joe comments on this that 'Bob just faced him down when he got aggressive one night at the YMCA. The thing with Don was that in fights he relied on the element of surprise – he got the first punch in, and with Don that would usually be the last one too. On this particular night Bob made it plain he was ready, so Don didn't push it. He was back the next Wednesday, though, telling us that "When that cunt Black Bob comes in I'm going to do him," but Bob didn't appear that night.' 'Black Bob' ended up as a genial and respectable primary school headmaster in the Manchester overspill estate at Hattersley – a grim place where the Moors Murderers Ian Brady and Myra Hindley committed their crimes.

Bryn Coch, the semi-derelict (now completely so) cottage above Llanberis which had become the Valkyries' and later the Rock & Ice's unofficial base. Don's reminiscences give a good flavour of the place and his feelings towards it, which are remarkably romantic for a man who was to gain a confirmed reputation as the hardest-bitten of pragmatists:

> Some of the happiest moments of my life were at Bryn Coch. I used to love waking up in the morning; the sun streaming through the holes in the roof, the sound of church bells floating up from Llanberis. I used to get out of my sleeping bag and pick my way between snoring bodies. I'd sit outside and just drink in the air and the view. Then there'd be the sounds and smells of frying sausage and bacon and us sitting there, laughing and talking and drinking tea and knowing that in an hour we'd be on Cloggy. Sometimes Nat didn't arrive until early Sunday morning. He'd have come on the train to Caernarfon, arrived there in the middle of the night and walked from Caernarfon to Bryn Coch. He'd come in quietly, creep over to Joe, who was always a sound sleeper, and grab him. 'Now then, youth,' he'd say. Joe had an old sleeping bag with holes all over it. He'd get out of it looking just like a half-plucked chicken, feathers and down all over him. And then there was Slim who was always one of the early risers. He'd come over to you and grab a handful of your cheek and hiss in your ear, 'C'mon, get out.' They were great times, those.

On this first weekend as the Rock & Ice, Joe and Don didn't go to Cloggy. They had another unfinished project in mind, and after breakfast they walked down to the village, tramped the four miles along the Llanberis Pass, and sweated up the 1000 feet of scree to the foot of Dinas Cromlech, where they scrambled up to the foot of Cenotaph Corner to renew the acquaintance made two months earlier with the crack-line on the edge of its right wall. Ray Greenall, his hands still suppurating and tender from holding Don's fall from The Peapod six weeks before, came with them to offer moral support and in the self-appointed capacity as 'official photographer to the Baron Brown'.

Joe led the first pitch, starting right of the arete, crossing round to beneath the crack and having no trouble this time with the difficult moves into it, where Don had pulled out the block. In the niche above, from which the holly tree used tenuously to grow before climbers came this way, he took a stance: 'We couldn't change places so Don led the second pitch which was truly hair-raising. All the way up it little flakes of rock broke off when we pulled or stood on them.'

Don's account is more detailed:

> The second pitch was just a crack up a vertical, smooth wall. I started off up this and Joe kept saying: 'Get some more runners on, get some more runners on.' He was stood in slings tied on to the holly tree. I got a few on and there were holds on the wall as well as in the crack; not too solid but as long as I'd got a good jam, I didn't mind standing on them. Inch by inch I got to the crux move where the holds on the wall seemed to disappear. I had a nose around for a while, reaching up and trying out possible holds. I saw one which was a sort of pocket. It looked really good, so I reached up and grabbed it. It turned out to be full of razor-sharp little flakes which cut my fingers pretty badly but I knew that this was the key. After a time I launched up and made the move and that was that.

Joe followed him to the tiny ledge out on the edge of the wall, and led on through up the easier top pitch. After 20 feet of climbing on huge, hidden holds, he stepped round the arete to a line of perfect flakes leading up easier-angled rock to the top. He shouted the news down to Don, who 'let out a shriek of triumph. Never before or since have I known him to show emotion in this way. He was normally taciturn after making a new route. Now he was bubbling over with pleasure.'

When they returned to the bottom, Joe got a lift back home to Manchester on a motorbike and Don hitched, without much luck, ending up by having to catch the 12.40 a.m. train from Crewe. The following Wednesday, in the café at Birchfields Skating Rink, Joe asked him how he liked a name for the route he'd seen on a bus in Chester whilst coming home – Cemetery Gates, to fit in with its neighbours Ivy Sepulchre and the still-unclimbed Cenotaph Corner? It stuck. Don added it in pencil to his diary entry.

The route was a milestone. Nowadays, the holly tree having departed – distantly attached to a falling leader – decades ago, the first two pitches are climbed as one, to Don's belay ledge. Technically straightforward, and with modern equipment very well protected, it remains one of the most-fallen-off – and one of the highest-quality – rock-climbs in Snowdonia. Routes with reputation generally suffer the reverse of them, but the Gates, as this one is familiarly and internationally known, retains the vestiges from a time when it was a psychological breakthrough – the first climb to breach one of the great vertical walls of the Welsh cliffs. ('Definitely E5, 1b,' was the verdict on it of John Allen, the finest technical rock-climber of the 1970s, emphasising both its relative lack of technical difficulty, and its continuing psychological impact.) Don's whoop of triumph was justified. His cool lead of the crux pitch opened the way to the Rock & Ice's great sequence of new climbs in the 1950s. He was now operating on equal terms with Joe, and the new climb's next important successor was not long in coming.

In fact, only a weekend intervened, in the course of which Don met Nat Allen, with whom he had become firm friends,[13] at Curbar, and repeated the latest of Joe's series of climbs there, the Deadbay Crack. This dream climb for the gritstone aficionado used to see very few ascents before the advent of camming-device protection, which has devalued the crack- and horizontal-break-based style of climbing on gritstone more than on most other rock types.[14] Joe had been quite proud of it. Whillans, according to Nat, flowed up it with barely a moment's hesitation.[15] He was pressing hard now at the master's heels. When they met midweek at the skating rink, the arrangement

---

[13] Allen recalled: 'Don used to write to me in the week – I suppose because he was a bit outside the Manchester group and so was I, and also because we both had to work Saturday mornings, being plumbers and not idle builders like the Baron Brown – and he'd say, "Meet you in the Plantation Saturday", or "See you at Froggatt," and of course you had to be there, because he could be very huffy with you if you weren't reliable. And most of the other buggers, by his standards, weren't that reliable, so in the early days I ended up climbing with him quite a lot.'

[14] And has also, in fairness, enabled some remarkable modern first ascents to be made and the plateau-level of climbing achievement vastly to have been raised. But with regard to the great climbs of the period under scrutiny, the point holds, and it is difficult for the modern climber to relate, in consequence, to the awe that these routes of the 1950s once engendered. Seven years after the Deadbay Crack's first ascent, Allan Austin – leading light in a new generation of Yorkshire gritstone and Lake District climbers – could still assess it as 'an extremely hard and strenuous crack climb'.

[15] On a subsequent ascent, when climbing with Joe, Don got the sequence of jams wrong in the crucial section, leapt off, and bruised himself quite badly.

was made to go to Wales on the Friday night and the understanding, given fine weather, was that they would go to Cloggy, where Joe had a long-standing score to settle with a climb which, two years before, had all but ended at a very premature date what many would consider to be the greatest-ever career in British mountaineering.

Their intended climb, Vember, lay up the first great break left of Curving Crack. Its first pitch, a deep face crack which acted as a sluice in wet weather and was invariably damp, had been climbed in 1938 by Arthur Birtwhistle, of Manchester's Rucksack Club, and was known as the Drainpipe Crack. Whilst attempting the next pitch under abysmal conditions in 1950, Joe had fallen from about 20 feet up. He had landed on the ledge and been fielded by his team, but had been badly frightened by the fact that two strands of his new hemp line had rubbed through as they dragged down a vertical edge of rock. However large a part reason might play in telling him that it was now dry, that he was using a much stronger and more abrasion-resistant rope, that he had found the first pitch infinitely easier than before, the sight of the sling which had held his fall and was still in place would have evoked painful memories. The effect on him is obvious in Don's account:

> Joe was going to lead all the way because, really, it was his climb. We got up the first pitch OK and I got myself solidly belayed on a tiny ledge. I'd heard enough about how Joe had come off the last time, and I was making sure that if he capurtled off this time, I wasn't going with him. Joe set off up the crack and reached the point where he'd fallen before. Then he seemed to be having some bother. I gave him time and then I called up to him.
> 'What's it like?'
> There was a long pause and then: 'Oh, it's all right.'

After some more conversation of a tense and minimal nature, Joe climbed on, and Don watched him closely:

> I could see he was definitely gripped up, which was unusual for Joe. Slowly he made the moves to the ledge.[16] When he'd

---

[16] One of the Brown myths current in the 1950s and 60s was that he had, in this section of the climb, whilst *in extremis* wriggled his fingers under a grass tuft, found a good hold, pulled on it, and replaced the tuft as he went by. I know at

got there, he turned round and called down, his voice shaking:

'Well, I'm up, but I thought I was off there.'

Afterwards, he said that he'd had psychological trouble when he'd reached the place where he'd fallen off before. You see, he'd never really fallen off anything else. I think he thought at the time that it was the hardest climb he'd ever done . . . I thought that if it was as hard as he'd made it look, then I was going to have to climb well to get up it at all. So I just forgot about everything except the rock in front and that was it; I found it reasonable.

Joe was a bit surprised at this.

'D'you think you could lead it?' he asked me.

'Aye.'

In that phlegmatic response, you hear the note not just of accepted equality, but of realisation that the master could be surpassed. Among British mountaineers, Joe's sole and unrivalled pre-eminence ended here, although it was established even more firmly in the imagination of the general climbing public of the time by his ascent a fortnight later of The Boulder on Clogwyn Du'r Arddu, in the course of which his seconds – Ron Moseley was one of them – couldn't follow and he led out 270 feet of rope to finish the climb.

The year descended into a succession of wet gritstone weekends. Don spent some of them with Joe, top-roping routes like Cratcliffe's Suicide Wall in the rain. Several weekends he spent revisiting the haunts of his walking days, ploughing over Kinder in the mist, sleeping at the shooting cabins in Torside and Ashop Cloughs.

At Christmas, they returned en masse – girlfriends, new members, hangers-on, as well as all the regulars – to Bryn Coch. The weather was dismal and the derelict house crammed. Don walked over Crib Goch one day with Brown, Moseley and Ray Greenall and came back soaked to the skin. Ray built up the blaze in the leaky barn section in which they were staying to bonfire proportions and Don noticed too late that his boots, which he'd placed by it to dry, were aflame, the toes burnt through.

---

least five people who have discovered the actual hold, on routes as scattered as The Boulder, November (not even a Brown route!) and The Mostest, and duly consigned its concealing tuft to the depths. Don's eye-witness testimony to its supposed source is the best commentary on the tale, and – elliptically – on the congenital propensity in climbers to bullshit.

On Christmas Day, in sodden clothes and with Don in his ruined boots, they went up to Cloggy. Joe, whose logical faculties have always been prone to the effects of damp, had decided that they should take a look at the Black Cleft. This huge left-bounding corner of the West Buttress may be the finest natural line on Cloggy. It is also a major line of drainage. A spring gushes out from beneath an overhang 150 feet up the corner to ensure that it is always wet, and sometimes very wet indeed, as Don recalled:

> Trudging up to Cloggy was a nightmare; every time I put my feet down, mud and slush squelched in through the non-existent toes of my boots and out again at the back. When we got to the snowline it was even worse, because my toes were just sticking out. There was another thing too: at some point, I'd ripped my pants from top to bottom on the inside leg.

Joe led a nowadays infrequently climbed pitch to the foot of the Cleft proper, where he made the curious but potentially useful discovery of a gardening hand-fork. His clear memory is that they decided not to go any higher. Don's version differs:

> I started up and got about 10 feet up the crack and then I'd had enough. It wasn't much fun jamming my bare toes into hard, cold, wet rock and in any case water was flushing down my sleeves and running out the bottom of one trouser leg and out of the tear at the top of the other leg. Talk about brass monkeys. Joe had had enough by this time too, his nose was like a road-mender's lamp and all his fags were damp. So we set off back to Bryn Coch, and that was the end of 1951.

It wasn't quite. On Saturday afternoon four days later, back in Manchester, Don took himself off to Brigham's and bought himself a new hat, windproofs, and a pair of Vibram-soled boots. He was the first member of the Rock & Ice to have rubber-soled boots. 'You'll rue the day you got those,' the Jeremiahs moaned at him later. They were stiff and square-toed ex-army ski-boots in best grey crome leather, not much good for climbing, and he'd worn them through in six months. He was at Wimberry the following morning with Joe and Ron Moseley to try them out. The snow was thick as they walked up to the crag, but the rock dry. He made an attempt to climb Freddie's Finale first, but succumbed to the cold and came down from beneath the roof to suffer excruciating hot-aches in his hands. Wandering along the foot, hands deep in the pockets of his new anorak, he noticed a new chockstone had been placed at half-height in Blue Lights Crack[17] and he led the other two up that. In their nailed boots in the bitter cold, Joe and Ron followed him. It had been a good year.

---

[17] Don later voiced the suspicion that Joe had put it there during the summer to protect a first lead of the route, but the latter's first ascent in 1948 is well authenticated, and Don's comment was made in the course of an extremely rancorous interview.

10

Mythical Heroes

Can heroes exist in climbing? I find myself more than a little conflicted around that question, and viewing it from all angles, so let me give you some context. Doug Scott, after a 1977 accident in which he broke both legs in the descent from the difficult Karakoram peak of Baintha Brakk ('The Ogre') – and which he survived with the assistance on the long crawl to safety of veteran Sheffield climber Clive Rowland – was put forward for some rather spurious-sounding media bravery award. He had the good sense and the right perspective ultimately to turn it down. Had Clive Rowland been suggested for the award, it might have seemed more proper, but he was not in the public's focus as recent 'conqueror' of the South-West Face of Chomolungma (Mount Everest).

A competent, quiet, retiring mountaineer who would anyway never have accepted or taken seriously such an award, Rowland lacked celebrity. Something of which the watching public – the audience for mountaineering – often seems unaware is that there is no intrinsic merit, no heroic value, in the mere struggle for self-preservation, however prolonged it may be. We can surely expect that of those who put themselves voluntarily into dangerous situations? To get yourself out of them when things go wrong is – or should be – simply part of the mountain deal. The point is no more complex than that of taking responsibility for our own actions. The great explorer-mountaineer H.W. Tilman, who was lost at sea in the South Atlantic in 1977, in his eightieth year and as an ordinary crew-member of a small boat sailing to a mountainous and uninhabited Antarctic Island, expressed this point most pithily and quaintly: 'In my view, every herring should hang by its own tail.'

As mountaineers, if we want to touch the void, we should make sure that, in the event of our falling into it, we get ourselves out; and having done so, we should not pose as heroes, should never believe in the constructs and the erroneous values that a public unacquainted through significant personal experience with the rigours and responsibilities of mountain activity may put on our actions. To get through by dint of our own efforts is why we choose to climb. When other reasons intrude – prestige, money, competition – the pure motive is clouded, the clear view lost, and danger can approach unseen, as witnessed by the corpses of guides and clients that litter the South Col and summit slopes of Chomolungma.

This is not to say that there are no examples of heroism in mountaineering. In the history of the activity there are countless examples of people quietly and selflessly helping others regardless of risk to themselves: Jack Longland safely shepherding his eight storm-blind Sherpas down from 27,400 feet on the North Ridge of Everest in a storm in 1933, his mountain sense guiding him down the right route; Tony Streather's doomed attempts to rescue his companions on Haramosh in 1957; Whillans himself, striving in vain to save the life of Harsh Bahaguna on Everest in 1971. These are real heroics, contingently enacted. But climbing itself is not. It is a form of play, and a public that views it ignorantly as heroism is palpably placing upon it false values. Or to take a more kindly and less austere view, it is mythologising the sport and its participants, inflating both to what becomes in effect the level of caricature, and as such to the sport's committed adherents is as comical, perhaps, as Homer's view of his petulant and meddling Greek gods.

This is certainly what happened to those Olympian weekend dwellers in hay-barns and derelict cottages and road-menders' huts, the early members of the Rock & Ice. We can even amuse ourselves by finding the old archetypes in the climbers' characters. Is not Brown an Odysseus, guileful and circumspect, ever-watchful and ever-wandering? Whillans as Achilles, temperamental, bellicose and quick to take offence, has already been suggested, and seems the more right the more I ponder it. But this, too, is for the future. For the moment, what I want to put forward is the extraordinary potency with which this supposedly secret society of the Rock & Ice seized hold of the imagination of the climbing world of the 1950s. '[We were] a close-knit body, intensely active in the mountains and avoiding the usual relationships with other clubs. We were not represented in any national mountaineering issues or debates and it was not surprising that other climbers viewed us as a secret society,' Joe Brown wrote, whilst Dennis Gray, who became associated with the club early in 1954, in the first and most literal and reliable of a highly entertaining sequence of memoirs, gives the following judicious overview:

> The more I saw of the club, the more impressed I was by its climbing prowess; nearly every member was an outstanding performer in his own right and those who were not front-rank leaders had other qualities which often complemented the stars' performance. The approach was essentially light-hearted and in keeping with my own previous experience.[1] Detractors of the Rock & Ice at that time and later were either motivated by envy or misunderstanding of the club's outlook. Charges were made of secretiveness, extreme competitive-ness[2] and even unfriendliness; these had no basis in truth. I was from another area, from a different group, but I was welcomed with open arms and treated with kindness and friendship.[3]
>
> Other people were building reputations for the Rock & Ice and claims were made that could not be substantiated, but it was no doing of their own. They never made extravagant claims, and some of their climbs were never recorded and other leaders have subsequently claimed the routes as first ascents.[4] They had no illusions of grandeur and other climbers

---

[1] Up to this time, Dennis had climbed with another informal group of working-class climbers, the 'Bradford Lads', whose activities were focused on Yorkshire gritstone crags and the cliffs of the Lake District, and whose outstanding leaders, Arthur Dolphin, Peter Greenwood and Harold Drasdo, were operating at more or less the highest standard of the day.

[2] Climbing, in the hieratic view of the activity's elders and traditionalists, was supposed to be above such trifles as competition. This view obtained until quite late in the twentieth century, and fuelled furious opposition to the introduction of competition climbing into Britain. Truthfully, of course, and as we have seen in the case of 'Ted' in Chapter Seven, competition, healthy or otherwise, has always existed in climbing.

[3] Shared social class was a factor in Dennis's reception, but even that did not constitute an unbridgeable gulf, as we shall see in relation to the Cambridge University Mountaineering Club of the time.

[4] This worked both ways – one of Joe's early climbs in the Llanberis Pass, the very popular Anthropology on Craig Ddu, had been climbed (as Rift Wall) several

who had, if they met Whillans for instance, were often disturbed by his uncompromising judgements.[5] But news-papers and other mass media were looking at this time for heroes from the changing social patterns of Britain in order to interest the public at large in new activities and to capture the attention of a massive new sector with great spending power.[6] This demanded personalities with backgrounds and culture values of their own, and the Rock & Ice supplied the demand to perfection.

In truth, the Rock & Ice was simply a historical accident. It took its focus from one outstanding climber, Joe Brown.[7] Personally

years before Joe's ascent by the great pioneer of 1930s climbing in Wales, John Menlove Edwards – a man for whose ability Brown had great respect. The culprit here – if it need be seen as such – is the very tardy and fragmentary nature of climbing information at the time, written reports of new routes in Wales only appearing in the *Climbers' Club Journal*, and often two or three years after their first ascents. On gritstone, the situation was significantly worse – reports of Joe's classic ascents on Wimberry Rocks from the late 1940s, for example, did not appear in written form until the early 1960s. And that in itself, as an adjunct to Dennis's argument here, was a fit breeding ground for rumour-mongering and myth-making.

[5] I would say this uncompromising element was general in the north of England climbing community for a quarter-century or more after the end of the Second World War. It certainly obtained in my own climbing apprenticeship at the end of the 1950s and beginning of the 1960s. Hard truths were the common currency, fragile egos were toughened or vanquished, attitudes were as rough and abrasive as gritstone itself, and that remained the case until the decades at the end of the last century brought in the so-called 'professional climbers', for whom realistic assessments of ability affected the saleability of their product. The activity's great regulators and truth-tellers – Patey, Burke, Whillans, Lewis, Anthoine, Nunn – had died or departed, often in the exercise of their craft, and among those left, the law became a kind of protection-racket for reputation and the writs began to fly. Significantly, gritstone climbing itself rather fell from fashion at this time. Though I'm glad to say that there does seem to have been a resurgence of its popularity since the late 1990s and the release of the influential and impressive *Hard Grit* video.

[6] What Dennis is arguing here did not really become applicable until at least a decade after the time under discussion.

[7] In the preceding chapter, I mentioned that, ironically, Joe was wholly opposed to the formation of the club. His argument against it ran thus: 'I clearly remember being against the idea from the start . . . My objections hinged on the belief that a club formation was unnecessary to keep the group intact. I pointed out that we would spend half our time tied up in red tape and rules: a club committee tends to busy itself with fund-raising schemes to purchase a hut or other permanent trappings, whereas I wanted the group to continue the self-initiated policy of

reticent in many ways, and understatedly charismatic, he drew around himself a number of talented performers, for the most part living in the same area of Manchester, who acted as a bank of seconds on which he could reliably draw for his early pioneering exploits. The convergence with this group of two other more or less local men, Ron Moseley and Don Whillans, who were also endowed with exceptional rock-climbing ability, completed the preliminaries, and by the start of 1952, the main narrative was about to begin.

As far as Don's climbing went, in the early part of the year it was dominated by a regular weekend diet of gritstone. The chief reason for this was an invitation he had received to go to Chamonix, in the French Alps, that summer with Nat Allen, Don Chapman and Don Cowan. So to conserve his funds – he was still only an 18-year-old apprentice plumber – he restricted his climbing to gritstone, where, in the canny company and under the discerning tutelage of Nat Allen, Ray Greenall and Les Wright for the most part, he worked his way through those classic outcrop routes he had not yet repeated from Joe's first phase of exploration pre- and post-National Service with the Valkyrie Club. He added a substantial line of his own to the gritstone repertoire early in the year too, and it was of high climbing quality, albeit in one of the less prominent and attractive venues along the edges. This was the Deadbay Groove on Curbar, and it had a certain significance. Hitherto he had shared the credit with Joe on his notable new climbs. But this one was unmistakably Whillans's own, bore what came to be recognised as his individual stamp, and retained a reputation for difficulty and quality for many years. It combined delicacy of footwork with strenuous use of small fingerholds, and required considerable boldness in its virtual absence of protection above a poor landing. The Whillans stamp was already upon it. Yorkshire climber Allan Austin, writing six years after its first ascent and at a time when the first cracks in the

---

sleeping where we found ourselves at nightfall and not becoming tied down with responsibilities. Deliberations on a meets programme and indoor functions at home, such as an annual dinner, promote stuffiness and argument. The reasons for wanting to start a club struck me as being futile because we were already pursuing all the functions successfully without an official committee telling us what we should do.' It might be noted as well that the initial enthusiasm for the club of Ron Moseley – who was, along with Don, one of the club's epochal triumvirate – had wholly abated by 1957. The fact that this left Don as the club's sole protagonist among its leading climbers is both interesting and telling, and will be discussed later.

Rock & Ice hegemony were starting to appear, considered it far superior to Joe's neighbouring Deadbay Crack and assessed it as 'a first-class climb of considerable technical interest. The climbing is remarkably hard and consistent, and this, combined with the utter lack of protection, makes Deadbay Groove, if not the hardest, probably the most satisfying and serious climb on Curbar.'[8]

Don's self-imposed limitation on visits to places other than the Derbyshire Peak relaxed at May Bank Holiday, when he and Joe met in Wales with the objective of another attempt on Clogwyn Du'r Arddu's Black Cleft. The spring that spouts from a crack high in the right wall of the cleft was still swollen with winter rain, the main crack and the slab to its left to all intents and purposes a waterfall. Added to that, one of the more esoteric delights of the Black Cleft is the luxuriance of its vegetation. Fortunately for climbers,[9] this consists mostly of large or even huge grass sods, uncertain of tenure, of a particularly slimy and unpleasant consistency, and no rarity value whatsoever. However, once embarked on the route, a leader has to detach them in order to get to the excellent jamming crack in the corner. This manoeuvre involves tugging them out of the crack and consigning the collapsing mass to the depths. The groove slants steeply from right to left, the climber has to face into it to reach the crack, so generally the sods fall between a leader and the rock and descend with unerring accuracy and considerable force on the unlucky second. On the first pitch of the Cleft proper, because it starts from a capacious pillar, the second has the chance to get out of the line of their descent. Which brings me to the point of this lengthy technical description – Joe Brown's Odyssean wiliness. Of course Joe would have pressed, flattered and manoeuvred Don into leading this pitch. He is

---

[8] 'Red Rose on Gritstone', *Climbers' Club Journal*, 1958. It should be noted with regard to Deadbay Groove, and its modern grading of E3, 6a, that the present-day climb incorporates a direct finish from the 1970s which is much harder than anything on the original route. This latter joined Deadbay Crack above its crux by a hair-raising swing from the left on a gravelly edge, and was very infrequently repeated before the advent of micro-protection.

[9] Clogwyn Du'r Arddu is one of the most important sites in Britain for arctic-alpine flora, many very rare plants growing here, and its hanging gardens in spring and early summer are one of the great sights of the Welsh mountains. It was this factor which drew the Reverends Williams and Bingley to make their ascent of the cliff's great Eastern Terrace in 1798 – one of innumerable 'first recorded rock-climbs' in Britain. If rare plants did flourish on the Black Cleft, they would draw an immediate ban on climbing there.

cunning. He weighs thing up, and will have noticed that there is less vegetation in the lower section of the corner, below a point at which it seems a stance may be taken. It will have registered with him too that the upper part of the groove is most abundantly grassed, and that little stance most likely to be in the direct line of descent for removed sods.

And so it proves. Don, in his ex-army, Vibram-soled ski-boots, in Joe's words 'excavated the first pitch slowly and tortuously, water running out of his trouser bottoms. When I reached him he was chattering with cold, wet through and shrivelled up.' Don for his part remembered feeling chilled, wet to the bone, all feeling gone from one thumb where he had hung for an hour from one particularly painful jam whilst cleaning the crack. He remembered the fusillades from above as Joe led the second pitch: 'The trouble was, you couldn't pull this stuff straight out; it was so full of water and mud that it just fell apart. Half of it he was throwing clear but the other half was landing on top of me. After about half an hour of this, I was being pushed off my stance with all the stuff piling up between me and the rock.'

Brown, climbing in nails, arrived at the overhang above, passed it using the crack on the right from which the spring gouts out, and continued to a stance on The Boulder – the climb which, on its first ascent the previous year, his seconds (Ron Moseley was one of them) had been unable to follow, causing him to run out 270 feet of rope without protection, and to struggle desperately when the hood of his anorak caught as he surmounted its top overhang. What happened next on the Black Cleft, in the generosity of Joe's recollection, demonstrates how resourceful and capable a climber Don now was, and the balance that was being established between himself and Joe as a team:

> Earth and debris rained on Don, spraying him with dirt from head to foot. He was in a sorry state on joining me at the Boulder stance. He stood there deliberating whether to continue. The last pitch was his. 'Oh, to hell with it,' he growled. As soon as Don started moving he was back in top gear. There was no stopping him now and in this sort of mood he rarely if ever made a mistake. He sailed over the overhang facing right, demonstrating what a mess I had made of the pitch when I had climbed the Boulder.

Don's version of events gives an interesting gloss on this. He describes Joe as worrying about the next pitch when he joins him on the stance, noticing that it was running with water, being concerned about how Don would fare in his Vibrams, and so offering to lead it. Don comments that by now he was completely fed up with the climb, was not going to stand around and freeze while Joe got to the top before him, so as a response to his offer he tells him tersely to get stuffed, races up to the overhang, listens as Joe explains how it is climbed facing left, shouts back down, 'That's a bit of an arse-about-face way of doing it, isn't it?', faces right, and is up in a flash. At the top, he grins at Joe – who is already assessing the climb as one that would be absolutely straightforward if ever it were dry[10] – and gives his considered verdict: 'That bloody thing's hard, mate – you can say what you want.'

How does posterity view this second of the great Welsh rock-climbs they did together? It grades Black Cleft at E2, and gives the two groove pitches 5c technical grades, which would make it arguably the hardest climb achieved in Wales until well on into the 1960s, and all the more remarkable for having been done in boots with virtually no protection. I have a little difficulty with the modern assessment. When I climbed it in the 1960s, wearing socks over rock boots and making sure of a partner, Rick Abbott,[11] who would not want to do any leading, it seemed to me that the groove pitches, had they ever been dry – which, even in the droughtiest of

---

[10] Joe can be a weird monkey at times, and his eccentricity is nowhere better exemplified than in his attitude towards the Black Cleft. He later climbed it with Ron Moseley during torrential rain, and was reputed nearly to have drowned at the top overhang, which he had to climb the difficult way – facing left – in order to keep his head out of the cascade and be able to breathe. In about 1964, on one of the wettest days I remember, Joe went up to Clogwyn Du'r Arddu with John Cheesmond and made the second ascent of Morty Smith's East Gully Grooves Direct Start – a big layback roof in impressive situation and at the time one of only two pitches graded 6a on the cliff. When they returned to the Cromlech Club hut in Nant Peris, their black Gannex anoraks dripping floods, Cheesmond's eyes were still contra-rotating with shock. Brown was his usual laconic self, and thought it 'not too bad'. This is not Joe's biography, however, but that of Don, who is a much more straightforward character . . .

[11] Rick, a fellow instructor at the National Mountaineering Centre, took up surfing thereafter, and to my knowledge has not climbed since. As to Black Cleft, I don't know of anyone having climbed it in years as a summer route. Since its first winter ascent by Martin Boysen and Baz Ingle in the marvellous freeze of 1962–63, it's now the domain of Darth Vader lookalikes wearing spiked boots and wielding psychopathically named picks.

summers, they never are – would have been fairly straightforward exercises in hand-jamming. But jamming and climbing on wet rock – the Black Cleft experience – are seriously unfashionable, and hence unpractised. Your Lycra gets dirty, they are uncomfortable, and they hurt. What is not remotely in question to my mind is that this neglected rock-climb is one of the finest and most characterful classic routes in Britain, perfect in its line, the climbing full of effort, technicality and interest, and the atmosphere overwhelming.

Having dried out from Black Cleft, bloated and septic hands returned to normal shape and clothes laundered of their residue of stinking mud, the next time we encounter Don in an outdoor context it is to have a very different, and personally far greater, significance. One of the early Rock & Ice members, Alan Taylor – generally known as 'Tater'[12] – had a girlfriend, Audrey Whittall. A couple of years older than Don, she had been born in Levenshulme in 1931, second of seven children. Unemployed in the depression years, her father had found work at Ford's Motor Company in Dagenham and the family had moved to London, where they had stayed until evacuated to Blaina ('And who robbed the miner?/Cry the grim bells of Blaina?' Idris Davies, *Gwalia Deserta* XV), in the South Walian valley of the Ebbw Fach. After 18 months there, in the old hill-enclosed colliery community with high moorland ridges all around, the Whittalls returned to Manchester. Audrey left school at 14 to work as a cutter[13] in the rag trade for a pound a week. Missing the freedom and open air of Blaina and the Welsh hills, from the age of 12 she used to camp out regularly in the air-raid shelter at the bottom of their garden. As soon as she could afford it, she bought a bicycle and started venturing out into the Derbyshire and Cheshire countryside. At the Alderley Edge copper-mines, which were, with their surrounding woods, a weekend magnet for the adventurous youth of Manchester,[14] she met Don Roscoe and Eric Price, and

---

[12] All the members of the Rock & Ice had nicknames, either alliterative or referring to some incident or character trait: The Baron Brown, The Villain, Count Neddy Goff, Morty Smith, Anderl the Brew, etc. etc. One unfortunate character even rejoiced (!) in the soubriquet of 'King Wank', for reasons which can properly remain lost to history.

[13] In Don's later life, necessarily in view of his then-obesity, Audrey turned this to good use and made all his clothes.

[14] The mine tunnels and rifts in the soft sandstone were an invaluable adventure playground for the street kids of Manchester even when I was growing up there in the late 1950s. After a few incidents where mardy kids got lost, had to be rescued,

through them the following week Alan Taylor, after which she was out climbing every weekend, very competently too, often in the company of her good friend Mavis Jolley, Joe Brown's girlfriend at the time. Here's Audrey's account of her first meetings with Don:

The first time I met Don was in Manchester city centre. Alan and I were on our way home from a day's climbing and we met Don and Les Wright on their way home too. Alan knew them, and had told me of Don's climbing ability. I did notice Don had bright blue eyes, and that he was rather short in comparison to Les and Alan, who were both over six feet tall. After that, we met Don from time to time at different crags. Then Alan had to go into the Royal Air Force to do his National Service. I continued to go out with Don Roscoe and Eric Price, who we had spent most weekends climbing with.

One weekend Don, Eric, another man I don't remember the name of and I went to Greenfield, to the campsite up at Chew Brook. We had two tents, one two-man and one three-man. We met Don Whillans on the way there. He hadn't got a tent, so the lads said he could sleep in one of theirs. Eric and I had already put our gear in the two-man tent, so Don was expected to go in the three-man tent with Don Roscoe and his friend. Don immediately put his rucksack in Eric's and my tent, which would have made it too much of a squeeze, so Eric put his rucksack in the three-man tent, which left Don and I, practically strangers, sharing this very small tent. Well, I thought he was a bit pushy, but I quite liked him, and of course, the night went like it does with fellas – it's like you're wrestling with an octopus. But anyway, we got a bit of sleep and woke to a lovely sunny day. Don produced a bar of chocolate and gave me half, said how about a kiss, today's my birthday. It was 18 May 1952, and he was 19. He said why don't I go to the Levenshulme Palais of a Wednesday when all the Manchester climbers met and it was only a shilling to get in. It was a very crowded and popular place. Jiving was all the rage. Most of the lads just sat around talking about climbing and that, but Ray Greenall was very good at jiving and taught

and their parents had made a fuss, the authorities put a stop to this, blocked off the tunnels and blew them up. Far too dangerous – Health & Safety couldn't approve.

me to do it, so I then taught Don, who got very good within a few weeks.[15] It came naturally to him. I was seeing Don regular like by then, so within a few weeks I had a decision to make, and I sent Alan the 'Dear John' as it were. Don was the one for me, and though it wasn't always a bed of roses, that's the way it was till the day he died. Unfortunately, Alan, who was a very nice fella and we'd stayed good friends, had died by then, too . . .

Three weeks after they first shared a tent, Whit Weekend came round, the weather was fine and sunny, and the Rock & Ice assembled in force at Bryn Coch. As a concession to his new status as an attached man, and a necessary part of the courtship ritual, Don led Audrey on ascents of Longland's Climb on Clogwyn Du'r Arddu one day, and the Great Slab on the following. And then the past and future pattern asserted itself – he went exploring with Joe, the two of them producing two good new climbs in successive days. The Pinnacle Flake[16] was the first of them. An exposed climb up the front face of the upper part of the East Buttress, it had a difficult and

---

[15] 'The good guys are the ones who went fishing, and the bad guys are the ones who went dancing. Brown didn't like dancing much so he went fishing. A nice, quiet sort of guy, and what can you say about a guy who goes fishing? Now Whillans, he was almost as good a dancer as I was (that will piss him off). Whillans thought he was the best rock'n'roller. We had many a good dance together. Actually, we used to practise together. We'd do these throws and things which the women wouldn't do, and nearly killed ourselves. We always thought we'd meet a woman one day who would do throws. It was more dangerous than climbing. Whillans wasn't a bad dancer, come to think of it. He was a much better dancer, then, than he was a climber.' Paul Ross, pre-eminent Lake District climber of his generation and one of the best performers on rock I have ever been privileged to tie on a rope with, interviewed in the 1973 *Leeds University Mountaineering Club Journal*. More of Paul anon.

[16] Peter Harding, the leading pioneer in Derbyshire and Wales of an immediate post-war generation, had strayed out on to this in the 1940s, when climbing with one of the doyens of 1930s cliff exploration, Ivan Waller. Waller had called him back, telling him that Colin Kirkus had once got himself into trouble that way. The mantelshelf move on Pinnacle Flake acquired a very dark reputation after a leader came off here in 1965. His scant protection failed, his second, who was belayed to an old peg which failed to hold on the Green Gallery at the start of the climb, was catapulted over the Great Wall of the East Buttress below, and both leader and second, after a fall of hundreds of feet, ended up on the scree under the cliff. The second was killed, but the leader, Terry Taylor, who suffered severe injuries, made a good recovery and went on to qualify and work as a highly respected mountain guide in North Wales.

poorly protected mantelshelf that both men found problematical. Joe led, and finished by a scrappy and vegetated line out to the left from the top of the flake itself. At a later date Don came back and added a better and more direct finish. The other climb, on which Joe and Don were joined by Nat Allen, was Spillikin, a route which used to be dismissed and downplayed as a scrappy little Very Severe (hard), was given a technical grade of 4c, and was frequently used as a pleasant solo escape from the Green Gallery after completing one of the harder climbs below. It takes the slabby lower right wall – the holds on it spiky and fissile – of a prominent groove in the left arete of The Pinnacle (this is the sharply triangular 150-foot-high upper section of the East Buttress), breaks out right to a ledge covered in a dense and beautiful growth of moss campion (*Silene acaulis*), and continues on some of the soundest and best rock on the cliff to the top. These days it is properly starred for the pleasure of its climbing and the drama of its situation high above the East Gully, and – an index, surely, of the modern generation's ability to cope with lack of protection rather than of the route's technical difficulty, which is negligible – graded E1, 5b.[17]

Both Spillikin and Pinnacle Flake were bagatelles – the merest trifles – compared to what happened on Clogwyn Du'r Arddu three days after the ascent of the former. This was one of the most singular events in the history of British climbing, even to this day perhaps the boldest lead relative to contemporary standards of difficulty ever made on a British cliff, and neither Brown nor Whillans was in any way involved. Whillans heard of it a week or so after its occurrence. He was walking along Regent Road in Salford with a member of the Cromlech Club, Sherwood Wiseman, who had just returned from a weekend in Wales. Wiseman mentioned that 'some bloke from Cambridge' had done the Red Slab on Clogwyn Du'r Arddu. This feature, soaring above the

---

[17] That this grade is patently a nonsense is made manifest by the same technical grade being applied to the route's far harder neighbours, Taurus and Pinnacle Arete. What happens in anomalies like the modern Spillikin grading is that the technical grade is usurping the role of the adjectival grade, which is the one supposed to reflect looseness, exposure, lack of protection – all of which qualities Spillikin possesses in full measure. But the modern guidebook writer seems seldom to have either the courage of his (invariably the gender is thus) convictions or the awareness of the tools at his disposal. Clearly, Spillikin should be E1, 4c, but to grade it thus is to invite derision, so the writer or his committee fudge the issue and undermine thus the rationale of the system.

Western Terrace, is the cleanest and most formidable sweep of unbroken slab on the cliff. Joe had been pondering it for a couple of years – he later went so far as to toss stones on to it, to see if they fell straight or merely slithered down, in order to assess its steepness. But by June 1952 he had done nothing about it. Don questioned Wiseman more closely, and was told that the man who had done it was in Britain on holiday, and that he had also led Cemetery Gates and the Black Cleft among other routes. Don gave the peremptory response to this information: 'I don't believe it!' Wiseman tartly reminded him: 'There's other buggers climbing besides you,' to which Don's rejoinder was, 'Aye, I know – but there's not so many climbing like that.'

But John Streetly *was* 'climbing like that', and as someone who became one of Don's closest and most unlikely friends, he deserves full recognition here. Even more markedly than Don, he had about him the unmistakable and – even to its possessors – incomprehensible trajectory of genius. Ali, Botham, Best at their peaks had something which set them apart, released them from the constrictions of ordinary possibility. Rock-climbing too produces once in every couple of decades a performer who raises it to the condition of perilous and ecstatic dance. Almost by definition they impinge only briefly. And few can match the extraordinary impact of John Streetly's short career on rock.

Streetly was brought up in Trinidad and Tobago. His father had trained as an engineer, but was later ordained priest in Barbados and worked in both Tobago and Trinidad until his death. For John and his younger brother, growing up on these islands was an adventurous idyll. They spent their time swimming, fishing and hunting, and seldom attended school. In all this their father encouraged them. Living on a clergyman's stipend they had little money, but fish were plentiful and their mother would send them off to the reef with orders for lobster or snapper for meals ('with a pair of goggles it was the closest thing to paradise for me,' John later wrote). When John was 14 he bought an old fishing boat called *Perfect Gift*, fitted it with a three-horsepower engine, and began his lifelong devotion to serious fishing. Somehow over the next few years he also found time to study, and in 1949 went up on the Barbados Island Scholarship to Queens' College, Cambridge, to read Natural Sciences. He was a boxing blue at featherweight, and swam and coxed for his college. Early in his time at Cambridge he had, in the words of a contemporary, 'been put off climbing by some damping remarks made by a well-known figure in the Cambridge University Mountaineering Club who did not appreciate the extent of his potentialities'. Some time in his last year at Cambridge, however, he ran into the Night Climbers.

This nocturnal tradition of pseudo-mountaineering on the college buildings dated back to the time of Longland and before him Mallory. Its practitioners occasionally found time in vacations to explore real rocks. John, with neither experience nor equipment to speak of, fitted in a couple of weekends in which he dispatched the hardest climbs on Stanage (Brown's new ones among them), Almscliff, and at Harrison's Rocks with some ease. Geoff Sutton recalls him at the latter nonchalantly 'hanging from an overhang with one hand whilst cleaning the soles of his rubbers with the other'. He visited Wales in June, raced up the crux pitch of Peter Harding's 'Exceptionally Severe' 1947 test-piece, Spectre, on Clogwyn y Grochan in 18 minutes, repeated a handful of other difficult climbs of the day, and then looked for the most challenging piece of unclimbed rock on which to make one of his own. The Bloody Slab, as the feature had been named in Peter Harding's 1951 guidebook,[18] is a beautiful and, in its atmosphere (compounded of architecture, remoteness, jagged line, and the weird coloration of the rock) rather a strange climb, which is still probably the finest slab climb in Britain. (A Scottish climber might well argue for some of the harder climbs on Beinn Trilleachan, but even on the rare occasions when absence of midges renders these endurable, there is a certain lack of atmosphere and monotony of movement about them.) A series of photographs exists of Streetly engaged on it. In the next-to-last, his single line stretched out through poor and occasional runners, the tiny figure makes a dancing step through to a grassy, uncleaned crack. As an image, it has iconic force in climbing – joy, danger and the unknown conjoined.

The route, as we shall see, soon acquired a huge reputation – and one which has never shared the common fate of those courses on rock whose currency is devalued by technological advance. Modern equipment notwithstanding, the Bloody Slab remains as powerful,

---

[18] *Llanberis Pass* (Climbers' Club, 1951). The 'Bumper Fun Book', as it was widely known, with its wonderfully florid gradings and lucid route descriptions, was relatively up to date and comprehensive, and provided a sound basis for the Rock & Ice generation's exploratory activities.

compelling and fearful a lead today as ever it was. The account of it which John later wrote up in the *Cambridge University Mountaineering Club Journal* has long been recognised as a *locus classicus* in the expression of the sangfroid necessary to the practice of the sport at its highest levels. It is worth quoting here at length as the most graphic description of the style in which the leading performers of the 1950s made their ascents. Nothing that Joe or Don wrote comes close to this as an exact bodying-forth of the conditions of pioneering on British rock prior to the revolution in protection techniques that began in the mid-1960s, and gathered pace to change the sport irrevocably during the 1970s. It is one of the great and honest historical documents in climbing history:

> The slab was very smooth and, under the overhangs, nearly always damp. Added to this was the fact that most of the climbing would depend on pure friction owing to the apparent lack of any holds. Those holds we could see all sloped the wrong way . . . rather a discouraging picture, but nevertheless still worth a try – I can remember thinking quite happily at the time, 'Never say die till you're dead.'

Streetly set off up the slab and after 40 feet of climbing arrived at the first crux section:

> From here on the climb becomes quite thin and now it is difficult to recall how the next 30 feet were managed at all. At one stage the only means of moving up was by reaching at full stretch with the right hand to finger-jam in the bottom of a vertical crack about 18 inches long and half an inch wide. By pulling on this and body-leaning to the left it was possible to swing up to the level of the top of the crack. At this critical point a quick call from an ever-watchful second pointed to the only possible foothold, about two feet away to the left. This allowed a moment's respite in a more or less bridged position which, itself being very tiring and with the previous move apparently impossible to reverse, left no alternative but to go on up. With the difficult move[19] below and the uncertainty of

---

[19] One of the very few points on the climb these days to have good nut protection – just to put Streetly's achievement even more clearly into perspective.

what was still to come, life at this point seemed to depend more upon faith than friction.

Still, after the second runner, the slab was dry and tiny flakes allowed pleasantly delicate finger- and toe-climbing to lead to a somewhat doubtful flake behind which the placement of the only piton manufactured another runner. This was about 70 feet from the start and about 100 feet from the rake directly below with still no possibility of a stance, belay, or even a resting-place. About 15 feet above was the first large overhang in the middle of the slab and the third runner made for much more confident climbing up to the base of this. At this point the first real handhold of the climb was manufactured by extensive gardening in the crack immediately below the overhang. Here the general dampness and moss made rubbers both useless and dangerous, so they had to be removed quickly and tucked away in case they were necessary later on. The climb was continued in socks, and with the newly found 'Thank-God' hold, a stretch round the overhang on the left enabled a small undercut handhold to be used by the left hand for a pull round the corner and up to a neat little ledge just to the left and above the bottom of the overhang.

After a rest here, on what was a reasonable stance, it became obvious that there were no belays in the vicinity. However, on the right along the side of the overhang an obvious layback crack of 15-odd feet led to the possibility of a runner behind a rather shaky flake. On return to the ledge the route became only too obvious! The ledge itself was on top of an overhang; there was an overhanging wall on the right; and directly above were what the guidebook terms 'the obvious overhangs of Bloody Slab'. The only way led diagonally upwards and across the smooth and exposed slab to the left. Fifteen feet away to the left was a thin vertical grassy crack and between this and the ledge the only holds were very tiny vertical ribs; in effect the ideal place for a horizontal rappel. This was done by using the rope through a runner on the shaky flake which allowed a precarious crab-like movement to be made across into the grassy crack.

From this point on the upper slab proper it was possible to climb diagonally up to the left on tiny finger- and toe-holds with the occasional use of a clump of grass growing in thin vertical cracks. At one stage when embracing such a strip of grass with hands and feet the top portion came away from the crack and started to peel off, rolling down from the top like a thin green carpet. With a 70-foot lead-out from the last runner – the shaky flake – the situation was critical and the piton-hammer was rapidly brought into use to cut off the detached part of the clump before the whole thing rolled right off. Quick movement off the grass was of course quite impossible owing to the thin and delicate nature of the climb. On the upper portion of the slab there was no trace of any real hold so all movements had to be carefully studied in order to maintain three good points of contact with the rock while looking for, or making, the next move.

Shifting carefully off the grass, movement could again be made diagonally upward to the left on very tiny rugosities until another large loose flake was reached. This appeared to be resting on a useful little ledge, so bridged on very small toe-holds, it proved quite a surprise when a tentative pull removed the whole issue – all 20-odd pounds of it! This presented an awkward problem, more so in view of the fact I was holding on it! One could, of course, hold the flake against the rock, but not for long, and it was too heavy to throw clear without falling off. Throwing would of course also remove two very good handholds – and if I dropped it – well, my feet were just below. Ted and Brian down below could not have known what was going on until, with a little push to the left, I half-dropped, half-threw it just clear of my left foot to slither noisily down the slab and over the overhang to crash, after a moment's silence, to the screes below.

Just to complete the picture, the groove from which the flake had come was rounded top and bottom with no trace of the hoped-for hold. Almost desperate examination of the rock, however, revealed a tiny flake the top of which was knocked off with the hammer to produce a neat little quarter-inch ledge. Using this as a finger-hold a move could again be made across and up to another grassy strip. Proceeding super-carefully up this (a 90-foot lead-out from the shaky flake runner), it again became possible to move on to the more rugose left edge of the slab which led up to a good grassy ledge . . .

Having led out 200 feet of rope on unknown rock, sustained at the very highest technical standard of the day, with scant protection and in poor conditions, he untied, his seconds being unwilling or unable to follow, and soloed off to the top of the cliff. Streetly was a tiny man – barely five feet two, a shade shorter even than Don, and slightly built – but he looked you straight in the eye, was modest, steely, direct in his speech, appreciative and rather kind. On the strength of Bloody Slab and an impressive 1952 Alpine season, he was invited on the successful 1953 Everest expedition. But he had to work to support his mother and pay for his younger brother's education, and Texaco, the company he worked for by then, having gone down from Cambridge in 1952, refused a junior trainee the protracted leave necessary. It later nearly fired him for standing on his head on top of a 200-foot derrick for a bet.

We'll meet Streetly again soon, but for the moment need to consider the effect of this climb on the Rock & Ice members. Initially, as with Don's response, many were incredulous. As its authenticity became plain, they became more curious. Within a year, the effect was galvanic, causing them to look anew at possibilities and to lift their own game.[20] The Bloody Slab itself had to

---

[20] I believe Streetly's example had a similar effect also on the Cambridge University Mountaineering Club in the 1950s – either that, or there was something in the air there at the time. Later in this book there will be the example of Bob Downes to be considered. And I might also mention, anecdotally, a meeting Peter Crew and I had in Wales in 1971. We were drinking one night in the bar of the Padarn Lake Hotel in Llanberis, at the foot of Snowdon, when a man walked in holding a copy of *The Black Cliff* – Crew, Wilson and Soper's history of climbing on Clogwyn Du'r Arddu which had just been published. He asked the landlord if he could tell him where Peter Crew lived. The landlord, Clive, said he could go one better, and directed him over to us. He was in his forties, about five feet four in height, powerful shoulders, tiny hips. He opened his book at a photograph of Pete's 1962 climb Great Wall – then still reputed one of the hardest in the country – introduced himself as David Nott, said he had just flown in from Caracas, Venezuela, was here to do this climb and would Pete guide him up it? Pete, who had not climbed for several years at this point, just burst out laughing, said 'no' or words to that effect, and in a spirit of mischief turned to me and added, 'But Jim will.' I had already led the climb on a couple of occasions and had no wish to do so again. Thinking quickly and wanting to save face, I said, 'OK – I'll do it, for a hundred quid.' This was an outrageous sum in those days, particularly to a climbing bum like me. David didn't bat an eyelid, said, 'That sounds reasonable – tomorrow, then?', offered Pete £50 to come along and take photographs, and the three of us ended up going back to Crew's house and drinking David's supply of duty-free whisky until the small hours.

In this time, David told us a certain amount about himself – poor Liverpool

wait two years before it received a second ascent. Don attempted it in April 1954, in conditions similar to those of the first ascent, and retreated from below Streetly's peg, having thoroughly frightened himself and all but fallen off. Later that summer, Joe led it not just once but four times, proclaiming it his favourite slab climb on the cliff and finding it, apart from a couple of moves padding up on friction, not particularly hard. On his return from Kangchenjunga a year later, in good, dry conditions he seconded Don for its sixth ascent.

As summer progressed, Joe continued his series of new routes in Wales, the presence of the unknown and formidable talent from Cambridge surely increasing the urgency of the quest. The wall-climb Llithrig and the major crack-lines of Octo and The Corner on Clogwyn Du'r Arddu were climbed within 10 days of Bloody Slab's first ascent, whilst Don was resigned to hearing the latest news at the YMCA on Wednesdays, and absorbed in a routine of dates with Audrey and weekends on gritstone. But there was consolation. His first visit to the Alps was rapidly approaching. Nat Allen, who was

---

upbringing, scholarship to Cambridge and so on. He had been climbing once before, apparently, 25 years ago and a year before he went to Cambridge. It had happened like this. He was camping as a 17-year-old by Idwal Cottage youth hostel, conceived a fancy for the young woman in the next tent, propositioned her, and she replied, 'I'll only sleep with you if you take me up Lot's Groove tomorrow.' This climb of Kirkus's from 1929 on Glyder Fach was still, in the forties, reputed one of the region's hardest. According to David's story, the woman took him up to the foot of the climb next morning, showed him how to tie on to a rope, belay and take in, he set off, did it without difficulty, and she duly fulfilled her part of the bargain.

The September morning dawned cold and grey, we took the Snowdon train up to Clogwyn station, and walked downhill to the crag. Mist wreathed it, the route was streaked with water, I led it slowly and with considerable difficulty. When it came to David's turn, he climbed it with ease and barely a moment's hesitation – his second-ever rock-climb, 25 years after his first. And he wanted more, so we went up the East Gully and did Joe's 1958 route Shrike, a very steep wall-climb of which I had quite recently done the first free ascent. After that, Pete and I had had enough, the rain was coming down and darkness falling, so we tramped back to the bar of the Padarn, where Brown himself was ensconced. He asked David what he'd done, and David proudly told him. 'And what did you do in the afternoon?' – traditional Rock & Ice put-down, this – the Old Man lanced at us, with a big, toothy grin. Then the talk got on to Streetly, and when David went back to Caracas, where he ran a press agency, we were left wondering what might have happened had these two examples of the extraordinary fund of talent at Cambridge in the early 1950s met during their time there (1947–50 for David, 1949–52 for John), whether Nott & Streetly would have had quite the same cachet as Brown & Whillans, and how rivalry might have spurred both on.

one of the party, remembers that 'He was keen as mustard and eager to get there, to find out all he could about them. And of course, he and Audrey had not long got together, so you could never flush those buggers out of their tent in the morning. There wasn't a lot of climbing getting done by The Villain that summer. They'd got the taste for something else, you see . . .'

Not according to Audrey, or at least not yet they hadn't:

Well, you just didn't do it right away with a fella in those days. You'd go through the stages, you know, keeping them at bay – necking and petting and that – and it'd be quite a long time before you'd let him go all the way, however much he was pushing for it, which of course is the way a fella is. I could tell with Don when he was expecting to get there, because he'd be off to the barber's[21] and there he'd be come the weekend with a short-back-and-sides and something in his pocket no doubt. We used to laugh at that, the girls, between ourselves. But you see, you didn't want to get pregnant, so you just had to be that careful. It wasn't like it is nowadays, unfortunately.

Despite the jiving and the haircuts and the trips to the cinema, by the end of July Don had enough money for the Alps. The most experienced member of the party, Don Cowan from Sheffield, who was a locomotive fitter, had booked them concessionary tickets on the train, and the four-man party from the Rock & Ice was on its way to Chamonix. Don's ambitions were huge. He wanted, in his first season, to repeat Riccardo Cassin's epic 1938 ascent of the Walker Spur of the Grandes Jorasses. The older and more experienced members of the party rolled their eyes, and to divert him talked instead of Ian McNaught Davis's having just traversed

---

[21] The only places you could obtain condoms – the only readily available method of contraception in Britain until the mid-1960s and easy access to the Pill – were chemists' and barbers' shops. To buy them from the former was fraught with embarrassment – young, reddening assistants calling for elderly pharmacists, who would grudgingly and disapprovingly complete the transaction after public interrogation. The barbers would always conclude your visit with the time-honoured formula, 'And something for the weekend, sir?' Having handed over your three-shillings-and-ninepence you'd walk out, newly exposed ears bright scarlet, clutching your precious packet. Very few young men in Britain had long hair before the advent of the Pill.

the Aiguilles du Diable.[22] They took him down to Snell's Alpine Sports shop to get him kitted out with new boots and crampons, and the four of them walked up through the pinewoods to Montenvers. It rained. They spent the night in a woodcutter's shelter. By morning the sky had cleared and a huge wall, dark and icy, patched and frosted with new snow, towered above them, reducing all the surrounding peaks to miniature scale. What was it? he asked Cowan. The Grandes Jorasses, came the reply. And could he see the great spur leading up to its highest point? Well, that was the Walker. Don was very quiet, in a kind of reverie, recording later how in that moment he felt his life would be dedicated to climbing the hardest and most inaccessible mountains in the world. Everything he had done so far assumed a new perspective: 'Now is my way clear. Now is the meaning plain.' The young star of Welsh and Peak District climbing, before his mentor Joe Brown had even set eyes on the Chamonix Aiguilles, had become a mountaineer. Not that much of this enthusiasm came across in his postcards home: 'Dear Audrey, The weather is good in the valley but cloudy for climbing. I think we are going up for a few more days today. Nothing much to say. A bloke fell down a crevasse last night and was killed. So long. Love Don. X.'

In terms of completed routes, their climbing this holiday was an excellent foundation for what was to come. They did the Ryan-Lochmatter Route up the East Ridge of the Aiguille du Plan, on which Don, in his new boots, came tumbling out of the Grand'Mère Crack and was caught on the ledge below by Nat and Don Cowan. Nat recalls that 'he did used to fall off quite a bit at first, and he fell the way they fall now, and would generally land on his feet and not hurt himself, he was that agile. After a couple of years or so with us, it stopped, I'm glad to say.' They also, in this season of 1952, climbed the South Ridge of the Pain de Sucre and the Mer de Glace Face of the Grepon. As a first alpine season, it can be seen in the long retrospective as enormously influential and in the main beneficial for the young Whillans. The unruffled affability and fund of experience of his older companions acted less as a curb on his

---

[22] The first British guideless ascent of this great Alpine classic had in fact been achieved two years earlier by one of the most endearing and potentially major figures from post-war British climbing, the young Cambridge communist Cym Smith, who climbed it with his future wife Nancy Heron. He was killed, shortly after their marriage, in a motorcycling accident in the snow in Edinburgh.

ambition, ignorant as this was at the time, than as sagacious instruction. He learnt from Cowan and Allen in particular the technical skills of alpinism, in which they were well versed, and which the young apprentice eagerly studied. Allen recalled, 'He was a nice young fellow in them days, and would listen to whatever you had to tell him, so long as you knew your stuff.' He also gained a sense of pacing himself, working within his limits, carefully studying conditions. These lessons from father-figures in the sport never failed him, though it could be argued that their stress on the need for caution in mountain environments, whilst it may have saved Don's life on occasions, perhaps also cost him some of the prizes he might have obtained without it.

As their last route before leaving, Cowan had determined to take Don on Route Major – Frank Smythe and Graham Brown's magnificent mixed route from 1928 on the Brenva Face of Mont Blanc. In perfect weather, they arrived at the Col de la Fourche bivouac hut on the Frontier Ridge. A young Italian guide with an elderly client arrived after them, they exchanged pleasantries, and it turned out that the client was British. His guide introduced him. It was Graham Brown, who had climbed the Matterhorn the previous week and was here to ascend the Old Brenva route. It was his seventieth birthday, and – contentious and curmudgeonly though he may have been – he was still active among the mountains. He must have appeared immeasurably ancient, the relic of a bygone age, to the 19-year-old alpine tyro. And his example no doubt also gave that tyro something to reflect on, and a certain measure of encouragement, as all four climbers descended next day, in snow that had caused both parties to give up their plans and beat a prudent retreat.

Back in Britain, there was another shock awaiting Don. In his absence, Joe had overcome one of his old bugbears and climbed the long-standing problem of Cenotaph Corner on Dinas Cromlech. Don might have had an alpine season under his belt, but he was losing out in the new route stakes. His response was to pester his father into putting up the money for a motorbike. It was a Royal Enfield 350cc Bullet – a solid, reliable single-cylinder bike to learn to ride on.[23] It cost £120, which Don agreed to pay back in weekly

---

[23] They still make them in India, and they can be re-imported back into this country. So for those who want to relive the total Don Whillans experience, start saving your rupees . . .

instalments, and had no pillion seat, so the long-suffering Audrey was assigned a pad strapped on top of the mudguard. The autumn put a damper on most rock-climbing, so the Rock & Ice launched into a new, Alps-inspired activity – artificial climbing. Most weekends they would go into the limestone dales of Derbyshire and Yorkshire, set up camp in a cave or under some huge roof, and start to peg round it, one of the party hammering in the home-made pitons and swinging from the crude etriers, the others lounging by the fire, smoking, making food, joshing and barracking. Limestone, which was traditionally deemed to be too loose for free-climbing activity, offered numerous opportunities for this kind of sociable play, but it had a useful psychological role to play also. For the significant alpine rock-routes on which their ambition and talk were beginning to centre, mastery of artificial techniques would be essential.

Wales did not figure largely in their plans during the wet autumn, but it did prove accurate Joe's prophecy about the direction activity took when a club was formed. In October the Rock & Ice held a dinner at the Pen-y-Gwryd Hotel. Most of the members were staying in the usual road-menders' hut accommodation by the Cromlech boulders in the Llanberis Pass, or in the howffs under the boulders themselves. When Don and Audrey came out of the hotel to ride back there, it was raining heavily. By the time they had reached the infamous 'Magnetic Bend', which has been the scene of innumerable climbers' crashes, Don's goggles had misted so he pushed them back, and as he steered one-handed round the bend, the magnetic effect of the wall came into operation. Don scraped along it, Audrey flew once into the air and landed back on the mudguard, flew again into the air and nearly pulled Don off the bike, flew for a last time into the air and disappeared into the gloom and rain. An oncoming headlight lit up a bundle of rags in the road, which was Audrey. She sat up, her left knee mangled, face as wet with tears as rain. The headlight belonged to Scotty Dwyer's combination, so he and Don helped her into the sidecar and took her to the Caernarvon and Anglesey Hospital[24] in Bangor. Don's

----

[24] This institution, thankfully long since defunct, had the highest incidence of post-operative gangrene in Britain. Its orthopaedic department – crucial where most climbing accidents are concerned – was a byword for setting limbs askew and hence necessitating further corrective surgery. Most climbers of my generation in Wales, if they were in any state to do so, would drive or have themselves driven back east rather than face the rigours and consequences of the C & A.

left knee was scraped, his bike had an oval front wheel, had lost its gear-lever and bent its handlebars, but was still just about rideable. What Tom Whillans had to say when he returned home on it is not on record. For all that, this accident very early in his motorbiking days does seem to have had a salutary effect on Don – he had few accidents thereafter,[25] and the most serious one, nine years later, was not his fault. This first one, however, put a temporary stop to Don and Audrey's romance – on which Mr Whittall had been less than keen from the outset, and in which view the bike accident and Don's subsequent behaviour in lying low and avoiding Audrey for several weeks thoroughly confirmed him.

The bike having been repaired, Don put his new, albeit temporary, bachelor status to effective use by joining Joe at The Roaches a few weeks later. The line of weakness through the massive overhang of the upper tier which they had discussed after first climbing together 18 months before is what draws them. They toss for the roof pitch and Don, to Joe's chagrin, wins, so Joe leads up to the pedestal on the slab 15 feet below the roof, where he takes a stance. Don follows him and they gaze up together at rock which jags out for maybe 12 feet above. Don steps up and places a heavy sling round a jutting block. A flake is attached to the underside of the roof. With a large audience gathered by now, Don eases his right shoulder into it, works out along it, hand-jamming in the crack splitting the roof as he does so, his heel still jammed behind the flake, keeping him in to the roof. Two body-lengths . . . He reaches round the lip, finds a hold, his foot suddenly slips out of the flake and he's left hanging from his hands to a gasp from the crowd. He muscles up, jams a foot in the crack to take weight off his arms, slips another runner on and pulls round to easier ground. Joe follows with ease. To the two of them, versed in the skills of jamming, it is technically straightforward, by no means the hardest of the gritstone roofs they will climb in their careers. But to those gathered below, The Sloth looks outrageous. Its execution is utterly dramatic, its situation hair-raising, it epitomises a new style. And so the myth of these little heroes compounds.

One of the spectators was Geoff Sutton, who left this account:

---

[25] Joe would dispute this: 'In my life, I've fallen off a bike ten times, and on nine of those occasions Don was driving.'

Seeing Brown and Whillans ascend the classic route to the Pedestal, [I thought to myself] how nice it was that on a cold day these two should be happy on a climb of Very Difficult standard. Suddenly everyone's eyes started out of their heads as Whillans was seen tackling the fantastic overhang itself, an unheard-of thing in those days. Dashing to the top of [my] own climb, [I] was in time to see a balaclava, followed by a tattered anorak, emerge from the depths. 'Was it hard?' [I] asked, rather foolishly. 'Not if you use your loaf,' came the reply, and [I] wandered away wondering whether this was a metaphorical statement or whether it referred to some new technique.

Sutton, who will figure large in later chapters, was a pivotal figure in the British climbing scene of the 1950s, and a hugely influential one in post-war writing about the sport. He was a large, powerful man with a personality to match. He had arrived to read English at Cambridge in 1952 with a colourful past already behind him. He had been invited to leave Harrow, a certain diffidence in accepting the constraints of authority having expressed itself in motorbikes and girlfriends, neither of which fitted easily into that school's curriculum. After this unorthodox school-leaving, he had come up against the further authority of a two-year stint on National Service, which he also managed to subvert. To his fellow undergraduates he recounted tales of voyages through the South China Sea, knife-fights with Chinese crewmen, travels in the Maghreb and Horn of Africa, and a commission in the Somali Scouts. He was almost sent down in his first term at Cambridge when a loaded revolver was discovered beneath his pillow by the woman who cleaned his rooms. In short, he was the stuff of young men's legends, and at Cambridge he glorified and flourished in that role, and helped amplify a few myths not his own along the way too.

11

Mighty Deeds

That the reputation of Don Whillans was firmly established by 1953, and had perhaps even marginally begun to nudge ahead of Joe Brown's in some respects, is made plain by a letter Don received before Easter from Ted Wrangham. Wrangham had been the watchful belayer of John Streetly on that first ascent of the Bloody Slab, and had a reputation as one of the supreme 'fixers' of the climbing world. The letter was an invitation to Don to join a new organisation Wrangham was proposing. Initially it was to be called the Face Nord Club, but this was quickly changed to the Alpine Climbing Group. Similar letters were sent to two other Rock & Ice members, Don's 1952 alpine companions Nat Allen and Don Cowan. Among the younger British alpinists of the period, a dissatisfaction had begun to grow with the senior representative body of British alpinism, the Alpine Club. In its august premises on South Audley Street, Mayfair, it had come to be seen as socially reactionary, an 'old school tie' organisation hostile towards and critical of a younger generation's activities. It seemed to embody all the attitudes of a pre-Great War epoch, when guided alpinism was a proper pursuit for the leisured gentlefolk. As to the working class, it scarcely came within the AC's purview, and the club's stance towards younger people and their unguided alpine exploits was distinctly stuffy. So a group of those younger persons – several among them, Wrangham being one, also associated with the Cambridge University club – determined on a policy of secession, and the idea of the Alpine Climbing Group was born. In its 20-year-heyday, before it was reabsorbed by a reformed and reinvigorated Alpine Club, the ACG was a remarkably radical and active organisation, the climbing record of members of which was distinguished, and the incidental role it played in breaking down the social barriers that had long existed in mountaineering being invaluable.

But when Wrangham wrote his letter to Don early in 1953, the ACG had not yet officially come into being. Don's response to Wrangham's letter was puzzlement, and it might be ours too. His alpine experience consisted of one short fortnight, in more experienced company, with no major climbs accomplished. Was he being recruited on his British rock-climbing record (which was not admissible as part of the stringent ACG membership requirements – had it been, Joe Brown would surely have been included in the approaches)? Had they heard of him by repute, and assumed that a 19-year-old – too young to be eligible for the Alpine Club of the time, incidentally – with his rock-climbing ability and a new-found enthusiasm for alpine climbing had the potential for significant achievement in that arena? Maybe Wrangham had been told of his most recent activities in Britain: the lead of The Sloth, or the new and difficult climb, the Subsidiary Grooves, that Don and Joe had just completed on the brooding buttress of Cyrn Las high above the Llanberis Pass; or in the Lake District at Castle Rock of Triermain, the ferociously strenuous variant line, Triermain Eliminate, on the great Jim Birkett's swansong climb, Harlot Face? Almost certainly the apocryphal story – long-established in climbing folklore – would have filtered through to Cambridge of Don and Joe's ascent, in nailed boots[1] and a snowstorm, of Surplomb, a severely impendent climb of terrifying aspect up the central and steepest section of Clogwyn y Grochan.

Whatever the reasons for his invitation – and every weekend in

---

[1] Don had not climbed in nailed boots since 1951. He and Joe made the actual ascent in rubbers and sunshine on the first day of March. On the day of the mythologised ascent, with Don in Vibrams and Joe in nails, and with snow falling, they climbed the first pitch of what is now Corruption to reach the overhanging chimney of the third pitch, which Joe led, bridged facing outwards, in his nailed boots and a snowstorm. Surplomb in its complete version was a significant and difficult climb – their hardest in Wales so far. Some might argue that the sling move to reach good holds on the first wall actually made the climb more difficult than it is without the aid. Joe appeared to have a penchant for these sling moves at one time in his climbing career, and I can think of several routes (Torero, Nimbus, etc.) where their use added substantially to the problems rather than alleviated them. As a pleasing cultural and generational link, it is worth mentioning that the first free ascent of Surplomb was made in the golden summer of 1959 by Phil Gordon, a great-nephew of Geoffrey Winthrop Young, who was one of the major figures in British mountaineering at the turn of the last century.

the spring and early summer of 1953 the myth-factory had something fresh to elaborate around his and Joe's activities – Don wrote back to Wrangham to point out how limited was his alpine experience. All he received in return was an invitation to the inaugural dinner. It was held at the Pen-y-Gwryd Hotel in April, and Nat Allen and Don Cowan were there. So too were a whole firmament of Oxbridge alpine stars: Dick Viney, Ian McNaught Davis, Hamish Nicol, Geoff Sutton and many others:

> This was the first time I'd got together with these university wallahs. I'd never had much time for them before . . . I could see that most of the lads at that first dinner were OK. They spoke differently than I did – fair enough, they were much better educated – but at least they seemed like genuine lads. They certainly had the right ideas and the courage to carry them out. I was just a 19-year-old monkey from the city then. They could easily have ignored me, but they didn't.[2] The climbing was the thing that mattered.

To prove which point, on the Sunday the three Rock & Ice members wandered up after breakfast from the road-menders' hut by the Cromlech Boulders to the foot of Carreg Wastad, and set to work on the unclimbed central corner line of the crag. Don led, ripping off turf and heather and throwing down flakes piecemeal, this being much the loosest of the popular Llanberis cliffs. The winter practice on limestone prompted him to put in a peg at the crucial bulge, the climb was named Erosion Groove,[3] and it seemed to spark off a wave of exploratory activity. For weekend after weekend the new routes came. Early in May, after an altercation outside a pub in Kendal (he was picked on by a six-foot-tall soldier, he leapt at him, wrapped his legs round his assailant's arms and knocked him to the pavement, where he proceeded to batter him

---

[2] Far from it – they elected him straight away on to the ACG committee.

[3] Don's later direct finish to this climb, led whilst he was on top form and working in Wales at the Pen-y-Gwryd Hotel in the summer of 1955, is an excruciatingly awkward, bold, unprotected and strenuous layback and bridging problem not notably more direct than the original finish (it might more properly be called the Right-hand Finish). It gained a savage reputation in the early 1960s as one of the hardest pitches in Britain, but this somewhat abated when the Oldham climber Doug Baines strolled up it in 1962 after a heavy lunchtime drinking session in the Pen-y-Gwryd and declared it pretty straightforward.

senseless), Don, suitably psyched up into the aggressive mode necessary for overhanging rock, and Joe climbed Dovedale Grooves on lonely Dove Crag, most impressive of all Lake District cliffs. It remained unrepeated for the rest of the decade, repelling the advances of several leading Lake District climbers.[4] A week later they were back on Clogwyn Du'r Arddu and, with Nat Allen and making good use of Joe's routes Llithrig and The Corner, they added the Girdle Traverse of the East Buttress[5] – a route which made up in length and character for what it lacked in original climbing, and the rope moves and abseils to link pitches on which were very much in an idiom that was to be useful in their future alpine seasons.

The next of those – that of 1953, which was Don's second, Joe's first – was approaching fast. Four of them set off from Manchester by motorbike. Don rode the Enfield, with tent and rucksack fastened on the tank and Audrey – whom he was seeing again by now – perched nervously on the mudguard for the best part of 1000 miles. Joe travelled on the back of Don Cowan's machine. On the approach to Chamonix, with Cowan dog-tired after the long, wet journey, a careless car caused him to lose control of the bike, which

---

[4] It needs to be noted that regional rivalries in British climbing have always existed. Before the transport revolution in the 1960s, restriction to a local area was general, and the rivalries were particularly marked. The new climbs done by Don and Joe – who were primarily identified with gritstone and Wales – in Scotland and the Lake District often aroused rancour, and were closely scrutinised by climbers from those areas. There was often a degree of coat-trailing in the naming of climbs, too – Don and Joe's Sassenach on Carn Dearg in 1954 is a prime example. So too is the name Welsh-based climbers Pete Crew and Baz Ingle gave to the new climb they added on Dove Crag in 1962, immediately after making the second ascent of Dovedale Grooves. They called it Hiraeth – in Welsh, 'a longing for home'.

Joe and Don's activities at Whit Week 1953 might also have offended Lake District regional pride: in heavy rain – snow at higher altitudes – Joe, Don and Nat climbed Routes 1 and 2 on Pillar, Scafell Central Buttress by the Direct Finish, Mickledore Grooves, Great Eastern and other routes – all very disrespectful. If you want to get an idea of the pair's all-round climbing ability, try that itinerary in nailed or Vibram boots and conditions so cold that the Flake Crack on Central Buttress 'felt like laybacking up an icicle'.

[5] Girdle traverses – climbs which cross cliffs horizontally – have fallen from fashion in recent years, perhaps as a result of climbing's increasing popularity, and the mayhem a party on a girdle can cause on a crowded cliff. Traditional thinking on them was that they were the last phase in a cliff's development, and a sign of its being worked out – which was not quite the case with Clogwyn Du'r Arddu in 1953.

sent its human complement flying into the River Arve. They arrived drenched at the Biolay – traditional flea-infested Chamonix accommodation for the British – to be greeted by Geoff Sutton with the comment, 'I say, old man – you look as though you've been in the river.' When Audrey and Don joined them, the former was put – according to the rules of the day, the Cambridge example of the likes of Cym Smith and Nancy Heron[6] not yet having breached the bastions of sexual chauvinism in climbing[7] – on cooking and sunbathing duties, and the other three made their plans. Cowan suggested the West Face of the Pointe Albert, a short and accessible rock-route on perfect red Chamonix granite, varied with several aid pitches and given the top alpine grade, VI, of the day. It boosted their confidence enormously, the free-climbing in a style of which gritstone had made them past masters, and the artificial climbing nowhere near the technical standards they were reaching in their winter play in the limestone dales. Cowan suggested they follow up the Pointe Albert with the higher and longer East Ridge of the Dent du Crocodile. It involved the long approach, with which Don was already familiar, up to the Envers des Aiguilles hut, that season in the course of reconstruction and quite comfortless, and a 2 a.m. start to get them to the foot of the route whilst the snow was still

---

[6] Actually a student at Leeds University, where she was a contemporary of Arthur Dolphin's, but when she and Cym married she moved to Newmarket, near Cambridge, where Cym was a student.

[7] That sexual chauvinism was strongly in evidence in climbing is made apparent by the fact that, even as late as the 1970s, most of the senior British mountaineering and climbing clubs did not admit women as members. Some even went so far as to exclude them from their huts, and the battle to change this situation was long, bitter, and drawn in large measure along generational lines. The reasons for preserving the status quo were for the most part utterly spurious. I remember one particularly angry debate at a Climbers' Club Extraordinary General Meeting called on the issue. The well-known Lake District climber of the 1930s, A.B. Hargreaves – in his seventies by then but still a notable lecher – stood up and proclaimed that when a chap came down after a day on the hill, he simply wanted to strip off, bathe, and dry himself naked in front of the fire. How could that be done with the ladies around?

As to the – often thwarted – ambitions of these selfsame 'ladies', it's well worth mentioning that whilst Don was otherwise engaged on the South Face of Annapurna, Audrey – along with Janet Davies, Nikki Clough and the wonderful Brede Arkless, mountain-guide and mother of eight – was out in the little-known Padar Himal, romping up a sheaf of peaks just short of 20,000 feet high. And that Audrey proved one of the strongest and most competent mountaineers on the expedition.

hard. The climb itself was a chapter of accidents. The shaft of Joe's ex-WD ice-axe broke as he was crossing the bergschrund guarding the approach gully. Higher on the ridge, poor rope-management on the part of the two Dons whilst Joe led a crucial artificial pitch caused their specially purchased 250-foot rope to jam behind a huge flake. It took them three hours to retrieve it – cut by then into four 60-foot lengths, which they clumsily knotted together with the inevitable result of endless further rope-jams, the impossibility of putting on any protection because the rope wouldn't run freely through it, and added problems on the abseil descent, in the course of which they dropped a torch.

By the time they arrived back on the glacier it was pitch-black and they had been climbing for 20 hours. With one torch and two ice-axes between them they set off down slopes that seemed, as always in the dark, twice as steep as they had done in the daylight. In the snow-basin below the bergschrund Don – not yet used to wearing them – caught his crampons in the leg of his trousers (who hasn't done that?), went headlong and knocked into Joe. The pair of them tumbled off down the slope, Don was held on the rope by Cowan, who injured his hand in the process, and Joe promptly landed crampons-first[8] on Don's backside. They limped back into the Envers des Aiguilles hut at 3.30 a.m., slept through the day, and descended back to the Biolay where bathing and dressing a score of puncture-wounds in Don's behind was added to Audrey's other chores. A rest day was called for, and they wandered down to the Bar Nationale,[9] where they met Cambridge University Mountaineering Club members Geoff Sutton, spectator at the ascent of The Sloth and known to Don from the ACG dinner, and Bob Downes, another outstanding young climber, who was then in his first alpine season and who was to play a significant role in Don's life over the next few years.

Other members of the Rock & Ice arrived. Nat Allen was among them and he gives an interesting view of Don's evolving attitude and his approach to communal living:

---

[8] One of the less obvious dangers of snow and ice climbing, this has been the cause of some grave injuries over the years. The brilliant young Liverpool University climber John Clements was killed in Glencoe early in 1966 when his companion, Tim Osgathorpe, fell and landed on his helmetless head in crampons.

[9] International feuding in this famous Chamonix institution over the years makes English soccer fans' hooliganism look like a Sunday-school outing.

We had our first dust-up on that '53 trip, Don and I. He'd started this later thing of his of doing the absolute minimum, and naturally this didn't go down too well with the other lads. He'd had a go at Ron and Joe over something, and then he said something to me, so I grabbed him by the throat, banged him against a wall with my fist in his face, and told him to behave himself. We didn't have any trouble later, him and me, but I know Ronnie Moseley went off him in a big way. He was tight, mind you, and it showed in lots of ways. Because his dad worked in the grocer's, he was always very well provided for – all Joe had in those early days was his off-ration bacon and cheese when he could get it. Ronnie was a good caterer, and very generous – made big brews, big butties. But not Don – he'd make things for himself, never do anything for anyone else on the ground. He was different on a climb, mind – he'd help you practically . . .

Joe had been indulging in the perennial off-day pursuit of climbers – thumbing through the guidebook. He had discovered that the hardest rock-pitch in the Chamonix Aiguilles was a crack called the Fissure Fix on the West Face of the Aiguille de Blaitiere, and that it was graded VIb. Neither he nor either of the Dons had yet climbed a pitch of this standard, but there was no reason why that should act as a curb on their ambitions. Sutton, who knew as much as any British climber of the time about the Aiguilles, told them that the face had suffered a huge rock-fall since the Allain-Fix route, on which the pitch lay, had first been climbed. He thought it might not now be possible. The incentives were crowding in thick and fast. Realising that they were determined on the objective, Sutton asked if he might join them, pointing out that they would climb faster as two ropes of two. Audrey was abandoned at the Biolay again and they flogged up to the foot of the Blaitiere's West Face. Low down on this, Joe, who was climbing with Cowan whilst Don and Geoff Sutton made up the other rope, led a wide, bulging, leaning crack that he quickly realised would not have been out of place both in style and difficulty on a gritstone edge. The four of them left a good deal of skin on it. This pitch, the Fissure Brown as it came to be known, once recognised and written up as part of a completed route, was soon to usurp the position of the Fissure Fix as hardest in the Aiguilles. But not this year. Above it they reached the scar of the rock-fall. Neither pair could determine on a line to commit the four of them to, the quality of the rock had deteriorated drastically, darkness fell, they bivouacked on the terrace at third-height on the face, and the weather closed in around them, spelling out that their brief season had come to an end.

Viewed simply in terms of achieved objectives, Don's climbing during the fortnight had only amounted to two routes: one prolonged epic, and one failure and retreat. In reality, the season was a very significant one. We learn best by our mistakes, and they had made plenty of them. They had also climbed at the highest alpine grade and found it straightforward. They had accomplished – though they were not yet to know this – the hardest free pitch so far in the Western Alps. In meeting Sutton – again, in Don's case – they had made close contact with one of the most elegant and insightful of all commentators on climbing, and one who would assist immeasurably in their elevation to mythic status. The auguries were good, and on the long, wet, painful ride home none of them need have felt unduly dispirited.

As the year slipped into autumn, the weekend pioneering routine re-established itself. Possessing his own transport was enabling Don to cast his net wide. For two weekends in October he was in Wales. On another, at the end of the month, he went to Deer Bield Crag in the Lake District – one of those rigorous venues where every succeeding generation feels the need to make its mark. Ron Moseley had already added the ingenious and bold Pendulum to the crag, and on this late October weekend he and Whillans joined forces for a difficult girdle traverse. On one of the Welsh weekends Don took a look at a strange, high cliff, untouched since the time of Menlove Edwards, on the south side of the Llanberis Pass – the aptly named Craig Rhaeadr, down the centre of which a waterfall sprays continually and on which the rock is disconcertingly compact and lacking in cracks. With Tom Waghorn, he embarked on a vague line left of the waterfall, events on the long first pitch of which nearly resulted in a very premature end to his career. Waghorn takes up the account:

I was following up the thinnish first pitch, which Whillans has just put behind him in his usual effortless way, when I slipped. It happened eight to ten feet left of the master while I was traversing into a one-foot stance. Before you could say

Jacques Robinson I was doing an involuntary *pendule*. Whillans was dangling upside down[10] with only a thin nylon sling looped round a knob of rock between us and the Llanberis mortuary. As I hung there pitons showered from Whillans's pockets on to my unprotected head. But, still suspended from the sling, he contrived to lower me to the ground. We eventually finished the 300-foot route, which I remember as perpendicular at times and dangerous because of the lack of reliable stances and belays.

With the onset of winter, the Rock & Ice members again abandoned the mountain crags and moorland edges for the comforts of the Derbyshire and Yorkshire Dales. Don Roscoe gives the rationale:

When bad weather curtails normal climbing, limestone is hardly affected; the overhanging faces remain dry in heavy rain or snow. Winter is, in fact, the best period for limestone because the crags are all situated in beauty spots and tend to be very congested with tourists in the summer months. The routes are all of a strenuous nature and the climber is kept warm by his struggles. The only sufferer is the second who is frequently called upon to manipulate ropes in atrocious weather.

Some of the winter activity was distinctly playful. Tom Waghorn again:

---

[10] The shoulder belay commonly used in the 1950s, and necessarily and correctly when tying directly on to a nylon rope, often resulted in incidents like this, particularly where there was a disparity in weight between climbers. Even as late as the 1960s it was still in use and giving rise to some frightening incidents. On an early ascent of one of the routes on Anglesey's Red Wall, for example, Lawrie Holliwell – a leading figure of the time – was belaying his brother Les thus from the top of the crag when the latter fell off clutching a huge loose block. Lawrie, who had a certain amount of slack between himself and the anchor, found himself up-ended, dragged over the lip, and looking straight into Les's eyes with a 400-foot drop to the sea beneath them. The rope had slipped from over his shoulder and he was holding on to it at full stretch beneath him with both hands, whilst Les still clutched on to the block that had caused the mayhem. 'For God's sake, let go of the block,' Lawrie yelled. The block was consigned to the depths, Les got back on to the rock, Lawrie righted himself, but both were considerably shaken. This was one of many incidents that led people to start looking more closely at belaying techniques in the 1960s and 1970s.

Our maddest escapade . . . was during a string of weekends when the Rock & Ice were exploring the fascinating limestone of Gordale Scar and Kilnsey Crag in the Yorkshire Dales. Tiring of the slow-motion stuff that the whack-and-dangle boys call climbing, we stretched a rope across the top of the Gordale gorge and aped across. At this spot the gorge was about 200 feet deep, but there was only a 50-foot gap between the lips. We couldn't hurl the nylon across because of the gusty wind, so we lowered a 200-foot rope from each side. A stooge at the bottom of the gorge linked the two, which were then hauled up to form the bridge. On one side the full-weight nylon was tied to a massive boulder; on the other it was pulleyed round a tree to take out as much slackness as possible. On to the bridge-rope we clipped two etriers, sat in them, and swung across one at a time. Taut as the rope had seemed before the crossing, it sagged alarmingly when one reached the middle, with 200 feet of fresh air below . . . I had to be pulled to the other side by the four strong arms manning the safety rope. Quite a hair-raising stunt which I wouldn't like to repeat. No wonder the Dales farmers thought we were crazy, and looking back they were indeed mad, zany days . . .

Light-hearted and daft these exploits may have been, but like much play they also had a more serious purpose: in habituation to situations of alarming exposure; in the acquisition of skills in rope-handling and improvisation; through them, Don and his companions were becoming ever more complete climbers. Another threat was looming, however, that seemed set to rob Don of two years of his climbing prime. In 1954, he would reach the age of 21, his apprenticeship would end, and he would thus be called up for his National Service.

He received his papers early in the year and duly reported to the Medical Board for examination. An unsavoury character fastened on to him as they went through the processes, and advised him not to put anything down about past illnesses when he filled in the forms they had been given lest they turned him down. Don promptly put in every illness, every medical condition he had ever suffered, including the 1950 bout of labyrinthitis and vertigo, which had at the time been diagnosed as 'stomach ulcers'. But at the same time he resigned himself to two years away from climbing – a pill the more bitter to swallow in view of the Rock & Ice plans for the summer of 1954. Joe, ever analytical and persuasive, had decided after the all-too-brief experience of 1953 that to succeed on the major climbs in the Alps it was necessary to spend the whole season out there. Ron Moseley and Ray Greenall were in agreement, and all three were living as parsimoniously as they could in order to save the necessary money. Joe had even given up smoking and was cycling to the Derbyshire crags to economise on bus fares. Regular weekends further afield had gone by the board. All this Don was having to sit back and witness, knowing that in all probability he would be excluded.[11]

The buff envelope from the Ministry of Labour and National Service landed on his doormat one Wednesday morning early in April. He opened it, and to his astonishment and delight found himself classified 'Grade Three – unfit for military service'. When he casually let the news slip at the YMCA that night, the Rock & Ice were incredulous – and in Don's account, one of them in particular was none too pleased:

'Oh-oh, this is it then,' taunted Moseley. 'Acting unpaid, unwashed, unwanted Private Whillans.'

I let the rest of the lads have a good guffaw and then I dropped the bombshell.

'I'm Grade Three, they're not taking me,' I said.

Talk about staring eyes and open mouths. Moseley went bright red and started spluttering.

'You what? What? You skiving get.'

'You jammy bugger.'

'You? Not fit? Let's have a look.'

I smiled quietly. 'Now who's going to the Alps?' I asked.

'Bloody hell,' said Moseley with deep disgust.

In celebratory mood, Don joined Nat Allen, Joe and Ron

---

[11] How well he was climbing at this time is made clear by Don Roscoe's memory of him soloing the Right Unconquerable, after Roscoe had failed on it, wearing a pair of 'brothel creepers' (thick, crêpe-soled shoes, as worn by 'Teddy Boys' – Don at the time possessed the whole 'Teddy Boy' regalia: DA, quiff, drainpipe, drapes and a shoestring tie). This habit of not dressing like climbers was common in the early Rock & Ice – mostly they would just make themselves look like walkers at weekends, and have fun on the bus or train to the crags by winding people up to bullshit about their exploits.

Moseley for an Easter trip to Ben Nevis. Moseley and Brown were intent on Point Five Gully, then unclimbed even as a summer route, whilst Don had his sights set on a line he had heard mentioned by a young Aberdonian medical student, Tom Patey, at the Biolay in 1953, an impressive sequence of corner-chimneys up the right-hand side of Carn Dearg Buttress, access to it guarded by a line of huge roofs. Patey had attempted it in October with fellow Aberdonian students Mike Taylor and Bill Brooker, reached an enormous loose chockstone in the base of the chimney, and sounded the retreat. Whilst Joe and Ron – who had climbed together a great deal in winter conditions in Wales and made ascents of many of the now classic ice routes – spent two fruitless and freezing days and one excruciating night in a home-made bivouac tent on Point Five Gully before being driven away by spindrift and powder-snow avalanches, Don and Nat probed for two days at the roofs guarding their intended line. On the third day, the two of them having got nowhere, Joe drifted over from Point Five and suggested a different approach. Using a couple of slings for aid, he came close to solving the entry to the chimneys before darkness fell. In the morning, Joe's efforts of the previous day having been so strenuous, they decided Don should climb up to the chockstone round which Joe had placed a sling on the previous day, belay there, and let Joe lead through. At least that was the plan: 'When he reached the overhang, Don told me that he felt quite fit, so I told him to carry on. He shuffled up and grasped a big stalactite hanging down from the roof. Hugging it like a coconut tree climber he vanished over the top.' Years later, looking back on this piece of climbing, Joe described it as 'like watching a ballet dancer doing something very special'.

Their ascent was now assured, and as they descended Number Five Gully to the left of the crag, George Ritchie, a Scottish Mountaineering Club luminary who was soloing Jubilee Gully and had been watching their efforts, shouted down to them, in not wholly jocular tones, 'English bastards!' Their rejoinder was to name the climb Sassenach. Before they had time to celebrate an ascent that was to rankle for years with Scottish climbers, a climber rushed into the camp to tell of an accident on Tower Ridge. A young woman had fallen from the Great Tower and was hanging from the rope. Despite their day's exertions, Joe and Don climbed back to the summit ridge, and at the descent to the Great Tower met Peter Bunney, a member of the woman's party of five. He told them that her name was Betty Emery, that she had fallen 40 feet, hit her head and been held on the rope by her companion, Anthea Russell. He gave them a spare rope, and in pitch darkness they descended into Tower Gap, continuing on along the Eastern Traverse until they came to a rope from which was dangling what they anticipated would be a woman's body. Quite apart from the conditions, which would have made exposure inevitable, the rocks below the Eastern Traverse – itself relatively straightforward – are extremely steep. In the 1950s, when the common practice was simply to tie on directly around the waist with a bowline, pressure on the ribcage and diaphragm would result in unconsciousness in minutes and death by suffocation usually within the hour.

The rocks were verglased, the rope from which Emery was dangling was frozen to them and a bitter wind was blowing. They struggled to pull up the woman's rope until their hands bled, debated whether one of them should abseil to her, and knew that such a course of action would almost inevitably result in another casualty. Not only that – there was no answer from below to their shouts, and both men knew that the woman they had come to rescue must by now be dead. Ray Greenall arrived with a stove and bivouac bag, and they spent a long night shivering and brewing up. At first light Joe abseiled down, chopped the frozen rope free and arrived at the dead woman: 'There was a great cleft in her head and it was obvious she'd been dead from the fall.' Joe freed the rope from an overhang and vee-chimney that had caused it to jam in the night, and the others pulled her body up to the traverse, from which it was taken off by the RAF Mountain Rescue team. The Rock & Ice members – for all their success on Carn Dearg and the mutual respect and reliance in differing conditions and situations the holiday had consolidated between Don and Joe – headed south for home that day in subdued and chastened mood.

Back in Salford, Don had three problems to face: how to explain to his traditionally minded father that he intended spending three months that summer in the Alps; how to get three months off work; and how to finance the trip, in which matter Joe, Ron and Ray had a head start in saving the necessary money. In the event, the solutions to all three problems neatly interlinked. Mr Emett, who regarded Don as an exceptionally neat and competent worker, agreed to his having the time off and assured him that his job would be open when he came back; this placated Tom Whillans, who suggested Don sell the Enfield and use the money from that as a further loan instead of paying it back to him. All this effort, however, seemed to have been futile in the face of rain in the valley and heavy snow on the mountains throughout their first fortnight in the Alps. On the occasions when it did brighten up, Moseley bullied them time and again on to the recent Bonatti Route on the East Face of the Grand Capucin – a climb at that time almost entirely artificial up a 1500-foot vertical face of perfect red granite. On one of these occasions, when only Joe and Don were attempting the route and Moseley was resting, the Britons were held up by a particularly slow Austrian climber whom they later recognised as Hermann Bühl.

On their last attempt, high above them as they set off from their bivouac in a makeshift and disintegrating igloo and commenced the climb, a French team was moving at snail's pace and removing all the pegs on the route as they went. Between Joe and Don, Moseley was also moving at snail's pace and neither placing nor removing pegs as he went. According to Joe:

> Don kept shouting at Moseley to climb faster because he was taking longer to climb each pitch with all the pegs in place than the time I spent putting them in and climbing, and the time Don spent climbing and removing . . . For some unaccountable reason I was sack-hauling without assistance and getting browned off. I was leading *and* hauling three sacks.

Dispirited, the British team gave the route up as a bad job, retreated, and were further goaded by the guardian of the Requin Hut enquiring – solicitously or chauvinistically – whether it had been too hard for them.

In the valley again, they regrouped and reappraised their objectives. Don suffered a bout of illness at the Biolay, and on his recovery from it he and Joe had a score to settle from the previous season with the West Face of the Aiguille de Blaitiere. They bivouacked at its foot; Joe led off up the Curbar-like crack that was soon to be known as the Fissure Brown; higher on the face Don located the Fissure Fix – then still reputed the hardest pitch in Chamonix – and Joe led it, as he had done every other significant pitch on the climb, including the Fissure Whillans, without difficulty. By nightfall the route – the hardest to be accomplished to that date in the Aiguilles – was complete. The names of Brown and Whillans were established at the forefront of alpinism as well as of British rock-climbing, and their season, really, had only just begun.[12]

Their next goal presented itself almost immediately. The three snail-paced Frenchmen who had forced them to abandon their climb on the Grand Capucin had gone on to make the second ascent of Magnone, Laine, Dagory and Berardini's major and celebrated[13] line from 1952 on the West Face of the Dru, the red spire of which had captivated Don on his first visit to Chamonix two years before. Not only had they been successful on it, they had cut the time for its ascent from Magnone's six days to a mere three. Joe and Don made their preparations carefully – this, after all, being the 'name' climb in Chamonix of the day. Joe borrowed a cagoule from Geoff Sutton, and the two of them visited Snell's shop where Joe bought a hammer-axe and they acquired an English translation of the route description from Magnone's book.

On a fine morning they took the 10.30 *téléférique* to Montenvers and crossed the Mer de Glace to the foot of the face. Above them a couloir stretched up for 1000 feet, the top 400 feet of it ice pocked with rock-shrapnel, a runnel gouged out of its centre by falling ice and stone. On the ice, Joe led out a full rope's length, and as he chopped steps, ice showered down on Don, who yelled up, 'Chop it into smaller bits, will yer?' The rope ran out before Joe reached a belay. According to the notably unreliable *Portrait of a Mountaineer*, 'because the Dru was essentially a rock-climb we hadn't bothered with ice-axes and crampons, though Joe had bought himself a new hammer-axe which would see us through if we encountered much ice in the couloir'.[14] Don, supposedly without

---

[12] As a prime example of French mountaineering chauvinism, when Gaston Rebuffat included the West Face of the Blaitiere in his book on the hundred best climbs in the range of Mont Blanc, he graded the Fissure Brown a lowly *Très Difficile*, recommending that it be climbed using very large wooden wedges. This theme will recur when we get to the tactics involved around the first ascent of the Central Pillar of Freney.

[13] Also heavily criticised in some quarters for having been done in two distinct parts. This French ascent was the first to be completed in one push. One of the Frenchmen involved died in the descent, which makes Joe and Don's going on it straight afterwards all the more bold.

[14] Joe's response to this is terse: 'That's complete bollocks – if Don hadn't been wearing crampons, I would have had to have given him a rope all the way down the Charpoua Glacier on the descent, and that definitely wasn't the case.'

crampons, in Vibrams, had to unfasten from the anchor and follow. It had started to rain. Don describes how he balanced up the streaming nicks Joe had cut in the ice to free more rope, both him and Joe now unbelayed and in the line of stonefall. At last Joe reached a rock ledge, clipped in to a peg, and both men could breathe more easily.

The storm increased, lightning flashing round the peak above them. 'We might have gone straight back down then, but the idea of going down the icy part of the couloir was so nasty we thought we'd better stay for a bit to see if we could go on up later.' They set to clearing the ledge they were on of ice for a bivouac. Joe's newly purchased hammer-axe broke, leaving one piton hammer between them. The rain stopped. They made food, slept fitfully, set off again at 5.30 and were soon at the start of the route's serious climbing, where they tied on to the 300-foot rope and began to lead through. Don arrived at the reputed crux of the route, the Fissure Vignes, and went up it without difficulty. 'It wasn't more than normal VS standard. If that's the crux, we thought, we're in for an easy climb.'

At the 40-metre crack above, overhanging and climbed on wooden wedges, it was Don's lead again, but after 20 feet he stopped on a better stance than the one at its foot and brought up Joe, who protested what a crafty bugger he was as Don handed over the lead. The wedges in the crack were all rotten. When Don came to follow, he rapidly laybacked the entire pitch. The climbing above, to the foot of the 90-metre diedre, was heavily iced and they had to cut holds. In the diedre itself, the rock was running with water and it had begun to snow. At its top, a huge vertical drop beneath them now to the glacier, they found the fixed traversing rope left by the original party and descended it to an uncomfortable bivouac ledge. It was eight o'clock, night falling, the ledge deep in snow. They hunched down and tried to sleep. Don, a Pacamac[15] covering his duvet, looked across enviously at Joe in his new cagoule – who was, unbeknown to him, also soaking wet as the garment leaked badly. All night it snowed. 'At last it began to get light. I could hardly see Don: he was covered with snow, with just the ridges of his Pacamac showing black. The dawn was grey and misty and it was still snowing . . .' They pressed on. At the line of overhangs across the top of the face they came across a wire caving

---

[15] A plastic raincoat that folded up very small; these were at least waterproof, but lacked flaps over the front fastening, and ripped very easily.

ladder left by the French party. It was a rope's-length long. They climbed it and emerged on to the North Face, the route beneath them but severe climbing on the snowed-up face still ahead.

Don hustled on, leading the most difficult pitch they had encountered on the route as he did so, not wanting to spend another comfortless night out in sodden clothing. They reached the lower of the two summits of the Dru. The only description of a descent route which they possessed was that for the traverse of the Drus, so they headed on for the higher summit. They wriggled up the last chimneys and roped off immediately down the face. Eight abseils on their 300-foot rope took them on to the Charpoua Glacier, their concentration the more focused by the fatality that had befallen the earlier French party here. It was dark on the steep and fissure-seamed glacier, with just a glimmer of moonlight. Don describes attempting to cross a big crevasse and falling in three times, swinging wildly on the rope: 'This is fun, but it gets a bit monotonous,' he quipped. 'It didn't happen,' says Joe. An avalanche from high on the Aiguille Verte swept past, blasting them with ice-spicules. With the broken hammer-axe Joe hacked an uncomfortable and inadequate ledge in the snow, and without food they spent a long and hungry night, watching the lamps crossing beneath as dawn neared. At daybreak, 15 minutes took them back to the Charpoua Hut. They dragged back down to the Biolay, ate until they could eat no more, and woke in the middle of the night to a campsite awash with flood water.

The following afternoon, a neat-pullovered and exquisitely stockinged Frenchman picked his way through the squalid quagmire of the campsite, sought out Monsieur Whillans and Monsieur Brown and introduced himself. It was the French guide and national hero Louis Lachenal, who had, with Lionel Terray, made the second ascent of the North Face of the Eiger in 1947, and the first ascent of Annapurna, first of the world's 8000-metre peaks to be climbed, in 1950. He was here to seek information and advice from a 21-year-old in his third alpine season.

12

Climbing Bum

To a British audience – whether the general public or the more knowledgeable one of the climbing community – still hung-over from the celebration of 'Coronation Everest', the impact of Joe and Don's 1954 ascent of the Petit Dru West Face was more excuse for national pride.[1] Even as they wended their way down from the Charpoua Hut, the two young climbers had been congratulated by Hamish Nicol, one of the driving forces in the Alpine Climbing Group at the time, for having achieved 'something for the Old Country!'. On the streets of Chamonix, once the news had disseminated, the Chamonix guides came up to them to shake them by the hand. Newspapers back in Britain carried the news. There was a full-page feature in the *Sunday Express* in which a host of later journalistic clichés along the lines of 'Manchester's pigmy climbing plumbers'[2] were first brought into use. Even the staid old *Alpine Journal* puffed out its patriotic chest and, in an account that strayed somewhat from the journal's usual accuracy and under-

---

[1] It also subsequently gave Don the pretext for considerable black propaganda against Joe. His account of the climb in *Portrait of a Mountaineer* is distinctly derogatory, building himself up as the strong member of the party at Joe's expense, and claiming things happened which Joe firmly disputes – that he was so weak at one point, for example, that Don had to carry his sack. It seems to me that the ghost-writer's hand lies heavily across this account, but it does raise the question of why Don did not see fit to correct a version that is palpably slanted, unlikely and inaccurate. None of the significant points of detraction in this version were present in the nearest joint contemporary account, as told to Anthony Rawlinson and published in the 1955 *Climbers' Club Journal*.
[2] Variations on this epithet were endlessly bestowed on Rock & Ice members during the 1950s and 1960s, despite the fact that the only plumbers in the club were Don and Nat Allen. Joe was not a plumber but a jobbing builder until 1961, when he became an instructor at the White Hall Centre for Open Country Pursuits in Derbyshire.

statement, declared that 'This perilous climb was carried out under the very worst conditions. For the most part they were climbing through thunderstorms. And they spent the night on a ledge so narrow that they had to snatch what sleep they could standing up.'

According to *Portrait of a Mountaineer*, another by-product of their achievement, and a more significant one than these ephemera of celebrity, came in the form of a visit to their campsite from the president of the ACG, Tom Bourdillon. Bourdillon had been one of the driving forces on the previous year's 'Everest' expedition, and with Charles Evans had been first to reach Chomolungma's south summit – the highest then attained. An amiable and unassuming giant of a man, who was tragically killed with Dick Viney on the Jägihorn in 1956, he is described in the Whillans/Ormerod book as coming out with a surprising invitation to the two leading lights from this scruffy band of Rock & Ice brigands.

An expedition was being planned for the following year to Kangchenjunga in Sikkim, third-highest peak in the world and – news having just come through of Lacedelli and Compagnoni's success of 31 July on 'K2' – the loftiest yet unclimbed. Would they be interested? asked Bourdillon. It was not a formal invitation, more of a sounding-out as to inclination and availability, and for the time being nothing more was said to either man about it. Even in 1953 there had been talk of Joe's going to Everest, but at the time this was simply the expression of class and regional sour grapes, Joe not even having visited the Alps when the expedition departed. Now, as the appalling weather of the 1954 alpine season – one of the worst on record, which makes the ascents they achieved in spite of it all the more remarkable – closed in around them and 'six weeks of cat-and-mouse games with storms and gales' sapped their appetite for any more climbing in the Aiguilles, the Rock & Ice decided to return home.[3] As they travelled back from France, Don

---

[3] Don wrote to Audrey just before they decided to leave: '9/8/54. Dear Audrey, I am still camping in the wood and dodging the rent man. We managed to do the Blaitiere and the West Face of the Dru – a first ascent and a third, me and Joe. I have got £15 left and I want to save £5 if possible for when I get home to spend a couple of weeks in Wales or Lakes. It has rained all today. Ron [Moseley] hasn't done a decent route and is fed up. I think £10 will last about a month or so. Sorry I didn't write sooner only you know me for writing letters. Ron Moseley tried the Capucin again and dropped the rucksack with the food 400 feet down the face so they had to come down. Good job – it stormed for two days. Cheerio for now. Best love. Don.'

and Joe established now as a formidable force in European mountaineering and a finely balanced climbing team, did they have a further goal on which to exercise their imaginations? Would they be going to Kangchenjunga together the following spring? Had either of them, in fact, then even been invited?

Not according to Joe they hadn't. Nor according to Val, his new girlfriend of the time and later his wife, who clearly remembers the arrival of the telegram of invitation from Charles Evans at Joe's home in November, a telegram she still possesses: 'Invited Kangchenjunga expedition stop Letter following stop Charles Evans.' There was no equivalent proudly propped on the mantelpiece of the Whillans household in Lower Kersal. Joe was going to the Himalayas. Don was not. To Don, his being left out rankled, and appears to have seemed both personal betrayal and against natural justice. Had he not been as strong on the Dru? – a conviction which later turned to him portraying himself as the stronger of the party and the one who had safely found the descent route. On their route on the Blaitiere, had he not been the one to find the crucial pitch of the Fissure Fix that led them to the top of the face (even though it was Joe who had led every difficult pitch on the climb)? So how could it be the case that Joe was chosen for the Kangchenjunga team, and he was not? Nat Allen remembers: 'We were all a bit resentful on Don's account. We knew that he was Joe's equal, and he was an incredible walker, incredibly fit in those days. But somehow he always went on second-class trips, whilst Joe – well, he was always close, hush-hush, so I can see how the suspicion came about.'

To the end of his life, with his close friends Don continued to express his rancour, his belief that Joe had 'stabbed him in the back'. Before his death from cancer in 1988, Ronnie Dutton told me, 'Don always blamed Joe for Kangchenjunga – reckoned he'd put in a word against him when if he'd spoken up for Don he'd have been on the boat. It was complete bollocks, of course, but he felt that strong about it you couldn't tell 'im, otherwise you'd have got a thump.' That Don's version is not the truth of the matter is pretty clear – as it is also the case that Don, in his one published record of his climbing career, either distorted the truth himself or allowed it to be distorted on his behalf without seeking later to correct it. Joe, in whose testimony I would place absolute trust and whose public assessments of Don have always been marked by a judicious balance of accuracy and generosity,[4] vehemently denies ever making any comment that would have jeopardised Don's chances of going to Kangchenjunga. His own place on that expedition had come about through Geoff Sutton's discreet lobbying – and Sutton, who knew both men, had not done the same for Don. The story of Bourdillon's overtures in Don's book simply does not ring true – was not the way the mountaineering establishment of the time operated.

Before Charles Evans's death in 1995, I quizzed him extensively around this point. Charles was one of the wisest, most honest and endearing characters ever to have graced British mountaineering. He told me that no provisional invitation would have been offered to either man at that time; that Bourdillon, who was punctilious in these matters, would not have considered himself empowered to extend one; and that there had never actually been any question of inviting Don. Because of his reputation as a hell-raiser? I suggested. Charles narrowed his eyes; his silence spoke volumes, and he went on elliptically to tell of how the expedition was designated as lightweight and reconnaissance, its personnel was pretty well decided by the early summer of 1954, and there was not room for two more climbers on it. Also, the contemporary thinking was that in general Himalayan performance improved throughout a climber's twenties; so Joe, at 24, might have seemed a risk worth taking whilst Don, at 21, was a more debatable one. In his book on the expedition[5] Evans makes this point implicitly: 'The youngest, and smallest [member of the expedition], was Joe Brown: he was 24, and is five feet six. The rest of us, both in age and size, came between. We were in our thirties, or late twenties.'

However disappointed Don might have felt, and however much force this was later to gather in his mind as Joe prospered in his climbing, in his marriage, in his business ventures, for the moment the two of them still had the euphoria of recent major shared climbs to draw on, and a few weeks of their planned summer climbing time left. Don borrowed more money from Tom Whillans, bought another motorbike – a fat, listless BSA 650cc Gold Flash – loaded it

---

[4] E.g., from *The Hard Years*: 'Don always gave the wrong impression of himself. He was lackadaisical yet dynamic, contented yet cunning. He was not exactly two persons; there were two sides to his nature and most of the time one overlapped the other, producing a mixture of he-man and saint.'

[5] *Kangchenjunga: The Untrodden Peak* (Hodder & Stoughton, 1956).

up, and set off to collect Joe with the intention of heading off for Scotland again. In the centre of Salford he collided with a newly erected traffic island whilst overtaking, demolished the bollards, the 'Keep Left' signs, and most of his new bike. It cost him £70 and a bad sprain to his ankle, so he was soon back – on a tradesman's pay now – at Emett & Smith to work off his accumulated debts. He was just out of his apprenticeship, and it was the last time in his life that he would hold down a regular job. When the spring of 1955 came round, he took the course later followed by generations of climbing bums, asked for his cards, packed his rucksack, headed across to Wales and was taken on as general handyman at the Pen-y-Gwryd Hotel.

News came through that Joe, with George Band, had reached the summit of Kangchenjunga on 26 May, and since most of the expedition members were Pen-y-Gwryd regulars, a party atmosphere prevailed. In what was turning into a golden summer, Geoff Sutton arrived and whisked Don away to Skye,[6] where he was instructing for the Mountaineering Association. Don met up with a couple from Tanganyika, and the woman expressed an interest in climbing, so she and Don went off for several days running to Sron na Ciche and repeated Integrity, Crack of Double Doom and other of the cliff's harder routes – the Tanganyikan woman ('a real tough-looking bird' according to Don) arousing a degree of interest and comment by climbing, very bravely given the roughness of gabbro, in her bathing costume. Sutton, having finished his instructional duties, teamed up with Don and they climbed the tottering and eccentric 160-foot pinnacle of the Old Man of Storr.[7] On the way

---

[6] 'Glenbrittle, 13 June '55. Dear Audrey, I am sorry to leave you in the lurch last weekend. I waited till 12.30 Friday night and you hadn't arrived. I still don't know if you went at all anyway. Sutton came and said he was going to Skye, all I had to pay for was my grub for the fortnight – no petrol or anything. I am sending you some money for the instalment which is overdue – you will have to lend me a couple of quid. I am sorry to say I will have to sell the bike shortly. I think my mam and dad are going on their holidays this Saturday. No need to say where I am if he thinks I'm still in Wales. I will call for you when I get home. Cheerio. Best love. Don.'

[7] An account purporting to be by Don of this climb appeared, of all places, in the correspondence column of *Country Life* a couple of years later. Too delicious to omit, it ran as follows: 'Owing to the rottenness of the rock for the first 20 feet, which overhangs, great difficulty was experienced in getting started. I was forced to adopt the expedient of arranging a sling between two projections, into which I stepped. Having stepped up a little further, I just managed to place a piton into a hole three inches deep. It could not be secured, but without this loose piton to

back to Wales from Skye, Don diverted to Wasdale and, in company with Johnny Sullivan, a Derby climber he had met in the bar of the Wasdale Head Hotel, he ambled up to Scafell and offered further affront to regional sensibilities still smarting after Dovedale Grooves when he climbed a striking crack-line on the East Buttress, Trinity, which is now regarded as one of the classic routes on this historical centrepiece of Lakeland climbing. His most dearly held ambitions on British rock, though, were still on Clogwyn Du'r Arddu, and the first significant one of them to be achieved without Joe as partner was soon to come to fruition.

One of the new members the Rock & Ice had attracted since 1951 was a young locomotive fitter from Sheffield who had been introduced to rock-climbing and the club by Don Cowan. He was called Vin Betts – 'Black Betts' according to his club sobriquet – and he had the reputation of being a madcap, tearaway character, fast on a motorbike and larger and louder than life. Vin takes up the story:

In the summer of 1955 Don Whillans was not very popular with the Rock & Ice lads as he was quite difficult to get along with. This was the summer Don took off work to devote himself to climbing, and it was also the year Joe was elected to go and climb Kangchenjunga with the toffs as the first of the working-class lads to go on a Himalayan expedition. So the rivalry between Don and Joe, which was definitely there on Don's side, could have accounted for Don's moods. Anyway, what it boiled down to was that if Don was in the Lakes we would go to Wales, and vice versa. However, we got it wrong this particular weekend. The Llanberis Pass appeared deserted, the crags were dry, and 'Lou' Waghorn and I decided to climb Bow-Shaped Slab on 'Cloggy'. We walked up to Halfway House, where Mrs Williams was very good to the Rock & Ice lads and would always knock something off the bill when we came to pay, and were having our tea and buns when in walked Don with Audrey, saw us, and said, 'What are you lads up to, then?' We told him our plans,

---

serve first as handhold, then as foothold, I could never have reached a ledge to the left that was the key to the summit. Having left the piton I experienced extreme difficulty in surmounting a bulge, using wrinkles as footholds . . .' etc., etc.

but he said we should come along with him and 'have a look' at a new route he'd seen on the biggest bit of unclimbed rock on the West Buttress. Knowing Don's surly moods in those days, we decided it was better to go along and humour him rather than get a biff round the ear or worse, and after all it was only 'a look', and there could be no harm in that, so we'd just be a bit late for Bow-Shaped Slab.

Well, we went to the start of this route, the four of us, and looked up. To me, it looked quite frightening. When Don undid his rucksack and pulled out the gear I realised that 'a look' meant an attempt. Anyway, Lou was his obvious second, or even Audrey, who both had more experience on 'Cloggy' than I had. Don proceeded to tie on, grabbed slings, karabiners, a few pitons and a hammer, and rasped out, 'Right ho, Lou – tie on!' Lou was a journalist, and not as developed physically as us manual workers, so he said, 'Don, this isn't my type of climb.' Don's face became black with rage. It was obvious he had set his heart on climbing this route. 'Right oh, Vin,' he snapped, 'you can tie on then.' I had no choice, as I'm sure he'd have beaten the pair of us to pulp, so reluctantly I tied on and Don proceeded to climb the access pinnacle. After he'd placed the first peg, I didn't give enough tension on the rope and came in for a torrent of abuse. I soon learnt to give tension and slack even before it was needed. Don climbed round the roof on to the slab and eventually across to the first belay. Now it was my turn.

I was not looking forward to this at all. If I came off the thin moves above the pinnacle, I would then be dangling from the 150-foot rope which would not have been long enough to lower me to the ground, and I was sure also that all the runners he had put on would have come out. Fortunately, Ted Wrangham arrived on the terrace at that moment, sized up the situation, and offered me a back-stop belay, seeing the danger I faced. So protected by Ted, I set off in my sandshoes, which were what we wore for climbing then, and got on to the slab better than I'd expected. The holds were thin, but I had no difficulty until I got to around 20 feet from Don's belay. He was out of sight round the corner so I asked for instructions, as there seemed to be no holds, just a huge void under my feet. Back came the reply: 'You see the big vertical crack?' 'What vertical crack?' I asked. 'The one you can just get your fingernails in – use that and swing across.' I made it to Don and he was very pleased with me – 'Not like those other ta-tas – they'd never have made it!' We rearranged the ropes and Don led off in good spirits up an easier rake, at the top of which, instead of taking a belay, he just kept on and soon ran out of rope, so I had to pull up the rope Ted was holding down below, which cut off my retreat, untie from Don's rope, fasten the two together with a fisherman's knot that wasn't going to get through any of the runners, and retie the belay. After a 180-foot run-out, Don made it to the top of the hard part and I had to follow. When he took in, that fisherman's knot jammed in a runner so I had to climb up the rake coiling the rope in one hand, release the runner, and then tie back on to Don's rope, which was long enough by then, and trail mine behind me. Everything went OK until I reached a short steep wall where there was a loose piton sloping downwards and a long stretch to holds above. Don shouted down and said he'd hammered in the piton, mantelshelfed on to it, and stood up on it: 'I was standing on one foot on the peg with my hands flat on the wall looking for a handhold, when suddenly the peg moved. I made a couple of quick moves and I was up, but don't ask me how!'

I managed to get up on a tight rope and reach the hold. I'm five feet nine inches tall, Don's five feet three . . . Anyway, we made it to the top of the pitch feeling very exhilarated, and Audrey met us there, having soloed down from the top of the crag. It wasn't repeated for five years, and then by Joe with Harry Smith, who were both suitably impressed by its difficulty. I remember being in a pub with Don a few years later and that guy Hugh Banner was there saying Don's second on Slanting Slab, as we'd called the route, had been Morty Smith and someone corrected him, so Banner drawled, 'Ah yes – Betts's only claim to fame!' Don was behind him and heard this, whereupon he whipped back at Banner, who'd gone pale when he realised he was there, 'And what's thine, Banner?' He was loyal to people who'd won his respect, and you didn't mess with Don in those days.

The route soon accumulated a considerable reputation, chiefly through the fear engendered in climbing that first exposed overhang, the two aid pegs still recommended for crossing it difficult to place in the shattered and untrustworthy rock. Twenty years after its first ascent, Dave Cook, writing about it in Ken Wilson's *Hard Rock*, could proclaim that 'Slanting Slab remains the most authoritative statement of bold route-finding made on the cliff in modern times.'

It was only the first in the definitive trilogy of Whillans routes on Clogwyn Du'r Arddu, and its successor was not long in arriving. Joe had arrived back from Kangchenjunga, and on a late July Sunday in 1955[8] he and Don raced up to Halfway House together. Joe had worn Vibram-soled boots in the Alps and on Kangchenjunga. Rather late in the day,[9] he was determined to try them out on British rock. He told Don he wanted to climb Sunset Crack, David Cox and Robin Hodgkin's winsome little pre-war struggle up the left edge of the East Buttress, and that he wanted to lead it all. Which he did, and – enervated by the effects of weeks at altitude, unused to the

---

[8] There has long been a degree of confusion around the date of the first ascent of Taurus. In *The Black Cliff* (ed. Crew, Soper and Wilson) and in the current guidebook to the crag it is given as 24 July 1956. The co-author of Don's autobiography, Alick Ormerod, also placed it in July 1956 and it went uncorrected, Don being away on Annapurna at the time of the book's publication. This is clearly a mistake, as Brown was about to board a boat back to Britain from Karachi on that date, after climbing the Mustagh Tower. In his biography, Joe makes it clear that this was his first climbing after Kangchenjunga in 1955. The 'New Routes' section of the *Climbers' Club Journal* for 1957 gives the correct date of 24 July 1955. To put the ascent of Taurus a year later detracts from Don's achievement in climbing his great trio of routes on the cliff within six weeks that summer.

Final point on this topic – you might well ask why not go to Joe and seek clarification? This is to misunderstand the nature of the Brown memory, which can on occasion be cloudy as the Welsh hills. He was listening to Don once as the latter was talking about the first ascent of Dovedale Grooves (see Chapter Eleven). 'Who did you do that with, Don?' he enquired, in all seriousness. 'You, yer daft bugger!' came the reply.

[9] 'I went on climbing in nails long after my companions had been converted' (*The Hard Years*) – in fairness, the received wisdom even as late as 1960 was that Vibrams were dangerously unreliable on wet rock and on grass, and nails the better all-round choice. A 1954 *Scottish Mountaineering Club Journal*, for example, carried the gravest of warnings by Dr Donald Duff about their use on the mountains in other than the driest summer conditions. The very precise foot-placing necessary particularly when wearing Joe's favoured tricouni-nailed boots resulted in exemplary neatness of technique. I remember climbing Vector on Craig Bwlch y Moch with an old Rock & Ice member, Don Roscoe, in the mid-1960s, and being hugely impressed by the delicacy of his footwork.

footwear – he made a complete mess of it. His feet skidded around wildly, the boot-edges rolled off nicks on which he could have stood happily in tricounis, and he did the climb on arm-strength alone. At its top, Don consoled him with the advice that like any kind of footwear, Vibrams needed their own technique to use well, and that came with practice. As they belayed among the loose and broken ledges above the dangerous descent into the East Gully, it was clear that Don's interest lay in the square-cut and overhung groove that ran up just right of the arete of The Pinnacle. They tossed a coin for the lead and Joe won. He plotted his way methodically up the unprotectable corner for 60 feet and, 20 feet below the capping roof, ground to a halt at a large, loose block. Unnerved, he shouted down to Don that if he so much as breathed on it, it would come off, and slowly he reversed back down the pitch. Don took his place at the sharp end of the rope, bristled up to the block, gave it a good thump, looped a sling over it and shouted back down to Joe that it was a good runner.[10] Then he pulled past it and continued to the roof, flicked a line sling on to another, poorer spike out left, shouted to Joe that the protection wasn't up to much but that he'd 'have a look' anyway, moved out to the edge and put in a peg 10 feet higher, then surged round the roof into a groove and out of sight. When Joe came to follow he found the climbing, on undercuts, layaways and thin finger-jams, to be desperate, and called for a tight rope. It didn't come. Joe shouted again. Still no negative gravity from the rope. He scrabbled round the overhang and a smaller one above, and at last the rope tightened. Don's face leered into view, and in cynical tones he declared, 'I reckon this will go down as *my* Cenotaph Corner.'

This little exercise in ascendancy over, the last climb in the Whillans trinity on the cliff came four Saturdays later, and broached a new and frightening piece of rock. The Far East Buttress is a huge area of cliff, the most distinguished feature of which is a fanned 300-foot-high prow of grooves and roofs overhanging the smooth and dripping 200-foot lower wall, and approached by a long walk round to the top of the cliff and descent down a terrace to its foot, where the situation is as impressive as any in Wales. Here Don and

---

[10] Its final demise came four years later when Phil Gordon (see page 134, note 1) pulled it off and came within an ace of ending rather prematurely the career of his second, Chris Bonington.

Joe roped up again. After attempts by both of them, Joe led a technical and strenuous pitch on poor rock through the first bulge into a slender, impendent groove and up to a ledge, on which Don soon joined him. The central groove of the buttress, obviously steep, swept away out of sight to their left, and Don, dithering a little at the entry, led into it. Thirty feet up was a large, loose flake which he flicked a runner on and hauled past. Beyond it, out on the left edge above a large roof, was another perched flake, towards which he advanced, retreated, advanced: 'Suddenly Whillans moved, got the flake, and hanging out above the void, hurriedly fixed a runner. Then he moved again and kept going until he disappeared into the groove above.' There is a photograph taken by Joe of Don as he contemplates the start of the sequence. A thin line runs out to him through a messy runner. In breeches and knee-length stockings, black rubber pumps on his feet, he's dark-clad, white-balaclava'd, peering up into the groove above with his left knee dropped for balance. There is a suggestion of mist, the rock sombre and steep, without obvious holds. It has a certain chill and a certain mystery about it.

When Joe came to follow, he reached the flake with ease, manteled on to the narrow, slanting ledge beyond and found himself fully extended, fighting for balance. Peter Crew, of the next Welsh generation of climbers, wrote that 'those few moves were the hardest yet done in so serious a position on the black cliff'.

It is easy to debunk with the wisdom of hindsight, but that does seem to me to overstate the case. Were they harder or more serious than Streetly's – climbed in socks and much worse conditions – on the Bloody Slab? The implicit point here is the interesting one. These three routes of Don's, Slanting Slab, Taurus, and Woubits,[11] as the last one on the Far East was named, had a kind of affective

---

[11] 'Woubits, Woubits – what the hell's a Woubits?' Don is reported to have said, on hearing what name the climb had been given (the Rock & Ice members at this time were particularly slow in writing up their discoveries in Wales and elsewhere, which certainly accentuated their mythic quality, and led to a running feud with the *Climbers' Club Journal* of the 1950s, where sniffy comments about their unwillingness to cooperate became the norm). As to the answer to Don's question, this is the longest-running tease in British climbing. 'They may know, but they're not telling' was what most climbers used to believe. In fact, there are two possible explanations. The *OED* gives this: 'A hairy caterpillar; a woolly bear.' Joe, whose allegiance is to *Chambers*, tells me it means 'small of stature, of shabby appearance', and was a good description of himself and Don at the time.

unity. They all climbed imposing lines, and had an aura of looseness, difficulty and seriousness about them. In the long retrospective, 50 years on from their first ascents, none of them has graduated to the status of great, popular classics. Slanting Slab is a powerful experience but at the same time quite an unpleasant climb, with some poor rock, nasty aid moves, a good deal of grass, and not much aesthetically to recommend it. It has little of the sustained quality, satisfying sequences and appeal of White Slab, Bloody Slab or – best of them all on the West – Bow Right-Hand. Taurus is still distinctly loose, and whilst the overhangs section is intricate and satisfying, few who venture here would bother with it in preference to its airy and dramatically positioned neighbour Pinnacle Arete. The best of the Whillans trio is Woubits, Don's pitch on which – technically the easier of the two, and these days the better protected – is one of the most enjoyable and impressively situated pieces of climbing on Clogwyn Du'r Arddu, and on rock so sumptuously rough and sound it could be gritstone itself. But Woubits is a long way from the other climbs hereabouts, circuitous to approach, and not many find their way up to its start.

Maybe there is a point hidden in all this. I have often thought – particularly when I was writing the biography of the pioneer of Welsh climbing in the 1930s, John Menlove Edwards – that the places we choose to explore act as an objective correlative to our own states of mind. The adjectives that suggest themselves to me in respect of these 1955 lines climbed by Don would be shadowy, forbidding, aggressive, unappealing, overbearing, insecure, flaky, fissile. Was that how he saw himself, after his imagined rejection for Kangchenjunga; after picking up maybe on the unwelcoming frisson the Rock & Ice members were giving out; after the bitterly voiced resentments of his Emett & Smith workmates at his taking time off and not settling to a steady job; after the strongly conveyed disapproval of his girlfriend Audrey's father? I wonder – and sense too that, for us climbers with our adrenalin-addicted egos, sometimes our climbing is as far as we can go into self-criticism, into self-knowledge.

In those four weeks between Taurus and Woubits Don managed to fit in his fourth alpine season. He hitched out to Chamonix where he met up with Audrey, Joe, Eric Price and Nat Allen. If the weather in 1954 had been bad, that of 1955 was indescribable. They attempted the North Face of the Grands Charmoz, Joe driving them on like the newly fledged Himalayan hero with a reputation to maintain that he had become. His three companions eventually ruled for discretion, and the four of them had to retreat in dangerous snow conditions. Don and Joe were also snowed out of the couloir beneath the Petit Dru as they were reconnoitring the South-West Pillar, then unclimbed and the current 'last great problem in the Alps' (Walter Bonatti, meanwhile, was biding his time and sitting out the weather in the Charpoua Hut on the other side of the Flammes de Pierre, by which route he would make his approach to the climb). In Snell's Field, sheltering from the rain, they met Berardini and Paragot, who had just returned, badly frost-bitten, from their epic ascent of the South Face of Aconcagua. The talk turned admiringly to Joe and Don's route on the West Face of the Blaitiere, on which these foremost French climbers had recently failed. But admiration didn't make the sun come out and the British team trooped off home.[12] Not before Don bumped into Ted Wrangham again in the Bar Nationale, though – and Ted had with him a stranger, who recorded the meeting thus: 'As we shook hands we looked each other in the eye. And each of us drew ourselves up slightly to our full five feet three until we caught each other at it, and both grinned – laughed at ourselves in fact. That was the start of our friendship, which never faded or faltered.'

If Don hadn't believed Sherwood Wiseman when he told him about the Bloody Slab in Salford three years before, he did now in Chamonix, face to face with John Streetly, the route's author, and the belief was tempered by respect too, having failed and all but taken a long and serious fall on the climb himself. Their next meeting was not long delayed. Back in Wales a week or so after the ascent of Woubits, Don was cooling off in the stream under Dinas Cromlech when a large sports car screeched to a halt in the lay-by. A tiny, animated figure bounced out of it and bounded over the wall, followed by an equally small and energetic companion, who

---

[12] With some valuable booty – on this visit to Snell's they all acquired pairs of the new, tight-fitting, smooth-soled blue-canvas-and-suede Pierre Allain rock-shoes, originals that inspired innumerable imitations and advances over the next half-century. Revolutionary in their time, and originally sold only from Pierre Allain's shop in Paris, they gave rise to the generic term in Britain for specialised light rock-climbing boots – 'PAs'. The first route on which Don put them to use after his return from the Alps was the ferocious Direct Finish to his earlier climb, Erosion Groove.

was introduced to Don as John's brother Arthur. They hustled Don into his clothes, down the Llanberis Pass, up to Clogwyn y Grochan, and for their first route did Joe and Don's most recent discovery there, the glowering and at the time dangerously loose wall of N'Gombo.[13] Instead of the original first pitch, they uncoiled the rope beneath that of an aided climb of Hugh Banner's, Ochre Grooves, which led to the start of the second pitch's big wall. 'Doesn't it go up here?' asked John. Don told him not, noticing that a peg then deemed crucial was missing from the first groove. 'Well, we may as well – it's a nice pitch to reach the terrace. I soloed it yesterday,' John breezed back, and Don had to free-climb the pitch, which he did with difficulty, to the foot of the one above. John danced up the high, overhanging wall of the top pitch, complaining of the loose rock and throwing holds over his shoulder by the dozen as he did so.

What followed, in Streetly's words, was:

a sunny fortnight of hard and hectic climbing, ticking off the then hard routes in Wales. What remains in my mind is the complete trust we had in each other's ability, and the almost unbelievable speed at which we climbed. Not the rapidity of the actual rock-climbing, but the impetus of the entire operation, the easy flow of competent rope-work, the speedy leading through – what we did find when leading through quickly on very hard climbs was that two hard pitches climbed non-stop left the leader somewhat bushed. We cut no corners and took few chances with safety, belays or runners. Certainly I could tell that when Don put in a runner what was in store was a hard move – possibly followed by a traverse, for he always took particular care to protect his second. One day we were on Suicide Wall in Cwm Idwal. I had started to lead the second pitch when Don's smoky comment came up from that little grass ledge: 'If you're going to come off, yell, so that I can jump too. This piton . . .' I looked down to the left, he pulled out the single belay peg and waved it at me. 'It's no bloody good.' Then he calmly carried on paying the rope out,

---

[13] 'It's Swahili for shit, and that's about right,' Joe told an earnestly enquiring young teenager, po-facedly, back in 1962. For the literal-minded who are reaching for their Swahili dictionaries, he was teasing . . .

having let me know. He could always relieve the tension in any climbing situation by a quick and pertinent comment that lightened the tension and gave confidence in tight places.

Arthur joined them for one climb, fell off, got back on, reached the top and was so excited that he unroped. The wind blew him straight back down the cliff, past Don, who was coming up: 'Bloody Streetlys, never know if they're comin' or goin',' he quipped. Arthur survived with just a few broken bones.

Holiday over, Don was briefly back in Salford, without a job, without transport, hearthside conversation with his parents centring around security and work and the future, autumn closing in with its rain and cold. The Rock & Ice routine was gearing up for another winter. One weekend Don, Joe and Don Roscoe made an exploratory attempt on the huge overhang at Kilnsey Crag near Grassington: 'Don led off, and managed to insert a peg at full stretch [in the roof]. He stepped up in an etrier and immediately swung clear of the rock. The groove was practically unbroken and he encountered great difficulty in placing his second and third pegs. The going was extremely strenuous and the pegs far apart. Exhausted by his efforts he descended and handed over the lead . . .' On another, the club was back at Bryn Coch for what was later termed 'the great pot-holing weekend'. Mrs Williams had told them the local story of two children who had wandered into a copper-mine entrance down by the lake at Nant Peris to emerge three days later near Clogwyn Du'r Arddu. Nat Allen remembered going in to one of the mine adits near the latter with one torch, three candles and a rope, wading streams, crossing stemples of rotten wood, and arriving in the roof of an immense cavern. He remembered too the race to ride down the rack-and-pinion railway track on specially selected flat stones with a bump in the middle to fit the central groove, and the speed they attained careering down the steeper sections below Halfway House.[14] Soaked to the skin from the mines, they took chairs from Bryn Coch, used slings to make them into rucksacks, pinched three bags of coal from the Snowdon

---

[14] Not many of these stones left now – sliding down the track was a traditional pursuit of Welsh climbers for so long that they're all at the bottom, and no one has yet had the nerve to ask the Snowdon Mountain Railway Company to organise a train to transport them back up (the activity not receiving much official approval after a few near-misses involving trains).

Mountain Railway and soon had a roaring fire going in the derelict cottage.

A letter from Johnny Sullivan arrived, suggesting that they head up to Glencoe and find work on one of the big power schemes being implemented nearby. They spent three days in Glencoe, where Don attempted a line on the then-unclimbed Creag a'Bhanceir but made little progress on it. With only £3 left between them, and the rain drenching down, they paid a visit to the Labour Exchange in Fort William and were taken on as tunnel labourers, living in Kingie Camp at Invergarry amidst the hard men of the Gorbals and the Irish gangs:

> It is easy to save here. At night you're too tired to have a good time, and anyway there is about four women to 500 blokes – not much use, eh? If you go to our house for the tent send me a pair of overalls and long underpants, and a photo of you. I might forget what you look like if I stay till Christmas. If I stick it till then we'll have £150 and should get a good bike for that if we look in the paper and buy from a private bod. I think I will have earned every penny too. It will be worth it to have a bike to go to the Dolomites next summer. Has Joe done my route on the West Buttress yet? What did he think of it if he did?

By December, Don had enough money for another bike, had had enough for the time being of this brutalising experience, and came home. There was still no plumbing work available in Manchester, so he teamed up with Pete Whitwell, one of the Bradford lads, and went back north. They hawked themselves around Scotland in the rain and snow looking for employment, hungry, their money running out, and finally were taken on as tunnel labourers again, this time on the Haweswater reservoir project in the Lake District. The work was hard, wet, dirty and dangerous, taken at full pelt under constant pressure of time, but it was well paid, and the two of them were earning on average £27 a week, which was very good money in those days: 'If I stay a month I will get a combination. If I stick three months we should be well off, all set for the Dolomites . . .' One of the younger Rock & Ice members, Morty Smith, came up one weekend, and together in the snow they climbed the compelling line of Delphinus on Raven Crag, Thirlmere – again offending

Lakeland sensibilities, this time by the amount of aid used on the alarmingly overhanging top pitch. Don made contact with some of the Lake District climbers, and one of them, Paul Ross, gives an interesting, and rather scathing, picture – surely tempered by the old Wales/Lake District rivalries, or the usual testosterone-poisoning at their ages then, or both – of him at the time:

> When I first knew him he was 22 and I was 19 or so. He wasn't Don Whillans then, he was just Don Whillans, a climber from Manchester, and in those days he was definitely a bit grumpy, not the witty Don Whillans of later years. When I began to hear in the 1960s about how funny he was and these brilliant lectures he gave, I didn't recognise the same man. He was completely uncouth in those days, and not really outstanding as a climber.[15] Pete Greenwood, for example, was definitely better. But Don was very determined. I remember him on one pitch in Borrowdale putting pegs in, and I thought it must be desperate up there. It turned out when I went to do it only to be VS. On another occasion I remember him having an absolutely desperate time and nearly falling out of the Devil's Wedge on Shepherd's Crag, which was supposed to be his kind of climb. Apart from the Bonatti[16] I never did that much climbing with him. We sort of fell out – I don't know why. He used to call in on his way down from Carlisle when he was working on Spadeadam. Then I heard he'd told Greenwood he was going to fill me in, and he called at my mum's house and took all his Bill Haley records away, so I knew he was upset with me. This stuff about him fighting all the time is nonsense. He probably had half a dozen fights in his life, but these legends grow. I remember doing Conclusion on Shepherd's one day with Pete Whitwell when they were on the Haweswater job. Whitwell was very quiet, smoked a pipe, didn't drink much. He was sharing lodgings with Whillans in Penrith, and Pete said, 'That cunt Whillans does nothing but

---

[15] I don't think these comments of Paul's are merely competitive debunking. This was the period at which Paul, who was an exceptionally fine rock-climber, first knew Don, who was working at the time in a gruelling environment which would have left him drained at weekends. Small wonder, then, if Don did suffer from vagaries of form at the time.

[16] See Chapter Thirteen.

whinge – if he doesn't shut up, I'm going to shut him up.' I saw Pete the next week and asked how it had been. 'Heaven!' he said. 'Whillans didn't say a word all week.' He wouldn't have dared cross Whitwell.[17] Another time in Keswick he was trying to get off with someone's wife and this fellow beat the shit out of him. Mind you, he was really uncouth where women were concerned. And he stayed that way. I remember going out for a fell-walk with him and a girl I was seeing. He kept trying to grab hold of the girl's hand and pawing at her, groping her and all that, even though he knew she was with me.[18] I had a couple of nose-to-nose confrontations with him, but he always backed off.

The weather, the work and the abrasive attitudes of the local

---

[17] Pete Greenwood has a recollection of happening into a country club outside Penrith at this time, and finding Don and Pete Whitwell coats off and back to back, battling it out with a notorious local fighting family, the women from which were looking on with connoisseurs' eyes.

[18] Don's reputation as a sexual opportunist was one of the contributory reasons for his unpopularity in the Rock & Ice. Nat Allen recalls that 'With other women, he'd always have a shot, whoever they were with. We were in the roadmenders' hut at the Cromlech one night and he slid in between a girl on the one side, and Audrey on the other. Now Audrey was a very sound sleeper, and it was a good job, because you should have heard the squealing that was going on. I had to tell him to pipe down eventually. We knew that, given half a chance, he'd have a go at any of our women.' He was a frequent visitor to the house of Colin and Annette Mortlock and Annette remembers that when Don was around, she had to be constantly on the alert when she was alone with him, and ready to fend off his wandering hands. The mountain photographer John Cleare, who was with Don on the 1971 Everest expedition, remembers another deeply unpleasant incident: 'While we'd been on Everest my then wife Viki had gone on a package holiday to Portugal with the baby. There she had befriended a girl of her own age who spent the season as a courier at the resort. They kept up a correspondence afterwards. The girl got pregnant in Portugal, her parents were Catholics, and Viki suggested a discreet abortion in London, collected her from the airport, took her to the clinic, brought her back to our house in Guildford and put her on a mattress in the living room (we only had three bedrooms – one was ours, one the baby's, and the other my office). Don, Audrey and I arrived back late from a party at the *Sunday Times*, and they put their sleeping bags in there too, Audrey's on the couch and Don's on the floor. Soon after dawn I was woken by screams and shouts. I pulled on a dressing gown and rushed downstairs. Don was lying naked on the floor, Viki was standing over him beating him with something and shouting, the girl was sitting up in bed, long blonde hair all over the place, waving her arms and screaming, and Audrey was curled up in her pit on the sofa, sound asleep and snoring loudly. I managed to stop the commotion and calm everything down. Viki ordered Don out of the house at once, but I insisted he was my friend and would have to have breakfast first. What had happened was that Don had woken in the

climbers seem to drive Don back to his more familiar Welsh routine. In February of 1956 he was back in the Llanberis Pass, where Joe, wearing his new 'PAs', led him up a sporty little route at the left-hand end of Dinas Cromlech. Eventually named The Thing, it achieved a degree of notoriety through a fulsome description[19] given to it in the first definitive guidebook to the 'Three Cliffs',[20] where it was one of only two climbs to be graded, in the increasingly compressed adjectival system of the time, 'Exceptionally Severe'. The next climb to be accorded that grade in Snowdonia was the Girdle Traverse of Dinas Cromlech. This had a curious genesis in the form of a letter from a young London climber[21] to Joe, asking for the loan of some of his artificial climbing equipment, so that he might attempt the Girdle Traverse of Dinas Cromlech that summer. Brown, thinking that maybe it was a joke, set to considering the problem. The main difficulties would obviously be concentrated into the crossing of the walls of Cenotaph Corner. On April Fool's

---

first light to this beautiful apparition, all blonde hair and white sheets, had checked Audrey was asleep and crept over to the girl to reconnoitre. She woke, with not the faintest idea who or what Don was – not that it would have mattered – and the nightmare began. After a very fraught breakfast, Don and Audrey climbed into their van and I went out to see them off. We said our goodbyes, Viki just glowered. Don, who always had to have the last word, leaned out, looked at Viki long and hard, said to her, "Get yer knickers changed next time I come," and drove off.'

　　If this isn't just a 'bus conductor' story, Audrey must indeed have been, as Nat says, 'a very sound sleeper'.

[19] 'Exceptionally Severe. Extremely strenuous. A short, vicious climb of great technical difficulty. Difficulty is sustained, protection poor, retreat beyond the crux uninviting and the ground below nasty to land on.' Neither Joe nor Don seems to have taken any particular notice of this climb, which takes an initially smooth and overhanging groove, at first on finger-jams and quickly leading to excellent jamming above – all very much in a gritstone idiom. I recall one day from my own prime as a climber in the late 1960s when I thought for purposes of comparison to make ascents of the supposed hardest route from each decade of the 1940s, 1950s and 1960s. Of the three climbs – Suicide Wall, The Thing and The Boldest – it seemed to me that the hardest technical moves and least protected situations were actually on the oldest of them, Suicide Wall, first climbed in 1945. But as Joe states – putting the mores of the time into context as he does so – 'You could jump off the crux of Suicide Wall and survive. If you'd tried that on The Thing, you'd have been dead.'

[20] An interim guidebook to Dinas Cromlech, Carreg Wastad and Clogwyn y Grochan, entitled *Three Cliffs in Llanberis*, had been published during the war years, and was written by J.E.Q. Barford and J.M. Edwards – the latter their earliest devotee and explorer.

[21] He asks to be spared the embarrassment of having his identity revealed.

Day, he recruited Don and they set off on the route. The first parts all linked together well. Joe led 'a superb pitch of no exceptional difficulty' across the left wall into Cenotaph Corner itself,[22] and climbed this to belay on the recently appeared 'pudding stone'.[23] He brought Don across, but for once the Whillans boldness was absent and his attempts to get established on the right wall were desultory and unsuccessful. He retreated to the foot of the corner. Before Joe joined him there, on the descent he took tension – which Don had refused – from the rope running up to a runner on the pudding stone, and managed to reach holds at the start of the ledge which continued across to the stance on Cemetery Gates. It was the key to the climb and next day they went back up to complete it, Don leading the pitch. It was the last new route they pioneered together in Wales, and the end of perhaps the most successful partnership in British rock-climbing history, though they climbed together subsequently in the Alps in 1958, on the 1973 Roraima expedition, and for several later television broadcasts.

The Cromlech Girdle came in for a certain amount of criticism from an old guard to whom artificial tactics were anathema. Don, in his later life, could scarcely remember it, apart from the oddity of encountering the corpse of a mouse on the ledge leading in to Cemetery Gates. In truth, it was not his kind of climb, was much more in the intricate and tricky style that characterises so many of Joe's first ascents: 'With me, it's always got to be a straightforward route with an obvious line,' Don declared in a 1971 interview. 'Vector . . . well that's the kind of route Joe would have done, not me. I tend to look at something and say, "Christ! That's

---

[22] Rapidly becoming a trade route by 1956 – in which year Bob Downes, who will soon figure large in this narrative, had led it with a woman, Geoff Sutton's sister-in-law Judith Clark, as his second. Clark was one of the best women climbers of her generation, but her first serious boyfriends, Downes and Mike Harvey, both died whilst climbing and she gave up the sport thereafter. The day before Bob Downes and Judith Clark did Cenotaph Corner, they had made the first ascent of Penamnen Groove, which they – rightly – found just as hard. When Don came to climb Penamnen Groove in 1964, he set Derek Walker to lead the crux pitch and sat on the ledge below chuckling and reading a western as Derek struggled with it. He'd fished the book out from his rucksack at the bottom of the cliff with the remark, 'Aye, I think this might be a long job – I'll take me book.'

[23] Carefully selected in Derbyshire and carried up, according to a legend I'm not sure I believe, in Jack Soper's rucksack, this beautiful round rock nestled for many years in the wide section of the crack leading into the niche, and was the salvation of many a leader tumbling out of the entry and exit to that feature.

impressive," and I want to do it . . . anything that hits you smack in the eye. You won't find many climbs of mine that are devious.'[24]

There was one compellingly obvious line still left on Clogwyn Du'r Arddu, and Don was very interested in that. He had even talked with Peter Greenwood about going on it, despite the fact that both Joe and Ron Moseley had made pretty serious attempts on the climb, which was known variously as the Hourglass Slab, the Concrete Slab, and White Slab. Even before them, Menlove Edwards, Jock Campbell, Peter Harding and Arthur Dolphin had all investigated it to a degree. Joe had come closest to climbing this cleanest and most elegant of features on the West Buttress, having retreated from partway up its final pitch feeling ill. The ethos in the Rock & Ice at the time was that if anyone wanted to do a route, no one reserved it as their own. So when, in the YMCA one April

---

[24] In this spring of 1956 he picked up the first ascent of a gritstone climb that epitomises the point. Joe and Don had been working on a – tricky and intricate! – line up the flakes on the severely overhanging front face of the Leaning Block at Higgar Tor, and Joe eventually succeeded to produce The Rasp. On the side of the Leaning Block was a feature that had become known as 'The Vicious Crack', which Don swarmed up with some ease to produce what gritstone initiates consider to be one of the definitive – and at VS surprisingly easy – jamming cracks, The File (and other climbers less acquainted with the gritstone mysteries find desperate – see Chapter Thirteen).

On The Rasp, Joe and Don had been making alternate attempts, and the latter had exhausted himself in threading the two crucial runners below the overhung niche just short of the top. When he retreated, Joe took over the lead and with the protection in place led the climb, which is one of the finest – and most strenuous – on gritstone. There is a point here that is significant, and needs bringing out. We learn lessons from our climbing that we apply not only to our future climbing but also, not always entirely appositely, to our life. Don lost out here on the kudos of having led the first ascent of an outright classic by having spent himself in cooperative effort. There may have been an element of guile and strategy in Joe's approach to the route – he is the subtlest of manipulators of his climbing partners. If Don learnt this lesson from Joe over the years of their partnership, his application of it, like his character, was more abrasive and direct. And in the aftermaths of Annapurna and 'Everest', where he played tactics in a team of very large egos, it was to have a negative and damaging effect.

There is a corollary to this, which is that Joe himself sometimes lost out on the successful leads by exhausting himself in preparatory effort. Sassenach, as we have seen, was a good example of that. So, too, was the first ascent of Erosion Grooves Direct Finish, from the bold and in-those-days unprotectable crux of which Joe spent himself in the effort of removing whilst on the lead a hanging flake weighing several hundredweight, which made the route impossible whilst it was in place. He later led this quintessential Whillans pitch on several occasions. 'We always climbed,' states Joe, 'with the intention of helping each other.'

Wednesday night after the rest had declared for a weekend in the Lake District, Don let it be known that he and Don Roscoe might go to Wales and 'give the route a try since you buggers have just been faffing about on it for years', none of the members' hackles were unduly raised. Later that night, however, back in Levenshulme, with Don safely over the Salford border, Ronnie Moseley told young Morty Smith, the club's powerful new apprentice, that on Friday night they would be going to Wales after all, and on Saturday 19 April Moseley consolidated all his earlier explorations on the White Slab. Taking the Narrow Slab start rather than the new and more difficult independent entry Joe had discovered, he led the lower main slab pitch, repeated Joe's lasso move[25] to cross a particularly smooth section at half-height, and continued up the narrow and difficult continuation slab to complete the climb.

Don, who had been working on Saturday and ridden down late in the evening, emerged from his tent in the Llanberis Pass on Sunday morning and, to his surprise, saw an exultant Ron Moseley. Don asked him if Joe was around too, was told that he was in the Lakes, and suddenly the realisation came. So a little later that morning, accompanied by Don Roscoe, a very angry Whillans wended his rather less urgent way to Clogwyn Du'r Arddu to pick up the consolation prize of a first complete ascent of one of the best rock-climbs in the British Isles. Roscoe recalls:

> Really, neither Don nor Ron had an outright claim to this route as most of it had been done before. What was upsetting was Ron's behaviour, knowing that Don planned to try it the

---

[25] This manoeuvre has caused much consternation and many delays over the years, and not a few outright failures on the climb. For those of you who have aspirations beyond those of an armchair mountaineer, here's the clue to the lasso move. The point is to get the rope round a small spike in a shallow groove at a slightly higher level beyond a particularly blank section of slab, and use it to cross over. The technique is not to aim for the spike, but to toss a hank of rope into the groove above it. The rope then trickles down, almost invariably lodges behind the spike, and can then be flicked straight and pulled tight. All that remains is to swing across with 400 feet of air beneath you. Remember, you aspirants to Extremely Severe climbs on Clogwyn Du'r Arddu, that you first read this here, and not in an instructional manual . . . (Please note that this advice has not been vetted by the Health and Safety Executive, so if anyone comes to grief in following it and feels inclined to sue me, ponder these two points before you do so: 1) What were you doing there in the first place? 2) I hold myself in no way responsible for your actions, and it's about time you did.)

following day. There was not generally any strong competition in the club, and if someone intended to try a route, he would have been left to do so. Ron's unusual action surprised us all, and Don saw it as an act of betrayal. On the day, Don led pitch one, I led pitch two, and Don led the rest. The crux pitch was very slippery, and of course very poorly protected in those days, and it stands out in my memory as an outstanding lead by Don.

By the time the White Slab was climbed, Joe was once more, and at very short notice, on his way to the Himalayas, to attempt the Mustagh Tower – a peak that the mountaineering authors of the early twentieth century had called 'Nature's last stronghold – probably the most inaccessible of all great peaks, for its immense precipices show no weaknesses.' The expedition members included two of the leading young climbers in the ACG, Ian McNaught Davis and Tom Patey, and again – even though this time he might more reasonably have expected one – there was no invitation for Don.[26] The rest of the Rock & Ice members, worn down by the sequence of wet summers, were taking a rest from alpinism. Don, however, ran into Pete Greenwood, whose climbing and fighting ability he respected as being on a par with his own, one weekend in the café opposite Ambleside bus station. The two of them began to climb together sporadically in Wales and the Lake District over the next few months. Greenwood had a guiding engagement in the Dolomites that summer, and Don remembered John Streetly's excited account of the Dolomites from the previous year. Greenwood's plan was to guide, then meet up with his girlfriend Shirley in Bolzano and stay out for some more climbing. Don bought a motorcycle combination, stowed Audrey in the sidecar – she having decreed against any more journeys perched on mudguards – as company for Shirley, and gatecrashed the party. The bike was not particularly reliable,[27] and

---

[26] According to McNaught Davis, the invitations were all very last-minute, Joe was asked to nominate another member, and it was he who suggested Tom Patey. Joe states categorically that this is untrue, and that he did not know Patey at the time: 'Mac knew him from the ACG and probably invited him because he was a doctor.' Both Joe and Tom had been at the Biolay together in 1953, but had apparently not met.

[27] No one who ever rode one could be in any doubt about the basic reason for the catastrophic 1960s decline in the British motorcycle industry. Whether it was Enfield, AJS, Matchless, BSA, Norton, Vincent, Velocette, Sunbeam or Ariel, they

broke down continually on the way to Italy, and they were three days late for an arranged meeting outside the 'Post Office' in Misurina (it turned out there was no post office in Misurina, so Greenwood found a shop that sold stamps and sat outside it for three days). An incident on the journey out there casts light both on his relationship with Audrey and his attitude to women:

> Kneeling in sticky tar on some road in France, I finally chucked my tools down in surrender. It was blindingly hot and I was covered in oil and sweat.
>
> 'Bloody stupid machine!' I cursed. 'I've tried everything I know and the bloody thing's worse than ever.'
>
> Audrey, knowing my mood, had remained silent during my futile labours; now she reached over and tried to pull the clutch in.
>
> 'You won't budge that,' I snarled. 'If I can't pull it in with two hands, I'm bloody sure you can't pull it in with one.'
>
> I grabbed the screwdriver and poked hopelessly in the gearbox. I unscrewed a small stud a couple of turns.
>
> 'It works now,' said Audrey casually.
>
> I looked up, prepared to tell her exactly what I thought of interfering women. She was moving the clutch in and out with nonchalant ease. Five minutes later we were on our way, singing at the top of our voices . . .

With Greenwood, Don climbed the Comici Route on the North Face of the Cima Grande di Lavaredo. Comici's philosophy that the ideal route should follow a line straight as a drop of water might fall from the summit was one with which Don was much in sympathy. This was the hardest climb achieved by previous British parties in the Eastern Alps, and Don was favourably impressed by the rock and the climbing, though he caused problems for himself by not using etriers on the artificial pitches. In the face of unsettled weather they abandoned plans to attempt the great Cassin Route on the North Face of the Cima Ovest, and left Misurina for Bolzano, where they

---

all spelt out one compound truth – winters in bits in the back kitchen, summer hours wasted squatting – usually in the rain – on some kerbside fiddling with oily, incomprehensible innards. But how, on those twisting roads so distant now in time, we would race on Friday or Saturday nights, meeting in the Rhuthun café and shaving the seconds off the latest crazy record time from there to Llanberis!

collected Shirley, who conveyed the news of Joe's success on the Mustagh Tower. The man with whom Don's name was inextricably linked had achieved, in successive years, two of the most notable ascents in the history of Himalayan climbing. What thoughts, what speculation on when his turn might come must that have produced as Don drove the ponderous combination over to their new campsite at Alleghe, underneath the mountain wall of the Civetta?

The first route they chose here was the North-West Face of the Torre Valgrande, which proved technically difficult and on rock 'like cube sugar stuck together with dried milk'. They halved the guidebook time on it, and were given sufficient confidence by that to come to grips with the Gabriel-Livanos Route on the North-West Face of the Cima Su Alto, first climbed in 1951 and one of the most difficult in the range. 'Pete is going home after another week, so we are going to try for the big fella, the Su Alto.' The climb was underpegged. At one point in what they found to be the crux roof, Don stuck his finger through the eye of a peg, and reached up to a wooden wedge above. Without letting go of the former he pulled on the latter, which came out, leaving him in the middle of an overhang suspended from the one finger in the peg. The sun baked down on the face, they had no water and were too dry-mouthed to eat. Don dropped their camera down the face, so there were no pictures to celebrate and record the climb. They reached the summit at sunset having climbed the huge face in a day. They had made the hardest British ascent by far in the Dolomites to that date.

With Pete and Shirley set on returning to England, Don and Audrey decided to head over to Chamonix. The weather there was bad for the third successive season, the Biolay once again squalid and awash. Nor was the atmosphere any more light-hearted, the news having just filtered through of Bourdillon and Viney's deaths in the Oberland. In the Bar Nationale Don met Bob Downes, with whom he was slightly acquainted and who was very rapidly establishing himself as a major force in British and Alpine climbing. He was one of the few who had repeated some of the harder climbs by Joe and Don in Wales, and had even added one of his own – Penamnen Groove on the isolated Carreg Alltrem – that was not only on a par with them in difficulty, but in later years drew the description of being 'Whillans-esque'. In the poor alpine season of 1955, when Don's bag of routes contained just two failures, Downes had made the first British ascents of the Cassin Route on the North-East Face of the Piz Badile – one of the classic north faces of the Alps – and of the great ice-route on the North Face of the Triolet. In June 1956, on Ben Nevis – a mountain which, in winter and in summer, obsessed his imagination – he had made both the second ascent of Joe and Don's Sassenach ('It's difficult to think of a route which has the character of Sassenach, or its grande envergure. Although the hard pitch is only half the length of Cenotaph Corner, to this party at least it seemed more tiring, more precarious, more baffling than that climb'), and also the first ascent of what is perhaps the finest medium-grade rock-climb on Ben Nevis, Minus One Direct. Downes's obituarist, Geoff Sutton, described him as 'small and puckish; his slanting eyes and pointed ears and scarred cheek gave the air of a sardonic yet twinkling elf'. He was the same age as Don, who described him as 'a quiet, reserved sort of man. I got to know him very well over the next few months and he was one of my kind. He had a strange scar running down one cheek, giving his face a sardonic look which, I suppose, tended to discourage people from making friendly overtures to him.'

They decided on a climb together, and Don put forward his bugbear of the 1954 season, the East Face of the Grand Capucin. They had made good progress to a point beyond the first Bonatti Bivouac and above the Forty-Metre Wall when one of the electric storms to which this face is particularly prone[28] rolled in and caused them to get out their bivouac gear. As the lightning flickered around them, Downes had the experience and mountain sense to stow all their ironmongery at the far end of the ledge. The hail fell so heavily it threatened to suffocate them in their plastic bivouac sack. Next morning, fingers numbed and the ropes frozen rigid, they descended through squalling hail to the foot of the face and down to Chamonix. Making arrangements to meet back in Britain for what they hoped would be some sunny rock-climbing, they quit Chamonix – in Downes's case for the last time.

Later in August, the motorcycle combination rolled up in Cambridge, where Downes's usual climbing companion Mike O'Hara was offered a seat in the sidecar but turned it down, and waved the two climbers off up the A1, en route for Ben Nevis. They

---

[28] Two friends of mine, Rick Kane and Arthur de Kusel, were killed in just this manner on the face in the late 1960s. A party below heard them screaming in the night as they were struck repeatedly by lightning. When they climbed up to them next morning their bodies were charred almost beyond recognition.

both had a line in mind, and if ever a climb 'hit you smack in the eye', this was it. Writing in *Hard Rock* in 1975, Robin Campbell described the climb they made together, Centurion, as 'undoubtedly the finest natural line on the cliff', 'one of the most challenging in Britain', and 'the classic modern rock-climb on Ben Nevis'. There are two crux sections, the more intricate and briefly technical of them high up on the seventh pitch, which Downes led. Ken Crocket, in his authoritative and comprehensive history of climbing on the mountain,[29] comments that 'the ascent of Centurion was a second Sassenach, a national disaster. To make matters worse, the very next day Whillans and Downes went out again and climbed The Shield, another Very Severe on the Great Buttress [where] wet conditions caused the pioneers some difficulty.' Don's balance in the bank of experience was steadily accruing, with a great classic route and radical alpine rock-ascents to his credit. He may have grown apart from one climbing partner, but in Peter Greenwood for a time, and now with the highly intelligent, highly motivated Bob Downes, he had found another. And one who was soon to offer him the key to the further sphere of mountain experience, entry into which he had been hankering after since 1954.

In the autumn of 1956 the Rucksack Club[30] in Manchester was busily organising an expedition to the Karakoram with the objective of attempting one of that range's highest unclimbed peaks, the 25,660-foot Masherbrum. Ron Moseley had been invited to join it, and talk at the YMCA on Wednesday evenings between himself and Joe was all of steamships and porters, seracs and leeches and rice, from which Don, again, was excluded. Until a surprise visitor turned up one night at the Whillans home in Kingsley Avenue and was ushered into the sitting room by Mary. It was Bob Downes, who had been working at White Hall Centre in Derbyshire since their ascent of Centurion. He told Don that Moseley had dropped out of the Masherbrum trip, that he – Downes – had been invited to join, and that in turn he had put Don's name forward, which the club had approved, and hence he had been sent round to make the formal invitation. All Don had to do was raise the required £150 contribution and he would be on his way to the Himalayas at last.

---

[29] *Ben Nevis: Britain's Highest Mountain* (Scottish Mountaineering Trust, 1986).
[30] This northern institution founded in 1902 is one of the so-called 'Senior Clubs' in British mountaineering, along with the Alpine Club, Climbers' Club, Fell & Rock Climbing Club, Wayfarers' Club and Yorkshire Ramblers' Club.

Inevitably, there was a hitch to this easy progression through to the next stage of a mountaineer's education. Don lost his job. However, his other new partner of 1956, Pete Greenwood, found him both work as a plumber on the Spadeadam defence project, and a bedsit in Carlisle. A few more months of mud and graft and he would have the money. And in the event, there was not even much mud or graft involved. No plumbing work being immediately available, he was set on as a labourer 'under the thickest bloke it has ever been my misfortune to meet'. A fortnight of that and the inevitable explosion took place, with Don pointing out to the project manager that he was a tradesman-plumber and not a navvy. So the latter sat him in a warm hut for three weeks doing nothing until pipework became available.

The time before departure passed quickly, and in April 1957, the boat was heeling out of Liverpool docks, Bombay-bound. The five weeks of the voyage were enlivened by other congenial company too – an expedition to Disteghil Sar, also in the Karakoram, and at 25,250 feet only marginally lower than Masherbrum, was also on board, and among its members were Alf Gregory, the photographer from John Hunt's 1953 Everest expedition, and John Cunningham, the near-legendary member of the Creagh Dhu club whose Glencoe route, The Gallows, Don had unwittingly disrespected back in 1951. In Cape Town Don and Bob scrambled up Table Mountain. From Bombay to Rawalpindi to Skardu the 24-year-old Salford lad's eyes were open wide. In the Skardu Government Rest House, the visitors' book contained the familiar slant of Joe's handwriting, left on his way to the Mustagh Tower. Herman Buhl had just passed through bound for Broad Peak, and the fatal cornice on Chogolisa that for him lay beyond it. Don wrote to Audrey:

Just a few lines to let you know how I'm getting along. I think of you very often and wonder what you are doing, whether you are still going out or not and if you are still dancing at the Palais, Ritz, etc. I don't know what has happened to the Rock & Ice lately but something is breaking it up or so it seems. Maybe you can tell me? If you have no one to go out with at weekends, try calling at Black Jack's. The old man has the bike now, but I am getting it back when I get home. Bob and myself are coming back overland if we get down OK and will arrive home about Christmas time. Cheerio for now. Don.

The attempt on Masherbrum was plagued by weather and indiscipline in the jockeying for summit-bid position. Don spent five weeks at altitude and came, as he thought, to within 500 feet of the top, before retreating to Camp Six, where he and three others spent five miserable days before retreating to base camp to recuperate. Whilst he was descending, the expedition leader, Joe Walmsley, passed on his way up to Camp Six with Bob Downes. From base camp days later, Don watched through binoculars and saw four out of the five climbers on the mountain descending. A night passed. At dawn he set off up the glacier to where they would come down. 'Where's Bob?' he asked Walmsley, and was told that he had died at Camp Six – of pulmonary oedema, it was later established.

Don was devastated.

Dear Audrey, Just another line to let you know how things are out here. I am sorry that the Rock & Ice are breaking up. I expect that by the time this reaches you, Nat will be married (I will drop him a line of sympathy). Pity you hadn't a spare £200 lying about for this trip round the world. Glad to know Joe is plugging along OK and from distant reports managing to get a grip on his wife and giving one or two orders himself. I have some terrible news for you in this letter. Bob Downes died in Camp Six a week ago. I suspected this yesterday when only four figures were seen through the glasses, and it was confirmed this morning when they arrived. I was in the base camp resting after five weeks of solid work. I went within 500 feet of the summit a fortnight ago and this may well be as far as we get. At the moment we are all at base camp. Bob is laying in Camp Six. It will be a fortnight before we get him to the nearest village. While we are up there if the weather is good we will try for the top. If bad we will be packing up for good. I am coming home by boat now . . .

The members of the expedition agreed to recover Downes's body and take it to the army hospital in Skardu. It meant that all the camps would have to be restocked, and a sledge dragged up to bring down the body. Don suggested that since they had to go so near to the summit, they might as well make one last bid for it. When they reached Camp Six, he, the exhausted Walmsley and the others took Bob's body on the sledge down to Camp Five, then the two of them

– Don and Joe Walmsley – climbed back once more to the higher camp, from which they headed on to a bivouac site 1000 feet below the summit. After a bitter night, they set off, Walmsley slow and hesitant, traumatised as well as all but spent. A wide and sunlit gully stretched up the final 500 feet to the col between the mountain's twin summits. The snow was soft, floury and knee-deep. At an altitude of 25,000 feet, Don opted to climb a rock-buttress to the side of it.

It took him seven and a half hours to climb 300 feet. Walmsley struggled desperately on the first pitch. The next lay up a layback flake that reminded Don of Joe's Right Unconquerable crack on Stanage Edge, back in Derbyshire. He climbed it, somehow, in his altitude boots,[31] and knew that Walmsley could not have followed him: 'If I'd carried on alone I could have got to the top easily. I was only 150 feet below the summit. But the bloke with me was at the end of his tether, and if anything had happened to me he would have been left sitting there. In a case like that you just have to weigh up the job and make a decision . . .' He made the only one he felt was open to him:

> I looked across at the summit, hardly a stone's throw away. If I climbed on, got there in quick time and then got back to Joe at the double, we'd still have to spend a night in the open which would mean certain frostbite and possible amputations. If I climbed on alone and fell, it would mean the end for both of us. I looked down at the silent figure, gazing at the world's most fabulous mountain scenery with unseeing eyes. If I called down to him, he would get to his feet and face up to the agony of a struggle which would surely finish him. No, if we couldn't make it together and return safely, I had no decision to make. We would have to go down.

So Don's first Himalayan expedition ended in loss, tragedy and failure, but the lessons so hard learnt were ones that would resonate throughout his future mountaineering career. And maybe one day, luck would be on his side.

---

[31] When I led my first Extremely Severe rock-climb (Brant Direct, probably the easiest route of that grade in Britain) in the early 1960s, my second – an older climber from Oldham – reverently pointed out the scratches reputedly left by Whillans as he was practising for Masherbrum. As I quivered my way up in rock-boots, the thought that Don had climbed it in altitude boots and crampons made me feel rather silly. And, of course, added to the Whillans myth . . .

13

Unlucky For Some: a Digression on the Sweet Science of Gritstone Cracks[1]

It is an interesting fact – and one by which Don would not, I suspect, be too favourably impressed – that the Whillans reputation in younger British climbing circles rests most firmly not on the alpinism and mountaineering in the greater ranges by which he set most store, but on his fighting (and how many of the stories around that may have gained in the telling we have considered in a previous chapter), and on perhaps a dozen crack-climbs on the gritstone edges and quarries, the most celebrated of which among climbers in the first decade of the twenty-first century is a full eight metres long. These cracks, taken together, represent so substantial a component in the Whillans legend that it is worth considering them as a separate topic, rather than letting them be immersed and lost in the main flow of the narrative. They have become, in rock-climbing terms, the definition of the man – to the extent that, if you hear climbers referring to 'a Whillans route', it no longer need be by the man himself, but merely possessed of his perceived qualities. Buffon's best-known maxim was never more clearly exemplified.

Sometimes this process overpowers reason and historical fact. Joe's route Blue Lights Crack on Wimberry Rocks, for example (see Chapter Nine), was attributed in one guidebook to Don in 1948, despite the fact that this was two years before he started climbing. The reason for this was quite simple – it looked like a Whillans climb, therefore it must be one. Any climber's stock of routes can fall prey to this posthumous predation and, if possessed of the right characteristics, be described as a Whillans route! – in which

---

[1] With apologies to A.J. Liebling.

description that exclamation mark for once is crucial. The Bob Downes route on Carreg Alltrem, Penamnen Groove, mentioned in the last chapter, is clearly a Whillans route! – as, much to his annoyance, is Paul Ross's off-width masterpiece on Eagle Crag, Langstrath, Post Mortem, despite the fact that Don failed and fell when he attempted to make the first ascent. They are wide, they overhang, you have to struggle, the protection is too distant or difficult for modern comfort, therefore by definition they become – Whillans routes!

What underlies all this wilful misattribution is a bristling little basket of outcrop routes that demand a particular attitude from the climber if he or she is to succeed on them: The Unprintable, Centaur, Goliath, Ceiling Crack, Sentinel Crack, The Sloth, The File, Forked Lightning Crack, and more, all of them in varying degrees painful, all of them offering affront . . . I have a faint suspicion that in regard to Whillans routes! the myth has taken over, and subsumed the generic reality of gritstone crack-climbing. In an essay written over 30 years ago, I tried to define that reality:

> The keynote of gritstone climbing is aggression: the climbs are short and steep; characteristically they deal out inordinately large quantities of pain and fear. Torn hands, scraped knees, strained arms and a dry throat are all in a gritstoner's day: the cracks in particular are armed with vicious teeth. They have about them a degree of static malignity which demands an equal display of controlled temper to overcome them. It's not that climbing on gritstone is more difficult than climbing on other forms of rock, it's just that the defences are more systematically designed to disconcert. Rounded holds, rough bulging cracks, and an overbearing angle; you just have to get used to them.[2]

In my own climbing heyday, this was by far my favourite rock. It reminded me oddly of boxing when I was a kid – the same brisk combinations, necessity to get the levers working, make the moves fast, slip in from the angles, get through your opponent's guard; the same need for fluidity and style. Gritstone is streetfighters' rock. I remember one very trivial incident, nothing to do with Don or his

---

[2] 'Right Unconquerable', in *Hard Rock*, ed. Ken Wilson.

routes, that typifies this. I was on Stanage one bitter winter's day with rain on a west wind winnowing against the crag, the cracks all running with water and green with slime. My companion was a young Exeter hotshot who had led all sorts of difficult things in the south-west. I hunched into my donkey jacket (as worn by building-site labourers, and de rigueur for climbers in this particular period), sought cover under a boulder, didn't even think of putting on rock-boots, and watched him tie on to double ropes, arrange his rack, put on his PA's, and look up at the appropriately named Green Crack – an emerald little corner then correctly graded Severe[3] that a competent gritstoner of the time would use as descent route from the technical face problems to its right.

The crack in the corner is wide and holdless at the outset, and you wedge or lay away on loose fist-jams for a few feet until better hand-jams arrive. The hotshot tried to bridge, dabbing at it as though it might sting. Green gritstone is very slippery. Two feet he ascended, his PAs shot off and down he sprawled. Same thing happened half a dozen times. He tried to layback, hands and feet greased off, and I had to abandon my shelter and catch him. 'For fuck's sake,' I snapped (having already been a little alienated by the bullshit about grades on the journey to Stanage), 'use the crack – fight it!' I demonstrated the required continuous flow of movement (preceding brief flash of temper very useful in generating this), half-climbed and half-slid back down, gestured him on to it again. He looked at me, baffled, looked back at the crack, and burst into tears. What would have happened had he been faced with a Whillans crack (or Whillans himself in one of his surly moods) scarcely bears thinking about.

I hope I might behave a little more charitably these days, but the point holds. If you're to climb a gritstone crack, you don't faff around, you slam in – having mastered the black arts of the jam in all its excruciating varieties beforehand. I look at the backs of my hands as I type this, and the pads of scar tissue across the knuckles are still livid-pale. Street-fighting rock!

---

[3] In common with far too many of the classic gritstone climbs which preoccupied my youth, it has been upgraded (I'm disciplining myself and not giving vent to an apoplectic fogeyish outburst here). Those that haven't – Moyer's Buttress on Gardom's Edge, for example, which used to be one of the most serious leads in Britain – have simply had their risk-factor reduced or entirely removed by modern protection equipment, leaving a pale shadow of the experience previously offered: 'A fear like birth and death,/When we see birth and death alone,/In a void, apart.'

To move the focus from generalities to actual Whillans routes, here is a tale from Ian Parnell, one of the best all-round performers in current British climbing and an acute observer of the scene. It concerns The File – the so-called 'Vicious Crack' on Higgar Tor's Leaning Block that Don swarmed up with ease in 1956:

Today The File really sorts out who has gathered the secrets of the forgotten art of jamming. I remember wandering up past the foot of the crag one Sunday to see a classic tussle ensuing. A hapless leader whose bulging biceps proved he'd paid a lengthy apprenticeship at his local climbing wall was attempting to layback the whole route – an indication that he'd perhaps been less studious in learning of the lowly hand-jam. Fortunately the climber's huge arms had managed to propel him 25 feet up, his boots slipping and sliding between the breaks. Unfortunately he'd done this without managing to make any of his protection stick. Due to his tenuous layback position, gear had been fumbled in blindly and had promptly sailed down the free-hanging rope. One camming device that looked to offer a glimmer of hope had been deftly flicked out by his pawing foot – in some ways the most stylish manoeuvre of his attempt. In a position of extreme concern, his bulging forearms seemed to swell even larger. He made a lunge for the final break, into which he wriggled as many of his limbs as possible and from which he refused to move. By now he had a substantial audience, and eventually several of the onlookers were forced to assist in his extraction, as the honed but humbled chap gibbered his incomprehension – particularly as his training had been going so well.

The File is a straightforward gritstone VS – probably the easiest route in the whole Whillans canon. But it could be thought of as a VS with attitude, if you don't want to engage, if you don't want really to slam in. Either you lose face, or you lose skin[4] – the choice, if you go on the route, is yours.

---

[4] The notion that expertise in jamming will ensure that you don't lose skin is completely erroneous. Simply, as you move, your hand will to a degree rotate and the crystals will gouge. Being able to do a steep jamming crack in control will lessen the amount of skin lost, but won't completely prevent it. If you disbelieve this, go and inspect Joe Brown's knuckles. There was a fashion – borrowed from

A little history now: walking along Burbage Edge – a trivial but pretty outcrop near Sheffield – with Doug Verity[5] one perfect sunny Sunday in 1958, soloing whatever took their fancy, Don came to a wide, and at first sight innocuous-looking, 25-foot crack and speculated on whether it had been done. He thought to try it, arrived at a chockstone, called down to Doug and said, 'It's a bit thrutchy, this – chuck us a sling.' He spent a fair time threading it with difficulty round the chockstone, then huffed and puffed his way up to the top. And didn't think very much of it, didn't bother to give a name to what he'd done.

Named or not, this particular Whillans progeny has acquired perhaps the choicest reputation of all his routes, 'rarely repeated, badly protected, thoroughly fierce'. Here is another of Ian Parnell's moral tales, from a *Climber* magazine article on Whillans cracks:

> Goliath [was] perhaps Britain's first E5 (although rated by some nowadays at E4, 5c). Whatever the numbers, this will be a stern test of anyone's character. The super-fit will attempt to layback the whole thing while the super-thin will attempt to wriggle internally. Those of normal stature will try a combination of both, relieved by the opportunity to place an unfeasibly large camming device before things get too hairy. In 1958 of course, technology didn't blunt the challenge. There has been talk of chockstones . . . the chockstones may have helped progress, as did three or four now departed pebbles for footholds,[6] but it was still another ferocious and

---

America, of course – in the 1970s for taping up before climbing a jamming route, but this was properly regarded by gritstoners as effete.

[5] Son of Hedley Verity, the great Yorkshire cricketer of the 1930s, and a recent import into the Rock & Ice from that county. A lovely, calm, genial man, Doug was for many years the golf professional in Pwllheli.

[6] These pebbles, the size of peanuts and quite common in gritstone, protruded at regular intervals from the left wall (facing this way is not the habitual modern way of doing the climb), and very substantially aided progress. Knee and shoulder in the crack, right arm wedged across, left doing anything useful that it could, you placed the side of your left foot very precisely on each succeeding pebble, eased your right limbs out of the crack, straightened up, slid whatever would fit back in and repeated the process from the next pebble. They had all snapped off by the mid-1970s when I last did the climb, making it much harder.

The reason why the climb had no substantial contemporary reputation is simply

very bold lead. Interestingly, Goliath wasn't that highly rated at the time, and was seen as a little short and scruffy. Dennis Gray made the second ascent and remembers underestimating it: 'Don said to me, "You'll be all right, Slippery Jim. You're so skinny you can get right in back of it." Of course, it wasn't that easy and I remember a right struggle at the top.'

One modern myth concerns a British Mountaineering Council youth meet during the mid-1990s.[7] A fledgling Ben Bransby, 14 years old, was understandably keen to make his mark with his first E5. Friends and onlookers gathered round and the bold whippersnapper set off with a confident layback. Reaching the solitary face hold – a rather disappointing flake – he whipped his Friend 4 out, readying the crucial cam in his teeth. More laybacking, this time showing signs of strain, saw the youngster eyeballing the vital placement 20 feet from the floor. It soon began to dawn on the crowd below that things weren't too rosy. Ben's hand would tentatively relax its grip on the crack to make a grab for the protection chattering between his quaking teeth, only to snatch back as his slight form began to barn-door away from the rock. Ben's dad Matthew encouraged him to go for it.[8] Feeling that his father wasn't perhaps fully informed of the situation, Ben replied in a quivering voice that he couldn't, at which point of course the vital gear plummeted to the ground. With no gear, and rapidly waning arms, Ben took the only option available, and fell off directly on to his dad. It's not recorded what his dad then said, but Ben was able to walk away without a scratch while the elder Bransby had various body-parts bandaged for

---

because it was so short – to Don, at a little over 20 feet long it was something he could jump off – scarcely more than a boulder problem. Joe has a memory of him jumping off from the crux move of Cave Wall on Froggatt once – at 35 feet, again quite a short route, but with a further drop below and a fearsome landing. He escaped quite unscathed.

[7] Definitely a myth – BMC youth meets, as a result of their inordinately high casualty rate, had been discontinued in the early 1990s.

[8] Amazing how often the spectators love to bay this phrase at a climber *in extremis* – as though the climber were unaware of that option. Generally, the best thing they can do if they want to encourage someone is to keep their mouths shut and allow the climber to concentrate. Richard McHardy, one of the mainstays of the Alpha Climbing Club in the 1960s, used to scream at people if they spoke to him whilst he was considering a move.

the rest of the week. I'm sure there's a moral about young stars, overexcited parents or camming devices there somewhere, but it does show that no Whillans route should ever be taken lightly.

Enough of Goliath – it may have the hardest reputation of all Whillans routes, but it is, after all, in current parlance only eight metres long. We should hear from the man himself:

Jamming technique [which all these climbs rely on in one form or another] is a natural thing. I met lots of bods who'd say, 'Oh, I taught Peter Harding' – you know, the guy who claimed to have invented the hand-jam – 'to jam', which is complete bollocks, of course, because if you climb on grit you can jam, end of story. Most cracks I could climb, but I had to be careful on faces because they were reachy and didn't have protection, and I didn't have a long reach for a five-foot-three bloke. I always used to trust a fist-jam where a lot of other people never would, and I definitely preferred climbs with overhangs because it represented a straightforward challenge. You didn't have to worry – it was there straight in front of you, and you could either do it or you couldn't. My climbs were obvious challenges, so maybe that does indicate a way of thinking. Things like crosswords and complicated manoeuvres – I'd rather it were just straightforward. With that Chatsworth thing [Sentinel Crack, climbed in 1959 – 'probably the most feared E2 in the country', according to Ian Parnell], I'd just done Puppet Crack and told the fellow I was with to go up and throw a rope down so I could look for some protection on it. Two moves and it was no bloody good anyway, with the rope not running, so I tied on and took a stone up, which I couldn't get in and there were only two moves above to get to the end. It was fairly bold with no gear – a bloody big rock on the ground below and you would just go splat and that would be it. There were two blokes on the road and they gave a big cheer.

Whillans cracks! Ian Parnell gets it right: 'This mythology is the only way that many of us can have any contact with the pioneering greats of the past.' Note Don's word – 'straightforward'. They are, mostly, whether it was Don, Joe, or whoever who first did them. They demand a lot of effort, they hurt, but you know what you're faced with. In front of your eyes on the lip of the roof of Sentinel Crack there's a fist-jam (unless you've been foolish enough to block it with a camming device). Just get the levers working right, haul up, leave some propitiatory skin behind as it twists round, don't falter even for a moment . . .

You should have the picture by now. Weigh the thing up and don't be outfaced by it. If you step into the ring with that attitude, you've lost psychologically before you start. Remember what Sugar Ray Leonard did when he stepped up a weight and went into the Marvin Hagler match, where all the fancy was prophesying he'd be slaughtered? He danced and taunted, slipped all the aggression, threw the bolo punch, and won on points. The effrontery of it was magnificent. Last thing to say about these Whillans crack routes on gritstone – affront aside, I've always thought Joe's were harder: The Dangler, Emerald Crack, Crack of Gloom, A35, Charming Crack, Roof Route, The Overhanging Crack, Brown's Crack, Ramshaw Crack, The Great Crack, Left Eliminate – OK, he may have used the odd sling on one or two of them, but we, with our easy-to-place camming-device runners, are in no position to disparage or even understand how difficult and exhausting these climbs once were to protect. On the first ascent of Ramshaw Crack, for example, which is arguably the hardest climb in this list, very seldom done, and in my view at least a full grade harder than Sentinel Crack, Joe used a sling for aid low down in order to arrange protection for the crux section, and having done this, then led the hardest section of the climb entirely free. Anyone who ever saw Joe climbing on gritstone in his prime was left in no doubt that, as a technical crack-climber, he was without a peer. The difficulty of Joe's climbs is something to do with keeping enough of that flooding aggression back to channel into guile and technical inventiveness – the boxer as opposed to the bruiser, Sugar Ray against Marvellous Marvin again. With Don's routes, you always knew that if you wound yourself up to a particular pitch of focused aggression, you'd get up them without having to think too hard about it. Which is surely enough for this particular digression.

Or maybe not quite. The best Whillans crack-climb of them all?

Forget about gritstone for the moment. It's Grond[9] on Dinas Cromlech, a wonderfully overhanging corner-crack coming out of a hidden little niche over to the right above Cenotaph Corner. The angle is unrelenting, the jams are perfection and don't even hurt that much, the protection used to be very sparse up to the chockstone (no idea what it's like now – haven't done it for 30 years), and Brian Royle remembers watching from below one day in 1958 as four little men – Don, Joe, Morty Smith and Dennis Gray – led it one after the other, dropping the rope down between each ascent, each of them climbing in one smooth, unfaltering flow of powerful, easy movement.[10] That's how you do them, wherever they are. Just make sure you learn to jam first.

---

[9] Since I've already mentioned Richard McHardy once in this chapter, I'll use that as the pretext to tell you about the fifth ascent – or as Peter Harding used to term it when a climb was done by someone other than its originators, the first independent ascent – of Grond. It took place in 1965. Richard was instructing at Plas y Brenin, now the Sports Council Centre at Capel Curig, when he pulled a block off one day on Ribstone Crack on Carreg Wastad whilst with students on a rock-course. He came on to his sole runner round a loose block; this also pulled off and landed on Richard's head where he had fallen on the scree beneath the crag. Bill Bowker, a friend of Don's from Blackburn, was climbing nearby and remembers scooping Richard's brain back into his severely fractured skull and bandaging it up before the ambulance took him down to the Caernarvon and Anglesey Hospital in Bangor. A week later, Richard was doing press-ups by his hospital bed in order to get fit. Three weeks after his accident, as his first route on being discharged from hospital, he led this ascent of Grond. Effrontery in the face of the contingent?

[10] Joe recalls: 'I was climbing with Morty and we noticed Don trying not very successfully to get up this crack with Dennis. We went round there and that seemed to spur him on. He got up it, and then all three of us led it.'

14

The Focus Shifts

As with most other sports, the intense phase of climbing is generally short-lived and a youthful phenomenon in a person's life. For those for whom it is not transient, but evolves into a way of life, along with that commitment there is a degree of loss. Friends of early days will become involved in careers, marriage, child-rearing – none of these easily done well alongside intense climbing. And also, of course, the higher the level at which you operate within climbing, the greater the number of your friends who will die.[1] By 1957, both of these self-evident truths were known to Don. Pete Greenwood had quit climbing to marry Shirley, and gone into business with the declared intention of making some money. He gave all his gear to Don to emphasise the finality of his decision. The Rock & Ice was

---

[1] I once, in a morbid moment, began to count the number of people I had known and climbed with who had been killed in the mountains. At 60, consumed by survivor-guilt, I stopped rather than reach a final figure.

[2] Climbed in 1957, it was then the hardest route on this centrepiece cliff. Moseley is the disregarded and under-rated figure in the Rock & Ice's trinity of outstanding leaders at this time, yet his new routes – Left Edge, Left Wall, White Slab, Pendulum, Phoenix, etc. – are all of exceptional quality. He was also Joe's most frequent partner for winter-climbing, and they made ascents together of the classic repertoire of hard Welsh gullies and socially, he was one of the most popular members of the club. Of similar stature and build to his two peers, in the physical contests in which Rock & Ice members continually engaged he also held his own, and could do more pull-ups even than Don. His climbing was notably erratic, however – one day he would fail to lead a VS, the next he would manage easily one of the new extremes. Why he failed to make so prominent a mark is probably through two main factors. He never formed so strong a climbing partnership as that between Joe and Don, which undoubtedly assisted them both to achievements they would not have arrived at so quickly as individuals. Also, in three very public arenas in which Don and Joe excelled – gritstone climbing and alpine and greater ranges mountaineering – his record was far behind theirs. His later complete break from, and dismissal of, climbing – to the extent that he refused all contact with

on the brink of breaking up. Ron Moseley had married and, apart
from a clutch of swansong climbs, Phoenix[2] on Scafell East Buttress
among them, was on the verge of giving up the sport and emigrating
to Canada. Joe and Nat, too, were married and – greatest of horrors
to the young Whillans! – were set on taking their 1957 holidays in
Cornwall. Bob Downes lay buried on a little knoll where the Indus
is young. But Don's direction was clear:

> The longer he continues to climb, the less he'll see of his
> original mates. They'll get married, or lose interest. This is
> really because they are just not very keen. I think in any field
> you really have to want to do something to do it well. As a
> rule I like any climber's company. You can make plans to do
> something and straight away they'll say: 'Yes, when do we go?
> How much will it cost?'

He had some reason for confidence in choosing to become – an
unknown term then, but perfectly acceptable to later generations –
a professional mountaineer. In 1957 an influential[3] essay by Geoff
Sutton – Don's rope-mate on the first Blaitiere attempt – had
appeared in the book *Snowdon Biography*, by Young, Sutton and
Noyce. It contained the following statement: 'Whillans . . . and
Brown climbing together have formed by far the most formidable
team ever to operate on British crags, and indeed perhaps anywhere
else, as they have demonstrated in the Alps.'
    'Whillans . . . and Brown' – there was a turnaround!

---

that community and its chroniclers – have ensured that, though still an important
figure, he remains an enigmatic and shadowy one.
[3] It was also widely mocked. This paragraph came in for particular attention from
the derisive brigade: 'Quickly it became apparent that rock-climbing had taken
another jump forward, and that even taking all modern aids into account the new
climbs were not only more exposed and sustained than anything that had been
done before, but more difficult – much more difficult. For the first time physical
specialisation began to make itself evident. Up to this time there had been great
climbers of every build: though there was a numerical bias in the direction of men
of medium height and wiry or muscular frame, the hardest climbs had been
available to and had been done by men of every build who possessed the necessary
technique and determination. It is dangerous to make predictions, but it seems
probable that future advances in rock-climbing will be made by men of less than
medium height but of strong and lithe physique, for apart from other
considerations only such men have the power-to-weight ratio necessary, above all
in the fingers, to climb safely up the angles and minute holds of new ultra-Severes.'

His ambition in this direction of a wholehearted commitment to mountaineering remained clear despite his marriage (the condition obviously being contagious in the Rock & Ice at the time) to Audrey, on 24 May 1958. They had been 'courting' for six years, he was just 25, she was three weeks short of her twenty-seventh birthday. The groom at his sister Edna's wedding in March had asked him when he was getting married. 'When I'm about thirty,' he'd answered. A week later he asked his mother, 'What are you doing on the twenty-fourth of May, Mam?' When she'd asked why, he told her, 'Me and Audrey was thinking of getting married. D'you want to come?' For their honeymoon they went to Glencoe with Creagh Dhu member Charlie Vigano and his wife Sheila, where Don – making no concessions to the occasion – promptly dragooned Vigano into 'taking a look' at the then-unclimbed 400-foot overhanging face of Creag a'Bhancair at the head of Glencoe, above the Creagh Dhu bothy of Jacksonville alongside which they were camping. Creagh Dhu members had been interested in this face for years, and had made little progress on it. Nor had Don on a previous attempt in 1955, but this time he found an ingenious and difficult entry on the left of the cliff that climbed an incipient pillar in the steep lower wall to a descending traverse line which led into the centre of the crag. Two things prevented him from continuing. To cope with the first – an eagle on its nest – he came up with a solution that would draw strong disapproval these days: he drove down to Fort William and bought a catapult (whether his old skills at smashing milk bottles had deserted him, and what the eagle's reaction was, are not recorded). The second factor was that Charlie Vigano was far from enthusiastic about seconding the traverse.[4] He was rescued, fortuitously, by the arrival of Don's acquaintance from the Bombay boat, the great Scots climber John Cunningham, the

---

[4] Anyone who has seconded this pitch will quite understand Vigano's qualms. The top of the first pillar is about 50 feet off the ground, the traverse right from it is 90 feet long and – in those days – devoid of protection. I did the climb in the 1960s with Martin Boysen, who had led the first pitch on two previous occasions, on both of which his seconds, Nick Estcourt and Mike Yates, had refused to follow. The first moves down from the top of the pillar are 5c, strenuous on the fingers, and to come off them for a second would have meant a ground-fall. I was perched atop the pillar, quivering and considering the problem, when there was an explosion of impatience and rage from the other end of the rope. I scuttled down the traverse more frightened of my leader than the prospect of a fall. These days, the sensible use a back-rope.

shipyard at which he worked being on strike. His account brings out very well the competitive attitude of the Creagh Dhu:

> Charlie was none too keen on the route, mainly I think because if the second came off on the traverse he was certain to hit the deck, and he asked me if I would climb with Whillans, and although I wasn't climbing very well I agreed. But I had most of the gear and as Whillans was supposed to be on his honeymoon he hadn't brought much up with him. We set off . . . passing an old sling left by [Jimmy] Marshall on his one and only attempt. A long traverse right brought us to the first ledge, home of the bird, and it was covered in the skeletons of small animals.
>
> Then came another hiccup. The belay peg was in an awkward corner and I couldn't shift it. And then I discovered that every difficult-to-remove belay or runner was my gear and the easy ones were Don's. I was running out of gear fast, so every time I found one of my pegs impossible to remove I helped myself to one of his. Eventually we were both stopped by a really nasty-looking crack and we decided to call it a day. Whillans whacked in another of my pegs and set off into space.
>
> When we got back to earth we put our gear in a little pile on the floor and Whillans was astonished to find he hadn't any pegs left. He said, 'Funny, Jock, I could have sworn it was all your gear I was banging in there.' The conclusion was that while I was roping off I saw a really good line wending its way through the final overhangs, but of course I didn't mention this to Whillans. Two weeks later I was back with Mick Noon and we finished the route off. What's more, we recovered a load of the gear too.[5]

After this débâcle, Cunningham and Don trailed down the long road through Glen Etive to the Trilleachan Slabs for an attempt on the tall, blank slab left of the original route of Spartan Slab:

> When we first tried The Long Wait I didn't know Whillans too well and he really impressed me. He shot up what is now

---

[5] Don (and Audrey) was incensed by this piece of playful Scottish chicanery – hence the importance attached to Don's 1962 direct finish to the climb (see Chapter Fifteen).

the crux pitch but got stuck about 100 feet up. So he just turned round and said: 'Watch the rope, I'm going to slide down.'[6] I had no gloves on and I wasn't having that so I told him so. When he persisted I took the rope off and tied it round the belay peg and then he had second thoughts and promised to climb down with me belaying him.

So Cunningham, as usual, was ahead on points in the gamesmanship stakes. However impressed he may have been by Don's climbing ability, other members of the Creagh Dhu were less so with his behaviour. Tommy Paul summed it up forcefully: 'When Whillans came up here on his honeymoon in 1958, he gave his wife a rotten time in front of us. I just thought, well, he may be a good climber but he is a right prick. He was trying to be the big-time climber but after that he never climbed with us.'

The newly-wed couple went to live with Don's parents in Lower Kersal, and Don, saving money for the Alps, lapsed into a weekend gritstone routine, climbing with whoever was around to make arrangements with at the YMCA on Wednesday nights. Joe was nursing a broken leg sustained in running down the screes from Clogwyn y Grochan[7] and it seemed unlikely that he would be going to the Alps. Don began to cast around for another partner, and found up in Keswick a very competent rock-climber who was hankering after some alpine experience – young Paul Ross, whose tally of new climbs in the Lake District was growing ever more impressive. Post Mortem, his brutal, overhanging crack-climb from 1956 on Eagle Crag, Langstrath, fast gained a reputation as the hardest in the Lakes, and Don himself had fallen out of it prior to Paul's successful ascent. There was a problem, however, in the degree of friction between the two of them. Paul was unimpressed by reputation and perfectly ready to stand up to Don in any situation. Don in return had taken to calling Paul 'the spoilt brat'. However, the two of them arranged to meet up in Chamonix, disregarding the universal truth that personal tensions increase

---

[6] Feasible, this, the slabs being set at quite a friendly angle (which is more than offset by their glacial smoothness and lack of protection or positive holds) – but distinctly not a pleasant prospect. We're back with propitiatory skin, in this case to be lost from a less public but more painful site . . .

[7] He had himself driven back to Manchester for it to be set – see Chapter Ten, note 24.

exponentially on climbing trips. Whilst Audrey stayed at home, Don rode out on his motorbike and Paul took the train. They camped at the Biolay, and Paul cooked for the first morning and night. Next day he suggested Don took a turn. 'Well, he got really grumpy at that and we ended up eating bread and jam and going down to Chamonix for hamburgers and pommes frites. We got ratted[8] for a week while it rained, and Don, just married or not, was chasing after this young French bird all the time.'

Their initial objective had been an ascent of the Walker Spur, which had still not been climbed by a British party, but the weather changed that. The route up the South-West Pillar of the Dru abortively reconnoitred by Don and Joe in 1955 had been climbed solo in August that year by the Italian mountaineer Walter Bonatti, in one of the most audacious ascents in Alpine history. Every other post-war climb in the Alps, Don and Joe's included, had been put into the shade by this achievement. In the season of 1958, it was an obvious target for the thrusting young pair, but as Ross recalls, they were not the only ones interested:

> When the weather lifted, it was only fit for rock routes so we thought we'd go for the Dru. We didn't have a description, so I asked Don if he knew where it went. 'Oh aye,' he said, 'it goes up the ridge.' Fortunately we met Bonington, MacInnes and two Austrians, Walter Philip and Richard Blach, in the bivouac under the Dru and they had a description.

The night was cloudy and the six climbers delayed their start till after dawn. Don and Paul were first away up the couloir leading to the foot of the pillar. Paul's lack of alpine experience showed as he tried to avoid the ice by taking to the rock at the side of the couloir. Don had to climb above and throw a rope down to extricate him, by which time the other four had overtaken them. On the ice higher up, equipped with ice-axe and crampons, they regained the lead, but the party was obviously merging and by the time they reached the foot of the pillar had become a unit. The three pairs swung leads as they climbed on. Bonington describes watching Don as he climbed one difficult variant pitch: 'He . . . just pulled up on the pegs and

---

[8] Don was drinking by now, and had started smoking whilst on the Masherbrum expedition.

wedges in the crack, and then seemed to walk across the slab on which Richard had dangled in etriers. He did not hurry: each move was smooth, calculated, and seemingly effortless, and yet when I came to follow, the rock thrust me backwards.' When Bonington started to follow, he found himself near the top of a pitch with a clean, vertical crack cutting through two overhangs in front of him, and Don's legs dangling over a ledge far above:

'Is it hard?' I asked.
'It's a bit strenuous,' came the reply, in a flat Lancashire accent, and the legs idly kicked against the rock.

Chris later recorded that he found Don's variant pitch, on which he all but came off, one of the hardest he had ever climbed. Higher up they arrived at the Grade Six chimney that was the supposed crux of the climb. Paul led, and when he began taking in the haul rope for the sacks it swung into a corner and clipped itself into a karabiner, effectively jamming the rope. Don shouted that he would climb up and clear it. Pushing the sacks in front of him he started the pitch, with Paul taking in the rope through a direct belay. 'How the fuck can you hold me and the haul-sack on that?' Don yelled. Paul shrugged and let him get on with it, and he collapsed on to the ledge gasping and exhausted. 'I had you on a static belay – you could have just hung on the rope,' Paul told him. 'He put his face right up to mine at that and hissed, "Don't you tell me how to climb."'

From the capacious bivouac ledge they reached shortly afterwards, they watched, chastened, as thousands of tons of rock roared down the approach couloir. 'Just as well that little lot didn't roll this morning,' declared Don, 'there wouldn't have been much left of us.' And then there came a whistling and a sickening hollow thud as Hamish MacInnes's skull was broken by a single falling stone. Bonington, ever-resourceful, produced an army field-dressing and bandaged his profusely bleeding head. They settled down to an anxious night. At dawn, with retreat down the couloir unthinkable and the only way out being up, the rope teams were rearranged. Don, clearly the strong man of the party, would nurse Hamish as best he could and lead him to the top. The fast Austrians would go first, prospecting the route. Paul and Chris would bring up the rear, taking out the pegs. After another bivouac, with Hamish doggedly fighting on and Don coaxing and helping him all the way, they arrived at the top of the face where they bivouacked yet again in deteriorating weather, waking to thick snow that obscured all the mountain features.

Walter Philip was the only one with prior knowledge of the difficult descent to the Charpoua Glacier from this point. He and Richard set off down, the others following. Above the Flammes de Pierre, in driving snow, the Austrians lost the route and Don, with his unerring mountain sense, scouted it out again. But there were frictions in the party that were coming to a head. Here is Paul's account of what took place:

> There was a point on the descent when the Austrians abseiled down the wrong one of two parallel grooves and got to a point they didn't recognise. We were over to the left at the bottom of ours. I wanted to wait so that the Austrians didn't have to fix up another belay in an awkward situation, which it had become with the storm and the spindrift blowing. Don just came over and said, 'Pull those fucking ropes down now!' As far as he was concerned, it was every man for himself, and the others could follow in his wake if they wanted. The young Austrian, Richard, was all-in and asking to be left then. But for Don, it was just, 'Pull those fucking ropes down.' Lower down, Hamish and I had been behind and pulling down these frozen 300-foot ropes on every abseil whilst Don and Chris went on. Hamish had made a remarkable recovery, but he was very weak. We came across Don and Chris resting – just sitting down in the snow – so I went across and said, 'Hey, how about coiling the ropes, doing something to help?'

Whatever may or may not have happened on the descent, it was clearly Don's strength and mountain sense which got the entire party down off the mountain alive. The continuing friendship between Don and Walter Philip is ample testimony to this. Bonington pays the appropriate tribute: 'We got up alive because [Don] and Walter Philip knew what they were doing.' All six men – Hamish with his broken skull, Paul on his first alpine climb, the 19-year-old Richard, Chris Bonington pushing himself hard to keep up to speed in this gaggle of prima donnas – performed magnificently to pull through together. But it was the end of Don's climbing with Paul:

Back down at the Biolay, Don and Chris moved into the big tent together and we didn't speak, even though I was in the tent next to them. There were a lot of Oxbridge types around who were stroking him, and he liked that. He was in his element. It was just silly stuff, really, very immature, but we were young guys. I couldn't have phrased it like this at the time – I was just a forestry worker and he was just a plumber – but he had a hell of an ego problem, a hell of a chip on his shoulder.

Whilst Bonington went off with Ronnie Wathen[9] to attempt the West Face of the Petites Jorasses, Don waited for Rock & Ice reinforcements to arrive. Joe's plaster cast had been removed, so ten days later he was on his way to Chamonix with the irrepressible Morty Smith, the boisterous Dennis Gray, and the uproarious Eric Beard. Don went down to join them one rainy night after their arrival in the Bar Nationale, which was packed with British climbers. Eric Beard[10] – 'Beardie' – was standing on a table belting out Elvis Presley impersonations when Don walked in: 'Beardie, is that song hard to sing?' he growled.

Quizzically, Beardie told him that it wasn't.

'Well it's bleedin' hard to listen to,' snapped Don, walking straight back out into the drenching street.

Joe was seriously unfit, but held to a philosophy that viewed training climbs as a waste of time. If you were going to suffer anyway, he argued, you might as well suffer on something worthwhile, and he cast his vote for another attempt on the route that had been the scene of their failure in 1955 – the North Face of the Grands Charmoz, which possessed the inestimable virtue for the limping Joe of a relatively short approach. So he, Morty and Dennis

---

[9] A delightfully eccentric and animated character who was published poet, uillean piper, student at Trinity College, Dublin, and general playboy and bon viveur, Wathen had recently returned from the chaotically successful expedition to Pumasillo in the Andes, on which he had been a linchpin to the entire party. He figures large in the last stages of Don's life, and died himself in 1993. I went to his funeral in the Wicklow Mountains, and on the way there from Dun Laoghaire the taxi-driver stopped to buy us an ice-cream (only in Ireland!): 'They say in there your Ronnie was a grand fellow,' he told us, getting back in the car. He was, and his death came far too soon.

[10] 'Beardie' was a natural entertainer and a legend in mountain athletics, who held, before his death in a car crash in 1969, the records for running the Welsh 3000s, the Cuillin Ridge (a record that stood for 21 years), the Three Peaks, and the Bob Graham Round in the Lake District.

moved up from the Biolay to the Montenvers wood-cutters' hut –
by now renamed Chalet Austria – where Walter Philip and Richard
Blach, Don's companions from the Bonatti Pillar, were already
encamped. Philip, whose physique was on the same massive scale as
his enthusiasm, listened to their plans and decided to join them.
Dennis fretted at the view of his first alpine-climb-to-be, Morty
consoled him with the thought that it would 'piss down tomorrow',
his prediction proved accurate, and they spent a day lazing around
at Chalet Austria, watching the Austrians retreat down the face, and
greeting Don as he arrived up from Chamonix in the evening. Plans
were reconsidered, and the four Britons decided to follow in
Bonington and Wathen's wake and go on the West Face of the
Petites Jorasses – then reputed to be even harder than the Bonatti
Pillar. They made the long walk up to the ruined Leschaux Hut,
pausing on the way to contemplate switching plans and going for an
ascent of the Walker Spur, but deciding against it in view of the
climb's serious reputation and Dennis's lack of alpine experience.

The following day, in two ropes, they started up the climb, Joe
with Morty and Don with Dennis, who was having problems
acclimatising: 'As we gained height I felt dizzy and had to inform
Don I was about to be sick. Don can be a difficult person to come
to terms with in a valley, but on a climb there is something of a
Quixote about him. He was worried about me, and when I began
retching he insisted [I] go down.' The three remaining climbers
carried on. With Joe's leg, wasted from months in plaster, still
troubling him, Don led up the vertical face. They arrived at the crux
section of the route:

> Don shouted down, 'I'm not surprised they have the cheek to
> grade this section A3.[11] You can't get any pegs in. There aren't
> any cracks. So when you get up here, lean across the overhang
> a bit and you'll find a mass of jugs.'[12] Once again Whillans's
> genius had divined the means whereby the hardest pitch of a
> very serious climb could be tackled in a straightforward
> manner.

[11] The highest grade of artificial climbing at the time.
[12] Not Dali-esque, but shorthand for 'jug-handles' – i.e. large, safe and satisfying
hand-holds. It's worth noting that Chris Bonington had shown the same route-
finding genius the day before, free-climbing the big overhang and being surprised
at how easy it was.

They finished the climb with an uncomfortable bivouac near the summit, made a perilous descent back down a couloir to the Leschaux Glacier, and carried on to Chamonix. Dennis was still awaiting his first alpine climb so he and Don walked back up to Montenvers, the railway being out of order, and Don let slip that their objective was to be – old adversary of his – the East Face of the Grand Capucin. When Dennis pointed out that it was artificial climbing, and he had hardly done any of that, Don tersely replied that it would be a good climb to learn on. His temper up, he drove Dennis snappishly up the climb, exploding into insults at him now and again when the previously avowed inexperience showed through. But they finished the route in the day, descended to the Geant Glacier in a storm – an eye-opening experience for the young Yorkshireman – and arrived back at their bivouac on a rock-buttress above the Geant ice-fall: 'How he climbed up there, in the dark, with the snow falling, I do not know, but I was glad of the tight rope he gave me when I had to follow him.' It snowed throughout the night and they wound their way at dawn through ghostly ice-falls and down a miserable, rain-washed Mer de Glace to Chamonix. However irritable and overbearing he had been towards his tyro companion, Don had looked after him, and shepherded him up an impressive alpine debut climb.

The two were met in the Bar Nationale by an agitated Nat Allen, who was brandishing a press-cutting from the *Manchester Evening News*. 'Cupid breaks up noted club', ran the title, and the story read thus:

> Cupid has helped to kill what was once one of Britain's leading climbing clubs. For Manchester's Rock & Ice Club, which produced the two 'climbing plumbers' – Joe Brown of Rusholme, and Don Whillans of Salford – is to be disbanded. The club was once all-bachelor. But Joe and Don have both married. So has 'leading light' Nat Allen. Others have gone to the altar – and left the club. And now treasurer Ron Moseley (married) and Doug Belshaw (engaged) are to share the club's assets among fewer than 12 remaining members. 'Most of the past and present members still climb, but no longer as a group,' one of them told me today. 'I blame women for the break-up. Please don't mention my name – my wife-to-be might object.'

Don, too, seemed to be growing uxorious, and wrote to Audrey, telling her, 'I will be coming home this weekend, so dress up and look your best. I have been missing you very much of late, so watch out when I get back!'[13]

Not only was an alpine season over – so, apparently, was the Rock & Ice. The break-up – long anticipated – didn't last long. By February 1959 the club had re-formed, and Don's name had been plucked out of a hat – the normal way of appointing to a post which no one ever wanted – to serve as its president. Don himself had started to perform on the lecture circuit, where his dismissive wit and laconic story-telling[14] were laying foundations for a substantial later reputation. After one lecture he gave in Oxford in May, he was approached by a crop-haired, blond, tall and powerful young man, Colin Mortlock, who told him that the University Mountaineering Club was organising an expedition the following year to Masherbrum. Would Don be interested in a return bout? It didn't turn out as planned, but the invitation was definitely something Don would consider, and he set to saving money, working as a plumber on the huge Manchester slum-clearance and rebuilding projects of the time. Meanwhile, there was the new problem of finding the right partner for the Alps in the summer of 1959. Joe was no longer an option, there being friction between Don and Joe's wife Valerie.[15] During a visit to Glencoe he encountered Hamish MacInnes again, who had recovered well from the fractured skull he sustained on the Bonatti Pillar, and they arranged to meet up in Chamonix. Jimmy Marshall, the pivotal figure in Scottish climbing at the end of the 1950s, remembers Don in the Kingshouse at the top of Glencoe at the time: 'We were all in the Kingshouse and

---

[13] Maria Coffey, in her book *Fragile Edge*, records how deleterious is the effect of altitude climbing on the male libido. Maybe the Alps just aren't high enough.

[14] Dennis Gray gives an interesting slant on this in his book *Tight Rope*: '. . . my father took to Whillans like a soul-mate . . . enjoyed frequent visits from [him] and occasionally took him on club dates. By that time my father was the epitome of the northern stand-up comedian and entertainer, and I believe that some of Don's later ability owes its origin to mixing in those circles.' Dennis has another fascinating take on the Whillans persona, believing it to have changed almost overnight after the appearance in the *Daily Mirror* of the first 'Andy Capp' cartoons. (Andy Capp, in the cartoons, is a heavy-drinking, feckless, conniving, chauvinistic, philandering, flat-capped Northern working-class male with a punch or a quip at the ready in every situation.)

[15] According to Don Roscoe: 'Don hated Valerie, and blamed her for taking Joe away from him.'

Whillans was being Whillans and upsetting people. A great big fat guy, an infamous puncher, was going to knock Whillans all round the bar and Johnny Cunningham just said very quietly: "No, you're not" and the guy backed off.'[16]

The arrangement with Hamish was complicated by a chance meeting with John Streetly at the Pen-y-Gwryd shortly before Don was to leave for Chamonix. John, in Britain on a flying visit from Trinidad, had not climbed since their orgy of difficult routes back in 1955. When the climb Don and Hamish had in their sights was made known, his enthusiasm was fired. Despite having no climbing gear with him, he made arrangements to meet up in Chamonix, and join them on the Walker Spur. Don rode out to the Alps, and made his way to Montenvers and Chalet Austria, where he found a solitary Hamish MacInnes. Hamish informed him that Walter Philip and Richard Blach had set out earlier to bivouac under the Nant Blanc Face of the Aiguille Verte. Despite the long ride from Salford and the slog up from Chamonix, Don rocketed off into the night to join them for a 'training climb' up one of the outstanding mixed routes in the Aiguilles, and one which had previously taken parties two bivouacs. The ascent and descent made for a 25-hour day. When Don reached Chalet Austria again, John Streetly had arrived. To avoid the difficulties of climbing as a rope of three, he and Hamish recruited a young Stockport climber, Les Brown. Don would climb with Les, Hamish with John. The ad hoc nature of the party was mirrored by the state of its equipment. John had scrambled together what he could, having arrived in Chamonix without anything. Les, through no fault of his own, had lost his rucksack, all his gear in it, on his last climb, and was forced to climb in the suit he had arrived in, carrying a pair of pyjamas to wear on bivouacs.

They shared out what equipment they had, topped Les's outfit with a discarded trilby found in the rafters of Chalet Austria, and on 22 July embarked on what they hoped would be the first British ascent of the Walker Spur. In the course of the climb Hamish was

---

[16] Cunningham, who was a champion wrestler as well as one of the most significant figures in Scottish climbing history, was revered even among the hard men of the Creagh Dhu for his fighting ability. For this and other anecdotes about Cunningham, I'm indebted to Jeff Connor's fascinating *Creagh Dhu Climber: The Life & Times of John Cunningham*. Cunningham was drowned at South Stack, Anglesey, in 1980 whilst trying to rescue a student under his instruction who had fallen into the sea.

affected by the recurrence of symptoms from his head injury, and he and John fell behind whilst Don and Les were delayed by a slow Czechoslovakian party in front. Les Brown tells of how the Czech party pegged and 'frigged' every move, and how, in one Grade Six groove, Don – in boots with a sack on his back – bridged past them and on to the stance. The wide-eyed Czech leader said to Don, 'Sir, you are tremendous, the most fantastic climber in the world.' 'No, mate,' responded Don, 'I'm not the best climber in the world – you're the bloody worst.' They were forced into a bivouac on a climb which, without these problems, they might have completed in a day, so fit was Don at this stage in his career. As it was, it gave him particular satisfaction and he thought it the most enjoyable climb he had ever done, but when they descended the Italian side and arrived in Courmayeur, his pleasure was shaded by a degree of disappointment. On the way up the climb, the observant Hamish had noticed some oddities: discarded Smarties packets, an abandoned jammed-knot sling. Had there been a British party on the route before them? he wondered. Back on the main street of Courmayeur two ragamuffin figures called out a greeting – Robin Smith and Gunn Clarke had finished the route the day before. Don had been beaten to the most prestigious first British ascent yet accomplished in the Alps by a couple of Edinburgh University students and a day.

In the face of bad weather in Chamonix, Don headed off for the Dolomites. At the Tre Cime he met Morty Smith and rattled off rapid ascents of the classic trinity of Cassin, Comici, and Yellow Edge, then followed his Austrian friends Walter and Richard to the Civetta. Don teamed up with a young Derbyshire climber who had recently joined the Rock & Ice, Steve Read: 'The weather is still not very good but all the regulars here say the end of August is always very unsettled and that it is always good in September.' Intrigued by an account in Hermann Buhl's recently translated *Nanga Parbat Pilgrimage* of a prolonged struggle in icy conditions on the South Pillar of the Marmolata di Penia, on 20 August they set off from their bivouac cave and plumped for a climb that Don would remember as one of the most dangerous in his mountaineering life.

Lightly equipped for a route given a guidebook time of 10 hours, they started it in cloudy, dismal weather. Eventually this improved, and they climbed steadily on, Read impressing Don with his ability.

The technical section of the climb was soon behind them, but Don grew increasingly puzzled by the number of abseil loops festooning the rock.[17] What must lie ahead? he wondered. The route description mentioned frequent ice in the upper cracks. They had no axes, no crampons, no bivouac gear with them, and had been unable to see the condition of the top of the face for cloud when they started. Suddenly ice-fragments cascaded around them, answering Don's question. And yet he still pressed on. Ahead was one crucial pitch – the last, if the description was to be believed, on which they might expect to encounter ice – leading into the final easy couloir. It was running with water, the rock beneath glazed with ice. A huge chockstone was jammed across the gully above, avalanches of powder-snow poured down and falling flakes thickened the air. In his book, Buhl recounts how he took two and a half hours to climb this pitch, and it had been less icy for him. Don launched out and – chopping holds in the six-inch-thick ice with his peg hammer – made a desperate lead over the chockstone and up the frozen gully-bed beyond. After 150 feet, the rope came taut. Without a stance, he belayed on pebbles jammed in a crack, braced himself in the corner of the gully, and called down to Steve to start climbing.

To pass the roof, Don had had to hammer in pegs beside rotting wooden wedges he uncovered from the ice to gain a vertical, slimy chimney just wide enough for his body that gave out on to the snow in the gully above. When Steve, who was much larger and heavier in build than Don, embarked on the difficult climbing below the chockstone, one of the pegs came out as he put his weight on it. He swung across the icy wall, snow swirling and the temperature below freezing. Meanwhile, a full rope's length above the roof, Don was slowly being dragged on to his hasty, poor belay. 'For Christ's sake, climb the bloody rope and take the weight off me!' he screamed down. Steve shouted up that he would try to get a peg in. As he chipped at the ice to find a crack, Don slid on to the belay. The pebbles grated in their crack, giving a little. Minutes passed. More grating, more give in the belay. Don waited for the instant of release, the sudden flight, the catapulting each other thousands of

---

[17] Read: 'The abseil loops were left there a month before by the cream of Scottish climbers at the time – John McLean, Jimmy Marshall, Dougal Haston – which indicates how tough the roof was.'

feet down the face that must come any second. Then the pressure on the rope eased, Steve's voice drifted up, telling Don that he'd got a peg in, was standing in etriers. Don scrambled back upright, banged in two belay pegs, and took up the slack as Steve attempted once more to climb round the chockstone. This time he reached the chimney. With the rucksack on his back, he was unable to get into it, fell off again and was left hanging from the rope Don had fastened over a rounded spike. Don was forced to secure the sack-hauling rope, climb down to the top of the chockstone, haul up the sack and then bring up Steve on a tight rope.

The pitch had taken them as much time as it had Buhl, and the daylight was fast slipping away. Don forged ahead up verglassed rock devoid of protection, running with water, making move after move where a slip would have resulted in death for both of them, and arrived at a final, desperate overhang. In Vibrams, his only ice-tool a piton hammer, he climbed it. Night was falling, their clothes were sodden and freezing. If they sat out the hours of darkness, the likelihood of their surviving till morning was remote. In the last glimmerings of light they climbed on, and suddenly in the overhanging wall on their left was a cleft, an entrance to a ribbon of snow leading up to the suggestion of a cornice. They kicked steps, arrived on the summit, found the hut Walter had told them of, and it was empty. Wrapped in blankets, they shivered the night away within its shelter. Don had survived his closest approach yet to disaster. And as a reminder of the costs of mountaineering, when they descended in morning sunshine they encountered a rescue team at the foot of the South-West Face, lowering the corpse of a climber who had opted to bivouac in the hope of better conditions arriving. Without Don's speed, obduracy, and exceptional climbing skills, he and Read would have shared that fate. On the Marmolata, he had for once been led into an error of judgement, and it made him a wiser mountaineer.[18]

Richard Blach had gone back to Vienna, so whilst Read rested, Don and Walter Philip teamed up again and made an exceptionally fast ascent, using very little aid and with Don leading all the way, of

---

[18] Don claimed later that: 'The climb that I did that came nearest to the real hard Scottish winter climbs, with a fantastic amount of ice on it and it was very, very hard, was the South Pillar of the Marmolata. That really was the equivalent of a Scottish winter climb. We didn't even have the proper gear on that, not even crampons, just boots and a peg hammer with a pick on it.'

the North Face of the Cima della Terranova.[19] Walter had been booked to guide for the rest of the season and the weather had deteriorated. Don and Steve set off slowly for home, by way of the Karwendal, where they made an ascent of another difficult climb enthused over by Buhl – the Rebitsch-Lorenz Route on the North Face of the Lalidererspitz.

In September, Don and Audrey moved out of Don's parents' home and into the house where they were to live for the next 10 years. The address was 222 Goodshaw Lane, Crawshawbooth – the same hamlet to which Don had been evacuated during the war. It was a primitive, little eighteenth-century terraced cottage high on the Lancashire moors above Rossendale, for which they paid £220. Tom Whillans lent them £200 – almost all his life's savings – and Audrey and Don scraped together the other £20. That Don, in 1959, was at his rock-climbing peak is made clear by his gritstone climbing at that time. The previous year he had made the ascent of Cave Wall at Froggatt Edge – a short but intimidating climb that follows an overhanging, boulder-problem start leading right out of the cave with a rounded and committing crux move, high up, unprotectable and involving a precariously long reach. Still graded E3, it ranks high among the Whillans gritstone canon, and is rarely climbed. In 1984 Don reminisced:

> We used to sit in the cave talking when it was wet weather, maybe having a bash at Cave Crack as something to do. One day I got out on to this ledge on the wall round to the right that was sloping, and like it was covered in ball-bearings with all the lichen. I thought, 'I could do this if it didn't have all the shite on it.' You didn't clean routes in those days from the top, like they do now, so I just went up and did it. It never registered that there was no gear, because it was very short.

Actually, the crucial section is about 30 feet up, the landing is poor, with a narrow ledge beneath and a further drop below that to rough ground, and the move is a huge reach from undercut holds for a flat edge on which to pull up and mantelshelf. It still impresses. So does Sentinel Crack from 1959, which we encountered briefly in the last chapter. Don's gymnasticism on rock at this time is well illustrated by an incident which took place on Black Rocks at Cromford. He was there with his Glencoe friend from 1952, Patsy

---

[19] This was the last climb he was to do with Walter Philip.

Walsh, wearing a pair of boots specially made for his forthcoming Himalayan expedition. Walsh soloed Peter Harding's 1949 test-piece Demon Rib, the problematical start to which still merits a grade of E2, 5c. Dennis Gray and Steve Read were also on the crag, and started to attempt the opening sequence of moves. Don, who had been lounging back in his duvet, smoking and spectating, roused himself to action, took off his duvet, and in his clumsy altitude boots demonstrated the start to his young acolytes. He strolled up the rest of the 60-foot-high route, employed a (very modern) sitting-on-your-hand resting technique on the top mantelshelf, and left the pair of them – both very competent gritstone climbers – open-mouthed with admiration: 'He was the most impressive climber I'd ever seen – just like an India-rubber ball in his gymnastic ability, with a phenomenal power-to-weight ratio,' recalls Read.

Martin Boysen, the outstanding technical climber[20] from the new

---

[20] . . . and the most enduring figure, whose achievements in climbing have spanned many decades. He was born in Aachen, Germany, in 1942. His father, a music teacher, was captured by the Russians on the Eastern Front, and was not reunited with his family, who had by then settled in Tonbridge, Kent, until years after the cessation of hostilities. Martin began climbing on the Wealden sandstone outcrops, and his early routes here are regarded as the difficult classics of the region. In 1959, as a 17-year-old schoolboy, he had seconded Joe with ease on Woubits Left-Hand – the last of his 1950s routes on Clogwyn Du'r Arddu – and had had the temerity to question if the amount of aid used by 'The Master' had really all been necessary. His subsequent contribution to British rock-climbing and mountaineering has been one of the most considerable ever, with major new climbs in venues all over the country as well as in the Alps, where his free ascent of the American route on the South Face of the Aiguille du Fou in particular was hailed as having – standard formula! – the hardest rock-climbing pitch of its day in the Alps. On ice, climbs like his 1962 winter ascent of the Black Cleft, using the antiquated equipment available at the time, were revolutionary and years ahead of their time.

Tall and bespectacled, chaotically untidy, widely cultured and with an amiable demeanour and slyly amused take on life, Boysen was quite unlike the usual preconception of the climbing 'hard man'. As a climber, he was possessed of a languid grace utterly disarming to watch – though his drive was nonetheless extremely strong, and could default at times to an explosive impatience (see note 4 above). Like Don – though with far less justification – he suffered rather from the politicking that surrounded the Bonington Expedition Circus of the 1970s and early 1980s, and a mountaineering career that might have flourished internationally failed to achieve that fruition. Unlike Don, it seemed not unduly to bother him; he retained a lifelong enthusiasm for rock-climbing, and as he approaches his mid-sixties he continues to lead routes in the high E-grades (usually in company with the almost equally grizzled former Creagh Dhu member Rab

generation that had come to prominence in the golden British summer of 1959, has a similar memory from a New Year's weekend in 1960. Don had inveigled the Rock & Ice to hold a climbing meet at Widdop, the magnificent and still quite infrequently visited gritstone crag on the Lancashire–Yorkshire border quite close to Don's new home in Rossendale. There were two barriers to much serious climbing being done. One was that the Manchester Gritstone Club had arranged a meet there, and its members were also staying in 'Dracula's Barn' – a huge, cold hovel worthy of the erstwhile Transylvanian peasantry, with a dripping roof, sodden beds, cracked walls, veils of grimy cobwebs draped from the rafters, and a rotting floor the holes in which revealed chickens ranging beneath. It had one significant advantage, in that staying in this squalor afforded residents' status – and hence all-night drinking – in the adjacent Packhorse pub. As wild men of their time, the MGC were on a par with the Creagh Dhu, and their champion, Barrie Kershaw, a demolition expert,[21] was the most feared man in Manchester from my climbing boyhood. I can recall few human beings who had around them so palpable a sense of threat. The wisdom was that if you were standing at a bar alongside Kershaw and he looked away, you ran, because when he looked back it would be to sight the fist or glass that was travelling your way. At this New Year of 1959/60 he and Whillans – long aware of each other's reputation, both spoiling for precedence – finally came to grips. Boysen laughs at the recollection of an 'OK Corral' atmosphere between the two clubs. The evening was spent in the

---

Carrington). Whillans held him in the highest regard, and in a comment which reveals where Don – at the time with every justification – regarded himself in the hierarchy, said of him, 'After me, it's Martin.' He went on to add, which again gives a very good clue to the Whillans mind-set, 'Martin's got no side to him. He's absolutely straight . . .' Which I think is a shrewd and fair assessment of the man who was, throughout most of the 1960s, the most accomplished all-round mountaineer in Britain, and one who has never really been accorded the credit that is his due.

[21] Do we choose our careers, or do our careers choose us? My favourite Kershaw story is of the time he was in court charged with biting a police dog. His defence, as reported in the *Manchester Evening News*, was that 'It bit me first'. Don was always very wary and respectful around him, and believed – with absolutely no evidence to support it – that Kershaw earned his living as a mercenary. He was very badly beaten up by a gang in Longsight one night when walking home drunk, it was discovered during hospital treatment that he had leukaemia, and he died in 1987.

usual physical contests, including arm-wrestling, and the final showdown – Rock & Ice champion against Manchester Grit's pet gorilla – suddenly went into meltdown with Whillans and Kershaw, fists still locked, careering crazily around the bar and on the point of exploding into serious violence. At which point the landlord, who had kept a low profile until his glasses started to get broken, leapt over the bar, grabbed a combatant by the throat in each hand, held them up at arm's length and told them to cut it out, pay for the glasses, or get their heads banged together. Don always being one to size up his adversary, and Kershaw too for once being circumspect, they obeyed – the posters on the wall advertising the landlord in his other capacity as 'The Blond Strangler', a heavyweight professional wrestler whose reputation in the ring marked him out as one seriously not to be trifled with.

Pub antics apart, the other barrier to climbing was the snow which lay thickly across the crag. Whilst the rest snored away their hangovers, Whillans and Boysen were the only two to venture out there. Martin, who had just matriculated at Manchester University to be near the gritstone outcrops on which significant ascents were the true sign of climbing pedigree then and now, remembers the power and precision of Don's climbing on the Widdop boulders, remembers him soloing up an awful crack in the frozen, wet conditions, and remembers him looking too in a meaningful way at the roof crack to the right of his own Ceiling Crack and marking it down as a challenge to which he would return.[22]

Don was not just climbing well on gritstone at this period. At Easter 1960, the new Rock & Ice were camping at Dale Bottom, near Keswick, 'doing a few routes of top quality and a large number of pubs of low quality'. On Easter Saturday a wet day's climbing on Castle Rock provided the pretext for a night's drinking in Keswick. Nat Allen, Derek Burgess, Colin Mortlock, Don and their wives or girlfriends were walking to a pub down an alley off the square when a passing man wolf-whistled at Audrey and called out, 'Hello, darling.' The little figure at Audrey's side took off and landed one punch on the side of the face which ripped the man's cheek open. 'I

---

[22] Sadly, he never came back, and the line did not receive a first ascent until 1974. Thirty Seconds over Winterland, it's now called, and the grade is E4, 6a, which would have put it very high in the Whillans canon. The leader was Mike Hammill – a formidably strong Yorkshireman – and he was seconded by one of Yorkshire climbing's gurus, Allan Austin, progenitor of Almcliff's Wall of Horrors.

have never seen so much damage done by one punch to a face. The recipient was a big lad, and out of order. He insisted on apologising,' records Nat Allen. Audrey administered first aid to him whilst someone else went to call an ambulance, and Don was quickly ushered away into another pub. This little bout – enshrined in Rock & Ice legendry as 'the dob of all dobs' – suitably primed him for a new route on Easter Sunday. He booted Mortlock awake at 8 a.m. and they 'shot round to Dove Crag on Don's bike. It was a perfect day, even if ruddy cold on a bike at that hour. An hour's walk, and the little cliff I had seen from the road loomed fierce and black.' They climbed what is undoubtedly the finest natural line of the crag, and one Don and others had previously attempted – its central corner between Hangover and Dovedale Grooves.

Mortlock[23] takes up the story:

> I hastily gave Don the end of the rope. He expected it, thank goodness. The first pitch looked deceptively easy. Don found a couple of runners and took about 20 minutes. I took the mickey as he was slow for him. He said nowt. When I climbed I said a lot – mostly purple in colour. The crack was very greasy and awkward, movement often largely by repetition. At the stance we took stock over a quick smoke. A large, black, sunless corner containing 100 feet of nearly vertical rock and steep slab, topped by about 40 to 50 feet of mostly overhanging rock. There were no escape lines and no place for a stance below the top. It took Don two and a half hours to climb this pitch. It must be the finest piece of rock-climbing I

---

[23] Don was spending a considerable amount of time with Colin Mortlock at this period, in preparation for their forthcoming expedition, and Colin has several vivid memories: of passing between a bus and a lorry on the back of Don's bike in Oxford, his shoulders touching the bus on one side and the lorry on the other; of winning his respect by being better at darts than Don in the pubs of Crawshawbooth; of being in a pub in Oxford where beer was fourpence more in the lounge bar than in the saloon, so Don rounded up his companions from the lounge, marched them into the saloon, and demanded their fourpences back; of Don's incipient racism (he once fell off his motorbike in Manchester, 'looked up and saw all these niggers peering down at me – I thought I must be in hell'); of the delicacy of his technique when bouldering at nearby Bridestones; of his dogmatic and inflexible attitudes ('those of a regimental sergeant major rather than an officer'); and of a life even then becoming soured by resentment of Joe and his easy ascent to what Don viewed as fame and fortune.

have ever seen. Don smoked incessantly in extraordinary resting positions. Two climbers passed the foot of the route:

'What route's that?'
'It ain't – yet.'
'Who are you?'
'Whillans.'
'Yer must be mad.'
This final pitch turned out to be just as long as our rope (150 feet). The slab was not only steep but greasy and minute ripples accounted for all the holds. Don cracked it by patience and magnificent skill. Despite being second and having a long reach I found it similar in difficulty to the crux of Great Slab on Froggatt Edge, though with greasy holds thrown in. Don climbed the whole pitch very slowly, with minimal protection, but inexorably . . .'

They named the route Extol, and it has become one of the enduring classics of Lake District rock, 'rather like Whillans – direct, uncompromising, and hard', according to Chris Bonington, who made an early ascent of it in 1964. After its completion, Don was immersed in preparations for the Himalayan trip on which he had been invited by Mortlock the previous June. The objective of this had changed since the idea had first been mooted. A leader, Wilfrid Noyce, had been appointed to whom the idea of following in the footsteps of others was increasingly anathema. So the idea of a second attempt on Masherbrum was shelved. Careful study of the maps Shipton and Tilman, Michael Spender and John Auden (brothers to the poets) had prepared from their Blank on the Map explorations of the Hispar-Biafo glacier systems in the Karakoram in 1938 suggested as an alternative an unclimbed peak called Trivor, the summit of which was at 25,370 feet. The expedition party comprised Noyce, Mortlock, American Rhodes Scholar Jack Sadler, Geoff Smith from Burnley, who had been on Masherbrum with Don, a doctor, Sandy Cavenagh, a botanist, Oleg Polunin, and Don himself ('a very small man with a slow Lancashire voice, a compact, almost streamlined figure, hair parted on the right and a direct, blue-eyed look, almost innocent you might say but very direct so that it would be hard to get away with anything undetected', in Noyce's description). Don left Liverpool for Karachi on board the SS *City of*

Perth on 16 May 1960, with all the expedition gear on board, and also his 650cc Triumph motorbike,[24] on which he planned to ride home to Britain ('Ask my dad to buy me a clutch cable and throttle cable for a 1957 Triumph Trophy. Also that book of British consulates abroad'). The voyage was uneventful and the ship's complement friendly: 'We had a good farewell party last night. I was dressed as a fairy, made up with lipstick. The best laugh came when most of us were tiddly. We were doing the conga round the swimming pool in the dark. I fell in, then we went up to the captain's cabin, where I sat making big puddles on the floor.'

On 1 June, the boat docked in Karachi, Don met up with Mortlock and – gear and motorbike finally rounded up – set off for Rawalpindi. Six weeks later he wrote to Audrey:

Have been very busy for the last week ferrying loads up from temporary base camp to base camp. We managed to find a reasonable route up the mountain and go up as far as Camp Three, from where the rest of the route can be seen clearly all the way to the top. The camp is on a col at 20,500 feet. To the right is Trivor at 25,330 feet and to the left Momhil Sar at 24,090 feet. With ordinary luck we should bag them both. Am now taking a well-earned rest and trimming the beard, which is coming along fine. Base camp is a fabulous place, on the side of a glacier on a bend. From the glacier nothing can be seen but snow, ice, rock and moraines. Just cross the moraine and there is a lovely flat plateau in a hollow. River, grass, flowers, butterflies – gets very warm during the day, and we take a bath. We are staying here till Noyce arrives – not enough gear to go any further, enjoying the rest and experimenting with the cooking . . .

Whilst the Trivor expedition was a success in that it put two men – Noyce and Sadler – on the summit, for Don personally it was a failure. He rowed with Mortlock – who won his respect by standing up to him, despite his complete lack of high-mountain experience – over the choice of route in the first stages of the climb; his relationship with Noyce, whose manner was rather fey and who

---

[24] The bike had been newly checked over by the Triumph factory in Meriden – Don was getting wise to the notion of sponsorship.

was a closet homosexual, was a little strained ('Noyce is much too easy-going,' he wrote to Audrey). And most disastrous of all was this: '21.8.60. Jack and Wilf went to the top, Jack taking my place because I had a temperature of 102 degrees. The doctor diagnosed polio[25] but I got over it OK and am now as normal.' There was consolation, however, in the prospect of his journey home.

He departed from Rawalpindi for his 7000-mile ride on 24 September, and after a few minor inconveniences with visas and stamps that caused some to-ing and fro-ing across the Khyber Pass, made his way through Afghanistan via Kabul and Kandahar, sustaining a broken mudguard along the way:

> I took the bike down to a welder in the bazaar and had the mudguard repaired, then bought oil for the oil change now due, and returned to the hotel. In the meantime, two girls had arrived at the hotel, one from Oldham, some 10 miles from where I live, and a girl from New Zealand, travelling together back to England. We combined cooking arrangements and I enjoyed several good meals. Hotels in these countries do not object to cooking in the bedroom. Two bottles of beer arrived, one each for the girls from a chap down the corridor who appeared concerned for them, though I think he became even more concerned when I downed both bottles before he could say knife.

Pressing on into Iran, in a town beyond Meshed:

> the entire police force arrived at my hotel in dribs and drabs until finally the chief himself arrived to see this stranger in the town. I was at first rather angry with the entire town in my bedroom, particularly as I had the front wheel off the bike trying to repair a puncture. Later it became so comical during my interrogation that I found it impossible to keep a straight face. Many severe glances were directed at me, which only added to my amusement. Finally with a stiff bow I was handed back my passport and the room emptied.

---

[25] Noyce was suspected already of being a carrier after two members of his earlier Machapuchare expedition, David Cox and Roger Chorley, contracted the disease.

In Tabriz, on his way to a welder's shop again, 'I had a head-on collision with a cyclist. In view of the threatening crowd, and the fact that I had been going the wrong way up a one-way street, I had to pay up a pound and try to look happy.' In Turkey, 'the most startling thing of all was that people were working. It was also nice to discover that the children didn't play the game of "stone the motorcyclist", as in Afghanistan and Iran.'

He wrote to Audrey from Istanbul:

Sorry not to have written before now but it's an expedition to find a PO in some of these places. I have reached Istanbul and expect to be home in 10 to 14 days. Afghanistan was very wild and lonely, though Kabul was a very nice place and the people quite hospitable. Iran I thought was duff – didn't care for the people or the country – all desert and every man a bloody twister. I went through the Khyber Pass into Afghanistan on a good asphalt road. Fifty miles into Afghanistan it disappeared and for the next 2000 miles was a bloody track to put the Cloggy one into the shade – a dirt road with corrugations, rocks, holes and dust. I looked like I worked in a flour mill. All that is over now – asphalt all the way home. I went into a shop this morning to change a note and met a bloke who studied at Leeds Uni. He fixed me up in a good cheap hotel and treated me to a fabulous meal in a posh restaurant. The only drawback in nearing home is that it gets very cold at nights. The last time I slept in the woods, I nearly froze to death – was covered in thick frost in the morning. The bike is going very well, the only trouble I've had was with the rear mudguard. Cash situation is OK. I have £45 left and if I get stuck in to some driving may arrive home with £20. I have stayed in quite a lot of hotels, so I could have done it much cheaper, but after three days riding in that dust a good bath is heaven. I suppose you have been home for a few weeks now. Hope you're not too lonely. Best get the tele back. Well, luv, that's all for now. Air my slippers and get a good meal ready – I think I'll need it. Better dust my cards,[26] too.

---

[26] National Insurance cards, that you had to give to your employer on taking up a job and collect on leaving.

At the Yugoslav frontier, the customs-officials aggravation he had encountered all along came to a head:

> Standing by the gate the customs officer gave me back my carnet and passport, then asked if I had any money. Thinking he intended to change my money . . . I handed him about £3.50 in leva. When no money came forth, I asked him about it. All he said was 'Confiscate' and as far as I could see, that was the end of the business. Roused to fighting fury by this cool cheek, I started a riot which finished with the guard running from the gate with fixed bayonet, and myself cursing the officer and telling him if he touched me with it, I'd shove it up his waistcoat.[27] Quite surprised that anyone should dare to say anything at all in this country, he wrote out an official form for me to draw the money from the Banc de Bulgarie in Erchard. Sure that no such bank existed, I drove into Yugoslavia still seething with rage. Ten minutes later a passing car flung a stone straight through my headlamp.

From Trieste to Manchester it rained. He slept in hayricks, crossed the Channel in a storm, had the last of countless punctures on the M1. 'At midnight in the teeming rain I stood outside the house I had left six months ago. A few pebbles at the bedroom window soon had Audrey . . . down to greet me with a pint of tea and a big fire. The date was Friday 4 November.'

Almost immediately, he was embroiled in plans for another expedition, to attempt Nuptse, a satellite peak of Chomolungma above the Western Cwm. He was not entirely convinced about the trip,[28] which was to be led by his Masherbrum companion Joe Walmsley: 'Has Streetly been writing to Walmsley,' he enquired of Audrey, 'because if John's not going, I don't think I'm interested.' In the event, a decision was made for him. On 30 January 1961, riding to an expedition meeting in Stockport with Audrey on the pillion, a lorry turned right without warning and the bike went

---

[27] Unlikely register, this; I suspect the sub-editorial hand of Wilfrid Noyce (the account of the journey appeared as an appendix to Noyce's book, *To the Unknown Mountain*).

[28] This expedition later became notorious for the 'personality conflicts' (i.e. punch-ups) that took place on it. What might have happened had Don been there is interesting matter for conjecture.

underneath it. Audrey's femur was shattered and she had to spend three months in hospital and a year in a calliper. Don's patella was badly broken, and from this time on he had a very weak knee. He wrote to Audrey, on a different ward in the same hospital, 'I'm sorry you are fed up. I am myself tonight. I just feel like buggering off now. The bloody big lump of iron on my foot stops me getting out. If you don't like it on that ward, maybe I can get that surgeon I know to have you moved. Little Tony Lyons came in with some fruit – you better have it, I never eat it.' The doctor told him that not only was he not going to Nuptse, but that he might never climb again. In view of which, Don accepted the doctor's first pronouncement, despite the fact that John Streetly was going, and made arrangements to meet Chris Bonington in Chamonix after the expedition had ended in July. He drove home the refusal to accept medical verdicts that spring by making the first ascent – in the course of which his knee was much needed and used – of the majestic off-width crack cleaving the overhanging Yellow Wall of Heptonstall Quarry above Hebden Bridge.[29] At Easter, feeling the need to make contact with the old community from which he had been drifting apart, he 'went to Langdale to look for the boys. I've never seen so many bloody yobs, coachloads of excursions, and cars before. I just turned round, went back to Ambleside, and stayed at Sid Foster's. Four blokes set about Barrie Kershaw in the Salutation and gave him a hell of a pasting. He was blind drunk, of course.' To Audrey, he wrote asking 'when you may be able to come home with the iron on? I'm always doing something,' he went on to complain, 'working, washing pots, sweeping, buying food, getting fed up with this already. I will try to get in to see you soon [Audrey was in Barnes Hospital in Cheadle, South Manchester, about 20 miles

---

[29] 'Most of the locals had, over the last couple of years, attempted to top-rope the stunning crack splitting the Yellow Wall. None had managed without falling off, so no one led it. [John] Hartley knew a chap by the name of Don Whillans, a strong and talented climber, whom they invited to try the route. The following Thursday evening, Don arrived at the crag, a top-rope was set up, and the line attempted. The same happened a week later, Don trying the crack again, this time looking more comfortable on it. It was on the third Thursday visit that Don abseiled the line, placed a wooden wedge in the first "zig" of the crack and proceeded to lead it, the wedge providing the only protection on the route. There was no doubt that Forked Lightning Crack was one of the most difficult climbs in the area. Hartley commented: "It must be hard, it took him *two* fags."' Greg Rimmer and Mick Ryan in *Yorkshire Gritstone*, ed. Graham Desroy.

away from Rawtenstall], but it's difficult from here. I'm really tired when I get home, falling asleep in the chair before I even get my tea. Well, sweetheart, mend up quick – I'm missing you more than I ever thought I could.'

A further crash on his bike in June prompted him to abandon two wheels and hitch-hike out to Chamonix, where he met up with an exultant Chris, who had reached the top of his second major Himalayan summit (the first had been Annapurna 2 in 1960). In terms of Himalayan achievement, the younger man was forging ahead of his companion.

> Have arrived OK though the sack nearly killed me. Chris arrived the day after me. By a stroke of luck he knows the chief of the mountain troops here at the Ecole Militaire des Montagnes. We have been invited to stop here free, grub as well and bloody good food it is. Chris thinks we can stay as long as we like. If you sell the bike, send some cash out with Ray Greenall. He is coming out with Fred in a few weeks. We are going round to Grindelwald and will stop a couple of weeks and hope the weather is good. After that we will come back here and live in luxury. The weather has been bad for the last week, before that good for a month.

They climbed a short route for training in the Aiguilles, and when Chris, who was gravely out of condition, argued for more of the same, Don – aware of how limited their joint funds were[30] – vetoed the suggestion and bustled them over to Alpiglen and the foot of the North Wall of the Eiger, the most notorious face in the Alps, the 'Wall of Death' of popular newspaper reportage, scene of numerous disasters, and still awaiting a British ascent. There they sat down to watch and wait – an activity at which Don was to become very proficient over the next couple of years: 'To climb the North Face, you've got to choose your moment, get on the mountain, get up it, then get off it as fast as possible.' With little money, they lived frugally on potatoes, vegetables and eggs, the question of who should cook them each day building into a quiet battle of wills: 'The trouble is, Chris, you're too greedy. You'll always crack before I

---

[30] They had £20 between them to last the whole summer, augmented by a loan of a further £20 from John Streetly.

do.' In the first book of his three-volume autobiography[31] Chris leaves a considered vignette of Don at the time:

> He had a rigid code of his own, that no one could make him budge from. He always thought carefully before committing himself, and then once committed could be relied on absolutely. He was intensely aware of his own rights, perhaps because he had to fight hard for them, and was bitterly aware of the limitations that his primary school education and upbringing had imposed on him.
>
> 'I'll meet any bugger halfway,' he often told me, 'but I won't go any further. I'm not going to be imposed on by anyone.'

Chris goes on to give a crucial insight not only into their climbing partnership, which for Don was to be the most substantial and productive since his early days with Joe, but also into Don's approach to mountaineering:

> This chip on the shoulder often made my relationship with him hard work; it meant that I had constantly to go more than halfway to find any point of contact. We couldn't have been more different in personality – where he was cautious, I tended to be impetuous, all too often undertaking something that, on mature thought, I could not fulfil. In the mountains I enjoyed making last-minute changes of plan, dashing off to climb this route or that, was restless if there was no climbing to be done. Don, on the other hand, decided the routes that he wanted to do, and was then quite happy to wait for them to come into condition, and was not prepared to fill in with anything second-best.

Their sojourn in Alpiglen proved to be in vain. One foray on to the face took them as far as the Hinterstoisser Traverse – the supposedly irreversible entry into the centre of the face:

---

[31] Their titles are: *I Chose to Climb*, *The Next Horizon* and *The Everest Years*. Taken together, although frequently and unfairly derided within the British climbing community – one review by the lancet-minded Scot Robin Campbell was of such memorable, breathtaking savagery it is a wonder Chris ever dared to venture into print again – they form one of the classic texts of modern mountain literature.

The Eiger came into perfect condition, we were ready, and the weather broke in the night, covering it in new snow. At the moment the weather is unsettled, and the face in mediocre state. If we don't climb it this time, I have learnt a lot about the face, and of the money angle to climbing it. Keep the money business under your hat! A newspaper has been in touch with us. We asked for £2000 for exclusive story and pictures. A telegram arrived which said they were interested and would make a concrete offer in a day or two, which although we may not get what we're asking, gives some idea of what it may be worth. Don't say a word to anyone . . .

They waited two more weeks: 'The snow level now is almost at the tents.' It was time to give up and move on, and Don had another ambition in mind, another 'last great problem of the Alps'. It was south-facing, on excellent rock, likely to come into condition very quickly, and had been attracting a considerable amount of interest in recent years – including an exploratory visit from Robin Smith after his ascent of the Walker Spur two years before. To counter-balance its more amiable characteristics, it was in as remote, high and serious a position as any in the Alps, high up on Mont Blanc, above the chaos of the Freney Glacier between the Peuterey and Innominata Ridges.

This was the Central Pillar of Freney. A serious attempt had been made on it early in July 1961, by a mixed Italian and French party of seven climbers which included Walter Bonatti and Pierre Mazeaud, and it had ended in the most catastrophic saga of post-war alpinism. Bad weather had caught them high on the pillar, below the final, overhanging 500-foot-high chandelle. With snow falling on them intermittently, they sat out the storm for three nights at an altitude close to 15,000 feet, hoping for the break in the weather that would allow them the easier option of escape over the top. The break never came, they were forced into an agonising retreat down the pillar, across the upper and lower Freney Glaciers, up to the Col de l'Innominata through deep snow in the continuing storm and over to the Gamba Hut. Four of them had died, only Bonatti, Mazeaud and Gallieni surviving.

Just weeks after this, Don and a Polish climber he and Chris had met in Alpiglen, Jan Djuglosz, decided (interestingly, in view of

Don's later chagrin at Chris's ascent of the Eiger) to attempt the Central Pillar. Chris did not initially join them. He had done no climbing since Nuptse, and felt in need of a training climb. He teamed up with Ian Clough, a Yorkshire climber he and Don had met in Chamonix of whom they knew by repute through an impressive alpine record, which had included first British ascents of the traverse of the Chamonix Aiguilles and of the French Direttissima on the Cima Ovest in this 1961 season, and his determined, if unethical, solution to the first winter ascent of Point Five Gully on Ben Nevis. Whilst Don and Djuglosz went up to the Col de la Fourche Hut, where they sat out threatening weather, Chris and Ian attempted and failed on the West Face of the Blaitiere before continuing to the hut at the Col de la Fourche to join them. The combined party was not the only one heading that way. The first ascent of this particular last great problem was becoming a race, with a strong team of guides from the Ecole Nationale de Ski et d'Alpinisme (ENSA) in Chamonix intent on the same goal. At the Col de la Fourche Hut, to remind them of the risks, a photo torn from a magazine of four climbers at the hut door was pinned to the wall. Three of them were dead and one – Pierre Mazeaud – was still recovering from his frostbite. And at midnight, like a phantom, a guide and his client entered, took up the hut book where Don had entered names and objective, read by the light of his head-torch, wrote, and slipped back into the night. When Don looked at the book next morning, the name leapt out at him: Walter Bonatti.

All this associative texture caused Don's thoughts to turn inwards as they mounted the lower slabs of the Central Pillar next morning. He thought, with regret, of Joe, and of how they had drifted apart, and he reflected upon the new partner with whom he was forging such a fruitful climbing relationship: 'We were an ill-assorted pair, but we balanced each other – his impetuosity, my stolidness; his volubility, my terseness. On a climb we made a sound partnership and I enjoyed climbing with him immensely. If Joe wasn't here, I could think of nobody better to share the climb with than Chris.'[32] They reached the foot of the chandelle and

---

[32] The reverse snobbery so prevalent in post-war British climbing has long loved to mock Bonington for his upper-class accent and his wholehearted attempts to communicate the nature of the mountain experience to the general public. He obviously became to an extent the victim of his own success as public

whilst the others prepared a bivouac, Don prospected the line ahead. A frantic studding of pitons led every which way, and hail began to fall. He retreated to the bivouac ledge. Chris returned to his high point in the morning and belayed as Don pressed on. One of the French guides with experience of the chandelle from a previous attempt had told them of a wide crack that would need thick wooden wedges. They had brought a sackful, but no crack of the right size for them appeared, and nor would the French party below, who had caught them up by now, lend them any that would be of use. After a pitch of extreme difficulty into an overhang-capped corner, Don took a stance in slings, brought Chris across, and made the decision to attempt to climb the impendent, thin corner crack without aid. At a desperate move into a chimney beyond the roof, Don fell off,[33] ending up 50 feet

---

spokesperson, encountering all the resistance that follows invariably in good fortune's wake, yet the degree to which he won Don's early respect is significant. As a rock-climber, he lacked the polished technique and gritstone pedigree of Whillans and Brown ('He's a clumsy bugger, Chris' is Brown's amused view), but was nonetheless, as his record of new routes in Scotland, the Lake District and south-west England shows, highly effective. As an all-round mountaineer, he has had few peers. One small instance from my own experience of climbing with him illustrates this. In the late 1960s we went to repeat a route on Anglesey's Red Wall – a 300-foot overhanging cliff of loose rock above a rotten zawn (i.e. rocky coastal inlet). This is usually approached by two long abseils down the opposite side from the cliff. By the time I had put my gear on and looked round for Chris, he had already started to climb unroped down the first of the abseils. We ended up soloing down into the zawn on appallingly loose, vegetated and slimy rock, the final section of it overhanging, with Chris relaxed and chattering away all the time as though out for a gentle walk on the fell. This enthusiasm of his and easy manner when out in the mountains or on the rocks has endeared him to most of those who have climbed with him, and helped counter the inevitable reaction within the anarchic community of mountaineers to his suaver management and promotional skills. I was once asked by the journalist and writer Peter Gillman, who was writing a *Sunday Times* profile of him, for an off-the-cuff opinion of Chris, and gave one which, over 30 years on, I see no reason to change: 'He's a really good guy, with two eyes on the main chance.' That the partnership between Don and Chris later defaulted – as with Joe – to bitterness and recrimination is, I think, more attributable to Don's sensitivity to perceived affront and betrayal, and demands for total, uncritical and unwavering loyalty, than to any particular failing on Chris's part, who has always made clear his primary allegiance to the activity itself rather than to any one individual within it.

[33] This raises the interesting question of wallet vs. hat, or who was the party treasurer. When he fell, Don lost his hammer and his hat. In *I Chose to Climb*, Chris records the hat-loss, and in his history of Mont Blanc, *Savage Snows*, Walt Unsworth relates how not only were Don's cigarettes in the hat, but also all the party's money, which showered down on the Frenchmen below. In his

lower and close to Chris, who then took over the lead. Cannily, using slings threaded round jammed stones and a peg on the lip of the roof, he climbed into the chimney and out on small finger-holds to a ledge beyond. It was the lead of his life from a man who, like Don, *in extremis* could be relied on to pull out every stop and blast through. Don joined him, and Ian and Jan prusiked up the rope. A couple of easier pitches lay ahead for the morning, the difficulties of the Central Pillar were behind them. Don had fallen from the brink of success. The limelight for solving the last great problem of the moment, inevitably, was going to belong to his younger companion. And Chris, the supreme communicator of mountaineering to the general public over the decades, both basked in it and turned it to advantage, securing sponsorship from the *Daily Mail* in return for an exclusive story – their next attempt on the North Face of the Eiger, to take place immediately. It proved more successful than the previous one, taking them to the Swallow's Nest, beyond the Hinterstoisser and below the first ice-field. But the temperature rose in the night, and the stone-fall that is so typical a feature of the face was whining down and pocking into the melting ice ahead. Chris, in his impetuosity, was keen to press on but Don ruled firmly for going down. 'There's always next year,' he stressed. 'The mountain'll still be here. The important thing is to make sure we are . . .'

A different mountain preoccupied Don in the last months of 1961. Whilst he was in Alpiglen, a letter had been forwarded to him from Frank Cochrane, a friend and fellow student of Ronnie Wathen's at Trinity College, Dublin. Cochrane had originally approached Joe with the proposition it contained, but Joe could not obtain leave from his new job as instructor at the White Hall Centre for Open Country Pursuits, and he suggested Cochrane approach Don. Would he like to lead an expedition of three Trinity students (one destined for holy orders – unlikely company for Don) and two

---

autobiography, however, Don – who was always keenly concerned about money – relates the following incident that happened as Chris led the roof pitch: 'During his big effort I had noticed something fall from his pocket and plunge down the couloir. "What was that that fell?" I shouted up to Chris. "My wallet," he replied sheepishly. The Freney was an expensive route: my hat, my hammer, and now all our money.' The other three climbers involved all being dead, on the grounds that 'He would say that, wouldn't he?', it seems unfair to ask for clarification from Chris.

Guinness employees – the brewery was one of the trip's sponsors – to attempt the unclimbed Aiguille Poincenot in the Fitzroy group in Patagonia?[34]

Audrey was just out of hospital, and Don asked her:

'I won't be able to go, will I?' I said you can go if you sell your motorbike. He wrote the letter straight away – 'I'm coming!' He didn't manage to sell the bike, of course, did some work for a local plumber, Eric Kershaw in Crawshawbooth, and when he went he had £12 to last him several months. Out of that he even managed to bring me back a small present. I lived on about two pounds a week sick pay. Friends used to say, 'I wouldn't let my husband keep going off for months like you do. I said, well, there's nothing to stop him. I'm quite capable of keeping myself, and I would go if I got the chance.

Don recalls that there was a slight problem that had been raised by the solicitor acting for them in the claim against the lorry driver in the motorbike accident:

[He] was very concerned about the report on my leg, which recommended that I don't go on the trip, and gave up climbing. Bit drastic. It says the damage is permanent, so if I gave up this trip it would be no better on the next, or any other trip at any time. So it is pointless putting off this. It stood a fair bashing on the Eiger and Freney and is only any trouble at all when descending, when I'm extra careful.

Another medical problem he and Audrey had to face before he departed for Patagonia was less easily circumvented. They had been married by now for over three years, no children had yet come along

---

[34] Derek Walker: 'The Irish students sent Don an article I'd written for the *Guardian* on the Towers of Paine and asked him to get in touch with me to see if they could change their plans and go for Paine instead. He and I and Chris met up in the Pen-y-Gwryd in October 1961, and I later showed Don my slides from the 1960–61 trip. Naturally, he was hooked but it was too complicated for the Irish to change their plans at this late stage. When I told him we were planning on going back to Paine in a year's time, his reaction was "Count me in!"' More on this in the next chapter.

and in 1961 Audrey entered her thirties: 'Don and I used to talk about when we had a couple of kids, but when it didn't happen we both went for tests. It was found that I had problems, and it would be a miracle if I produced any children. Don said that he wasn't that bothered, which I suppose most men might have been, so that was it.'[35]

Patagonia enthralled Don: 'The panorama had everything: the lake, dense green woods, glaciers, and the clean, honey-coloured ramparts and spires of the mountains. Overhead, huge condors glided effortlessly on the air currents. The beauty of the scene was breathtaking.' From an advanced base camp in a snow-hole, with Tony Kavanagh (one of the Guinness employees), Don equipped the first stages of the climb, and then the weather in this land of tempest intervened, playing cat-and-mouse with them for weeks until the very last day before they had to leave. Frank Cochrane suggested a last-ditch attempt, and they raced up the previously climbed approach to the shoulder of the mountain, and in rising winds began to climb the rock-ridge that led to the top of the peak. Pitch after pitch up strenuous chimneys and cracks, the snow eddying around them, suddenly gave out on to a brief ridge.

> A long traverse left, under some big blocks, led to the bottom of a slightly overhanging 20-foot corner. Don led up and still the rope ran out. My turn. I found the blocks pushed me off balance. I followed a pair of slanting cracks upwards and to the left and found Don wedged in a windy socket between two blocks. 'What now?' I called out. 'I think this is the top – I can't see anything higher.'

They were there. On his third expedition, Don had at last reached a summit. The descent, abseiling impossible because of the fierce updraughts, was exhausting. Don shepherded a tiring Cochrane all the way and after 18 hours of climbing they regained the safety of the snow-hole.

The Poincenot expedition was a significant one for Don.

---

[35] I've long pondered this, its focus, and the hurt, flat acceptance in Audrey's voice as she related it, which she did to me on several occasions. One woman friend of hers, who had better remain nameless, commented rather trenchantly, 'I wouldn't say Audrey never had a kid – she just didn't happen to have given birth to one.'

Impromptu though it had been, and with inexperienced climbers who were completely unknown to him before they left for South America, he had achieved a bold victory against weather and time on a dramatic peak in a remote and, at the time, little-known area. There is an underlying point here that is telling. On the Aiguille Poincenot the burden of responsibility for route-finding and leading fell entirely on Don, and the ambience of the expedition (Guinness employees and all!) was entirely unthreatening, the only perceivable adversary the objectified one of the mountain itself. So the Whillans persona that the situation brought out was the most effective and benign one. John Streetly, with whom he formed perhaps the most enduring and mutually respectful friendship of his life, left this brief note on the question of Whillans's personae: 'Don was a composite character and mixture of personalities. One was the calm and competent climber with whom it was an exciting pleasure to be. Another, less attractively, was the aggressive, cynical member of the pub crowd; yet another was the relaxed home person, happy in himself and a fund of funny stories.' Perhaps we're all thus, but Don was more so, more extreme in the divisions of character and their manifestations, than most. Where people were concerned, his guard initially was always up. He was not a man to tread lightly and circumspectly through the minefield of competitive egos that is mountaineering.

Perhaps the run of good fortune begun on Poincenot would continue. There was one obvious venue where it would be needed, and in July 1962 Don and Chris were back in Alpiglen to put it to the test:

> Don picked me up in Hampstead on his motorbike and I travelled pillion with him straight to Alpiglen, riding the bike all the way to the farm up the footpath. Conditions on the face were so bad that we just turned round and started down. Don's brakes failed halfway and as he accelerated, he shouted, 'Jump, Chris!' When I hesitated, he pushed me off, leapt himself, and the bike crashed through a fence. He repaired it on the spot, but I opted to walk the rest of the way down. We then drove to Chamonix and went on to the south side of Mont Blanc, climbing the South-West Face of the Aiguille Noire de Peuterey before returning to Grindelwald and Alpiglen.

No sooner had they arrived back, fit and climbing well, than they went straight on to the Eiger North Face in the afternoon of 25 July, and up to the Swallow's Nest Bivouac. Chris, newly married, clearly did not have his mind entirely on the job. A careless flick of the rope caused him to send his ice-axe clattering down the face, leaving one between the two of them. In the bivouac, water dripped all night and they woke to clouds wreathing the upper face and a heavy sky. With the leader taking the single axe ('For Christ's sake don't drop that, or we really will be in the cart!'), instead of retreating immediately as they had done the previous year, they elected to go a little further up the face, front-pointing at the side of the first ice-field to the Ice Hose – the gully connecting the two ice-fields. With stones starting to come down, Chris led out 150 feet of rope without protection on difficult and verglased rock to the side of the gully, belayed at the foot of the second ice-field and brought up Don. The face above was thawing, stone-fall increasing and the ice running with water. There was no option but to retreat. Just as they were coming to terms with the decision, they heard shouts from below and looked down to see a rescue party of Swiss guides approaching fast. They let them know that two British climbers were in trouble above them, and would need help. Don led off carefully on to the ice-field, cutting bucket-steps to facilitate their retreat. After a rope's length he shouted down to Chris that he could see somebody – a tiny red dot hundreds of feet above at the top of the ice, edging his way downwards. Don shouted up for the figure to stay where he was, and he and Chris led out rope-length after rope-length up the streaming and stone-pocked ice, laboriously hacking the big steps as they went. As they made their slow way up, there was a rushing and flapping in the air above them, and a rag-doll of a body thumped and cartwheeled down past them, bouncing finally off the lip of the ice-field and disappearing into space and void.

After a dreadful, heart-stopping pause, they looked up. The tiny red figure was still there. They climbed on, Chris in the lead on the last run-out. There are photographs in existence of the climber they had reached – Brian Nally – which bear out the latter's testimony that Chris's action on reaching him was to retrieve his camera from his rucksack and start taking pictures. Nally is poised, elegant even, a tangle of rope round his neck, making his way across sugary-looking ice, his eyes fiercely intent. An impression of competence in that medium starts out at you from the picture. This, it tells you, is a proficient ice-climber. As indeed he was, with the first British ascent of the North Face of the Matterhorn in 1961, another very determined winter attempt on the same route which all but succeeded in February 1962, and other difficult alpine ice-routes behind him. Nally claims that Chris's first words to him were, 'What paper are you with? I'm with the *Express* . . .' In Chris's account Nally asks, 'Are you going to the top? Can I tie on to you?' As far as Brian Nally's recollection goes, I do question whether there is a natural element of telescoping of events going on here. Bonington comments thus: 'I've no recollection of this conversation, but Nally's version sounds totally out of context and character with what I would have said at that moment – though at some later time, perhaps just before we met the assembled press at the window, I might well have asked him that.' For more on this, see note 37 below. Also, what really matters is not words here, but actions, and Chris's were wholehearted in climbing up to Nally and accompanying him safely down. Whatever the truth of the matter, clearly they were going down.[36] Nally's climbing partner, Barry Brewster, was dead, conditions were extremely dangerous on the face and deteriorating, and Nally himself would necessarily have been in shock. The incidental detail in Chris's account – of taking 20 minutes to untangle Nally's 300-foot rope – tallies with the photographic evidence. They started to descend, Nally being hit on the head by a

---

[36] '. . . we were just on the point of turning back ourselves, because it was obvious that bad weather was on the way. Then we saw the guides coming up and they told us there was a bloke needing help. When we saw him at the other end of the second ice-field I calculated we'd reach him just as the weather broke – and that's what happened. We were going away from safety in that situation, rather like going the wrong way down a motorway, knowing you can't turn round and getting further and further away from the place you want to go. Our only alternative was to abandon the bloke, and we obviously couldn't do that . . . it turned out . . . a bit unpleasant . . . stones falling all around, hail sweeping down the ice-field and water streaming down the face.' Don, interviewed in *Mountain* magazine, 1971.

'If I'm going on a serious climb, and things start to go wrong one after the other, one after the other, before I really get anywhere I will say, "This is no good – we'll come back." It's the basic feel of the job. If it's wrong, I think, "Come back another time – try again." You can only afford so many slip-ups and it's not many. [With Brewster and Nally] things were going wrong for them and yet they didn't come back, they just went on into a worse situation. With a bit of cunning you can always get back. When we got Nally off I found one abseil of 70 feet that cuts out half the first ice-field, the Swallow's Nest and the Hinterstoisser Traverse. If things start going wrong, you're over the worst of a climb and it's getting easier, then go on. But not when you're climbing into a worse situation. . .' Don, interviewed by T.I.M. Lewis, 1972.

Whillans and Bonington on the bivouac ledge at the top of the Central Pillar of Freney, 1961

Whillans and Bonington
alpine-bound in the
summer of 1962

Brian Nally at the top of
the Second Ice-field on the
North Face of the Eiger –
after Barry Brewster had fallen
to his death and at the moment
Chris Bonington reached him

Annapurna South Face 1970 –
Don belays Dougal Haston.
Note the Whammer at bottom
right. The mountain in the
background is Machapuchare.

Don and Mike Thompson arrive
at Camp Two on Annapurna –
a Whillans Box is between the
two tunnel tents

Torre Egger, typical of the
rock spires of Patagonia
(*Inset*) Mick Coffey jumars out
of the crevasse on Torre Egger

Making the headlines again, 1975

Daily Mail Friday, April 25, 1975

The day Tiger Whillans took on the law

THE Sherpas of the Himalayas don't call climber Don Whillans 'Tiger' for nothing — as five policemen discovered when they tried to arrest him after he was seen driving erratically early one morning.

For Whillans — only 5ft. 4in. tall, but built like a mountain—grabbed one round the throat, lashed out with his fists and feet and cursed and swore at the top of his voice, a court heard yesterday.

It was only after he had been handcuffed and two of the policemen sat on him in the back of a panda car that he was restrained.

At Rossendale magistrates court in Lancashire, 41-year-old Whillans admitted speeding at 60 m.p.h., driving with excess alcohol, assaulting a police officer and damaging police property.

Inspector Jack Withnall said that PC Ian Stanney saw Whillans driving his BMW saloon on the Bacup relief road at around 4 a.m. on March 26. The car was going fast and was 'sailing from side to side.'

He followed, and when the car accelerated, radioed for help. Near Haslingden, where Whillans lives at Grasmere Road, PC Stanney stopped the BMW.

When Whillans was told he had been speeding, he got out of his car 'with some difficulty,' swaying and leaning on the bonnet. 'He was, in fact, drunk,' said Inspector Withnall.

Shouting

'Then he quite deliberately lunged forward and pushed the constable backwards. Both his hands were around his throat as though he was trying to choke him.'

Another police car arrived and an officer managed to pull one of Whillan's hands away. But he kept hitting PC Stanney with the other hand.

Eventually he was handcuffed—all the while shouting obscenities.

As the officers tried to get him into the panda car, Whillans ripped the constable's coat, and pulled buttons off a sergeant's uniform.

Inside the car 'he was repeatedly kicking the passenger seat and the interior panels. He was continually lashing out with his feet and trying to smash the side windows.'

At one stage he kicked the panda driver on the head.

'It was only after two officers literally sat on him that he was restained—and all the time he was shouting obscenities.' said Inspector Withnall.

DON WHILLANS ... two policemen had to sit on him.

How to be 9 stone or less again –
Don in the Red Sea on the wreck of the *Umbria*

Gangotri 1981 – a portly Don meets a sky-clad yogi

Doug Scott's 1983 Karakoram ensemble

Don's last climb, Bill Peascod's last minutes – Great Slab, Clogwyn Du'r Arddu, May 1985.
Don's and Bill's climbing together had been arranged by Bill Birkett for a
magazine profile of the latter.

Back where it all began – and still goes on. Modern climbers Martin Crook and
Ed Douglas on the top pitch of Matinée at the Roaches – Joe's and Don's first climb together.
The Don Whillans Memorial Hut is situated just below the crag.

stone as they did so. When they reached him, Don greeted Nally with the line, 'Come on, lad – let's get down and have a cup of tea.' A brief storm ripped across the face and they cowered on their ice-peg belay. With an unerring instinct for mountain route-finding, Don discovered a line by which they could abseil to the lower end of the Hinterstoisser Traverse, and from there hurry across to the Stollenloch, the window on the Eiger North Face that leads to the Jungfrau railway line, where a press party and a special train were waiting. Within hours, Don and Chris's names and faces were splashed across the front pages of the European press as rescuing heroes of the Eiger. And Brian Nally's growing mountaineering reputation and future ambition were utterly destroyed as the uncomprehending and reductive gentlemen of the press bodied him forth in the disempowering role of helpless and hapless victim.[37]

---

[37] Understandably, this experience left Brian Nally extremely bitter, and he continues so to the present day, particularly against Chris. Yet there is no contradiction between the accounts both Chris and Don give of his state when they encountered him: 'I could see that the worst was going to happen: Nally would be a complete liability on the descent. His eyes were blank and his expression wooden. Shock, exhaustion and exposure had reduced him to a robot state.' (Don, in *Portrait of a Mountaineer*.) He was later reconciled to Don, and they became good friends. Nally's grievance against Chris seems rooted in a perceived lack of common humanity in the matter of that first purported question and greeting. To put that into one context, lower down on the climb, before the retreat, Don had accused Chris of 'being away with the fairies' over the matter of the dropped axe. His recent marriage, his having given up his job with Unilever to commit himself to professional climbing, his new contract with the *Express*, all would surely have been preying on his mind and – faced with a very dramatic photo-opportunity and story – this new direction may perhaps have over-ridden conversational niceties. My view is that the shock and confusion of events ensure the truth will never clearly be known.

For all that, it seems to me that Nally received brutal treatment at the hands of both the Swiss authorities (who presented him with a massive bill for a 'rescue' they failed to complete) and the British press, who portrayed him in an unfavourable, overambitious and incompetent light. He was clearly a very fine ice-climber who, given the good luck which the Eiger so often denies, would have developed into one of the leading figures of his generation. His companion, the 22-year-old Bangor University student Barry Brewster, was a brilliant rock-climber, possibly the most talented of the 1960s generation. They were a good team, had a right born of experience and competence to be where they were, had done their research and in better conditions might have pulled off an extraordinary coup. In the aftermath of Brewster's being hit by stones, taking a long fall, and probably sustaining lower spinal injury, Nally's care of his companion was beyond reproach. He deserves not only sympathy for the loss of his partner, but also far more credit than he has ever been given. I believe that the friendship Don later extended to him was based on recognition of that.

The publicity and commercialism they ran into sticking in his craw, Don persuaded Chris to go with him to the Kaisergebirge and Karwendal groups near Innsbruck (where Audrey and Wendy, who had hitched out from Britain, finally caught up with them), for some rock-climbing on steep limestone, after which they climbed the Cassin Route on the North-East Face of the Piz Badile in the Bregaglia in the phenomenally fast time of six hours. Both men were at the peak of their form, and conditions in the Alps were steadily improving, but Don had run out of money, a lecture date was pressing, he felt that the season was over and he needed to head back to Britain. Chris stayed on in Chamonix and met up with their previous year's companion from the Freney Pillar, Ian Clough:

> Ian and I just planned to do the Walker Spur. We climbed it so fast we reached the top about three in the afternoon, decided to bivouac on top, and next day traverse the Grandes Jorasses and the Rochefort Ridge to the Torino Hut with the thought of continuing the enchainment by doing the Route Major on the Brenva Face. But that night in the hut I realised we were both going as well as we ever would, and that with the good weather we were enjoying the Eiger would be in condition. I put the idea to Ian, and next morning we were on our way to Alpiglen . . .

With two bivouacs, in perfect, freezing conditions, they made the first British ascent of the North Wall of the Eiger. Only three weeks after his name had first been splashed across the newspapers, one of those 'heroic rescuers' was back on the front page with a new companion beside him. Public recognition as the face of modern British mountaineering was Bonington's as Don was heading once more back up the motorway to Crawshawbooth.

15

Too Much of Nothing

When a person in any field of endeavour starts to believe in the infallibility of their own judgement, the excellence of their own ability or their automatic right of precedence, however slowly it may come the inevitable consequence is the onset of decline. In the long view, 1962 can be seen as perhaps the cusp of Don's climbing career. Certainly there were successes thereafter, and among them two of the most notable ones he achieved. And yet, in 1962, before he is even out of his twenties, the Alps are beginning to fade from focus and his rock-climbing pioneering is over.[1]

---

[1] His last new routes on British rock were Forked Lighting Crack (1961) and the Direct Finish to Carnivore (the latter done with Derek Walker in June 1962) – some routes to sign off with! But given his ability, why were there not more? Why did it end there? The contrast with Joe Brown, whose pioneering curiosity and simple-hearted enjoyment of rock have sustained his interest and stimulated his activity into his seventies is stark.

With the Carnivore finish, both Don and Audrey had been angered by Cunningham's snatching the route, which he had completed by way of a long traverse right, using half a dozen pegs, to the edge of the crag, and another rising traverse back left above all real difficulties. Don did the forbidding direct finish using only one protection peg. Here's Derek Walker's account: 'The third day was gloomy and threatening . . . rain was sweeping across the valley again but fortunately we and the rock stayed dry under the overhang. Don hammered in a peg at the foot of the crack and laybacked out of sight. I had a desperate struggle following, weakening my feeble arms trying to remove the peg, and being hauled up the crack. When I emerged from under the overhang he was 40 feet higher, and after slipping and sliding up the wet, lichenous slab – also very hard – I joined him after the hardest pitch I had ever done.

'We walked down to the Kingshouse in the pouring rain. That was only the Tuesday, but we didn't climb for the rest of the week – he wasn't interested – and we went up north, touring, five-up in a mini-van. Audrey had heard there were palm-trees growing in Poolewe so we went there in hope of finding tropical sunshine. I climbed with him again about a week later at Tremadog. We were walking along the bottom of the crag, he looked up, and saw a climber falling

In Wales and on gritstone, a new group of climbers from yet another loose-knit and anarchic organisation, the Alpha Climbing Club, had taken over the mantle of the Rock & Ice and was making its own series of vanguard ascents. Clogwyn Du'r Arddu in particular was the scene of an orgy of exploratory activity by Pete Crew, Baz Ingle, Jack Soper, Martin Boysen and others. Their new routes from the early 1960s – Serth, Bow Right-Hand, Pinnacle Arete, The Pinnacle Girdle, West Buttress Eliminate, Daurigol, Great Wall, Scorpio and others – suddenly made those of the Rock & Ice era look rather amiable. There was a feeling around that climbing had moved on, though this was still tempered not only by the dark and brooding menace of Don's Clogwyn Du'r Arddu trio from 1955, but also by his technical masterpieces on Welsh rock like Grond and Erosion Groove Direct Finish, both of which retained a reputation well into the 1970s. On gritstone, of course, as we have seen in Chapter Thirteen, in their particular style – which is in the main inimical to modern climbing taste – his routes have an enduring status.[2]

To counterbalance this shift, Joe Brown, 'The Master', had embarked on a new exploratory phase of his own, and on the low-lying crags south and west of Snowdon had produced a series of technically difficult, sunny and entertaining little classics – Vector, The Fang, Hardd, Vertigo, Dwm, The Grasper, The Wasp among them – that subsequently attained great popularity. Don, mean-

---

repeatedly from the top groove of The Grasper. "That looks like 'Arry [Rock & Ice member Harry Smith] up there, and I reckon he needs a top-rope," Don said, and he flashed up the climb – then supposed to be the hardest on the cliff – and gave him one.'

There seems to me something curiously telling, motivationally indicative, in the fact that Don's last major new climb on British rock was essentially the settling of an old score. The Carnivore finish did not receive a second ascent until 1971, when the brilliant young Scottish climbers Rab Carrington and Ian Nicholson succeeded on it, and having done so spoke in awed terms of its difficulty and exposure.

[2] It seems to me in retrospect that the notion of climbing having taken a step forward around this time – predicated chiefly on the solutions, often in questionable style, being found to current 'last great problems'- was illusory. The hardest of the Alpha routes were of much the same order of difficulty as the harder ones climbed by Joe or Don. Although hints of progress had been given in the early 1970s by Syrett and Pasquill, the next major advance in standard to take place in climbing was not to come until the mid-1970s, was led by Livesey, Allen, Bancroft and Fawcett, and was underpinned by a complex revolution in protection, training and approach.

while, was basking in the adulation of his lecture audiences, playing up to the image of cloth-capped, beer-swilling Northern hard man, forsaking the habit of regular climbing,[3] and allowing himself to be consumed by bitterness about the outcome of his 1962 Alpine season. His partnership with Chris Bonington, which had begun so productively, in that season of 1962 stood revealed as one of climbing expedience rather than based in firm-rooted friendship and affinity. When not climbing, down in the valleys the two men had barely spoken to each other, and never socialised together. Don – aware though he was of the alpine weather-pattern that so often gives good, settled conditions in September – had lacked the flexibility of thought and action shown by his younger partner. He had held to his view that the season was over, missed out on the crucial climb he expected them to make together, and lost the return on it in terms of income and fame that he had outlined in his letter to Audrey (see Chapter Fourteen) and that were now Chris's alone. His resentment and chagrin exploded into a vicious letter, in which he accused Chris of cheapening the climb and selling out to commercialism. It was neither fair[4] nor diplomatic, and it was particularly untimely in view of the fact that both men were about to embark on a lengthy expedition together.

The invitation for the expedition had come from Derek Walker and Barrie Page. In 1961, as graduates of Bristol University, these two had taken part in a climbing and survey expedition to the Cordillera del Paine in Patagonia. It was the first British expedition to this mountain group, and the written accounts and photographs of the trip by Walker published in the *Manchester Guardian* and the *Liverpool Daily Post* had aroused considerable interest. Walker and

---

[3] 'I think your tastes in climbing change as you get older. Mine did anyway. I climbed on gritstone when I was young, but nowadays I can't be bothered to make the effort; it doesn't seem to have any challenge for me. When you have done a lot of one sort of climbing, the challenge goes out of it; you want to go further afield and find another challenge on different mountains and in different situations.' (Don in 1971 – expounding the philosophy of Casanova . . .?)

[4] Had Don been the successful one instead of Chris, he would assuredly have been subjected to the same misquotation and sub-editorial distortions, the same exaggeration into vainglory of what he had written, as was the fate, post-Eiger, of Chris. Those who yearn for celebrity and its rewards need to be ever-mindful of its more negative implications – which latter Bonington, for whom there is no need to act as apologist but about whom I feel this needs in justice to be said, has handled with considerable skill and aplomb throughout his career.

Page (the deputy leader in 1960–61) were planning to return there late in 1962 with the objective of two unclimbed peaks in the group of dramatic rock-spires known as the Towers of Paine. A natural diplomat, self-effacing and enthusiastic, Walker was not only a highly competent climber, he was also an indefatigably efficient organiser. A very experienced team was assembled, with Chris and Don, Ian Clough and John Streetly as its main climbing strength. Barrie Page, a geologist and fine natural rock-climber, was the leader; Vic Bray was photographer, and – controversially – there were three other people accompanying the trip: Chris's new wife, Wendy; Barrie Page's wife Elaine; and their two-year-old son Martin, the 'base-camp baby'. Even before the team left Britain, the frictions were evident. Nancy Banks-Smith, nowadays the veteran TV reviewer for the *Guardian* but then a junior staff reporter on the *Daily Express*, captured them humorously:

> The Patagonia expedition is taking two wives and a two-year-old child – a unique and unthinkable break with the tradition that Mountains are for Men. And if the experiment succeeds it will prove more, I feel, than the man with his flag on the mountain. For the women and the baby at base camp will have moved a whole mountain of prejudice. Elaine Page, the 28-year-old wife of the leader, and 24-year-old Wendy Bonington, five months married to the Eiger-breaker, could have grown into the kind of women who surround themselves with brick and bric-a-brac for security. If they hadn't married mountaineers . . .
>
> To Wendy, Patagonia is the wind in her hair and riding the half-broken horses of the nearest ranch. To Elaine, the mother of Martin, the base-camp baby, it is turning the wilderness itself into home: 'I can cook very good bread and cakes in a hole in the ground. I have made myself an efficient hairdresser with only cold water and a few rollers . . . Barrie and I always wanted to have children young, and still do all the things we'd talked about together. So . . . he's coming to Patagonia with us.'
>
> 'To Pa-ta-gonia,' nodded Martin, wisely.
>
> Like the demon king with crampons on, Don Whillans leapt into this idyllic scene. Page and Bonington grinned as he gave them his opinion straight and Lancashire fashion: 'Women are

out of place in a base camp. They fuss. They expect attention. They'll cause trouble among the Chilean cooks. It'll be "Do this" and "Have you done that?" till, ah . . .!'

He shoved the whole world of women from him with the flat of his hand.

'My wife's going as far as Trinidad and that's near enough for me.'

The more-trouble-than-they're-worth women said nothing. They were too busy cooking curry, cutting cake, brewing tea for 20.

'You'll see,' said Whillans indistinctly, having finished his curry and started on his wife's helping. 'Any more of this . . .?'

Page's grin, and Bonington's, were wider than ever.

Whilst Chris was enjoying his new-found financial freedom and the prospect of writing articles on the expedition for the *Daily Express*,[5] Don was filling in the weeks before their departure date by working for the outdoor company Black's of Greenock, at their Glasgow store:

> I am glad to say that I have begun to master the job of shop assistant. The first two days were terrible. Couldn't reckon up, give change, find the articles or the price, etc. etc. But today I finally mastered the cash register (bloody machine . . .!). One of the Creagh Dhu boys' wives works in the shop. I have to work Saturday mornings so will be going out to a small local crag on Sunday.

On 23 October[6] Don, Audrey, and the other team-members apart from John Streetly, who was in Trinidad and would make his own way to the base camp, embarked on the SS *Reina del Mar* in Liverpool and set sail for Valparaiso, Chile. After brief calls in

[5] The presence of 'Eiger conquerors' Bonington and Clough on the expedition, and the consequent link-up with the *Express*, meant that it was exceptionally well supported financially (the BBC was also providing funding). After their Eiger climb, Clough and Bonington had both been touring the country lecturing to audiences which frequently numbered thousands.

[6] It's worth mentioning that they were heading right into the heart of the Cuban missile crisis. The night before they sailed, Derek Walker and his future wife, Hilary, were listening to John F. Kennedy's hard-line speech together. They parted not knowing whether they would ever see each other again.

Santander and Vigo, on 4 November the boat disembarked Audrey in Port of Spain, where she was to stay with the Streetly family for the duration of the expedition. On 19 November it berthed in Valparaiso, and the team travelled on to Santiago. Don was met there, and wined and dined by a Rawtenstall textile millionaire ('I didn't manage to scrounge a million but I did have several fabulous meals on him'). The men with wives present went sightseeing, whilst the unattached expedition members organised transfer of equipment for the flight down to Punta Arenas from Santiago between variously making the rounds of official engagements and the city's bars and brothels.[7] A letter arrived from Audrey, and Don wrote back to her before the flight south:

> Dearest Audrey, I was most upset to receive your letter, and find things haven't worked out. I'd love to have you here with me, because I love you much more than you've ever thought, and to have dumped you somewhere for so long is misery, hurts me very much. If you came here, all the money we have would be finished, with nothing to back us when we get home. If you cannot bear to stay alone when John and Elizabeth leave, get your ticket transferred and catch the boat back home. I don't like the idea of you in an isolated spot with no white people about you for a long spell – it might be dangerous. If you feel you can't face it, go home – at least you will have friends about you . . .

Audrey duly and dutifully went home, John Streetly travelled to Paine to join the expedition, and the team set to work on the Central Tower, the most impressive of the group: although the South Tower is marginally higher, the Central Tower was regarded as the real prize. On Boxing Day 1962, Don again wrote to Audrey:

> Hope you had a good trip home in the *Reina*. We have been stuck in base camp for the last ten days. Bad weather. So far have only made 80 feet of climbing from the notch. Chris and John went up in fairly indifferent weather and knocked in a

---

[7] 'Not me!' protests Derek Walker. 'Remember that I was in love at the time. But I do remember that – especially later in Punta Arenas – we were all a little concerned that Don was leading Ian, who was very innocent, a little astray.'

few pegs, but it was too cold to do much. We had a good booze-up and Christmas Dinner yesterday. The Neilsons from the Estancia Cerro Guido came over. Had a letter from Dennis [Gray] saying the Rock & Ice dinner was a great success and with news of Vin Betts,[8] who's only worked 11 weeks in 18 months. He says he's enjoying life, drinking and wearing grass skirts . . .

The expedition progressed on the tower with excruciating slowness, pinned down by tempestuous weather and put under additional pressure by the arrival of an impressively equipped Italian team which included some of the leading Dolomite climbers of the day. Tents being useless in the conditions, Don and Vic Bray designed and built a prototype of what was to become the Whillans Box (see page 3), and it was erected in place of Camp Two. It had become obvious that the expedition's strong pairing would be Whillans and Bonington, who were barely on speaking terms. Chris made the first move, initiating the following, slightly Goon-ish dialogue:

'You know, Don, we've avoided each other up to now – I think we'd best get together.'

'Aye, I've been thinking on the same lines. We'd better do the next spell on the hill together.'

A brief lull in the weather having arrived, the teaming-up of the two most forceful climbers, with Page and Streetly in support, was immediately successful. With the Italians using their fixed ropes and closing on them fast, in scenes reminiscent of their ascent of the Freney Pillar the previous year Don and Chris raced up the Central Tower. At one point in a holdless position on a feature they had named The Big Slab, a hemp fixed line on which Don was pulling up snapped. Faced with the prospect of a 150-foot fall he somehow kept his balance, knotted the broken ends together and climbed calmly on. They left all their excess gear on the shoulder of the tower and reached the summit as daylight faded, before descending to bivouac on the shoulder. In the face of intense competition, and once again sharing the credit with Chris, Don had reached one of the most spectacular of the world's hitherto-unclimbed mountain summits.

The expedition drove home its advantage during continuing fine weather as Ian Clough and Derek Walker made the third ascent of

---

[8] Betts had emigrated to Australia initially, and later New Zealand, in 1960.

the North Tower of Paine. Don, Clough, Page and Walker also reached a point within 400 feet of the summit of the Cuernos de Paine, and Don, Clough and Page made good progress up the South Tower before the storms started up again. Don's letters to Audrey from the latter stages of the Paine trip are more than usually eloquent, and – Central Tower or no Central Tower – express strongly his continuing resentment of Chris:

Thanks for the letter and photo (glamour puss!). I don't blame the photographer for grabbing you! As you will have known long ago from the *Express*, we climbed the Central and North Towers in a spell of good weather, beating the slimy Eyeties to it. Chris was most upset when he fell and sprained his ankle and couldn't get down the mountain for his publicity, and even more so when he found that we had told the press about it (same as he did with all our little mishaps). He is not able to take a bit of praise without it going to his head. The boys and most of the people I've met here are sick of his name. Anyway, the sprain turned out to be a bad one and he left a few days ago. I don't think the girls enjoyed the trip at all, and as far as the expedition is concerned, they have been of no assistance in any way, and women in base camp has been a bigger flop than anyone expected. I knew it would be because of the type of females they are . . .[9]

---

[9] Derek Walker comments that 'the major problem was that Barrie who had apparently been given an ultimatum by Elaine along the lines of "We all go or no one goes" – had given us all the impression that the girls and the child would be accommodated in the estancias and not at base camp, but quite naturally this was too much to expect of the owners and managers of the farms, so after four weeks they were in base camp, where they had a pretty torrid time. Most of us felt, with Don, that they shouldn't be there, and we weren't very nice to them. Elaine, with the baby to look after in a tent in that weather, had a particularly hard time of it. She and Barrie divorced not very long afterwards, which I don't suppose was entirely unrelated . . .' Chris adds the following gloss: 'The original plan had been for the girls to stay on the Neilson ranch – this is what Barrie assured us and what attracted Wendy to the expedition. When it became evident that there had been no such invitation and that they were overstaying their welcome, they worked as unpaid domestic help for Pedro Radic for a time. He got fed up with Barrie and I staying on the nights we were down from the tower, so they had to move up to base camp. The boys refused to let them enter the communal tent, so Wendy and I camped a hundred yards away – very pleasant – and ate in a separate mess-tent. It's not surprising we ate at separate tables in Buenos Aires.'

We made an attempt on the South Tower, Page, Ian and I –
but were travelling alpine-style and after reaching a point
where we thought all difficulty finished found we needed
fixed rope in order to retreat safely in case the weather turned
bad. The Italians reached the top from the other side though
we didn't see them. They said their route was very dangerous
(ours wasn't dangerous). One of them, Taldo, had a damaged
head and hand and was whisked away for a check-up. His
crash-hat was split completely in two. It was a pity as he was
the only good bloke among them.

We attempted to climb the Cuernos the other day, but
couldn't get up the last 500-foot tower – bad rock, very steep,
not able to get a good peg in and snowing. Bonington has had
a rough time from the boys about his articles. Everyone is sick
of hearing about 'the bold explorer'.[10] He went to Punta
Arenas to be X-rayed and has cracked a bone in his foot – not
very serious. I think his fall shook him very badly.[11] It was a
miracle he didn't fall down the face.

It was a shock to hear about West and Spike.[12] I didn't care
for West, but Spike was OK. Ian has a letter from the
American Alpine Club offering a warm welcome to us (me,
Ian and Chris – we're not telling him!) if we are going to the
States this summer. It would be worth thinking about as we
may be able to cover our expenses with the showing of the
expedition film. Fancy a tour of the USA and Canada . . .?

---

[10] Having seen the press-cuttings from the trip, this seems to me unfair and bitter
comment. The phrases at which Don takes such offence are clearly of sub-editorial
origin, Bonington's articles themselves concerned not to grab attention for himself
but to give credit all round.

[11] During the descent from the Central Tower. The very last section of fixed rope
he was descending snapped as he was reaching the rest of the party at the notch
between the towers. Had he fallen the wrong way, it would have been down a 500-
foot face to certain death.

[12] Graham West and Spike Roberts, two leading members of the Manchester
Gritstone Club, were killed in an avalanche in the exceptionally hard British
winter of 1962–63. They were snow-climbing at Wilderness Rocks, just up the
valley from the Chew campsite which was the focus of Don's early climbing
activity. Graham West, a dynamic and ebullient character, was one of the most
accomplished artificial climbers in the country. His 1962 guidebook to *Rock
Climbs on the Mountain Limestone of Derbyshire* did much to dispel the mystique
and often-undeserved reputation for looseness that had discouraged most climbers
before that date from sampling limestone's leafy delights.

He gives a last glimpse of an expedition that was both successful and in some aspects rather fraught[13] in a letter from Buenos Aires: 'We met up with Chris and Wendy in BA and are now one big happy family (I don't think!). The Pages are on a different dining table, as are the Boningtons. Ian got himself in desperate heart-trouble over a female in Punta Arenas[14] and was nearly driven to distraction at leaving, mooning around for days wondering whether to go back.'

In the spring of 1963, his reputation in this sphere steadily growing and more material now to draw on, Don was heavily booked up for lectures, most of them organised under the aegis of Black's. He found time for occasional outcrop climbing. Whilst in London for a week he went down to High Rocks and Harrison's Rocks – the Wealden sandstone outcrops around Tunbridge Wells – and dismissed their routes tersely as ''ard, scruffy little climbs'. Mid-July saw him back in Alpiglen, in the company of Tom Patey and still hankering after an ascent of the North Wall of the Eiger. Patey records that his 'preparations for the Eiger – meticulous in every other respect – had not included unnecessary physical exertion'. He had whiled away the days in Chamonix, en route to Kleine Scheidegg, with 'sunbathing at the Plage till opening time', after which he would down six pints of beer a night, smoke 40 cigarettes, and play table football until closing time. The attempt on the Eiger with Patey – Don's fourth – ground to a halt at the foot of the second ice-field, from which they beat a rapid retreat. Although the climb ended once again in failure, it did have one notable outcome in the form of Patey's article for that year's *Scottish Mountaineering Club Journal* entitled 'A Short Walk with Whillans'.

This vignette by the finest comic essayist in climbing literature played a considerable role in establishing the persona of Whillans as doom-laden quipster and drollster, and in a mellow but perceptive way also brought out the character traits that were ultimately to contribute to the widespread disaffection with him among the companions on his later expeditions: the strategic indolence, the

---

[13] Despite all the resentment Don expresses in these letters against Chris, at the Easter shortly following their return, he and Audrey, the Boningtons, the Walkers and Mike Thompson all spent a very convivial long weekend together at the Boningtons' first home above a barn at Loughrigg.

[14] See note 7 above.

racism, the incessant scrounging,[15] and the propensity for dogmatic utterance that would brook no contradiction. It also, in a brief and masterful final paragraph, captured beautifully the sense that here was a man who, for all his unique abilities and exceptional achievements, had hanging around him something of the atmosphere of failure, something of the sense of one unloved by those gods who bestow good fortune and easy chance on humankind; and perhaps also the sense of one who was growing 'tired of knocking at preferment's door': 'We got back to the Alpiglen in time for late lunch. The telescope stood forlorn and deserted in the rain. The Eiger had retired into misty oblivion, as Don Whillans retired to his favourite corner seat by the window.'

To compound that sense, as Don left Kleine Scheidegg for the sunnier climes and campsites of the limestone Alps, two young men were making their own way up to Alpiglen. In the last days of July 1963, Dougal Haston and Rusty Baillie[16] made the second British ascent of the face, in conditions far from ideal, and the English press were there again to record the climb and celebrate the 'heroes' who had accomplished it. No one was going to be much interested now in who might make the third British ascent. There was some solace when Don returned to Britain in the form of a planned outside broadcast for television – the first of its kind on this scale. It was to take place on Clogwyn Du'r Arddu at the end of September, the climbers involved being Joe and Don, Ian McNaught Davis and the Frenchman Robert Paragot. The climb they were to do was a composite affair. It started up Joe's 1952 route on the East Buttress, Llithrig, moved right into the upper cracks of the 1927 climb,

---

[15] Don's virtual refusal ever to buy anybody a drink was legendary within the climbing community. Bill Smith of the Creagh Dhu has a good story on this: 'Whillans arrived at [a] do where there was plenty of drink and he was helping himself until the drink ran out and we had to go out for more but there was no sign of Whillans putting his hand in his pocket, which to us was the worst crime you could think of. The next day we all go back, about 20 of us, and shout the drink up. I had a whisky and a half-pint of beer, most of the lads had the same, and then we all stood back and said, "He's paying." He had a habit of that. I think he had been spoiled in the Lake District and Wales, people sucking up to him. It didn't work with us.' Derek Walker has a rather more kindly take on this, and suggests that Don never liked going to the bar because of his size, but would always, in his company, produce the cash when it was his round and say, 'Get 'em in for us, will yer?'

[16] Baillie was in fact Rhodesian by birth, though by this date he had settled in Scotland.

Pigott's, and finished above the Green Gallery with Joe and Don's
Pinnacle Flake of 1952.

The journalist and Olympic gold medallist Chris Brasher –
himself a good rock-climber in his day – was to provide the
commentary, Joe was to climb with McNaught Davis as the first
rope, Don with Paragot on the second. They spent three days
'rehearsing', which mostly meant skulking in pubs out of the rain
whilst the technical team set up camera positions, and on Saturday
28 September the broadcast went out live. It was by no means an
unqualified success. The rain was falling, wraiths of mist streamed
across the cliff, and most of the time the climbers could hardly be
seen or heard. 'Several hours of watching dirty cotton wool
twitching in a draught' is how one reviewer described it. But it had
a high point. The team had assembled on the big ledge atop the
massive pillar of rock in the corner taken by Pigott's. The final
cracks above were streaming with water. Anyone unacquainted
with cliff and route might think this 70-foot stretch of climbing at a
lowly grade of Very Severe to be straightforward. In fact, it is one
of the rare bits of devilry in the Welsh rock repertoire. Off-width is
the term, smooth is the texture, and green with lichen is the hue. Joe
took his craftsmanlike and considered time, Mac huffed and
floundered and gasped, Paragot was plainly ill at ease. Don shot up
in one continuous burst of movement so masterful and dismissive it
made the others' efforts look for the most part amateurish and
ineffectual. He had stated his case for pre-eminence as a rock-
climber in front of the largest audience yet for the sport, and he had
comprehensively ruined his chance of much further employment in
that medium. Brutally, he had just made it all look too easy.[17]

A week later, his potential income took a further blow when he
was admitted to a Scottish hospital:

I am OK but as usual fed up. All the trouble fixing the lectures
and the lot gone in one go. I cancelled the first four at Carlisle,
Newcastle, Old Dungeon Ghyll and Littleborough, but have
left the Women's Institute Lumb-in-Rossendale still open.
Though may have to cancel that and the next one as well. It's

---

[17] Don and Joe had made a winter ascent of this climb in heavily iced conditions
10 years before. On the evening after the broadcast, Derek Walker recalls meeting
Don and Audrey in the Pen-y-Gwryd, and a jubilant Audrey proclaiming that
'You showed 'em you can still do it, didn't you, Don!'

cost us £40 already. I'm not sure what the trouble is. It may be appendicitis. But I feel dizzy whenever I sit up. I've missed my week at the factory as well. I don't think it could have happened at a worse time. Still, enough depression. I thought you'd find paper-hanging more difficult. Which room have you done, and what colour? About the car, I think leave it till I arrive back at 222. I can't really see that our choice is a bad one. It's the same as the Mini, but with much better finish inside and out, and I think a better design, boot, radiator, etc. I can't write much more as me eyes are getting dizzy and this makes me feel sick. Cheers the noo, sweetheart.

The cause of his hospitalisation proved to be another bout of labyrinthitis – the vertigo-inducing condition that had troubled him recurrently since the age of 17. That he was not going to let it curtail his continuing mountaineering ambition is made plain by his contacting Dennis Gray soon after his discharge from hospital, and inviting himself on an expedition of Rock & Ice members that Dennis was organising to the Nepalese peak of Gauri Sankar.

Thirty-six miles to the west of Chomolungma and straddling the Nepalese–Tibetan border (a fact that rendered choice of route on the mountain politically sensitive, Tibet being closed at the time), Gauri Sankar is clearly visible from Kathmandu. With its summit at an altitude of 23,440 feet, and its defences on the Nepalese side savagely unbroken, it was a peak very much in an idiom that was to become popular from the 1970s onwards – of lesser height than the giants of the Himalayas, but far more technically demanding by any line than the ordinary routes to their summits. To attempt its ascent, Dennis – a fine rock-climber who had amassed alpine and Himalayan experience since his 1958 introduction to mountaineering on the Grand Capucin – had assembled a team which included Dez Hadlum and Terry Burnell, two gifted young rock-climbers from the new Rock & Ice; Ian Howell, a forceful and competent climber who had spent much of his life in Africa; Ian Clough, with whom Don had formed a strong alliance on the Towers of Paine expedition; and Don himself. Most of the party were to travel out to Nepal by Land Rover, and their leaving party was held in Don's local pub, the New Inn, on 12 July 1964. Don, according to his diary, bought a large barrel of beer (other sources have it that the

barrel was donated by a local brewery, which seems more likely).
Tom Patey arrived in his Skoda on his way down from Scotland to
collect Joe Brown for what was to prove a very successful alpine
season. The pub door was smashed in the course of what the legends
tell was a violent altercation between Don and a woman by the
name of Violet, and Don had to spend the following Monday
pacifying local sensitivities by 'cleaning up the mess after the party,
replacing the broken windows', and returning her shoes to another
woman.

The Land Rover departed from Leeds three days later and Don
himself set sail from Liverpool on the RMS *Celicia* with the
expedition's baggage late in July. He wrote to Audrey ten days later:

> I'm already as red as a lobster even though I try to keep out of
> the sun. The ship is a good one, all one class which makes it
> much better. The bloke from the other expedition is a card,
> looks like Alistair Sim. I've begun reading *How Green Was
> My Valley*. I have been playing deck tennis quite a lot, and
> think I'm getting a bit thinner. Keeping the booze down to
> reasonable amounts too. I've made a start in writing the
> book,[18] but will have to see how it goes.

The boat called at Port Said, Aden, Karachi – where Don fell ill
with a stomach infection – and finally Bombay in torrential
monsoon rain on 13 August: 'Bombay is better than Karachi – at
least what I've seen of it . . . I was reading yesterday that there are
70,000 prostitutes (keep me busy!!).' He arranged for the forward-
ing of the baggage, travelled by train to Calcutta to see it through
Indian customs, oversaw its packing on to a lorry, and accompanied it to Kathmandu via the border customs post of Raxual – a
by-word for official officiousness, where Don's diary tersely
records his spending three days and having to call on the services
of the Nepalese military attaché, Charles Wylie. The undisclosed
subtext here appears to have involved the snapping of Don's
patience and a resultant savage mêlée with armed guards and

---

[18] Commissioned by Heinemann and eventually written in cooperation with the
journalist Alick Ormerod and published as *Don Whillans: Portrait of a
Mountaineer* in 1971. Then, as now, mountaineers are notoriously slow at
delivering their manuscripts . . .

Gurkhas that necessitated Wylie's intervention to keep Don from a gaol sentence.

In the immediate post-monsoon period, the expedition set off on a 13-day approach march that all involved were to remember as one of the most unpleasant experiences they had had in the mountains. A nightmare of leeches and mud, it resulted in infected bites and blood poisoning for both Don and Hadlum. When they finally reached the mountain, there were further unseen difficulties awaiting them. The aerial photographs the expedition had obtained proved gravely misleading in the matter of viable lines of ascent. Their projected route up the west ridge of the mountain was plainly not feasible, and in conditions of intense cold the logistical chain was stretched to its utmost in traversing across steep ice and difficult climbing on the north-west face to a gully line giving out to the more reasonable north ridge. The mountain held its surprises right to the last. The gully proved to be hard ice at an angle of 70 degrees, and it was not in good condition. Only Don and Ian Clough were still sufficiently strong after the arduous approach to attempt it. From a camp in an ice-cave in the steep face at its foot, Don reached a bulge in the gully a rope's length from easy ground. His mountain sense somehow alerted him to danger. He stopped, considered, listened to the eerie silence. Suddenly it was broken as seracs peeled off from above and huge ice-blocks came cascading, bounding and ricocheting past them, roaring over the ice-cave camp and ripping out their fixed ropes. Miraculously unscathed, Don and Ian retreated to the ice-cave to spend another frozen night, and then descended to a lower rest camp that had been fitted with a heavy manufactured prototype of the Whillans Box.

Four days later they moved back up to the ice-cave and made a further attempt. So cold had it been that both men were dangerously close to frostbite as they left the cave. Spindrift lashed them as they huddled in the gully. They had not even reached their previous high point when Ian – as durable and resolute a mountaineer as Don had ever climbed with – signalled his need to retreat or face serious frostbite. It was the first day of November, temperatures plunging. They went down, packed up the camp, and as they were retreating off the face a stupendous avalanche sheared off from high above and scoured the route they had just taken: 'The climbing must have been as difficult as any done in the Himalayas,' Don wrote to Audrey. 'Our best Sherpa – dozens of big expeditions

– shat himself[19] and went down three camps after one day. If we hadn't packed up on the mountain, another of the New Inn locals might have been missing.'

On the descent from the mountain Don tore a cruciate ligament. The march back to Kathmandu was agony. With a degree of understatement and irony, he wrote to Audrey, 'I enjoyed the trip, but will be glad to start for home.' He sold and bartered his gear in Kathmandu, climbed into the Land Rover with the rest of the expedition apart from Dennis, who was sailing home with the equipment, and set off to drive back to England through Pakistan and Iran. In Munich – Don's old obsession reasserting itself with a possible new twist – they tried, but failed, to make contact with

---

[19] This, if literally true rather than figurative, is an insensitive thing to write or say about a Sherpa, and seems to me a fair point at which to comment on two things. The first is the strong thread of racism in Don's responses to people of different cultures at times (though it also needs to be noted that he did get on well with the Sherpas on his 1970s Himalayan trips – the mutual addictions to boozing and womanising giving them much common ground). This doesn't seem to me innocent or stemming from ignorance – though in another sense it is exceedingly ignorant – but rather a product not only of his own Lancashire working-class culture, and having grown up in that myself I can testify to its racist propensity, but also of a supposedly comic, assumed bigotry, very much in the Bernard Manning vein. Nat Allen told me of Don's habitual response when he descended on Nat in Derby and was given one of Nat's standards – egg and chips for his tea: 'Not fucking nigger's lips again, is it, Nat?'

The second, and more general point to be made here is regarding the treatment by western mountaineers and expeditions of the indigenous hill-peoples upon whom they rely heavily for logistical support. All too frequently this defaults at best to insensitivity, at worst to mockery and insult. The vilest example of this that I came across was during a period of a couple of months that I spent at the exquisite high meadow of Tapovan, above the source of the Ganges with Shivling – arguably the world's most beautiful mountain – soaring beyond. A Czech expedition attempting a new route on Shivling was also camped there, with a liaison officer, Haresh Thakur, from Himachal Pradesh. Haresh was an exceptionally pleasant and intelligent young man and a devout Hindu. The Czechs continually taunted him by feeding him beef. He eventually moved into our camp – we were living on cabbage curry and aloo paratha – and with our 17-year-old liaison officer, both of them in borrowed and inadequate gear, ran up and down Shivling, the ordinary route on which has some quite technical climbing, in a day. Which says something not only about western rudeness, but also about the scale of our pretensions in these environments. If the physiologically adapted local people had the technical training and equipment of western mountaineers, they would make all our efforts seem paltry. Final point – the bad example set by some western climbers in the greater ranges is not, I'm glad to say, universal, and some of the projects initiated by mountaineers like Sir Edmund Hillary, Doug Scott and Dr Jim Duff are both altruistically motivated and socially beneficial.

Toni Hiebeler, who had made the first winter ascent of the Eiger North Face in 1961, and whose book about the climb, *North Face in Winter*, had just been published in Britain. On 17 December, in good time for Christmas and with another momentous effort expended on a climb that had come so close to success, the most gifted nearly-man of British mountaineering was home. Don was back in Crawshawbooth and rehydrating in the New Inn.

His knee continued to trouble him and restrict his activity, until eventually, in March 1965, he gave in to the inevitable, opted for surgery and was admitted to the Northern Hospital in Liverpool, where he spent three weeks. He was also, throughout 1965 and 1966, being troubled by frequent and severe attacks of vertigo. Determined, nonetheless, to pick up the threads of his alpine ambition, he travelled out to Chamonix with Derek Walker in July, intent on climbing the North Face of the Dru. The weather was bad, and hanging out in the Bar Nationale they met up with Gary Hemming,[20] who suggested they head for the Dauphine, where they climbed the classic Pierre Allain route on the South Ridge of La Meije. Their bivouac before and after the climb was on the site of the old Promontoire Hut, which had been destroyed by an avalanche and was under reconstruction. The workers had stored copious quantities of beer under the platform on which they slept, to which Don and Gary helped themselves. Back in Chamonix, the weather was still bad, so Don and Derek set their sights on Zermatt. Having failed so repeatedly to climb the 1938 route on the Eiger, Don downscaled a little, and with Derek and Ian Clough's wife Nikki decided on a centenary ascent of Edward Whymper's 1865 route on the Matterhorn, the Hornli Ridge: 'It's like Blackpool Promenade,' he commented, viewing the continual procession of summit aspirants with a jaundiced eye.[21]

The attractions of Zermatt having quickly been exhausted, and Derek having arranged to pick up his wife Hilary in Geneva, Don returned to familiar ground in Chamonix and the Biolay, where he

---

[20] For more on the character of this influential American climber, see Mirella Tenderini's excellent *Gary Hemming: The Beatnik of the Alps*.

[21] Walt Unsworth: 'In a Zermatt bar with the Cloughs and Derek Walker, Don demanded the band play "Ramona", which he swore was his favourite song. Lighting up a fag, he said ruminatively, "I gave these things up once." "Why did you start again, Don?" I asked. He thought for a moment and said, "I reckon it was the tension of me 'olidays."'

teamed up with another young star of the Rock & Ice, Jimmy Fullalove, and tested his repaired knee a little further with an ascent of the Frendo Spur. Usually a straightforward climb, in the face of terrible snow conditions on the final, long arete it proved to be more arduous than Don had expected and they returned to Chamonix exhausted. Short of money, they were faced with the choice of eating or drinking and opted for the latter. The decision was fortuitous. All the butchers of Chamonix were in the Bar Nationale playing football, so Fullalove issued forth again, lifted all the barbecued chickens displayed on stands outside the butchers' shops, and he and Don feasted on them back at the Biolay that night.[22]

A conversation with Dave Bathgate, one of the 'Edinburgh Squirrels' who had become a driving force in Scottish climbing by the mid-1960s, led to Don's heading over to Leysin, near Geneva, where he encountered the two men who had beaten him to the second British ascent of the Eiger two years before. Chris Bonington was about to officiate as best man to Rusty Baillie, and invited Don along to the wedding reception, where he was introduced to the

---

[22] Sociological fact: shoplifting was endemic among British climbers in the 1960s and 1970s – a part of the prevailing anarchic ethos of the activity at that time, and a competitive sport in its own right. French supermarkets were a particular target, and jackets with poacher's pockets an essential item of equipment for the provisioning of alpine seasons. Climbing equipment stores were also ransacked wholesale, gear often being stolen to order, and many of the leading figures in the sport were involved. This thievery was not only restricted to abroad – I remember being strolled through an Ilkley liquor store by one of the great names of British climbing in the 1970s. At the spirits shelf he carefully manoeuvred me between himself and the security mirrors, pocketed two bottles of Glenmorangie, and without a moment's hesitation walked out, leaving me open-mouthed at the sheer brazenness of it all. This same climber used to do his regular shopping in the same way, total up what he had 'spent', and ask his girlfriend for half the cost. Never trust a climber!

It's worth noting that the reaction of Joe – who remembers his tent at the Biolay having strangely filled up with lettuces one day – and Nat Allen to the thieving activities of the younger Rock & Ice members in Chamonix this season was strongly censorious, the good name of the club being invoked, etc. Don's attitude was more ambivalent. As with the beer 'found' at the Promontoire Hut, he seems to have been prepared to avail himself of the booty but not to engage in the crimes. On a trip to Alaska in which he took part in the 1970s, the provisioning of the expedition involved a van, a supermarket, and no exchange of cash. It's not recorded that Don went hungry on this expedition, though his eyes were out on stalks and he proclaimed later that he'd 'never seen 'owt like it!'.

pre-eminent American climber of his generation, Royal Robbins. Royal was working as Sports Director at the American College of Switzerland in Leysin – a finishing school essentially, but co-educational and with something of an outdoor bent – and he invited Don to stay with him and his wife Liz: 'Don stayed with us in Leysin and Liz complained to me about his leaving cigarette ashes about. The bravest thing I ever did was to ask Don to mind his smoking habits. Actually he was surprisingly gracious about it.' Royal had just taken on Mick Burke – a young climber from Lancashire – as an instructor, and enquired whether Don would be interested in working there too. Compared to the prospect of returning to Crawshawbooth and looking for plumbing work again, the offer was enticing. So Don became instructor, PE teacher and proctor at a school for rich young Americans, and in October, Audrey came out to join him there. Also in Leysin at the time, and running the newly founded International School of Mountaineering, was a former USAAF pilot called John Harlin. An outstanding athlete who was building up an impressive record of climbing in the Alps,[23] Harlin had one over-riding obsession. He had already tried to entice Don on to his instructional staff with a view to involving him in the project. Now that Don was in town, he put the proposition to him. Was he interested in attempting a direct route up the North Wall of the Eiger that winter of 1965–66? Don listened, weighed up the attraction, the difficulty and the likely problems, and after a week's consideration told Harlin flatly that he was not interested.

Harlin, meanwhile, had recruited a formidably talented American aid-climber, Layton Kor, with whom Don had recently been climbing around Leysin, and the young Scot Dougal Haston. Chris Bonington had been commissioned by the *Daily Telegraph* to photograph the climb, Chris in his turn enlisted Don on to the *Telegraph* payroll to act as his 'minder', and so another chapter in Don's involvement with the Eiger North Face began. As involvements go, it proved to be rather a brief one. In February 1966 a team of eight Swabian alpinists suddenly turned up and began to lay siege to the face. The newspapers sensed a race between them and the American–Scottish team.

---

[23] This included the American Direct on the Dru, the Hidden Pillar of Freney, the South Face of the Aiguille du Fou and the North Face of the Eiger in 1962, shortly after the Whillans/Bonington/Nally episode. He had also, amusingly, once tried to persuade the Sherpa Tenzing Norgay to attempt it with him. As with Don, the invitation had been turned down.

Harlin and his two companions set off for Kleine Scheidegg, and Kor and Haston made some progress on the projected line, whilst the gentlemen of the press made much of the competition expected to take place. Don, who had buckled down with Chris to the unaccustomed role of load-carrying and provisioning camps on the face, cast a sardonic eye over the proceedings, proclaimed that 'if it's a race, it's the slowest race in the world', and after three weeks returned to Leysin, where Audrey by now had arrived. The remaining climbers joined forces, and Kor and Bonington led two crucial and difficult pitches that proved to be the key to the route. And then, as the Harlin team was pressing home its advantage, tragedy struck. Two days after his return to Leysin, Don had to face the task of going round to the Harlin flat with Audrey and telling Marilyn, John's wife, that her husband was dead. A fixed rope had broken[24] whilst he prusiked up it and he had fallen 3000 feet to the foot of the face. He was buried at Leysin on the afternoon of 25 March. That morning, in savage conditions, four of the Swabians and Dougal had reached the top of the Direct, and the wild-eyed young Scot had become the new national mountaineering hero.

The arrangements between Don and the American College did not prove mutually harmonious. He had taken over as Sports Director – rather to the pique of Mick Burke, who had been there longer – from Royal Robbins when the latter returned to America in April. There was thereafter a good deal of bickering about money, about Audrey's employment, about Don's frequent absences, and a certain amount of disapproval had been engendered too by Don's habitual character traits. His marital infidelities and crude passes at women strained loyalties in a small community where Audrey was both known and liked, and his capacity for violence on occasion transcended anything that could remotely be taken as comical or heroic. On one occasion in the bar of Leysin's Club Vagabond, Mick Burke

---

[24] One of the many reasons Don had for not getting involved in a serious climbing capacity with the Eiger Direct route was because of his reservations about the diameter of rope to be used for the fixed lines – too thin, he had argued, to withstand the abrasion consequent on storm and heavy use. He also had an altercation with Harlin which he recounted to Leo Dickinson years later in the following terms: 'D'you know what that fucker said to me? He said, "I don't want you on this mountain." So I went up to him and said, "Listen, cunt, when you own this bloody mountain, then I'll listen to ya – and until then I'll go where I bloody well like. Got it . . .?" '

witnessed him smashing a glass in a South African's face.[25] Nor did his attitudes to the students endear him: 'There were many occasions when I would dearly have loved to have belted some of the troublemakers.' All this seemed to the college authorities a little too much like trying to house a nest of rats alongside the food in the larder. He left the American College, worked briefly at the International School of Mountaineering, and by mid-August he was back in Crawshawbooth and preparing for his next move. Whilst in Leysin, he had made contact with several of the most prominent American climbers of the era: Harlin himself, Royal Robbins, Layton Kor, Yvon Chouinard. On 20 August 1966, he flew out for an indefinite period from Paris to New York on a ticket he had been given by an American whilst climbing in the Calanques at the beginning of the month – and he flew alone. Audrey's correspondence to him at this period makes it quite clear that the years of neglect, of being taken for granted, and on occasion of public undermining and abuse were beginning to tell. She and Don were beginning the longest separation in the course of their marriage.

Don was met in New York by Royal Robbins and they drove west, fetching up on 26 August in Boulder, Colorado, where they stayed at the home of an extremely strong and talented[26] young climber called Pat Ament and next day went climbing in Eldorado Canyon, where Ament lured the two older stars on to his recent testpiece, Supremacy Crack:

> Leading above Royal and me, Whillans passed by all the fixed pitons in a virtually unprotected solo lead. His rope hung down free along the yellow rock, passing between the rock and Royal, who was unanchored on the belay stance. In my presumptuous way I informed Royal that if Whillans fell the rope would pull Royal off. Royal answered in a kind of cold way, 'I'll take that chance . . .'

[25] Don himself had a slightly more innocent account of this: 'I remember one occasion when I smashed a bloke in the face with my fist with a glass in it. I never even thought about it. I couldn't get at him quick enough. But most of these situations are caused by a bloke being unreasonable. I don't like it, because often you find yourself going into a scene just to save face, and really you feel like telling the bloke to clear off.'

[26] Multi-talented, in fact – Ament's output as climber, musician, film-maker, writer and poet has been distinguished and prodigious over four decades. At his best, Ament seems to me one of the most delicately gifted of all writers on the sport.

Two days later, Don and Robbins arrived in Yosemite and Don was handed over into the care of a man many have seen as his American counterpart, the squat, bald and bearded Chuck Pratt. At the time, British visitors to Yosemite were few. There were points to be made and points to be scored. He and Pratt downed a few six-packs, slumbered in the sun, and roused themselves towards evening for a climb called Pharaoh's Beard. Pratt led out 150 feet of rope without any protection. Ament's impression of his performance on Supremacy Crack notwithstanding, Don was unfit, overweight, having difficulty adjusting to the rock, and found it desperate. Next day he went to ask a drink-befogged Chuck about it. 'Did we do a climb?' was all the response he got, together with a puzzled look. But the day after, the sand-bagging began in earnest as Chuck and Don and two keen younger climbers, Tom Garrity and Eric Beck, all took a trip down-valley to Elephant Rock to pay their respects to the Crack of Despair. Garrity and Beck led off first, and despite having done the route previously, struggled on the first pitch and took falls off the second. Chuck invited Don to lead the first pitch: 'I concentrated on the moves ahead and, climbing quite well, I completed the pitch without much trouble.' Pratt led on up a crack previously climbed on bongs.[27] When Don's turn came to follow, he managed it with some difficulty. It was the route's fourth ascent. Honours were even as Don left the valley to join Royal at Tahquitz.

For the next two months Don stayed mostly at Camp Four in Yosemite Valley, partying, swimming in the river, sunbathing, listening to Bob Dylan, Mozart and the Rolling Stones, and rock-climbing more intensively than he had done in years. New people, new cliffs, and routes that followed classically pure lines on perfect rock rekindled his enthusiasm. With Pratt he climbed Enigma and the Left Side of Slap Happy Pinnacle; others partnered him on Moby Dick and the East Face of El Capitan; he climbed Braille Book on the gleaming, ice-scoured slabs of Higher Cathedral Rock, the Steck-Salathe on Sentinel Rock, the Lost Arrow Spire and the

---

[27] Large pitons that looked and sounded like cowbells. It took American climbers some time to realise that wherever you could place one of these, you could also find good jams. Martin Boysen's 1967 free lead of the crux artificial pitch of the American route on the South Face of the Aiguille du Fou – a climb on which several very strong French parties had failed – caused great consternation Stateside, but proved exactly this point.

North-West Face of Half Dome with Dez Hadlum and Terry Burnell from the Rock & Ice, who had arrived in Yosemite on their way home from a successful expedition to Alpamayo in the Cordillera Blanca of Peru.

With the first frosts of the fall settling in Yosemite, Don took up an offer from Yvon Chouinard to work in the factory he had set up at Ventura to manufacture climbing gear. 'Fitting slings on hammers, fitting gates on krabs – Yvon off surfing!' He bought a Chevrolet, found a place to live, dated nurses, partied hard, had the occasional fight, ground rurps all day, or hammer-heads or Lost Arrow pitons, and a week before Christmas Chouinard gave him the sack. Royal Robbins again: 'Apparently Don wasn't up to snuff and Yvon had to let him go. Chouinard says, "Firing Whillans was the bravest thing I ever did."'

Whilst Don was away in California, back in Crawshawbooth Audrey was receiving from another source the attention Don had so long denied her: 'Saturday 7 January 1967. Went to a party at our Mavis's. Good night. Harry went funny. I said I would pack him in. He asked me not to.' For week after week in the first months of 1967, Audrey's diary focuses entirely around Harry. He takes her out to the cinema, they go dancing and for walks together, attend his running club dinner, he buys her antiques and trinkets, has her fire lit and tea ready when she gets home from work: 'Harry didn't go home', 'Harry stayed the night', she assiduously records. He follows her around devotedly, all their weekends are spent together, they have rows when she goes out for the evening with her women friends: 'Picked up Harry straight from work. Had words about me going out with the girls. Made it up after.' They visit each other's parents and relations, stay together with mutual friends, are daily – and frequently nightly – in each other's company.

Having spent January and February drifting around the States, and with his six-month visa on the point of expiry, into this brief idyll suddenly on 9 March the return of Don intrudes. For the next few days Audrey's diary is full of references to Harry phoning her at work, writing letters to her there or his aunt writing to her on his behalf, meeting her in pubs in the evening or at his aunt's in Rochdale. After a month of surreptitiousness, finally on 3 April this: 'Went to see Harry straight from work. Told Don about Harry.' Don's response was to be 'hurt and upset'. For a few more weeks Audrey struggled on, seeing Harry, tending to Don, trying to sort things out, until she finally broke with the former in mid-May: 'Don went to hospital for his vertigo. They put him on pills. Went to see Harry. Told him I wouldn't see him for a month. Harry upset. Wouldn't let me go home.' Six weeks later, having resolved his marital difficulties and collected a substantial royalties cheque from Karrimor for the 'Don Whillans Alpiniste' rucksack the company was manufacturing to his design, Don was flying back out to America.

In June and July of 1967, Don hung around New York City and the upstate crag of the Shawangunks for a month, bouldered in Central Park, partied, even went to rock concerts in the 'Summer of Love', and finally lit out for the territory and drove west to Wyoming, where he visited Yellowstone National Park, bathed in the hot springs, climbed the North Face of the Grand Teton, went fishing at Grizzly Bear Lake ('Caught five trout. Rained all night'), saw a rodeo and came off worst in an encounter with a cowboy. Don had made a disparaging comment about the brevity of the rider's display on a bronco, the cowboy – who was even shorter than Don, but in much better physical shape and even more prickly – took exception, the situation fired up, and Whillans was battered all round the parking lot before finally being laid out cold.

Chastened by the wildness of the West, Don took refuge for a while with Pat Ament in Boulder, climbed a little at Eldorado Springs, and by the end of September was once more in Britain. The first foot and mouth epidemic ensured that no climbing could take place through most of the country that autumn and winter. I have a vivid memory of Don in the midst of a crowd of more-than-usually boisterous climbers attending the Alpha Club dinner[28] at the Railway Hotel in Buxton that November. One of the end of evening rituals was 'jousting' – a big guy got a little guy on his back, thus paired everyone took to the floor, and the rest was assault-and-battery, all-in wrestling, vendetta settlement and serious fisticuffs

---

[28] This – attendance at which was by invitation only, and those present were carefully chosen – was the wildest event in climbing's social calendar in the 1960s, and an excuse for general mayhem of such intensity that it could never be held in the same place twice. An attempt was made to reinstate it a couple of decades later, but by that time most of the members had become respectable professionals and businessmen and it was all rather staid and disappointing – no fighting, no broken bones, no teeth being spat out on the floor, no drunken car crashes on the way home. No longer any point to it at all, in fact . . .

combined. The late Paul Nunn – a big, exuberant, red-haired character of Irish descent – was usually prime mover in all this, and in 1967, with a still relatively slim Whillans on his back, he was unassailable. Social diversions aside, Don was planning for another expedition. Dave Bathgate, the Edinburgh carpenter he had met in the Alps in 1965, invited him on a small Scottish expedition to attempt the South Face of Huandoy Sur in Peru's Cordillera Blanca. Don, who had not been to this part of South America before, quickly accepted, and having studied the map came up with the romantic notion of Bathgate and himself returning by raft down the Amazon. The other two members of the team, Brian Robertson and Ian McEacheran, were, like Bathgate, from the Edinburgh Squirrels. They beat the publicity drum for the trip by terming the South Face 'the Eiger of the Andes'. Although the face itself was – at about 3000 feet – small relative to the Eiger's, the mountain's top lay at the breathless altitude of 20,210 feet. And small did not mean easy.

The expedition reached the foot of the face in June 1968, and initially made good progress in climbing and fixing rope up an obvious ice-ramp that led into its centre, whence there was a choice of routes onwards, all of which looked equally improbable and uninviting. Don retreated from this point down to base camp. A day later, the other three were on their way down to join him. A traversing section above the end of the ramp had proved so loose as to be unjustifiable. Don watched from below as they retreated, taking down the fixed ropes as they did so: 'I cannot say I was too pleased at the decision, but since I wasn't there, there wasn't that much I could do about it.' The team had clearly been too small and too ill-equipped to attempt what turned out to be one of the most difficult challenges in the Andes, and one that only finally succumbed to Japanese, Italian and French teams working on three separate lines in June and July of 1975. So Don had yet another failure – and a pretty desultory one at that – to add to his tally and brood upon as he and Bathgate left for an equally disappointing return journey by river-boat – Don wearing his pyjamas throughout – down the sweltering, mosquito-plagued watery thoroughfares they had conceived of as the unexplored Amazon.

By the late 1960s, to any objective viewer Don's career as a mountaineer seemed at best becalmed, or perhaps even at an end. He was drinking every night, and seldom climbed apart from the briefest of forays out to his local outcrops of the Bridestones,

Widdop, Heptonstall or Hugeoncroft, where he might hold
someone's rope or advise them on how to do his favourite problems
from the start of the decade. (Getting them to 'quack' on The Duck
– a painful little jamming problem at the Bridestones – was his
favourite piece of sadism. He seldom chose now to demonstrate it
himself.) His expeditions to the Himalayas, for all his stalwart
performances on them, had brought no personal success. His great
Alpine and British climbs were receding fast into memory. His
income was derived from an endless grind of lecturing to clubs,
schools and the Women's Institute on trips and ascents often made
a decade before, or from equipment royalties or plumbing work.
His few achieved summits on expedition were perceived as being in
a relatively minor key. His physical condition was parlous –
growing obesity and a smoker's cough added to the vertigo and the
knee problems – and he was living in a ramshackle house without a
bathroom that the council in 1969 had condemned as unfit for
human habitation. If there had been a form guide for mountaineers,
you would not have been racing down to the bookmaker's to place
money on a classic win.

To add to the generally depressive picture, his erstwhile climbing
partners were doing notably well for themselves. Dougal, after the
Eiger Direct climb and the 1967–68 Cerro Torre Expedition, was
the mountaineering pin-up boy of a generation, and ran the International School of Mountaineering in Leysin. Chris Bonington's
writing and journalism was fulfilling a popular demand for tales of
derring-do. Joe Brown, owner of a successful chain of climbing
stores in Wales, and an engaging and frequent performer in live
outside television broadcasts on climbing, had entered yet another
exploratory phase, arguably the most remarkable even in his long
history, and on the sea-cliffs of Anglesey had excelled himself with
a series of new, imposing and difficult climbs – Mousetrap, Primate,
Red Wall, Wendigo, Winking Crack,[29] Dinosaur and dozens of
others – that were garnering for him the respect of new generations
of climbers. Joe and Don met briefly at the end of January 1969, as
the latter was about to walk up to Clogwyn Du'r Arddu with Alick
Ormerod, the co-writer of his biography:

---

[29] Wonderful climb, this – definitely a Whillans route!, with a sweet little
gritstone-style and protection-free off-width at the very end of the long, steep top
pitch. It was much fallen-off for a while in the 1960s and 1970s, and nowadays is
seldom done.

'D'you fancy a climb tomorrow?' Joe asked. 'We could go over to Anglesey. It's always sheltered on Gogarth.'

I thought for a bit. I guessed that Joe had made a big effort to come out with this invitation. Alick stood in silence waiting for the answer. I looked at Joe: he was obviously extremely fit, whereas I was vastly overweight and not at all in condition. I couldn't see myself struggling up a sea-cliff behind him.

'No, I don't think so,' I replied. 'I'm not fit.'

'Ah, you'd be all right,' said Joe.

I shook my head. 'No, not this weekend. We'll be having a booze-up – I won't feel like doing anything strenuous tomorrow . . .'

A fortnight later Don received another invitation from Chris Bonington for a couple of days' climbing midweek in Scotland, and this time he didn't turn it down. Chris arranged to pick him up in Crawshawbooth at 10 p.m. on Shrove Tuesday. When he arrived from his home in Bowdon, Don was out at the Calf's Head in Rawtenstall. Audrey entertained Chris with cups of tea before going to bed herself. At 2.30 a.m. Don rolled in, having drunk 11 pints of bitter. In high dudgeon, his mind registering this against the as-yet-undisclosed reason for the trip, Chris bundled him into his Cortina GT and drove through the night to Ian Clough's house in Glencoe, Don snoring peacefully beside him all the way. Tom Patey joined them at Clough's, and early on Thursday morning the three of them set off for the unclimbed-in-winter Great Gully of Ardgour. Walking into the corrie and up to the foot of the climb, Don dawdled along behind, eschewing undue exertion as the other two sped on to the route. They soloed up, Don taking a rope from time to time on the trickier pitches. The very last pitch was a wide chimney, sheathed in ice, steep, forbidding and with a cold blast of wind funnelling up it.

To the surprise of the other two, Don commandeered the lead, and with his legs out almost at right angles as he straddled between its walls he forged up the pitch without bothering to arrange any protection, swung out on the iced-up boulders at the top, and brought up Chris and Tom, who both struggled to follow:

The last bit of climbing I did in Scotland in winter was with Chris and Tom in Ardgour. This to me was just the same as the climbing I'd been doing on the higher mountains. I didn't feel at all out of place. It was very cold, hard climbing, and the wind blowing straight up the crag. My gear was fairly good but Tom's wasn't and his legs were frozen stiff at the top of the route. He could hardly walk – in fact he was staggering. I had a pair of thick, heavy ski-pant material breeches on that we'd used in Peru – snow doesn't stick to them. Long woollen pants under them, and a windproof jacket and ski-goggles. The goggles were really useful: they were wide-angle and my eyes were all right, whereas Tom was really suffering with frozen eyelashes.

They went back to the house of Ian Clough, who was privy to the purpose of the visit, Patey drifted off home at 4 p.m. and Chris, having made up his mind that Don was still capable of turning in creditable performances and knowing that he was 'certainly the finest all-round mountaineer that Britain had produced since the war', came to the point. An expedition was being planned for the following year to the South Face of Annapurna. Chris showed Don the photographs he had obtained from Jimmy Roberts, and invited him to join. Don studied the face for a while, said to Chris, 'It'll be hard, but it should go all right. I'll come . . .', and was promptly offered the position of deputy leader – an act of remarkable trust and generosity given the previous rancour between them, and a clear indication of Chris's commitment to ensuring the best chance of success for the trip. After a five-year absence, Don was on his way back to the Himalayas, and as a key member in the most ambitious expedition in British mountaineering history.

16

Major League

The 1970 expedition to the South Face of Annapurna, even over a distance of several decades and after innumerable other major climbs, still holds its status as one of the most radical enterprises undertaken in mountaineering history. It came after a period in which the Nepalese Himalayas, because of strained relationships and sporadic frontier clashes between neighbouring countries, had been debarred to climbers for several years. So a whole generation of British mountaineers had grown up unacquainted with the conditions that prevailed on the world's highest peaks, and without high-altitude experience. The imponderable of how well or otherwise an individual might perform in the rarefied air hung over most of the chosen team. To a degree, it even hung over the leader himself, for Bonington's last experience of going high had been on Nuptse in 1961. By contrast, Don and Ian Clough's sterling efforts above 23,000 feet on Gauri Sankar in late 1964 – the hardest technical climbing to that date in the Himalayas – seemed far more recent.

The idea for Annapurna South Face had arisen in conversations between Chris, Nick Estcourt and Martin Boysen, who all lived quite close to each other in Cheshire and climbed together regularly in the late 1960s. These three, after canvassing possibilities, had decided on an objective that for its time was staggeringly ambitious – like several Walker Spurs set one on top of the other and ending above the 8000-metre mark. No such difficult face-climb had previously been attempted in the Himalayas; the scale of the undertaking dictated the size of the team to attempt it, and the approach that team would take. The Cheshire three formed the nucleus. Dougal Haston, who had been with Boysen on Cerro Torre in the winter of 1967–68, and had stood out as the driving force of that expedition, had already discussed the idea with and been enlisted by

Bonington when they had shared a snow-hole on the first winter ascent of the North Face of the Aiguille d'Argentiere in the winter of 1969.

To these four were added Mick Burke, an obstreperous little dynamo from Wigan who had also been on the unsuccessful Cerro Torre trip and was proving, despite his technical limitations as a rock-climber,[1] to be one of Britain's most effective alpinists; and Ian Clough, who Bonington knew to be as indefatigable and equable as he was entirely dependable. An American, Tom Frost, was added at Bonington's agent's behest in the interests of the American market – this expedition may not have initiated the end of mountaineering's age of innocence, but it strongly flagged it up. Don made up the climbing team of eight, and Chris augmented it with the trio of Dave Lambert, Mike Thompson and Kelvin Kent to manage medical matters, provisioning and base-camp running. Bonington's organisation, and his ability to delegate and enthuse, were impeccably professional. And Don played his part prior to the expedition's leaving by applying himself assiduously to equipment design. The expedition took with it not only a new, lighter-weight version of the Whillans Box, manufactured by Karrimor, but also a pack-frame and down-suit he had designed, the 'Whammer' (Whillans hammer),[2] and the prototype Whillans Harness.[3]

---

[1] Rock-climbing ability is not, perhaps, the most crucial factor in deciding an individual's aptitude for mountaineering. Few of the outstanding names in British alpinism and Himalayan climbing over the last 40 years have operated at the highest standards of their day on rock. In this, Don was an exception – though it can be pointed out with justice that even by the time of Gauri Sankar in 1964, his great days as a rock-climber were behind him.

I have always had a suspicion that lack of rock-climbing pedigree bred a degree of insecurity and a kind of siege mentality in some of the members of the large-scale expeditions led by Chris Bonington in the 1970s and 1980s. And I suspect, too (though this will obviously be denied by all involved), that whatever the dark hints dropped or rational reasons properly adduced, a degree of Kleinian envy was present to lubricate the machinations by which Whillans and Boysen – the only two members of that circus whose rock credentials were impeccable – were elbowed out. That the lesser ability/greater ambition syndrome bore fruit in death after death seems to me an interesting and arguable point.

[2] Don's reply to Hamish MacInnes's famous hammer, 'The Message'. The 'Whammer' never really caught on, and although issued with them, few people on the trip used them – perhaps because not many wanted to hit things the way Don did. Nowadays they're quaint, rare and unwieldy museum pieces.

[3] Manufactured by Troll Safety Equipment, this became standard equipment for British climbers from its introduction in the early 1970s, and is still taken on some

Don even stirred himself so far as to venture out to the Alps with Mick Burke (whom he had first met in Langdale in the late 1950s) in the summer of 1969, to re-kindle the old enthusiasm and see how he was performing on the longer routes. On 5 August, the two Annapurna team-mates-to-be stayed at the Argentiere Hut, and ambled rather slowly next morning up to the foot of the North-East Spur of Les Droites – a hard, high classic of the Aiguilles. Another pair of British climbers – Eddie Birch and Dave Little from Manchester, young members of the Black & Tans Club – arrived shortly after them at 5 a.m., having been delayed by the inveterately absent-minded Little's apparently having forgotten one of his crampons, a descent to the hut to collect it, an impromptu decision

---

expeditions. So popular did it initially prove that royalties from it became a mainstay of Don's income. Designed for mountain work, it was widely used for a time by rock-climbers, for whom it had one serious disadvantage for the male of the species in the form of a strap that came up between the climber's legs to fasten at the front. Otherwise-comfortable falls from overhanging rock could sometimes result in a nasty tweak if you were wearing a Whillans Harness, and one leading climber even lost a testicle after a long plummet in the Avon Gorge. If the same happened to anyone in contemporary times, lawyers for a squeaky-voiced victim would try to have the shirts off a designer's and manufacturer's back. There might, of course, have been an element of self-fulfilling prophecy in all this, given Don's privately held view that 'climbers these days 'ave got no balls'. (Comment reported to author by Ronnie Dutton, 8 May 1988.) Tony Howard, the director of Troll, gives the following measured and positive assessment of Don's involvement with his company:

'When Don first called at Troll about his idea for a harness for Annapurna, we were based in a little shed in Greenfield, close to the entrance to Chew Valley. I was the only full-time (between climbs) employee at that time (late '69), knocking out nuts and getting harnesses made from old mill belting sewn by the local cobbler. Don wanted a harness that would make life a bit more comfortable when prusiking, and had brought along what could only be described as a nappy – more as a discussion point than anything else. Together with my partner, Alan Waterhouse, we put together a working prototype which was based on Don's pattern, but terribly uncomfortable. Nevertheless, it identified the need for something that would lift the legs to a sitting position when prusiking yet offer no restrictions when climbing. This was the key to what eventually became the Whillans Harness – the world's first climbers' sit harness. Not only did it do what was needed on Annapurna, it also provided an accessible racking system for the increasing amount of protection gear being invented. Furthermore, falls previously taken by a rope round the waist, or at best a belt, were now supported in comfort. It rapidly became a world best-seller, shifting thousands a month and held a top place in the market for almost 20 years – quite remarkable in an era of rapid gear development and improvement. As such, it paid Don a nice royalty on sales right up to his death, and afterwards benefited Audrey. Don continued to keep his Troll connections, calling in regularly to have a new harness made as his

to go without,[4] having discovered it was not there, and the chance recovery of it from where it had fallen off Little's sack on the way up the glacier in the dark.

Birch and Little raced ahead and arrived at the crux pitch – an awkward, iced-up wall, technically difficult but reasonably well protected, beneath which Don and Mick Burke caught them up. Birch and Little suggested Don led it, which elicited the prompt response, 'Fuck that – get on with it.' So Birch led the pitch, and Don gladly accepted a top-rope. At nightfall they bivouacked on adjacent ledges above all difficulties and below the final snow-ridge. According to Birch:

> We spent the night brewing up, chatting away with Don holding forth in his usual vernacular, dozing a bit, and next morning after we've cooked breakfast Don decides to assert himself and takes the lead, since he's not done any leading so far. It's only an easy snow-arete, mind, but he's going to lead to the top, because he's got it into his head that it's not in good condition and no one else is to be trusted with the safety of the team where it really matters. He ties two 150-foot ropes together and leads up without any protection whatsoever. Well, we just let him get on with it. It was all very amicable . . .

The next six months passed in a frenetic whirl of activity. Don and Audrey, having been given £25 compensation for the compulsory purchase of their old, condemned cottage – a payment which both infuriated them and enabled them to pay back the last

---

waist continually expanded, or for a brew and a chat with us and Sylvia Kershaw, a Troll machinist and wife of 'Dobber' Kershaw, one of Don's more notorious friends.

'I should also say that whilst Troll was doing reasonably well prior to Don's first visit, and whilst making climbing gear was supporting my climbing addiction, it was undoubtedly Don and his harness that put Troll on the world map. The harness which eventually made inroads into the "Whillans" market – the Troll Mark 2 – actually used the Whillans principle of lifting the legs into a sitting position after a fall but achieved the result by using a belay loop in place of the front strap of the Whillans. This front-loop system, connecting waist and legs, became the basis for almost all the world's climbing harnesses – a great legacy.'

[4] 'We just said, 'Ah, fuck it – it's shit or bust, we'll do it without,' recalls Eddie Birch. Sound mountaineering philosophy, this . . .

of Tom Whillans's loan from 10 years before – moved house to a new, split-level, end-of-terrace local authority maisonette. This did not happen without a certain amount of intransigence on Don's part, of course – the incursion by authority being very close to home in this instance – but Audrey eventually persuaded him of the benefits of the new house, and the developers were already building around the old one. Number 6, Thirlmere Way, Loveclough, was high up on the moors above Rossendale and looking out west. She and Don having furnished and decorated, Audrey involved herself with the planning of Breda Arkless's women's expedition to the Padar Himalayas. Don buzzed around between equipment manufacturers, foundries, sessions with Alick Ormerod on his autobiography and expedition meetings with a down-to-earth zeal and application that completely belied the lackadaisical reputation built up around him in the previous few years. On 26 February 1970, he left London Heathrow on the 1700 hours flight to Bombay, and on 4 March travelled on to Kathmandu. After a fortnight of delayed equipment-transport and other logistical nightmares, the expedition arrived in Pokhara[5] on 19 March.

Don had reached there on the 15th, and at Chris's behest had headed on up to the old Machapuchare base camp from 1957, at the entrance to the Annapurna Sanctuary, in order to study the route. His diary briefly records, 'Mach. base camp. Deep snow. Yeti. Moonlight.' He had been pitching tents with the Sherpa Pemba Tharkay when Pemba told him a Yeti was coming. He looked round and saw a black shape disappear beyond a ridge. In the diary entry for the following day, 'Snow soft. Saw Yeti tracks. Saw Yeti and weasel during night!' Don had in fact spent a long time watching from his tent the brightly moonlit slope on which he and Pemba had seen the Yeti, had seen movement, and watched through a monocular as a powerful, ape-like creature bounded around hunting across the snow. The next day he had examined the

---

[5] In anything but its entirety – its gear was still on the high seas after the ship carrying it had broken down in the Indian Ocean, Ian Clough was in Bombay waiting to expedite its unloading, and in the meantime replacements had been air-freighted from Britain with a British Army expedition to the north side of Annapurna, and this team kept the South Face expedition provided with enough army rations to keep them from starvation whilst they waited for their own to arrive.

footprints it had left, photographed them,[6] questioned the Sherpas with him very closely, and observed their reactions, all of which had convinced him not only of the existence of the Yeti, but also of its shamanistic status with the Sherpas. Rattled as well as moved by the sighting, Don's own view was that if the creature, whatever it was, had managed to exist in that cold place down the ages, it should be allowed to continue doing so undisturbed.

Don, at 37, was the oldest in a team half of the members of which were in their mid- to late twenties, and were looking up to him and learning from his measured and tactical approach to risk-taking. Martin Boysen recollects that because of his lack of previous successes in the Himalayas, Don was completely determined to feature this time. There was an uneasiness, Boysen recalls, between Bonington and Whillans, though they were respectful around each other, and the decision to take Don had been arrived at in large measure not through personal affection but because of his perceived soundness of judgement. This was quickly borne out when time was lost by Bonington and Frost low down on the route in climbing a difficult ice-ridge, and Whillans and Haston then found an alternative traversing line half the length of the ridge. The critical matter initially, Boysen considers, was the forming of the partnerships, and one attraction became very obvious. Don was 'skulking in the background', Dougal, 'a weak character in some respects', was watching and allowing situations to evolve to his advantage, and both men were weighing each other up. Davey Agnew, who was close to Haston in his time at Leysin, has a very telling insight into the relationship that sprang up between the two of them:

---

[6] The curious matter of the 'Abominable Snowman' has entertained and preoccupied Himalayan explorers and climbers for a century. H.W. Tilman, the great mountaineer and explorer of the 1930s, believed in its existence, corresponded with *The Times* on the subject and wrote a learned treatise on it as appendix to his *Everest 1938* book. His frequent companion Eric Shipton, who was of more playful disposition, included a very crisp full-page photograph of a 'Yeti footprint' in his book on the 1951 Everest Reconnaissance expedition. In the mid-1980s I interviewed Sir Edmund Hillary, who was with Shipton when the photograph was taken. Hillary told me that Shipton went round a vague mark in the snow improving it with his knuckles as a gentle tease against his great friend Tilman. When this story came out, journalists got hold of it and there were some huffy and indignant pieces in the press accusing Shipton of being a cheat, a liar and a fraud, etc. Which seems a very humourless reaction to a piece of fun. But then, mountaineers . . .! Very serious people, only laugh at their own jokes. Heaven help you if you cross them . . .

Dougal said to me, 'Whillans is the man' . . . There was this compassion about Don, which a lot of people don't often attribute to him. On Annapurna, and on Everest later, when they ran short of food, it was Don who would open up the last can or tin of pâté and say: 'Here you go, Jimmy, you eat this.' Don survived on tea and cigarettes, and as far as Dougal is concerned, he told me later that Don saved his skin. He looked after Dougal, [who] called him 'Dad'.[7]

The fascination was mutual, Whillans not quite knowing what to make of the driven, self-contained young Scot who was fast soaking up all the lessons his own example provided: 'It's as though he were behind glass,' he told Ingrid Cranfield. 'You can see him but you can't touch him.'[8]

The expedition buckled down to the serious climbing in hand and made rapid progress up the first stages of the climb. This early thrust was blunted by the difficulties of the 2000-foot rock band above Camp Five (which had been placed at 22,750 feet), and by the extremely arduous nature of the carry up to that point from Camp Four at the top of the ice-ridge. Nearly 4000 feet of climbing of unknown difficulty lay ahead. Burke and Frost were in Camp Five, and the leapfrog system Bonington had initiated whereby pairs of climbers would alternate between load-carrying to the highest camp and the easier and more pleasant task of lead climbing was showing signs of breaking down as altitude, illness, exertion and fatigue took their toll. In the long, cold nights in the high camps, the calculations would be weighing on the men's minds. How well would they be going, how much strength would they have left, how high would they be when it was their turn to be in front? It was mid-May. The monsoon would be rolling in by the end of the month. The situation was becoming critical.

Don and Dougal, after days of resting at base camp, had climbed back to the camp at the foot of the ice-ridge. In the evening of 13 May, Chris went on air for the customary end-of-day, between-camps radio conversation, and the effect was galvanic. Asserting himself in his position as leader, he told Mick Burke that Don and Dougal were coming up to Camp Five next day to take over the

[7] Quoted in Jeff Connor's *Dougal Haston: The Philosophy of Risk*.
[8] Quoted in Cranfield's *The Challengers*.

lead. The pugnacious Burke argued back strongly, pointing out that it was now the turn of Boysen and Estcourt, who were at Camp Four, to take the lead. But these two had borne the brunt of the high carries, and Estcourt in particular was close to exhaustion.[9] Burke tried to insist on Don and Dougal carrying between Camps Four and Five for a period, Chris accepted a compromise for his rested and strongest pair of one carry, and then Don switched on his handset and rounded on his fellow Lancastrian:

> Dougal and I left Camp Five a week ago. It isn't even consolidated, and progress towards Camp Six has been so poor it's had me and Dougal depressed all the way up the mountain. I don't know what Mick thinks he's playing at, but time's short and we want to get the route pushed out. Unless they can establish Camp Six, or at least find a way, they should make way for someone else.

With the wisdom of hindsight, this conversation can be seen as one of the defining moments in Don's career. A time for plain speaking it may have been, and he and Chris were proven right in the strategy they forced through. But in doing so, feathers had been ruffled and the leader's compromise decision – and hence his authority – had been questioned and changed. When Bonington, on his way up to support the lead climbers, met Burke and Tom Frost on their way down, and tried to explain to them how, in the interests of a team success, expediency must sometimes take precedence over principle, he was left in no doubt as to how hurt and disaffected those who had been out in front were at the turn of events. The team rapidly regrouped around the new protocols, but ripples had been caused, enemies had been made – a scapegoat, ultimately, would be found and his reputation assiduously blackened in the cabals of the ambitious world of professional and semi-professional climbers.

---

[9] One source from the expedition has it that Don, who was always most loyal to those he regarded as friends, felt very guilty about stepping in front of Martin Boysen like this: 'He didn't give a shit about Estcourt, but suggested to Martin that he team up with him and Dougal. It couldn't have worked with three, of course, and Martin was buggered at that point anyway, with all the carrying he'd done. Martin was one of the real stars of that trip, working for the team throughout. Don worked for the team too, but always with an eye to the top.'

Don and Dougal duly climbed to Camp Five, and pressed on up the ropes fixed by Burke in the magnificent leads up the flank of the 'Flat Iron' feature into which he had been needled by the conversation with Don. By general assent these were the most difficult of the entire climb, and gave Burke authority in the criticism and backbiting that later went on between him and Don. With sterling logistical support from Bonington, Clough and Estcourt – support without which they would not have been able to sit out the weather and wait for the moment to go for the summit – the pair established Camp Six – a single blue RAFMA tent – at 24,000 feet, on top of the Flat Iron and at approximately half-height on the rock band. After a day spent by Dougal in replacing gear lost when his rucksack had fallen, they began to prospect the route ahead. Following terraces that ran out left, they found a gully that led to the top of both the rock band and the smaller rock band above. As the days passed, and the two of them were alone and far out on a limb at Camp Six, above the monsoon that had arrived below, the rest of the team – the strength of which by now had all but fizzled out – grew increasingly concerned for them. On 24 May, they climbed for a second time to the top of the gully and tried to establish Camp Seven there. Don recalls:

> We'd been looking at the place for months through binoculars, but when we finally arrived it was just going dusk and snowing. We had shovels and a tent so we thought we'd fight it a bit. We got to the bank of snow at the foot of the rock and started digging. About a foot down, it was ice.
>
> 'That's it. Get out of here. Back down the ropes . . .'
>
> 'We'll find a place,' Dougal said.
>
> 'No chance,' I said. 'It's going dark.'
>
> 'Can't we bivvy?' he said.
>
> 'Christ, no!' I said. 'We'll be back down those ropes in half an hour and in the tent.' We were up there at 25,000 feet in a blizzard. Absolutely lunatic idea to stay. We dumped the gear and went back down the ropes.

Dougal, who had been doing all the trail-breaking and leading, wrote in his journal, 'It's a case of one leg after the other. What a senseless existence. W behind me, but unable or unwilling to go to the front. It's too much to hope, I suppose, that he will ever get his fucking finger out and make a brew. Too late to change now . . .'

They returned to Camp Six, spent two more days living on sparse rations or cigar smoke, and then came dawn on 27 May. In the thin, cold air, without benefit of supplementary oxygen, around one o'clock that afternoon, 'W' did change, did 'go to the front', and in an entry set with tragic symmetry between '25 May – Tom Patey killed[10] – 38 years', and '29 May – Ian killed', his diary simply records, 'Top of Annapurna. 2.30.'[11]

By the time Dougal had arrived back at Camp Six, Don was already tuning in the radio to relay the news back down to base camp. He handed the set over to Dougal, who told Chris they had finished the climb and reached the summit. Martin Boysen, listening in to the conversation, remembers the team's response:

Everyone, just everyone – even Nick – was pleased. We were pleased that at last he'd pulled it off, and in a situation where success might so easily once again have passed him by. They'd been so far out up there, the rest of us obviously concerned, so the relief was immense. And Don himself, of course, was delighted. I remember him in the pub months afterwards, just grinning still. It was an age of innocence then, and though Don was the only non-innocent one among us, he wasn't yet the cynic he later became. He exuded confidence, and was good company. And we learnt from him. He was such a meticulous man, everything kept shipshape. He loved boxes and his camp was always so clean. He looked after himself, looked after his equipment, and of course he particularly looked after his own chances of success. However it was later viewed and however those lessons were later applied, in that moment when the news came through, it was just simple

---

[10] Whilst descending by abseil from a Scottish sea-stack. Patey's was a flame that burnt very bright through two decades of climbing, and the collection of essays (published as *One Man's Mountains*) that he left is one of the jewels of mountain literature.

[11] Interesting piece of trivia – Don went to the top of Annapurna with no socks on. He believed that constricted blood-flow to the feet was the most likely cause of frostbite, and trusted therefore to the felt inners of his altitude double-boots for warmth.

delight that he and Dougal had done it, and that we, as a team, had done what we'd come to do too. 'It'll go,' he kept telling us. 'We'll get the job done.' I suppose if you look at that language, it sounds reductive, but 'doing a job' with Don was a figure of speech. He abhorred overt sentimentality, and I think he was quite incapable of verbalising his attachment. It wasn't a job that you get paid for that he meant by the phrase. The job really was the craft – it was just a way of expressing his craft, and it was one at which, in his time, he was supremely good.

There is one crucial phrase in that judicious overview of Martin's. He lets it slip almost by chance. It is one to which we shall return. For the moment, mark out that 'even Nick' as one of the bells that are quietly beginning to toll for Don's career: 'This Troilus is clomben on Fortune's wheel,/And litel weneth that he moot descenden.'

Although the summit had been reached, the expedition was not quite over. Others had their ambitions, too, and were bent on their fulfilment. Burke and Frost – still high up above the monsoon – wanted to make their own attempt to reach the top, even though conditions on the lower face were rapidly deteriorating, and there would be no help available and no possibility of anyone climbing to their assistance if things went wrong. On 28 May they started to move up to Camp Six. Don and Dougal passed them along the traversing ledges on their way down. In the little tent at 24,000 feet that night, Burke slept the sleep of a spent man, whilst Frost woke at 1 a.m. and made his preparations for the summit, setting out at 4 a.m. with Burke following shortly afterwards. Whilst the latter's effort petered out after a few hundred feet, Frost reached the snowfield at the top of the gully at 8 a.m. and viewed what lay ahead. The snow was knee-deep, a rising, fierce wind whipping it across the slope. Discretion over-ruled his desire, the savage cold bit into his body, and he turned back. The stripping and evacuation of the mountain could now begin in earnest, and not before time. Below Camp Three, a huge avalanche had already scoured away Don and Dougal's descent tracks. Wet, heavy snow was swirling all around, temperatures low down were rising, and the mountain itself seemed to be in motion, sloughing off its old pelt. As two of the team retreated past the crucial danger point below Camp Two – a ramp with unstable seracs towering above – one of the seracs collapsed, and Ian Clough was killed. So guilt and sadness were added in to the cocktail of emotions – envy, pique, disappointment – of which the players in this production were variously to drink. For Don himself, there was the loss of a valued partner and friend to allay the sweetness of success, and harden that resistant, thick carapace of his a little more as the team packed away the base camp that had been home for two months, and left their friend's grave behind them.

The response to the climb back in Britain was overwhelmingly enthusiastic. There was general recognition of its significance and difficulty. Dougal's public wonderment at the 'length of Don's neck' in the last stage of their climb added to the Whillans reputation. The team was met at Heathrow by John Hunt and Douglas Busk, so the wholehearted admiration of the Establishment of mountaineering was also made apparent. For his part, Don frisked around London for a couple of days – Audrey was still travelling back overland from her own Himalayan trip – before returning to Rossendale to pick up the threads of his life. Within a week, he was climbing out on his local gritstone again, at Widdop with his Lancashire cronies Albert Ashworth and Dave Barton.

The celebrity consequent on Annapurna took some unexpected forms. Don featured in an article on motorcycling in the Automobile Association's *Drive* magazine, riding trail-bikes along the Icknield Way in the company of Sir Ralph Richardson (who seemed in an amused and patrician way to enjoy himself and ally with his squat, forthright and bearded fellow bike-enthusiast – Prospero and Caliban on a pair of Montessas!); and his picture was splashed across the front of the *Sunday Times* review section as Bonington told the story of the expedition. The fitness and confidence of the South Face climb still with him, a film crew in tow and old scores to be settled, late in July he set off for Alpiglen with his Huandoy Sur companion Ian MacEacharan and a couple of the other Edinburgh 'Squirrels', Bugs McKeith and Kenny Spence. They went up to the so-familiar Swallow's Nest, bivouacked, and retreated – in Don's case for the last time – next morning as snow and rain fell.

In August, Don fulfilled a long-standing obligation with photographer John Cleare in Wales, working as Sherpa-gaffer on *The Climbers* – a marvellously shot film of the Holliwell brothers[12] managing a sheaf of hard Welsh routes of the time (Grond among them – see Chapter Thirteen). The climbers and crew were staying in a hostel, Bryn Du, in Llanberis, which Don had recently replumbed. Hot water came out of the cold taps, and vice versa, and the proprietor, Richard Stanley, warning of this quirk, explained that, although the workmanship was superb, Don had got something wrong and was refusing to put it right on the grounds that it all worked so long as you were colour blind. Don's own expectations took a knock in the course of the filming, when 600 feet of rope he had put in place on Dinas Mot for John to abseil down and film from in the morning was found to have gone when they went to use it in the afternoon. 'We looked down, and noticed several hurrying, rope-laden figures approaching the road,' Cleare records. 'We'll catch the buggers,' Don growled, and set off in pursuit. The man in the hamburger van at Pont y Gromlech beneath saw an aggrieved Whillans plunging down the hillside, gave him the registration number of a suspicious Ford Anglia estate car that had just driven away, and whilst filming was suspended Don went hunting for the culprits – who, fortunately for them, were not found, though the rope was rumoured to have turned up on the North Wall of the Eiger a week or so later.

Don was filming again late in August, but this time in front of the cameras. A climbing outside broadcast had been arranged from the Anglesey sea-cliffs. Whilst Joe Brown and McNaught Davis swung around on the Spider's Web and the Holliwell brothers and Janet Davies cavorted on Tyrannosaurus Rex, Don and Pete Crew plodded up the rather less dramatic Wen. All five climbers on the slab side of the zawn were landed at the foot of their routes by Joe Brown's inflatable Zodiac in an operation the commentator Chris Brasher, in his best gung-ho mode, had termed 'The Assault from the Sea'. With the tide rising and waves crashing in, one of the riggers, Robin Turner, remained at the bottom with the Zodiac, the plan being that Don and Pete Crew would abseil down into it and sail away into the sunset to end the programme. Crew led the more

---

[12] Lawrie and Les Holliwell were a pair of vibrant, raucous and energetic Cockney brothers – Lawrie in particular one of the very best climbers of his time – who revitalised Welsh climbing during the latter half of the 1960s. Lawrie died on Craig yr Ysfa in August 1973, when the sling to which his abseil rope was belayed slid from a rounded spike as he was inspecting a line he hoped to climb on the Lower Amphitheatre Wall.

difficult first pitch of Wen, and Don the second to where an easy traverse ledge slants off right to the path along the top of the slab. By now, the outside broadcast was running late because of the weather conditions and associated technical problems. Alan Chivers, the producer, came on to the radio link to instruct Don and Pete to start on the closing action. The wind was getting up and the notorious rip-tide was racing round the North Stack promontory. Don took one look and growled, 'Sod that!' Crew, who could not swim, decided to go down alone, so Don – taking the view that Pete was a competent climber accountable for his own actions, and himself being a little weary after prolonged pub sessions during the week of set-up and rehearsal – untied, soloed off the cliff, borrowed the keys to a Land Rover belonging to one of the support crew, and went off to take a nap in it.

Crew, meanwhile, had abseiled back down the pitch to join Turner in the boat that was heaving and bouncing around at the foot of the cliff. Committed by now, and without Don above to help them escape, the pair quickly found themselves in trouble. They were unable to start the Zodiac's engine and the boat itself was awash in heavy seas. Hamish MacInnes, on the opposite side of the zawn, saw Crew and Turner in the bucking boat being doused in the surf at the base of the cliff – and so also did a walker on the path round the head of the zawn, who sped back to Holyhead and reported what he had seen to the coastguard station. Hamish had alerted Joe, who – chuckling away as usual – got a 500-foot non-stretch rope down to Crew and Turner, and they, soaked, chilled and far from pleased, set off slowly jumaring for the top in the gathering dark, at which point a coastguard craft arrived below with a searchlight, coastguards appeared above with a thick hemp hawser which they tried to lower down and which proved too short, and various representatives of the local and national press arrived, to the BBC's considerable embarrassment and displeasure. If Don's prospects of further television employment in 1963 had been scuppered by his competence, now they were completely sunk by the perceived negligence he had shown in this pantomime. He was officially reprimanded for abandoning Crew and creating an incident.

It was a curious incident, too, which rebounded rather on Don and gave rise to a certain amount of negative gossip about his selfishness and callousness – terms chiming a little too nearly with the negative fall-out from Annapurna that was already starting to seep into climbing circles as the other returning climbers renewed their local acquaintances. Reports of a row with Mick Burke on the return trek to Kathmandu, in which the aggrieved Burke had in colourful language told Don that he was 'past it', took on more credibility as the television audience watched the unremarkable performance of a plump Whillans on a climb that was clearly very easy by comparison with the others on offer. And to compound that impression, there was his action in leaving at the top, where for once Don – though it was surely not the case nor how he would have viewed it – seemed to have failed to look after his companion or hold his safety paramount.

Offers of work were now pouring in. For the first time in his life, Don was becoming relatively affluent. He traded in his Mini and bought an orange Ford Capri GT:[13] 'It's great for running the missus down to the bus stop in the morning when it's raining.' The autumn and winter of 1970 saw him lecturing on Annapurna almost every night. A beaming and besuited Don adorned the front page of his local paper, shaking hands with the mayor as he was presented with a silver salver 'on behalf of the people of Rawtenstall'. Talking to the local press, he grew quite expansive: 'Rossendale hasn't got the beauty of the Lake District, and even though when I come back and it's raining it can look a bit grim, it's a place where I feel at home. It's a close, small area almost cut off from the rest of the country, and with an atmosphere that I like.' He went on to add that 'I hope to go on climbing for some time yet. Sometimes I feel I ought to do something more responsible, but responsible things bore me so I go off on another expedition.'

Another invitation had already been extended to him when he and Dougal had reached Kathmandu after Annapurna. It was for the 1971 International Himalayan Expedition, which was to involve 31 mountaineers and film-makers from 13 different nations. The first Briton to have been invited had been Joe Brown, who had, with characteristic percipience, quickly declined. If the mountain gods, laughing at human foibles, had chosen to put the Annapurna

---

[13] Students of Barthesian semiotics will understand the significance of this. All Ford Capris came with sun-visor strips which read 'Wayne' and 'Tracy'. Bonington's car of choice, after his brief 1960s flirtation with Cortina GTs, was always a Volvo. Students of Barthesian semiotics will understand the significance of this, too.

climb through a particularly crazy hall of mirrors, this baroque fiasco is how it might have looked. Where, in 1970, there had been unanimity of purpose, there were now a score of divided national and personal ambitions. Where there had been one of the most elegant lines ever to have been tackled on a great mountain, there was the presiding, phoney shibboleth of 1970s Himalayanism, the 'South-West face of Everest'. Bonington, as astute and mindful of his image as ever, resigned from the venture twice before it even left its diverse shores. That Don took it quite seriously is demonstrated by the fact that, after a request from the co-leader Norman Dyhrenfurth that all members should pay homage to international accord by striving to learn a language other than their native one, he enrolled at night-school in Rossendale in order to learn German (though he did question privately why he would need any language at all – even his own – since he would be climbing with the taciturn Dougal). A barrage of criticism was directed against the project. Eric Shipton, the once-and-future hero of mountaineering's avant-garde, rounded on the publicity it was generating:

> I have seen people's attitudes to climbing ruined by publicity, so one can say they haven't got any enjoyment out of [the experience] at all. All right, you can whip up the vicarious enthusiasm of the great world public – the press makes news, the press can whip up interest in a flea race. It's the very fact that these people are forced into that position that I find objectionable. The psychological value of climbing is a subtle one, it must ultimately depend on enjoyment. As soon as you allow extraneous things to come in, it destroys it.

Shipton continued with the thought that the International Expedition contained all the prerequisites not only for suffering and failure, but also 'for a great deal of ill-feeling'. 'I should think it would be absolute hell,' he concluded.

Don, in his sanguine way, brushed all this aside. He had climbed before with foreigners and had no problems there. Altitude and burn-out would put paid to all the potential difficulties of the expedition, 'so forget national rivalries. The mountain sorts them out.' As to Shipton's continuing belief in the value and effectiveness of the smaller expedition, Don gave that short shrift:

You don't crack a big nut with a little hammer. If you could do this job with a small expedition, it would be more appealing, but you can't. At the next stage you may be doing it with small expeditions, but that stage hasn't arrived yet. If you try to jump a stage you are likely to kill yourself. At the moment, because they don't have a reserve, small expeditions cut down the safety margin.

Shipton, as usual, was wise before the event, and as usual – the juggernaut having got under way – his wisdom went unheeded. The world press, in its unfair and simplistic way, had such a field day with the various and conflicting xenophobias of the 1971 International Himalayan Expedition that it is still, over 30 years on, a by-word for confusion, misbehaviour and mismanagement.[14] Where Bonington had given serious thought to the question of how effectively and amicably his team for Annapurna might operate together, Dyhrenfurth – an amiably ineffectual idealist – opted for a pick 'n' mix strategy that simply assumed the individuals' cooperation and altruistic effort, instead of assessing their likely capacity for these. The fun started right from the outset, and Don was in the thick of it. He had a lecture tour planned for January and February, and his autobiography was due out at the beginning of March, so he was almost a month late leaving for Delhi. By an unfortunate coincidence, passenger transfer at Heathrow placed another late-joining member of the expedition who had flown in from Paris on to the same Delhi flight on 7 March. Somewhere over the Caspian Sea, Don spotted him as he walked down the aisle. It was the French Gaullist deputy Pierre Mazeaud, whom we last encountered in this narrative on the disastrous 1961 retreat from the Central Pillar of Freney.

Ten years on, the success of Whillans and Bonington still rankled with this proud Frenchman – that his prize, for which his fellow Europeans had made the supreme sacrifice, should have been snatched, and by that doubly damned demon, a working-class Englishman . . .! Unaware of any rancour on Mazeaud's part, and

---

[14] Had Dyhrenfurth read the runes, he might have been a little more cautious. His father, Gunter Dyhrenfurth, had led a multinational expedition to Kangchenjunga back in gentlemanly 1930. According to the British member Frank Smythe, 'It wasn't a happy expedition at all. I think if they had got into a critical situation it might have been very difficult indeed.'

with no axe of his own to grind at this point, Don attempted to engage him in conversation, to which the deputy responded with coolness, though he thawed a fraction when Don offered to buy him a drink. A Pernod and a can of light ale duly arrived, and Don – as usual without money – offered the stewardess a traveller's cheque, which she could not accept. So Mazeaud, who took this as a grave personal insult and connivance, ended up having to pay – and not only that, but the fastidious deputy had to endure Don's company, incomprehensible conversation, and incessant cigarette smoke in Delhi and on the flight in a specially chartered UNO Cessna to the air-strip at Lukla, seven days' march from the expedition's base camp. By the time they finally joined the expedition, a personal rift had opened up before the climbing had even got under way.

There was a further problem, which was Don's physical condition. It had been bad enough before Annapurna. What fitness he had recouped on that trip had been annihilated by eight months on the lecture circuit (his diaries for this period record the pubs he went in every night, and are leavened with frequent comments like 'drunk', or 'very drunk', or 'hangover – felt ill all day'). He was quite unashamed about the state he was in. 'You get fit by actually climbing,' he told John Cleare, who was along to help film the adventure. 'You're at your peak when you need to be then. That's my philosophy and it seems to work.' Others were more perturbed. His beer-belly flopped over his belt, he was unable to fasten the top button of his trousers, walking blistered his feet badly, he both coughed and puffed away on acrid little Indian cheroots continually, and when not called upon to stir himself in any way he lapsed into buddha-like contemplation outside his tent, where he expected his every need to be attended to. To compound all this, once at base camp he suffered a severe and prolonged attack of the old, incapacitating vertigo. The betting men of the world's press, for whom he was odds-on favourite to reach the summit, looked at him askance and shook their heads in disbelief.

His climbing partner, meanwhile, had been busy. When he arrived in Kathmandu in February and had been issued with the official equipment for himself and Don, Dougal had taken one look at the job-lots and bulk-buy deals – German boots that wouldn't take the Austrian crampons, oxygen face-masks that wouldn't fit the Sherpas – that Dyhrenfurth had assembled, grabbed what he could and took it down to the bazaar, where he managed to exchange it for the still-unsold Annapurna equipment that they had off-loaded there the previous July. So he and Don were by far the best-equipped climbers on the mountain.

No sooner had Haston arrived at base camp than he set to work, spending two weeks carrying loads and establishing the route through the ever-dangerous Khumbu Ice-Fall – in particularly bad condition in 1971 – to an advanced base camp in the Western Cwm, from which the team's two objectives could be approached. After a great deal of heated discussion, which had caused one resignation[15] before the expedition even left its native countries, these had been fixed as attempts on the South-West Face and the West Ridge Direct of Chomolungma. The first had been reconnoitred twice by Japanese parties in 1969 and attempted in 1970. The West Ridge itself had been climbed by Hornbein and Unsoeld in the course of a 1963 American expedition also led by Dyhrenfurth. Neither of these routes was consonant with the ambitions of all the members of the expedition. Some had already fallen under the malignant spell of 'Everest'. Indeed, one faction, comprising Mazeaud, the Italian Carlo Mauri and the Swiss couple Michel and Yvette Vaucher, were much more interested in gaining the world's highest summit by any route, and thus being the first from their respective nations to do so. (The expedition ultimately imploded around this issue, the co-leader Jimmy Roberts finally rounding on the deputy and simply telling him, 'Fuck off, Mazeaud!' Which he, Mauri and the Vauchers promptly did.)

The early phase of the climbing is best known for the connected facts of a great storm that blew for 10 days, marooning climbers in high camps, and the death of the Indian Harsh Bahaguna. If Whillans had been looked on with a degree of criticism before the second event, he was to absolve himself and further his reputation in his actions around it. With his companion, the Austrian Wolfgang Axt, Bahaguna had established a Camp Four for the West Ridge climb. In their descent from that point, they had decided to resite Camp Three, which they did in the face of a gathering storm, whilst others from the West Ridge party rerouted the climb to Camp Three and established a rope traverse across a 40-degree ice-slope

---

[15] That of Rusty Baillie, who had written of the West Ridge/West Ridge Direct to Dyhrenfurth: 'The former has been done and the latter is splitting hairs . . . the time will come in Himalayan history when variants will be climbed. But it is not now.'

before themselves retreating to engage in haranguings of the leadership at advanced base camp. Having finally moved the camp, Axt and Bahaguna set off down, heading for Camp Two at 21,700 feet in the Western Cwm. With the wind rising and snow blowing, Axt waited for his friend at the end of the new rope-traverse, saw him appear and wave as if to gesture all was fine, and – himself exhausted after his efforts on the West Ridge and for the previous weeks in the ice-fall – was just about to reach Camp Two, 300 feet below, when he heard Bahaguna's screams. He alerted the climbers at Camp Two, and crawled into his tent and sleeping bag. Immediately, a team geared up and set off, with Odd Eliassen and Michel Vaucher, who had rigged the traverse and knew the route, in the lead, to attempt to rescue the man.

Don was among the 13 climbers in Camp Two at the time. John Cleare was also in the camp, and gives this impression of what happened:

> Everyone rushed off at once into the blowing snow on a rescue bid, except Ian Howell and myself, who delayed long enough to put a movie camera together, and Don: 'It's going to be bloody cold up there, fellas,' he said. 'Make sure you're properly dressed and bring your torches – them bloody continentals have only got half their clothes on.' He then got Ian and myself to help him collect together all the ski-poles we could find. 'It'll be dark and a white-out when we're trying to come back and we won't find camp again unless we leave markers.' So we hurried up, planting the poles in a line as markers as we crossed the glacier, from which all the tracks were being rapidly obliterated. Without those poles, I don't have any doubt that there would have been further disasters that night.

When Don reached the other rescuers, according to Cleare, he 'automatically took over the leadership of the party, showed great forethought, much moral courage, and considerable pragmatism in getting all the ill-prepared rescuers back to camp alive'. For Bahaguna himself, he could do little. Don balanced across the ice-slope on the front points of his crampons to where the Indian hung from the rope, righted him, for he had turned upside down, and looked into his face. He was blue, unconscious, barely alive. The rescuers had been unable either to lower him to a place where an attempt at resuscitation could be made, or pull him to either side along the rope because of its sag between anchor points. Don assessed the situation, knew it was hopeless, that other lives would now be lost if they did not regain shelter from a blizzard at 22,000 feet, and said goodbye: 'Sorry, Harsh, old son, you've had it.' With which he scrambled back along the rope and shepherded the party back down to the tents, where the great storm that had rolled in raged around them for 10 days and food and fuel ran low or ran out.

Several of the famous continentals were rushing about waving their hands in despair. Don just calmly explained that there was nothing to do but wait for the weather, not use more food and fuel than was essential, and use the time to good effect. So the South Face team, under Don's tutelage, produced detailed logistical flow-charts for the route to the summit whilst the West Ridge lot did nothing but moan and grouse and hold endless inquests on the accident. Don just took the stance that 'We're here to do a job of work – let's not bugger about, let's just get on with it.' It was his simple common sense that kept most of us going.

By the time the storm abated and the wind had blown away the new snow, of the 13 men at Camp Two, 12 were sick with a variety of ailments. They limped and staggered back down through the ice-fall to recover at base camp, leaving one fit man behind at Camp Two. It was Don. The pariah – the fat man – had won through, and was waiting for his partner to arrive to continue the climb.

The expedition, however, was falling apart. Affected by the death of Bahaguna and ravaged by continuing illness and the departure of the deputy's contingent,[16] its ability to support the four lead climbers – Whillans and Haston, and the Japanese pair Ito and Uemura – as they attempted the face was severely restricted. The co-leader Dyhrenfurth was sent home on health grounds by Peter Steele, the expedition's doctor. Jimmy Roberts took over the

---

[16] Done with Gallic passion and flair, Mazeaud's final utterance has gone down in mountaineering folklore: 'They expect me, Pierre Mazeaud, Member of the French Assembly, aged 42, to work as a Sherpa for Anglo-Saxons and Japanese. Never! This is not me, but France, they have insulted!'

leadership, with Don as climbing leader, and the depleted team struggled on up the wide snow couloir of the South-West Face to the foot of the rock band at 27,000 feet. Prospecting on each side at the base of this, they climbed a difficult ramp and established Camp Six at 27,200 feet. The British pair spent 21 consecutive days above 24,000 feet – which broke all records for endurance at altitude. When the weather allowed, they issued forth from the tent and Don peered round a corner to the right, where he spied a straightforward traverse line leading across slabs and scree slopes to the South-East Ridge, with the summit of the mountain easily accessible above.

We'd stuck to our South-West Face route all the time, right through all the squabbles about swapping routes and all that. All along we had said we would climb the Face or fail. When I found that it would be easy to walk across slopes from our high point to the South Ridge, I knew it was a real possibility. But we weren't far enough up the Face for that way to be called the Face Route. If the traverse had appeared a few hundred feet higher, it would have been all right.

They turned instead to a gully leading up through the rock band above. It was easy climbing through deep powder-snow. Don led a last pitch, looked up at the continuation of the gully,[17] realised that it was far longer than he had thought, told himself then and there that he was neither going to get up the mountain nor come to any

---

[17] On the post-monsoon expedition in 1972, this was again the line the climbers intended to attempt. On that trip, however, Bonington noticed the possibilities of circumventing the rock band by ramps leading up to the top snow slopes at its left-hand end. This was the line taken by Haston, Scott, Burke, Boardman and Pertemba on their successful ascents in 1975. Either way, given their circuitous and marginal natures, raises the question of what Don was doing, involving himself in this climb: 'With me, it's always got to be a straightforward route with an obvious line.' The South-West Face of Chomolungma is anything but that, and in engaging with it he surely reneged on his principles in the interests of his professional career in mountaineering. Ivan Rowan, commenting most astutely on the climb in the *Daily Telegraph*, pointed out that 'Whillans accepts all the implications of the Everest South-West Face. Mountaineering, for him, if not Big Business is Business. He lives by climbing, says that professionalism is increasing in British mountaineering, and believes that some commercialism is inevitable.' So for Don, 'the job' that he was always so concerned to get done had become just that – a job; and quite a complex one for which others were always at liberty to tender . . .

harm upon it, tied off the rope and slid back down to Dougal. 'I think we've had it, lad.' Without food, oxygen, rope, all of which they had run out of, to climb on up the line was not feasible. 'What d'you think of it?' he asked Dougal, nodding to the way ahead. Not so very difficult, Dougal thought, but long, and they would need much more rope, and of that there would be none forthcoming unless they went to get it themselves.

'How about buggering off?' Don suggested, which was exactly what they did, and after another night virtually without food in the cold and discomfort of Camp Six, on the way down they met John Cleare just above Camp Two in the Western Cwm.

I watched Dougal come down the fixed ropes and stagger towards us down the Cwm. He was zonked. He looked like a Belsen victim and dragged his feet through the snow. Pemba rushed out to meet him with a big kettle of hot fruit juice. Dougal flopped in the snow to drink it, and then, supported on Pemba's shoulder, he staggered into camp – shot.

Ten minutes later Don swung off the bottom of the ropes. He strode down the trodden path towards camp humming a tune and dribbling a snowball at his feet. Pemba ran out with the kettle and Don dismissed the friendly little Sherpa with a friendly slap on his shoulder: 'Thanks, Pemba, but I'll have what's left of the real stuff.' He reached inside his down suit, pulled out what was left of a half-bottle of Glenfiddich, and knocked it back in one gulp. Then he chucked the bottle over his shoulder and strode on down to the accompaniment of a loud belch.

In the tents later, whilst Dougal slept, Don talked to Cleare:

There was me and Dougal like sparrows in a gutter, and I looked round the corner and lo and behold! We could have traversed across easily on to the ordinary route just below the South Summit. It weren't very far and we could have climbed to the top of Everest. But how many times has Everest been done by that bloody route? We was there to climb the South Face. That's what Norman raised all that money for . . .

Cleare asked him how he had got on with Dougal for so many days alone together in a small tent.

> You can't go wrong with Dougal if your diet's just porridge and whisky – that's all he needs. That's all we had, at any road. You know one thing – Dougal would've made the top, but he wouldn't have come down again. It was old Grandpa Whillans that kept him alive, otherwise he'd have killed himself up there. But I've no time meself for dead heroes. You know, John, always remember that in the Himalayas it's softly-softly-catchee-mountain. Watch and wait and don't go till it's right, otherwise you're bloody dead, and that lasts a long bloody time.

There were many reasons – none of them to be laid to Don's account – as to why the 1971 expedition failed, but fail it did nonetheless. And on his return to England there were some question marks being raised too about the most notable success of Don's career. During his absence in Nepal, the Thames Television 1970 Annapurna expedition film, *The Hardest Way Up*, had been shown to widespread acclaim. One of its most telling sequences was the interview with a dejected and exhausted Nick Estcourt on his arrival back at base camp, spilling out his sorrows and complaints after being shouldered out of the way in the race for the summit. It was footage that could not help but elicit a warm response. Don certainly impressed with his mocking pragmatism: 'I approach this climb like a job of work – now Dougal here has a much more intellectual approach'; or again, to a background of avalanches thundering down the face, 'I don't like taking risks. I try to get out of the danger area as quickly as possible.' But there was a sense from both film and critical reaction to it of the balance of sympathy not being for the 'victors' but for the team-workers – a sense too that the issue of fair opportunities for all, and especially for the younger climbers then coming through, was one that would run and run.

To back up that vague generality, there was also the very informative, expressive and comprehensive expedition book that had appeared soon after the publication of Don's own auto-biography. The devil that would pursue Don from this source lay in the detail – more specifically in Appendix A, and a section of it entitled 'A few statistics' compiled by Estcourt. In this, he wrote some apparently flattering comments about Don:

> Don had spent nearly the least time above Camp Three, and yet was going strongest on the final day when most other people were burnt out. Perhaps this shows that deterioration due to altitude sets in only just slower than acclimatisation, and in fact Don, the wily old mountaineer, had timed things just right.

The most telling inclusion in this appendix, however, was a table of various facts relating to each expedition member – how many days in the lead or spent carrying loads, for example. Estcourt and Boysen had spent five days each in the lead, and 22 carrying loads. For Haston, the respective figures were 22 and 10. For Don, they were 19 and 7. Your reaction to this might depend on how you view statistics, but mountaineers are inveterate controversialists and the editor of the prestigious *Mountain* magazine, Ken Wilson, well briefed as ever, was straight on to this point when he invited Don into the Star Chamber of one of his interview sessions in the winter following his return from Chomolungma: 'It is said that there was some discontent on Annapurna because you didn't carry as many loads as everyone else.' Don knew exactly what Wilson was getting at:

> What amused me was that statistics list of Estcourt's, which showed that I didn't carry many loads between the lower camps. As far as I know there aren't many people who can be in two places at the same time, and if there are, they're a dying bloody race. All my statistics were from higher up the mountain. If I was high up, how the hell could I be low down? ... this business of being wise after the event is beginning to crop up more and more after expeditions. Most of mine, like Masherbrum and Trivor, have been no bother. On Trivor I didn't try for the summit because I was sick, and that was that. I missed out. But I've never said that I wasn't sick and that I could have gone on; and I've never tried to bend or twist it afterwards.[18]

---

[18] I was present when this interview was being taped, and with Wilson wrote the preamble to the published version. Don was remarkably prickly and defensive

A barrister, faced with that response, might well invite the speaker to try answering the question. The mountaineering community, ever sensitive to the slightest affront, whether real or imaginary, would have picked up on the comment directed against Estcourt and pondered where it stood in the narrow spectrum between plain speaking and speaking ill. The wheelers and dealers in world mountaineering, already planning the next campaign to attract sponsorship for however many trips it would take to vanquish this 'last great problem of the Himalayas', would have noted with dismay Don's brutally frank disparagements, and wondered if they needed a chap on their team who had so little faith in the product they would have to sell to their sponsors:

> We could never claim our route was ever going to be a
> direttissima once we veered off to Camp Six . . . I think it's all
> a bit of a farce: I can't take it seriously. At one stage when it
> looked as though the previous Japanese expedition might get
> up, Dyhrenfurth sent out a newsletter saying that even if they
> climbed the face we could still do the true direttissima . . . all
> this direttissima stuff is a load of cobblers as far as I'm
> concerned.

Cobblers or not, after a winter the high point of which was an appearance on the kitsch television show *This Is Your Life*, where he was joined by Bonington, Haston, Brown, MacInnes, and a Munich doctor by the name of Karl Herrligkoffer, the spring came round and Don was preparing for Chomolungma yet again – this time without the prospect of Dougal to climb with.

The 1972 European Expedition led[19] by Herrligkoffer proved to be even more of a débâcle than that of the previous year. Whereas

---

throughout, and afterwards Wilson remarked that he felt he had been lucky to get away without being thumped. One question-and-answer – the latter not atypical of the Whillans wit – that was left out of the printed version gives an interesting glimpse into Don's attitude towards younger climbers of the time, as well as revealing quite an unpleasantly dismissive and arrogant streak. Wilson asked him what he thought of the younger rock-climbers then coming to prominence – John Syrett, for example, who had just made the second on-sight lead of Almscliff's Wall of Horrors, or Alan Rouse, who had soloed The Boldest. 'Aye,' Don responded, in his best nasal sneer, 'I've 'eard ducks fart before.'

[19] Interestingly, Herrligkoffer only spent three weeks out of the trip's three-month duration with the expedition.

1971's team had established – after the departure of the fractious contingent – an *entente cordiale*, relationships on the 1972 expedition were fraught, its organisation suffered from a crucial lack of understanding of the particular problems posed by mountain and route, and the language barrier between German and British members was never more than tenuously bridged. Added to that, there was an almost paranoid suspicion of Don on the part of the Austrians, Kuen, Huber and Haim, and the Italian, Breitenberger – all of whom had been warned about his machinations (or tactical nous, if you wanted to put a positive slant on it). The fact that Don again fell ill from vertigo in the early weeks, and had to rest at base camp whilst the way through the Khumbu Ice-Fall and the early camps were established by the Austrians, fuelled their suspicion that he was – again, as they presumed – operating to a work-avoidance strategy.

Whether that was strategy or habitual mode is a moot point, but certainly it made the Austro-Italian team of lead climbers even more wary – of Don especially, but also of his two fellow Britons on the 1972 team, Hamish MacInnes and Doug Scott, the latter a 30-year-old Nottingham schoolteacher who was, despite a great deal of climbing experience worldwide, on his first expedition to the highest mountains.[20] So instead of a Whillans plot, an Austrian one was hatched to keep the British trio from reaching the top. It worked, too – by dint of collusion with the leadership, plain obstruction, a continual barrage of carping criticism and the subversion of every sensible proposal put forward by Don on the

---

[20] Don had insisted on the invitation of Doug, telling Herrligkoffer that he would not go if Scott wasn't invited. The two had first met when Doug was 15 and staying at Wasdale Head. In the rugby matches the climbers played in the barn to keep out of the rain, Doug kept coming up against Don, and the final tally between them was a black eye to Doug, a broken rib to Don. On the 1972 trip, the amiable Doug was subjected to the usual Whillans prevarications in all matters pertaining to the use of stoves. 'It was an interesting experience sharing a tent with Don. He wasn't one for camp chores and spent most of his time sleeping or thinking or adapting equipment. Above base camp I cooked all the meals. I never minded that as I quite enjoyed cooking. But after a big solo effort to Camp Five I came down the ropes and yelled, "Get a brew on" to Don. When I got to the tent Don was still tinkering with his equipment, and no brew. I gathered snow, melted it down, got a brew on, passed it round and then prepared the evening meal – mashed potato, sausage and peas – and handed that to Don. I said, "I'm not your mother, you know, Don." He said, "Oh, are you one of those people who moans about a bit of cooking?" He was so outrageous I had to smile.'

grounds that each suggestion or proposed new plan would have some veiled motive by which he would be seeking to propel himself into the lead. For once, because of a now-international reputation for Machiavellianism that had preceded him and grown inexorably in the contemplation, Don was prevented from playing any effective part in the climb. The supposedly international team were working to the plan that this particular striker must never be fed the ball, the Britons knew it, and the frustrations and tensions rose ('Doug and Hamish fuming,' Don wrote in his diary on 21 April).

Eventually these came to a head over schedules for the deployment of climbers in summit bids. The Britons were sidelined in these, and rather than working in the support role offered, they descended and left the expedition. Kuen and his team, strategically victorious, climbed up to the site of 1971's Camp Six using that year's fixed ropes, a storm came in and – without even reaching Whillans's 1971 high point – they retreated, leaving the mountain to draw its breath and await the next assault. And the pundits of the mountain press to hold forth on 'pampered, highly strung prima donnas acutely aware of their own ambitions and unable to display even basic team spirit when the chips are down'. In the summer of 1972, as he returned to Britain, Don too had begun to be included in that spreading perception.

That he was, on the 1972 expedition, 'a man more sinned against than sinning'[21] is quite apparent from all accounts. But he had nonetheless established a reputation that had some very strong negatives attached, and the repercussions from which would very soon become obvious. He was home from Chomolungma in June,

---

[21] 'Hamish MacInnes recounted how, during Dr Herrligkoffer's European Expedition to the South-West Face of Everest, Don, apart from nicknaming his leader "Sterlings-coffer", did in fact behave with astonishing forbearance in the face of almost unendurable provocation and never once stepped out of line – until the expedition was over. Apparently, during the earliest stages of the expedition, when the members were just getting to know one another, they heard on the base camp radio that Germany had just beaten England in the World Cup. "Aha," cried the dour Felix Kuen (the climbing leader) to Don, "we have beaten you at your national game!" Don paused, looked around, narrowed his eyes to the merest slits, leant forward, paused again, and said in a harsh whisper, "Aye, but we've beaten you at your national game twice now."' Mike Thompson, in 'Out With the Boys Again' (included in *The Games Climbers Play*, edited by Ken Wilson). Sports historians will naturally pick up on the vital clue here that consigns this anecdote to the file marked 'Whillans stories!' There was no World Cup in 1972 . . .

and within days of his arrival, a new expedition to attempt the South-West Face had been announced. Bonington had previously secured permission for a lightweight team to try the Lhotse Face/ South Col/South Ridge route in the post-monsoon period of 1972. When news came through of Herrligkoffer's failure, he switched his plans and permission to the South-West Face, appointed Jimmy Roberts as his deputy leader and announced his climbing team: Mick Burke, Nick Estcourt, Dave Bathgate, Dougal Haston, Doug Scott and Hamish MacInnes. Beth Burke, Mick's wife, was to be there as base camp nurse. The absent name shrilled out, the press reacted with amazement; the saga of Don's involvement with the South-West Face climb was over.

What had happened? Dark hints circulated: 'Whillans's abilities at high altitude are well known, but other events on both the Annapurna and the 1971 International Expedition are understood to have prompted his exclusion. It appears that a significant proportion of the team was worried about his membership . . .'

'Even Nick', Bonington's closest friend, perhaps?

The commentator continued: 'Bonington is clearly taking a gamble in sacrificing proven ability at high altitude for higher morale lower on the mountain, and there are some who will question his wisdom in this.'

Bonington himself, in *The Everest Years*, his clearest account of how he came to the decision, with quiet understatement makes the situation that obtained between him and Don quite clear:

> I had left out Don Whillans, the one person both the media and the climbing world expected me to take. We had done some of our best Alpine climbing together . . . in 1970 he had . . . been my deputy leader and had contributed a great deal to our success. His forthright, abrasive style had complemented my own approach, but it had also created stress. One of the problems had been that when we had climbed together in the Alps, Don had indisputably held the initiative. He had been that bit more experienced and was also stronger than I. It would be very difficult for him to accept a reversal of those roles. He was a strong leader in his own right, had now been to Everest twice, and knew the mountain much better than I. It would not have been easy to run the expedition in the way that I wanted with Don taking part . . .

That the expedition failed even to pitch a tent at the Camp Six site he and Dougal had established in 1971 was small consolation to Don as the comment-seeking press kept his phone ringing all day on 15 November, after the failure of the Bonington expedition had been announced. He had made more enemies than friends among the new order of British Himalayan climbers who were to dominate in the 1970s. Burke, Haston and Estcourt did not want him along,[22] and who, on the evidence, could gainsay them? They were eager, ambitious young men with their own reputations to establish, their own ambitions to work towards. Why, any longer, should they have borne with the blatantly self-serving strategies of a climber who, in their eyes, had had his day? For Bonington, these were the men with whom he climbed in the Alps and each weekend at home, and around whom his future plans centred. Loyalties had shifted. Old debts had been repaid with interest and it was time to move on. For Don, his brief time as a player in what the media viewed as the major league in mountaineering was over. Not yet 40 years of age, he was shunted out of the limelight and consigned to the periphery, where legends best thrive.

---

[22] It needs to be recorded here that Scott and MacInnes, with whom Don had so recently and strongly been united in the struggle with the Germans and Austrians, did vigorously press his case for inclusion; the argument adduced to defeat their case was that the dynamics of a single-nation, closely knit team would be entirely different, and likely again to reveal the flaws rather than the strengths in Don's approach.

17

Cult Hero

For much of its history there was a hallowed tradition of gracious debunking in climbing literature that gave a voice to the activity's anarchic and extra-societal leanings.[1] It is, I suppose, neither accident nor coincidence that two of its finest exponents in their best essays turned an amused and ironic gaze upon Don Whillans. Tom Patey, in his 'A Short Walk with Whillans', concentrates on the man, his Eiger obsession, his humour, and the whiff of detachment and ill-fortune that hung around him. Mike Thompson, in his comic and mischievous 'Out With the Boys Again', touches on Don more glancingly, but his brief, trenchant commentary also captures something central about him: 'No wonder the individualistic, subversive Whillans became the cult hero of the B team. Never was anyone more present by his absence.'

The particular absence Thompson is referring to here is that of Don in 1975 from the last act in the cod saga that went under the title 'Everest South-West Face'. By the time that took place Don had been surplus to the requirements of Chris Bonington's massively publicised and sponsored Himalayan project for three years. And as Thompson recognises, far from consigning him to oblivion, the effect of this removal from the limelight was to elevate him to that realm which had always been very dear to the seditious world of

---

[1] Though it still exists to a degree, it has been put in abeyance rather by the increasingly litigious social climate of the 1990s, and the rise of the image-conscious 'professional climber'. In recent years it has tended for the most part to emerge from climbing's marginal and 'underground' media. Chris Bonington states the point behind this neatly when he writes that 'even anarchic climbers can be very prickly where their own egos are concerned'. He goes on to add, judiciously, that 'as far as I see it, I've had stacks of brickbats and piss-takes over the years, none of which have done me any real harm and which I have to accept as the price of success'.

climbing – outlaw status. If he was not wanted by the glossy and the select, well, neither for that matter were the vast majority of climbers in Britain. If he was too awkward, uncouth and disruptive for that glamorous and chosen world, well, were they for the most part not also thus?[2] And as to the values of those enterprises of the select that seemed to take such short spoons to sup with the devils of business and banking, countrywide there was an undercurrent of debate as to whether they were the traditional ones of mountaineering. Did they exemplify the motives of those who upheld mountaineering's great tradition and that had impelled Longstaff, Shipton, Tilman – curiosity, spontaneity, self-reliance, closeness to people and land?

My own view of this widespread grassroots perception is that it was an oversimplification – both traditions had in fact coexisted for decades – and in its relation to Don one that stemmed from particular circumstances. Chief among these was that Bonington and the members of his teams acted with considerable forbearance and discretion in not making public the reasons why Don had been dropped (these will re-emerge quite clearly in the course of this chapter). It was easy, in the absence of explanation, for conjecture to hold that the abrasive little Northerner's face didn't fit with a glamorous, high-profile enterprise, and in the absence of reasons to the contrary, conjecture could establish itself as fact. Never mind that Boysen, Braithwaite, Burke – each of them grassroots climbers, hardly glossy or select, and in Burke's case just as abrasive as Don himself – did not want Don along. The loyalty of their continuing public discretion gave Don's reputation a degree of protection, and drew upon themselves, their fellow team-members and their leader

---

[2] In an address to the National Mountaineering Conference in 1974, Dave Cook made clear the British climbing community's susceptibility to a distinctly Whillans-derived cultism: 'If you had wanted to compose an identikit, advertisement-style prototype of your aspiring hard man in, say, 1963, you would have included the following: first, the "h" on "hard" would have been dropped; certain insignia, ranging from flat 'ats to Morris 1000 vans, would have been adopted; in the Alps it would have been compulsory to be very dirty, and in bars everywhere to drink loud and long. An intensely chauvinistic attitude to British climbing was essential. By definition, the continentals were unable to free-climb hard rock, while the Americans only got up cliffs because of the power drills on their backs. The most essential ingredient of this style was a sort of exaggerated "workerism", and throughout the 1950s this grew until eventually it replaced the public image that had gone before.'

a sense of opprobrium – for having acted unfairly and disloyally.

From this unclarified situation the notion gained ground that although Don, forsaking for a while his Odyssean mode, had forgotten to have himself lashed to the mast and had wandered a while on the Sirens' shore, he had somehow escaped. His rejection was seen as his liberation, and through it, by a neat side-step to evade personal responsibility, he came to speak for the community of climbers. Not only that, he moved freely among that community. Unlike the increasingly professional and slick big-venue lecture tours after big-venue expeditions – each of which added weight to the sense that Don's character, and not any declining ability, had led to his exclusion – year in and year out from the late 1950s he was lecturing nightly countrywide, guest-speaking at club dinners, drinking till all hours with whoever was around to keep him company.[3] He was available, and he was formidable, with his piercing blue eyes and forearms like hams, and he had been rejected, and he was funny and cutting and disrespectful, and the B team, which in effect is all of us, began rather to pamper him and court him and love him. Also, an element of pathos had begun to intrude. He clearly had a drink problem, and a weight problem too,[4] which

---

[3] Bruce Goodwin: 'I was at a party of Al Harris's in about 1972 with a group from the Black & Tans – Brian Sullivan, Eddie Birch, Richard McHardy among them. We'd all – apart from Richard, who was very concerned with health and fitness – been doing the Padarn Lake [this was the Llanberis climbers' pub of the period] swill routine, Whillans had been there and come back to Harris's with us. At about 2 a.m. Richard, for whom Don had a pretty fond regard and who was still sober, said to a red-faced, profusely sweating Whillans, who was still downing ale like the breweries might go out of business any day, "Why do you drink so much, Don?" "I've got a morbid fear of dehydration, Richard," came the reply, to the usual accompaniment of guffaws from those who were hanging on his every word, and that was the end of Richard's solicitous enquiry. But Richard was genuinely interested in the why of the drinking because he was, in his own idiosyncratic way, concerned for Whillans's health. And rightly so, as it turned out.'

[4] The assumption might be that these two were related, but this is not necessarily the case. Don also liked his food and Audrey was well versed in supplying that need. When I first took on this biography, I went round to the Penmaenmawr guest house she then ran to talk it over with her. She sat me down at her table and – scarcely eating anything herself – commenced to feed me. On the table in front of me appeared a large pudding basin full of rich, thick soup, very good too, and half a loaf of bread thick-cut and thickly buttered. I waded through. It was cleared away, replaced by a vast dinner plate with two immense pork chops, stuffing, apple sauce, roast potatoes, carrots, cabbage, sprouts, mash, all swimming in gravy and cooked to perfection. Now I like a challenge, whatever the sphere, and I cleared my plate and groaned silently and felt very much like the anaconda that

exacerbated the problems he suffered with his knees. The frequency
of the incapacitating attacks of vertigo from which he had suffered
since he was a teenager was also increasing. And then there was the
burden of failure. Ronnie Dutton remembers an aggressive young
Manchester University student coming up to him at a club dinner in
The Swan pub at New Mills in Derbyshire.

'You've been on a lot of expeditions, haven't you, Don?'

'Aye,' Don replied, waiting for whatever deferential comment or
question came next.

The student curled his lip, lanced, 'Most of them failures . . .' at
him, and walked off without another word, leaving behind a silence
in which Don, speechless, simply bit his lip and shook his head. One
of the crucial keys to the Whillans character is how easily he could
be hurt, how necessary he felt that habitually aggressive front to be
– and how ill, perhaps, it ultimately served him.

If there was no prospect of anything to offset that undercurrent
of negative perception about his mountaineering career in 1972, no
invitations to take part in Himalayan expeditions forthcoming,
there were at least the material signs of success in which to take
comfort. At the end of October he and Audrey left their council
maisonette at Loveclough and moved across the valley to 58
Grasmere Road, Haslingden – a bungalow they had bought on a
new estate of identical properties. John Cleare called there on his
way north a month later, and left the following culture-shocked
impression of life in the Whillans household at the time:

> As I pulled up in front of the modern, ticky-tacky box on a
> private estate, I was surprised to see a large caravan parked
> behind Don's orange Capri. The living room was chock-full
> of ethnic goodies that Don had brought back from all over the

---

ate the pig and thanked Audrey profusely and told her I wouldn't need to eat again
for a month, and she beamed and said she liked to see a good appetite on a man
and disappeared into her kitchen again, reappearing seconds later with a
Brobdingnagian bowl, six inches of creamy rice-pudding like my grandmother
used to make in its base, set into which were four ring doughnuts, each of them
filled with a scoop of ice-cream and topped with a fist-sized dollop of jam. I had
my old labrador with me that day, who was the greediest dog who ever lived. The
phone rang and Audrey left her dining room to answer it. I lived to eat another
day. Behind every great man . . .! At Don's funeral the old Rock & Ice member
Harry Smith, in a piercing Brummy accent, delivered this verdict: 'Well, Audrey
got her revenge – she fed him to death!'

world. Carvings, paintings, rugs – there were some very tasteful artefacts. But on one wall the three china ducks were in full flight – it was real parody. Don and I were sitting talking in the big soft easy chairs in front of a huge television set when Audrey came home from work in Manchester. He hardly acknowledged her. She went off and came back with Don's slippers, which she carefully fitted to his feet as we sat there. He continued talking, saying not a word to her, and she went off and started making the supper. In the morning she brought us both breakfast in bed before going off to work again. Eventually we got up and went off to climb on a nearby gritstone outcrop, and then on to the pub – I found it all quite an eye-opener.

A visit to Don by Leo Dickinson at the same period strikes similar chords: 'Don was stretched out on the sofa with his feet on the cat to keep warm when Audrey came home. She made us a cup of tea. Don took a swig from his and immediately spat it out. "'Ave yer lost the use of yer 'ands?" he barked at her. "This isn't stirred!"'

The caravan proved useful when spring came round, and Don trailed around Wales and Scotland[5] in it, busying himself with organising not one but two expeditions for the closing months of 1973. The hint for the first of these – and maybe the strangest expedition Don ever went on – had been given in a film made by Derek Bromhall for the BBC's *World About Us* series:

The film I had made [was] of an expedition to the plateau of Roraima – one of a number of plateaux forming a cordillera running from Venezuela to Guyana and Brazil and the inspiration for Conan Doyle's book, *The Lost World*. I had filmed the 'prow' of Roraima from Guyana and Don wondered

---

[5] One of Don's earners post-Annapurna was the directorship of a Lancashire clothing company, 'Top Togs', a speciality of which was making golfing apparel. So after visiting Hamish, the next port of call for Don and his caravan was the Open at Troon. On the Roraima expedition itself, Hamish records that 'I watched Don unpacking his clothing. He had a fascinating selection of colourful apparel, obviously influenced by the trendy international golf scene. One garment – a shirt which he held up – was utterly fantastic; it had vertical stripes in bright rip-stop nylon, like a multicoloured bull's-eye. I collapsed in a paroxysm of laughter when I saw it and it was some minutes before I'd recovered sufficiently to ask him what on earth it was.'

if it was climbable. A 1500-foot overhang, emerging from the rain-forest to over 9000 feet, shrouded in mist and daily drenched by torrential rain that spilled off the plateau in magnificent waterfalls appealed to Don as a challenge very different from his more usual experience of climbing snow and ice.

Don started to assemble a team. The obvious first choice for an expedition in that part of the world was John Streetly, and he quickly signalled his willingness to go. Hamish MacInnes, their companion from the Walker Spur, proved a little more difficult to entice, but eventually was drawn in through the involvement of a close friend of his, film-maker Neil McCallum. The trip's appeal to the insatiably curious Joe Brown was immediate, and he put forward his friend and acolyte of the time from the climbing community that had grown up around Llanberis, 'Mo' Anthoine.[6] The inclusion of Mike Thompson made up the team's climbing strength. 'We were,' Hamish records, 'as our friends had been at pains to point out, most of us a bit long in the tooth.' It was an odd mixture of personalities, and was not to prove an entirely happy one. Although it was the first expedition that Don and Joe had been on together, it failed to bring about any rapprochement between them. In his book[7] about the trip, MacInnes makes the delicately barbed comment that 'Don has unfortunately a very bad reputation, most of which is ill-founded.'[8]

---

[6] One of the pivotal figures on the Welsh climbing scene for many years, 'Mo' was a scabrously funny, savagely witty, cherub-faced, muscular little man who had no truck whatsoever with any of the pretensions and minor or major dishonesties of climbers and excoriated them personally at every opportunity. Brutally honest about his own shortcomings, he expected the same from everyone with whom he came into contact, and if it was not forthcoming from them, the public flayings that ensued were cruel spectator-sport. He died of a brain tumour in 1989. The distinguished critic, poet and novelist Al Alvarez was one of his close friends, and wrote a subtle, graphic memoir of him, published in 1988 under the title of *Feeding the Rat*.

[7] *Climb to the Lost World*, Hodder & Stoughton, 1974.

[8] The rest of Hamish's pen-portrait is a masterful summing-up of the Whillans character, worth giving in its entirety, from one who knew him well and had reason to hold him in high regard: 'Blunt and shrewd, tending to introversion, he is at the same time gregarious: at his best in a desperate mountain crisis or holding forth in a pub where he can talk and drink at great length. I have always maintained that Don, in his day, was one of the greatest mountaineers. Frequently

That reputation was not salved in any measure on Roraima. There were certainly extenuating factors. Import restrictions on bringing foodstuffs into Guyana, which were only relaxed hours before the boat carrying the expedition's supplies left Liverpool, meant that provisioning the trip was a last-minute shambles. Don's great friend John Streetly had to have surgery on a knee, it was not successful, and he was forced to withdraw. The climbing partnerships were thus thrown into sharp relief. Joe, as had become his Welsh and Himalayan habit at the time, was going to climb with Mo, so Don would have to team up either with Mike Thompson[9] – wonderfully relaxed and amusing company but not the most naturally gifted or experienced of rock-climbers – or with Hamish, whose all-round mountaineering competence was unquestionable, but whose rock-climbing had suffered a degree of neglect from the long years of his domicile among the snows and mists and temperate monsoons of Glencoe.

The central dynamic here is a very old one by this stage of Don's life, and a compounding one too. In a talk that he gave at the Royal Geographical Society in February 1987, speaking about the end of their climbing partnership in the 1950s Joe made the wry quip that 'It was either Don, or a wife.' The emotional truth in that off-hand comment is important, and is one that Ronnie Dutton, a good friend to both men and an extremely perceptive observer, makes plain:

Joe and Don had a strange attitude towards each other. Right at the beginning, Don was seriously setting out to court Joe,

---

he remains in the background, almost free-wheeling, until the odds are against him, when he comes forth with unbelievable reserves of will-power and endurance. It was an education to climb with him on "Everest". He was grossly overweight even when he arrived at base camp, having previously stated in a television interview when asked when he stopped drinking, "At the last pub – in Namche Bazaar."

'He took his time, acclimatising slowly and summing up the situation, which he always does with great perception. It is when others are starting to feel the strain of high-altitude climbing that he comes into his own. He is pared down to his proper weight, having lost about two stone in five weeks, and starts going like a bomb . . . Don is an amazingly straight bloke. There can be no pretence with him, he sees right through any hypocrisy: that is the time to beware for he won't beat about the bush, no matter who is involved. I have been in many dangerous situations with him . . . I cannot think of anyone better with whom to share a tight corner.'

[9] Mike Thompson also had to leave the expedition at about its halfway point, after sustaining a foot injury whilst having gone to replenish supplies.

but when they grew apart after Kangchenjunga, it was almost as though Don felt he'd been jilted, and he grew very, very jealous of Joe[10] – to the extent that it became very hard to be friends with the two of them. Don would always be complaining – 'He's crafty, he's got money no one knows about.' I remember once when Don was round at our house and we had a five-hour row until eventually I had to shut him up. 'Because it's Joe you're having a go,' I told him. It was 'hell hath no fury like a Whillans scorned', and he did feel that was how Joe had treated him, even though both of them were always circling round trying to find a way to make it up. They were just too different, in the end. One thing that was very apparent from that Roraima trip, though, was that Don hated – and I mean hated – Mo. He thought he'd taken his rightful place with Joe, and that he was just using him – which he wasn't, of course; Mo really looked up to Joe. But that wasn't how Don saw it, and he was very critical . . .

At the beginning of October this explosive mixture of an expedition, founded in the notion of old friendships and focused on a leaning prow of sandstone that raked up for 1500 feet out of tropical rain-forest, left Gatwick for Guyana. A worse destination for someone as fastidious as Don had become in the years since long-gone summers in the squalor of the Biolay is hard to imagine. The approach was a nightmare of swamps and mud, swarming with every kind of strange and dangerous creature that ever bit and blooped and nipped and stung and crawled. There were bird-eating spiders the size of a man's fist, poisonous snakes that sought out the warmth of sleeping bags, dense undergrowth teeming with bizarre insects with telescopic antennae which Joe – inveterately curious – collected in cigar tubes,[11] to Don's disgust and frequently voiced complaints. Among his peers, the indolence and opportunism with regard to the daily chores that was now ingrained in Don's

---

[10] In the heyday of the Rock & Ice, Don's rudeness and surliness towards Joe's girlfriends was very marked, and on at least two occasions led to remonstrations and threatened thumpings, from Doug Verity and Alan Taylor – both of them big, mild, friendly men not easily roused to anger. Nat Allen, too, recalls that particularly towards Mavis Jolley Don was unforgivably rough and personally insulting.

[11] Joe revelled in this trip and the strangeness of it, still regarding it over 30 years on as one of his favourite adventures.

behaviour was strongly on display ('Don came round – an excellent sense of timing – just as the billy was boiling'), and was met with a kind of attritional irony all round. If there was no option but for the others to tolerate it, at least they would comment upon it. To the drum-beat of daily downpours, frictions escalated into rows. Neil McCallum came in for criticism from Don for his individual style of film-making, and infuriated him by calmly telling him to 'Get lost!' instead of displaying the normal deference of those who feared they might get thumped. The whole ambience had quickly begun to grate on Don: 'Can't stand all these blighters farting about like blue-arsed flies. There are too many plans flying around. It's like crapping on a fan blade . . .'

There had not been the usual Himalayan walk-in, with its opportunity to gain fitness, so Don, faced with 1500 feet of impendent, vegetated, slimy rock, was unable to pull the considerable weight now contained within his 44-inch waistline and was restricted to a supporting role.[12] This placed the burden of hard climbing on Joe and Mo. The former led some extremely difficult free pitches low down, after which the climbing on the compact, quartzy sandstone

---

[12] That it was not only Don's climbing ability that had deteriorated, but perhaps also his judgement and his awareness of inherent danger, is suggested by an incident during a descent from a belay above a feature known as the Africa Flake. Fixed ropes up to this belay had been fraying over a sharp edge, which Don had rounded off with his hammer. When Hamish came to jumar up the ropes, one of them was so worn it began to part, and he had hastily to transfer to another as Don watched the proceedings. In the descent, Joe – with Don beside him on the ledge – began to abseil on this rope: 'As he launched himself over the edge he felt the frayed rope under his hand as he fed it through the descendeur. He didn't know then that I [i.e. Hamish] had had such a narrow escape on the ascent, and that the rope had almost parted. In the darkness, Don hadn't realised which ropes he was using. Joe had been about to descend on two ropes: a loose corlene used for sack-hauling, which was hanging over a bromeliad beside Don – not anchored – and the faulty rope which had already scared the daylights out of me! Quick as a flash, he saw his mistake and attached a jumar above the damaged section of rope, then moved up and transferred to the new rope. It was a very close thing.'

It seems to me absolutely fair to ask why – given the darkness and the scare with Hamish earlier in the day, about which Joe may not have known – Don had not warned Joe to be careful which ropes he used for the descent. The omission was surely innocent, but it was most definitely culpable, and came very close to resulting in the death of Britain's greatest-ever climber. As Don would once have known, and Joe's responses demonstrated, when you venture into these situations, your every sense must be on red alert.

relied heavily on aid and the task of leading fell to Mo – 'Without Mo, Roraima would not have been climbed,' states Joe. So overhanging was the prow that once sections of the route had been established and prusiking back to the high point each day became the norm, on each pitch the climbers had to jumar outwards for 30 feet from the face before making any vertical progress. After having reached two-thirds height on the prow, Mo and Joe felt others should make an effort and decided to delegate leading on the last sections of the mainly artificial climb to Don. Mo was assigned to deliver the message:

> 'I've been talking with Joe . . .'
> 'Aye,' Don said noncommittally.
> 'We feel that you should lead to the summit now.'
> 'Oh? You mean that when things get a bit tough you want to back out?' started Don aggressively.

The crisis was negotiated by some diplomacy from Hamish, who played a crucial and driving role in the completion of the climb, leading the final pitches. All four climbers reached the summit of the Roraima plateau, to give Don another title and a fund of stories for his lectures list. But it was not an entirely successful expedition in terms of its human dimension. Eighteen months after being given the bum's rush from the Bonington extravaganzas, Don now found himself marginalised, his behaviour viewed askance, even by his own peers. And to any reader of Hamish's account of the trip, the figure of Whillans that stepped out of it – though Hamish had shown charity and a pursed-lipped forbearance in the portraiture – was difficult, selfish and lazy, the wily clarity dimmed, the old glory of his ability all but extinguished. With a dozen years of living still left to him, a record and reputation that still commanded respect and a physique and natural talent that, had they been nurtured, could yet have brought success and reward, the negatives inherent in Don's character had won control. Roraima, really, was the end of Don Whillans as a serious contender in the world of mountaineering.

Fortunately, there was a degree of redemption at hand on the second expedition in which Don took part in 1973/74. Whereas Roraima had been a success in terms of its objective and something of a failure in terms of its human dynamic, that to Torre Egger was just the reverse. A very strong British–American team of Martin Boysen, 'Tut' Braithwaite, Eric Jones, Mick Coffey, Leo Dickinson, Keith Lewis, Dan Reid and Rick Sylvester was joined by Don, who had flown down from Guyana, in November for an attempt on this difficult and unclimbed Patagonian peak to the north of Cerro Torre. The idea for the expedition, Leo recalls, had come from Doug Scott: 'You should make a film about Don before he gets past it, youth.' In the early 1970s, Leo had built up a considerable reputation in adventure film-making, and he seized the hint with alacrity. He takes up the story:

I wanted something fresh, and Don liked the idea of Torre Egger, although his recent roles had been better played out at high altitude climbing. The problem was money, and I assumed that with Don in the team it would be easy. Wrong! For some reason, his name seemed to close more doors than it opened. 'What we need, Don,' I said to him, 'is a millionaire.' 'Well I know a couple – I'll have words,' he responded. Sure enough, two weeks later he had enrolled Alan Heap, who was secretary to a car-dealer millionaire, Ian Skipper. Both were dyed-in-the-wool fans of his down-to-earthiness and his dry humour. We met up in various pubs to discuss progress, or rather for me to tell Don what had been happening as I don't recall him doing much work after the cheque came through. Starting out in this line myself at the time, I was interested to know how Don did make a living, and enquired how much he charged for lectures:

'Three 'undred quid,' he told me, and, after a pause, added, 'plus expenses.'

'But surely you wouldn't charge expenses if it was in the local town hall?'

Don leaned forward to stress the point: 'Aye – but I might be in Kathmandu the night before!'

Don had interesting opinions on almost everything, but on one particular day the only topic of conversation was Mark Spitz, who had won eight gold medals at the 1972 Olympic Games. 'Incredible to win eight gold medals – impressive isn't he?' I suggested to Don. 'Well, no, not really – he's obviously good at the 100 metres, and 200 metres is only a bit further. Then there's all those bloody relays . . .'

Don put things in perspective like no other – you had to go a long way to win his adulation.

The tax inspector was clearly one who didn't impress Don, and began rather to plague him after Annapurna: 'Mr Whillans – I can't understand how you manage it! You have a BMW, a caravan, you've recently bought a house, but you never appear to work. and then you keep disappearing for four months at a time on these climbing trips . . .'

'Aye,' came the response, 'if you disappeared for four months, no fucker'd miss you!'

The approach to Torre Egger was guarded by a dangerously crevassed hanging glacier,[13] the face-climbing above on verglased rock proved very difficult, and was under continuous bombardment from falling ice. Braithwaite suffered a broken arm from this, and the climb was abandoned. Earlier in the attempt, however, Don – back in his more accustomed realm of ice and snow rather than among jungle mud and fauna – played a crucial role in what came uncomfortably close to being a disaster. Mick Coffey, one of the most amiable and engaging characters on the British climbing scene in the 1970s, gives his own account of what took place:

Don and I got on very well in Patagonia. He arrived down there after the jungle trip with Mo, Joe and Hamish with an amazing amount of fancy gear including cosy wet-weather boots which were ideal for advanced base camp. By chance, Don and I took the same size of boot, so I availed myself of them at every given chance. Now Don, as you will know, was piss-poor at load-carrying or general work around camp. He excelled at ram-rodding the excavation of the snow-cave that we used higher up, giving many instructions but little or no physical assistance. You forgave all this as his sense of

---

[13] Two years later, and just before the peak's first ascent by the Americans Bragg, Donini and Wilson, there was a fatal accident to the New Zealander Phil Herron on this glacier. He and his companion Tim Whethey fell into a crevasse, the latter quickly rescuing himself, but Herron fell 180 feet and was wedged where the crevasse narrowed. Whethey roped down to within touching distance of him, but was unable to pull him free by himself. After struggling to do so for four hours he went for help, returning at first light with a rescue party. By that time Herron had slipped further down, and was beyond reach or help.

humour was just outstanding, together with his story-telling. In fact Don was basically a seanchai.[14]

On this occasion when he saved my neck, he was outstanding. He, Rick Sylvester and I were moving up the hanging glacier towards the snow-cave under Torre Egger on a hot sunny day. I was wearing an open, sleeveless shirt and carrying a heavy load of hardware, ropes and petrol. Rick and Don stopped to take some photographs and I pushed on up the glacier. Suddenly, I popped into a crevasse up to my waist. I swung my legs to try to gain traction, but as I did so the snow around me collapsed and I fell into what I could see was one large mother of a hole. The weight of the sack was turning me upside down, I blacked out temporarily, and that's how I came to – jammed solid, and almost upside down. I knew that the rope was in my sack, and that the other two had little in the way of gear. By twisting my head I could see the perfect, round hole which was my entry into this icy pit. Then I heard Don shouting down, so I yelled back that I was stuck. Don told me to hang on – as if I had any option! – and said he'd get help. Then he was gone, leaving me to contemplate the shit state I was in, and knowing that I had no chance of surviving long in my current state of attire.

It's funny to remember now, but fear was no longer a factor, and generally isn't as you realise that the chips are well and truly down. I guess I must have been getting drowsy as hypothermia set in. Next thing I recall is Don shouting 'Hang on!' again, and then there he was standing on top of me.[15] He had abseiled down on an assortment of slings and wires, and proceeded to pull and heave and yank to free me from the ice. At first I was stuck as tight as a nun's crotch, but then suddenly I popped free like a cork out of a bottle. Don stood me upright, got the rope out of my sack, and tied it on to the makeshift

[14] 'Story-teller' in Irish – Mick Coffey is Irish, and lives nowadays in Co. Kerry. His sister is Maria Coffey, a very gifted writer on mountain and other themes. This point of Mick's is a particularly significant one in explaining the degree of tolerance extended to Don even after his effective climbing days were past. He had become a consummate entertainer, with a fund of humorous and historically interesting stories to tell and retell and embroider and elaborate upon.

[15] Don: 'There wasn't anywhere else to stand, he was fairly well jammed and didn't seem to be going anywhere.'

abseil line that he'd come down on. Rick pulled it up, and all I had to was jumar up from my tomb into the warm sunlight. Don quickly followed me up and they rubbed me vigorously while warning me to expect pain with returning circulation.

Coffey was very lucky to have someone as strong, experienced and determined as Don at hand, otherwise his fate would surely have been the same as that of Phil Herron later (see note 13 above). But the whole incident inevitably highlights how attitudes had changed during Don's mountaineering lifetime. I asked Mick Coffey whether they had considered roping-up on an obviously dangerous glacier, and whether Don – whose early alpine tutors would have instilled in him the wisdom of doing this when crossing snow-covered glaciers – as the senior member of the party might have suggested this. His reply makes some very telling points:

The whole expedition had been moving unroped across the glacier for weeks prior to this incident, and everyone was highly experienced. We also had well-known solo-climbers in the team, in addition to very poky guys who would tell you that they could smell a crevasse a mile away. Our ice-cap expedition the previous year[16] also did not rope up unless crevasse danger was highly visible. With due respect to him, Don at this time would no longer have been accepted as the senior member of the team – Tut, Martin, Eric, Rick Sylvester, Leo and Dan Reid would agree with me on this. The cruel fact is that people in high-risk sports get complacent with danger – look at the list of guys we know who have died in crevasse falls, including Phil Herron two years later – same glacier, same location. The year after my accident I was in the area again with Donini, Bragg, et al., and rope-up was rare on the glaciers. I wouldn't hang any degree of responsibility for my mishap on poor old Don. His cool head saved my skin.

Leo sums up the expedition – and the role Don played in it – thus:

---

[16] In 1972–73, with Eric Jones and Leo Dickinson, Coffey had crossed the Southern Patagonian ice-cap and made first ascents of Cerro Lautaro and Cerro Mimosa.

My problem was, the mountain proved to be harder than we expected, and my star-studded team made slow progress. I tried to film it as fly-on-the-wall documentary, and clearly trod on some toes – Don's included. My rushing around with a cine-camera had started to annoy him: 'You know what your problem is,' he told me, 'you try to be in two places at the same time. The last person who tried that trick died on the bloody cross!' One day I was filming a torrent duck that lives in the icy streams of Patagonia. The chicks were bobbing around like champagne corks as they danced and fell over waterfalls. Don was fascinated by their antics. 'These are some of the rarest ducks in the world,' I told Don, who, without missing a beat, came back with, 'Aye – that's not surprising.'

It was clear from the outset of the trip that Don was not going to carry many loads to the Advance Base Camp – the three-hours walk he felt was a bit far. Even when he decided to make an intermediate camp, we didn't mind – after all, he had found the meal-ticket. But what really took us by surprise was when Don stocked this camp from a higher one downwards . . .

Don returned to Britain in February after having been away for four months, and immediately pitched back into a nightly social round in which the focal points were the Jester, the Woolpack and the Shoulder of Mutton. He was soon on the lecture circuit again, and with new material to draw on. John Cleare attended one of his shows in Winchester in March, and gives the following appraisal:

I went over to Winchester at Don's invitation to have a drink with him when he was lecturing there. Bob Pettigrew, then the Principal Adviser for Outdoor Education in Hampshire, had originally brought Don there several years before, and by 1974 Don's annual lecture had become an annual fixture at the fine, Gothic town hall. The capacity-audience seemed largely to be composed of genteel elderly ladies, retired colonels and masters from Winchester College. Don waddled on stage from the wings, in jeans, white shirt with sleeves rolled up nearly to his shoulder, flat 'at on his head and a cheroot in his mouth. The audience leapt or creaked to its feet in a standing ovation.

The subject was the Roraima climb – all snot, rain-forest and foulness – and the audience hung on every word and cheered virtually every sentence. The lecture wasn't especially good. It certainly wasn't professional. But the show was superb. Don's timing was brilliant, he was extremely funny, rather coarse, and larger than life, playing up to the comic Northern image. And he had that genteel Winchester audience just where he wanted them, they relished every word, and loved him for it. It was an impressive happening.

Don's addiction to pubbing back home in the North was overriding. Frequently he would be driving out to drink into the small hours in the Shoulder of Mutton above Todmorden and elsewhere, often in the company of Barrie Kershaw, the two of them indulging in favourite games like 'nutting' holes in the ceiling (which, fortunately for their skulls but not for the ceiling, was of plasterboard). These nightly bouts inevitably led to the apogee of the Andy Capp persona, and one of the most notably anarchic events in Don's life – 'the rough-up with the Rawtenstall rozzers'[17] as it was widely referred to in the Lancashire climbing community at the time. More perhaps than any other, this particular incident has endeared him to climbing's subversive faction, and been elevated and amplified to mythic proportions. It took place at the end of March 1975. Audrey was in Rossendale General Hospital for an operation[18] and Don was in the Woolpack with Barrie Kershaw. The court list having been posted, the first report of what took place appeared in the *Manchester Evening News* on 21 April and read thus:

> Don Whillans, the Salford-born Everest climber, will appear in court in Rossendale on Thursday accused of a drink-

---

[17] 'Rozzer' is slang for policeman – the whole register of the phrase seems intended to mock the newspaper reports of Don's trial.

[18] After Audrey had come out of hospital, and before his court appearance, she and Don had taken a fortnight's holiday in Tunisia, where Don met a fellow climber, Roy Hardcastle, and they went to do a route together: 'At one point on a fairly steep rock wall, I was above him and looking down at a point where upward movement was temporarily eluding him. "There's a good hold just above you to the left," I shouted down. "I don't need no bloody advice," was the riposte. Suitably chastened, I kept quiet while he climbed the rest of the pitch. I was shaken by the immediacy and directness of his response. After that, I kept my mouth shut, and we got on fine.'

driving offence and police assault. Whillans . . . is accused of speeding, driving with excess alcohol in the blood, assaulting a policeman, damaging a police panda car and policeman's uniform, and £35 damage. Whillans said today, 'I'm saying nowt about the job. It will be sorted out one way or the other on Thursday.'

The story in the *Manchester Evening News* for Thursday 24 April was much more forthcoming. '5 ft 2 ins Don, "King of Everest", took on five Pc's' read the title of the second lead (beneath 'Hanoi denounces new terror bombs'). If Don felt at all displeased about being robbed of an inch of stature, he might have found consolation in the career-boost that followed:

Climber Don Whillans is only 5 ft 2 ins tall but he has conquered Everest twice. And a court was told today that he had a series of struggles with five policemen the night he was caught speeding and drunk in his BMW car.[19] It was said that Salford-born Whillans: had both his hands round a policeman's throat; kicked a policeman in the head; tore police clothing; damaged a panda car; and shouted obscenities. Whillans was fined a total of £220 and banned from driving for two years by Rossendale magistrates at Rawtenstall. He had 213 mgs of alcohol per 100 mls of blood compared with the legal limit of 80 mgs.

His solicitor said that at the time he was worried about his wife who was in hospital for an operation. She was now all right. Whillans, who pleaded guilty, was fined £10 for speeding and £100 for driving with excess alcohol in his blood. For assaulting PC Ian Stanney he was fined £100, and for damaging police property worth £35.65 he was fined £10 and ordered to pay compensation. Including a doctor's fee, Whillans was told to pay a total of £273.66.

Chief Inspector Jack Whithnell said Whillans's car was spotted at 3.25 a.m. near Bacup Road. It slid slightly from side to side. A policeman followed at 60 m.p.h. before stopping the car. 'Whillans was in fact drunk,' said Chief Inspector Whithnell.

---

[19] Don had traded up from the Ford Capri by this time.

He then grabbed the policeman around the throat 'as though he was trying to choke him'. Other policemen called and loosened one hand, but Whillans had kept hitting the policeman with the other. He was repeatedly shouting obscenities. When being put in a panda car Whillans ripped a policeman's coat, and inside the car he repeatedly lashed out with his feet. The car was stopped, and another policeman got in the back with Whillans. 'Only after two policemen sat on him was he restrained,' said the chief inspector. At the police station, Whillans went berserk, throwing punches and lashing out with his feet. He was put in a cell, where after 20 minutes he calmed down.

Mr Ward said Whillans had an income of about £4000 a year derived from lectures and interviews, and he depended upon a car to travel to lecturing appointments.

The national newspapers ran the story, complete with pictures of a sun-tanned Don sporting a neatly trimmed beard, white shirt and cravat. To the *Daily Mirror* reporter who was present at the court, Don commented, 'I'm disappointed with the police. It was just a bit of a tussle, but they threw the book at me. The best thing I can do now is go off on a two-year climb.' However, he was, incontrovertibly, two and a half times over the legal limit, and by present-day standards got off with this and the other misdemeanours pretty lightly. What actually took place may even have been downplayed in the police testimony as being something of an affront to their manhood. According to Ronnie Dutton, who was another of Don's regular drinking companions during his time in Haslingden, Don's opening salvo once the panda car had stopped him was to tell Constable Stanney to 'Get that fucking car off my bumper.' He had then, in Dutton's account, laid out three policemen in the initial fracas, and calmly waited around for the next shift to arrive. In his diary, Don records without comment the fine he had to pay,[20] and

---

[20] The incident apparently also cost him an MBE in the Queen's Birthday Honours list immediately following his court appearance, for which he had been recommended by the British Mountaineering Council. The Prime Minister's Office is reputed to have rung the BMC General Secretary, Dennis Gray, to enquire whether the Mr Whillans who had just been convicted of drink-driving and fighting with policemen, and the gentleman put forward for an honour by the Council, were one and the same. Neither then nor subsequently did Don's name appear in the honours lists.

notes that four days after his court hearing Barrie Kershaw was also breathalysed. The good burghers of Rawtenstall had obviously been taking careful note of the nocturnal activities and companions of their most famous resident.

Within a year Don and Audrey had uprooted from Rossendale and moved to Bod Hyfryd, a large Edwardian villa above Penmaenmawr in North Wales. 'Don Whillans leaves the Valley,' proclaimed the *Rossendale Free Press* early in 1976. Audrey quit her job as cutter in a Manchester clothing sweat-shop, her boss peeling a fiver off his wad and handing it to her in recognition of over 20 years' loyalty to him. The Penmaenmawr house had been bought from Ivy Davies, the estranged wife of Frank Davies who owned climbing equipment shops in the Lake District. Ronnie Dutton believes that Don moved there to be nearer the social hub of the very active Welsh climbing scene of the time, the focus of which was Llanberis, where Joe, Pete Crew, Mo Anthoine, Al Harris[21] and many others lived. Yet just as with the Salford home of his youth, it was at a remove, over 20 miles away from the centre of activity. And the invitations to go on expeditions that had their genesis in the Llanberis community, which Dutton believes was a primary reason for Don's moving to Wales, were not forthcoming. For obvious reasons, he seldom drank in the pubs of Llanberis.[22] The expeditions he did go on seem to have been pretty desultory affairs. One to the easy Hindu Kush peak of Tirich Mir in 1975 reached its

---

[21] If Joe was the guru of the climbing scene centred on Llanberis from the mid-1960s onwards, Al Harris (1944–81) was its lord of misrule. He was the best playmate I ever had, and his wildness was legendary across continents. A very talented, but completely undriven, climber, he lived at Bryn Bigil above Deiniolen and his exploits continually tested the boundaries of the socially and legally acceptable: the great JCB joust; the chicken game at Bus Stop Quarry where we drove cars into a deep, water-filled quarry-hole in the dead of night, jumping out at the last moment; the crazy racing, incessant partying, competitive solo-climbing, the keeping-going on booze and speed and coke for days at a time – all these led to the inevitable ending: a drunken, fatal crash on a dark, wet road. He was a Dean Moriarty character, ultimately trapped and destroyed by his own image and the community needs and cravings he was expected to fulfil. One of my closest friends, I loved him dearly and miss him still. See my essay, 'Prankster, Maniac, Hero, Saint and Fool' in *On and Off the Rocks* (Gollancz, 1986).

[22] Breathalysing the climbers was one of the favourite activities of the local police, between whom and the climbing community a mutually amused antipathy seemed to exist. In one of the years in which I lived in this community, I recall being breathalysed seven times – once at nine o'clock in the morning – and I scarcely drank. Had Don lived here, he would probably never have driven again.

unexceptional summit.[23] 'As you get older, you look for new challenges,' he told *Daily Mail* reporter Sinclair Newton in talking about the trip, and when drawn on whether he wanted to go back to Chomolungma, suggested that for him the mountain was 'losing its mystique', its approaches awash with 'hippies'. 'As far as I can see, there's no chance of me going there again in the near future. It's all booked up for years with other people who want to climb it.' Chance or no chance, his interest in the mountain does seem to have continued. At about this time he suggested to Joe that the two of them went to do the South Col route together. 'We'd piss up that,' he told Joe, and went on to tell him to get it organised. Since Joe was averse to organising, to the whole 'Everest' brouhaha, to big trips, and to the prospect of going on one with Don by this time, the idea didn't come to fruition.

In 1976, Don was one of nearly 500 climbers in 85 teams who were on Denali ('Mount McKinley') – at 20,320 feet the highest mountain in North America – in the Central Alaska Range. Whilst the likes of Scott, Haston, Charlie Porter, Messner, Braithwaite and the Burgess twins were climbing new lines or making ascents of the Cassin Ridge of the mountain (and whilst, out in the Karakoram, Joe, along with Mo, Martin Boysen, Malcolm Howells and Tony Riley, was succeeding in the first ascent of the dramatic, technically difficult and slightly higher Trango Tower), Don, who had not even reached the age Riccardo Cassin had been when he made his ascent of his great ridge on the mountain, was plodding up the Western Rib – one of the straightforward voies normales to Denali's summit. Iconic within the British climbing community, at 43 he was a spent force. In mountaineering terms, what remained was simply leftover life to kill.

He didn't entirely stop climbing: early in 1977 he was in Kenya, rock-climbing with Ian Howell in Hell's Gate Gorge, doing the Ice Window route on Mount Kenya with the landlord of the Shoulder of Mutton (who wore crampons for the first time on the route), and later making a notably slow ascent over six days by the tourist route of Africa's highest mountain, Kilimanjaro. On the way to Mount

---

[23] 'Ta for the invite to the housewarming – just a shade late in replying because I was busy plodding up Tirich Mir, a 25,230-foot peak in Pakistan when it came, and have been busy "hydrating" since I got back four weeks ago. I see the boys earned Christ Jesus Bonington his knighthood, and Stinky Burke provided the ingredient to ensure a best-seller.' Don to Ingrid Cranfield, 7 October 1975.

Kenya the jeep the party was travelling in became bogged down, and local Masai men were recruited to push it out: 'Don wouldn't lift a finger to help, and when the Masai had finished, and were standing round hoping for a reward, he leaned out of the jeep and just said, "Right, you lot – fuck off!"' When he regained his driving licence in April of that year, he returned to his old trade and began to do emergency plumbing work all over north-west England, sleeping in a Volkswagen van that he had painstakingly fitted out for that purpose. He was settling into a pattern that was to obtain for the rest of his life: well-paid (often in ready cash that need not be declared to the tax-man) emergency plumbing; some lecturing; trips away each year to geographical locations or to try activities that interested him; spectating at the Isle of Man Tourist Trophy motorcycle races each June and September; a very occasional rock-climb. The Penmaenmawr house, run by Audrey as a bed-and-breakfast establishment, was busy with a regular clientele of Don's friends and admirers, and because of this, ironically, there was no room there for Don himself in the holiday season. Audrey slept on a sofa and Don took to the road. When not sleeping in the van in pub car parks (which at least allayed the fear of being booked again for drink-driving), he had a country-wide round of acquaintances he could visit for a bath, a meal and a bed. Nat Allen recalled:

Right through from the 1950s, he never had any compunction about living off you, but then, the Alps and all those expeditions was a very expensive lifestyle, and his income was pretty variable, so you sort of understood. Baths he'd use to the maximum, with living in the van and working I suppose, and I'd just say to Tinsel, or Ruth later, 'It doesn't matter what he does, just let him do it – less trouble that way.' I suppose in a way we looked on him as a cross we had to bear, but he was good company, and entertaining – even if you had heard the stories a dozen times and not always in the same version. He just had a way of telling them.

When not behaving suitably domestically at friends' houses, he was keeping wild company: 'February 3: Barrie rang – in nick all last week – bare feet, dogs, Saddleworth,' he recorded cryptically in his diary, and continued, 'Harris crashed mate's Mini. Broke nose again. In Padarn throwing drinks.' Subsequent entries sustained the theme: 'February 25: Harris broke nose again, fighting.' 'July 22: Vaynol – Harris, Birtles, Barrie – "strawberry milkshakes".' 'July 23: Barrie out of it on milkshakes.'[24] 'July 24: Delph – warrant out for Barrie.' 'August 13. Row with Audrey[25] about Barrie.' 'August 15: Barrie "lifted" at The Bull in Delph.'

Don's climbing in 1978 amounted to an ascent of the Old Man of Hoy, by the original route climbed by Baillie, Patey and Bonington 12 years before. Don acted as anchor-man to a rope of five led by Derek Walker. 'You get us all up, Derek, and I'll get us safely down,' he told his leader before they started – a reassuring proposition given the inexperience of some of the team and the trickiness of the abseil descent. At the end of 1978 he went on a lecture tour of Australia and New Zealand, in the course of which he climbed Mount Aspiring in the Mount Cook range with two Americans, Bob and Anne Schneider. Back home again in May his diary gloated over two events in which no right-thinking person could take any pleasure: 'May 3: TORY WIN!!!' 'May 12: Manchester United lost FA Cup.' On the further evidence of the diary, he seems to have spent those periods he was at home during the rest of the year in watching – and carefully recording their results – boxing, snooker, football and even indoor bowls on the television, whilst getting in serious training for a lecture tour of South Africa in December.

The active highlight of this, a week before Christmas 1979, was a descent of the Kango Caves – a tourist attraction which, although electrically lit, does have a sporting element in the form of a squeeze through a narrow slot between two of its sections. Don's weight by now having ballooned to over 14 stone, the inevitable happened and he got stuck, unable to manoeuvre his belly through the slot and having in consequence to turn back and climb out the way he had come. And so a decade which had opened for him with one of the most audacious ascents in mountaineering history ended with failure even to manage something holidaymakers took daily in their

---

[24] Don't be misled by the innocent name – 'strawberry milkshakes' were a lethally alcoholic concoction of spirits and liqueurs in a pint pot, the recipe for which Harris had brought back from America. On two of them you'd be drunk. Three would render you unconscious.

[25] Not uncommon between them at this period. Ivy Davies remembers calling round at Bod Hyfryd one day to find Don out and Audrey locked in the attic, hammering and screaming to be let out.

stride – in the space of 10 short years he had gone from Premier League to Third Division relegation zone.

Maybe the failure in the Kango Caves had a galvanising effect, for in 1980 there were signs of a resurgence of interest in rock-climbing and mountaineering. Cornwall – on which he had poured scorn as a climbing venue 20 years before – he visited twice, on the second occasion running into his old friend John Streetly in the bar of the Gurnard's Head Hotel. In October, he took part in a very curious trip to Gibraltar to climb on the famous Rock. A party of climbers mostly from North Wales, and including Ben and Marion Wintringham, Smiler Cuthbertson and Pete Allison, with official permission made a climb up the limestone face, and asked to be allowed to call it Regina Mater, in honour of the Queen Mother's eightieth birthday, which had been at the beginning of August.

The tribute was duly accepted, and the tribe were invited to the Government Mansion for a celebration dinner. Ronnie Dutton, who was also with the party, recalls the liaison officer asking perfectly politely whether the lads could get cleaned up a bit, and Don taking umbrage at this.

His pants had been made by Audrey and were too short, and he wasn't wearing socks: 'I wouldn't wear socks for the Queen of England,' he said, and he didn't. When the waiter, in gloves and a white jacket, served soup, Don – still riled by the LO's request – turned to him and said, 'Bring us a bit o' fucking bread to go with the soup, pal.' The room went absolutely silent. But Don was like that – didn't care what he said when he was in that sort of mood. He wasn't very nice company on that trip and a lot of the lads took against him. We had a breakfast kitty, and he and Audrey wouldn't put anything in. Every day she took him breakfast in bed. I was in chatting to him one day when she brought it in. 'Not fuckin' egg and bacon again,' he said. 'I'll look like an egg and bacon.' He picked up the plate and just threw it against the wall. I was laughing at the daftness of it and he sees me. 'What the fuck are you laughing at?' he says. 'I'm laughing at you,' I tell him. 'You'll be laughing the other side of your face in a minute,' he snapped. I just shook my head and walked out, it was that childish. Another time I was helping him with the technical stuff at a lecture – hundreds of people present and there was a power-cut. 'What the fuckin' 'ell 'ave you done, Ronnie?' he yelled out. Just then the picture came back on. 'Thank fuck for that,' he growled, for everyone to hear. He just didn't care what people thought of him, and at times it was not much. He could be very nasty, very cutting at times when there was no need. There was one time when we'd been sliding down the Snowdon railway on slates like they used to do, and we'd passed three girls. Later on we saw them in the Padarn and they were giggling so I asked them what was up. 'We saw these old men sliding down the railway on stones,' one of them said, so I told her who Don was and she went off to get his autograph, and started talking to him about climbing. He ignored her after a bit, turned to me, and said, 'Aye, another one in fucking cloud-cuckoo land. She'll be on Everest next.'

The meeting with John Streetly in Cornwall had resulted in an invitation for Don and Audrey to spend six weeks out in Trinidad and Tobago over Christmas. Streetly left a brief impression of Don during his time in Tobago that provides a welcome counterbalance to the many negative accounts of his behaviour:

Perhaps less well known among the many facets of Don's character was his well-reciprocated love of children. My family thought the world of him and can retell every detail of his entertaining antics. Fourteen stone of Don miming Audrey's 'cockroach dance' was very, very funny, but after he had swum over a very large sting-ray in very shallow water, his subsequent tip-toe version of the 'sting-ray dance' left Marcel Marceau at the post and had the rest of us weeping with laughter. He became very competent while with us as a scuba diver, kept a marine aquarium at his own home, and was always adding to his knowledge of natural history. Part of the drive to this, he admitted, was the picking-up of the threads of an education he regretted missing as a young man. Those who knew him well also knew that the universities had missed a good mind, a mind still active in later life and with a wide range of interests.

That mountaineering still featured strongly among those interests is borne out by Don's having been casting around in the autumn of

1980 for another Himalayan trip to go on. Mo Anthoine was planning one to Gosainthan, and Don went to see him in Llanberis to enquire about it, but Roraima was still too recent a memory, and no invitation was forthcoming. He had better luck with Doug Scott, who was planning to attempt a new and difficult line alpine-style on Shivling in Garhwal in the early summer of 1981. Typical of many of Doug's later expeditions, this one comprised a disparate group of mountaineers with differing objectives heading for a challenging venue, and one that – with its Shipton/Tilman associations – typified the retroactive radicalism that was being hailed as the style in British and American mountain activity in the 1980s, and proclaimed as a reaction against the perceived corporate ethos of the 1970s.[26]

One of the team's members was a young Australian climber, Greg Child, recently transplanted to the Pacific North-West of America, and soon to make a name for himself not only as one of the best all-round climbers in the world, but also as one of the most stylish, lucid and exciting of writers on the sport. Clearly fascinated by the self-ruined archangel who was his expedition companion, Child gives vignette after vivid vignette of the latter-day Whillans. The expedition made its way from Delhi to Uttarkashi, and took the most terrifying, dramatic and dangerous bus-ride in the world in one of the pilgrims' conveyances from there up the gorge of the upper Bhagirathi river,[27] main source-tributary of the Ganges, to

---

[26] I have my doubts about how well these generalised perceptions current at the time hold up to detailed scrutiny. For example, the 1975 'Everest South-West Face Expedition', underwritten by Barclays Bank, made a substantial profit which was ploughed back into the Mount Everest Foundation and hence benefited the smaller expeditions and mountaineering as a whole. The 1981 Kongur Expedition was sponsored by Jardine Matheson, and it climbed the mountain – which has only had one other successful ascent in the last 20 years – in fine alpine style. Bonington himself made a notable, alpine-style first ascent of Shivling's West Summit by the West Ridge with Jim Fotheringham in 1983. And conversely, even our retroactively radical heroes have their livings to earn – Greg Child, for example, is a member of the North Face clothing and equipment company's team, as is another 'climber's climber', Mick Fowler. To stereotype, as the mountaineering press often does, can all too easily create false and unhelpful perspectives, and the danger of that in considering 'expedition politics' and the way they impinged on Don's career needs constantly to be borne in mind.

[27] I remember a night journey up this nightmare road, waking to the driver missing a gear change, the bus sliding backwards, glancing out through the window to see the boiling river 2000 feet below and the edge of the road crumbling away beneath the bus tyres just as the driver managed to get it into gear.

the settlement of Gangotri – an atmospheric and magical place. From behind the temple in Gangotri, they wound up through the groves of deodar at an altitude of 11,000 feet and followed the pilgrims progressing the dozen miles up the valley to Gaumukh, where the infant Ganges rushes forth from ice-caves in the snout of the Gangotri Glacier and the great peaks of Bhagirathi, Shivling and Meru crowd all around.

> Whillans strolls along the trail, shielding himself occasionally from the beating sun with a red umbrella. As he rounds a bend on the path he confronts a gaunt, ash-covered yogi. It is a meeting of worlds. They stare at each other for a moment, then the yogi raises his open palm for Whillans to drop a coin into. 'Hmmm,' Whillans says, 'are you on some sort of sponsored walk?' Whillans then grasps the yogi's hand firmly and shakes it, utterly confounding the Indian.

Along the same trail, at Bujobas, Doug Scott remembers lying in the shade of trees by a dhaba resting, and seeing Don, who was unaware of his presence, hobbling past, his knees rendering his progress slow and painful – something he was too proud and stubborn to mention to anyone else on the trip as explanation of his inability to keep up with others' pace.

The expedition reached its base camp at the flowery, wide meadow of Tapovan, above the glacier's lateral moraines and beneath the crystal spire of Shivling[28] itself. There the expedition divided into two teams. Greg Child, Doug Scott, Georges Bettembourg and Rick White were to attempt alpine-style the East Pillar of the mountain, Steve Sustad, Merv English, Colin Downer and Don would go on the West Face route, with its frightening serac barrier, up which the mountain was first ascended by an Indian–Nepalese expedition in 1974. Bad weather and varying responses to acclimatisation (their base camp was at an altitude of 14,800 feet, and many of the members had no experience of altitude) caused initial problems; a lot of time was spent sitting

---

[28] 'What exactly does Shivling mean?' [Don] asked Balwant. 'It's a fertility symbol. It refers to Lord Shiva's phallus – his "linga", or organ of generation.' 'Is that so? Well, let's hope his lordship doesn't get brewer's droop and fall down on us during the night,' replied Don.

around, mutually spectating and – traditional expedition activity –
griping:

> '. . . Old Don – he won't carry a load,' says Merv. 'He fills his
> bloody pack with his sleeping bag. If you ask him to carry
> something he says, "It's not the weight – it's where to put it."'
>
> 'Well, Don's getting on in years. He had trouble with his
> knees,' counters Doug, in defence of his canny old friend. Don
> had long ago decided that his seniority excused him from
> carrying heavy loads.
>
> 'And he wouldn't brew you a cup of tea if your life
> depended on it. He expects us to do all the bloody cooking,'
> snarls Colin.
>
> Doug smiles at Colin's complaint. 'Ah, well I warned you
> about Don and cooking before we left. It's his generation and
> upbringing. There are certain things he simply won't do, and
> cooking is one of them. He thinks it's women's work, or
> something like that . . .'

Whilst the by-now long-established non-contributor complaint
was receiving another airing, Child is concerned to balance it with
the by-now equally long-established positive of Don's entertain-
ment value; and even if some of the routines have been in the
comic's repertoire for a substantial number of years, there is
nothing an audience likes better than an old, familiar story. Not to
leaven the well known with too much novelty is one of the prices of
popular acclaim:

> If Don's idiosyncrasies flustered his team-mates, his humour
> galvanises us all. At midnight a yell from his tent rouses the
> camp.
>
> 'Hey! Wake up! I just realised it's me fiftieth bloody
> birthday!'
>
> The climbers all crawl from their sleeping bags and out into
> the freezing night.
>
> As a full moon rose over the Bhagirathis, we gather about
> in the cold, passing round a bottle of Irish whiskey. It wasn't
> really his fiftieth birthday – it was his forty-eighth – but he
> liked the well-rounded half-century figure and claimed it as
> his own. Soon Don's tales began to flow.

The night wears on, the bottle grows empty, and the stars above began to sway. Don harks back to Annapurna: 'After we came down from the summit, somewhere on the way out we had a victory celebration. I don't remember how many bottles of whisky we polished off, but it was quite a few. The Sherpas watched us get wilder and wilder. Dougal disappeared for a while – he'd fallen in a latrine and couldn't get out. One by one we passed out. By morning we were sick as dogs – a terrible sight. The Sherpas loaded us on to a tarpaulin, dragged the entire expedition to the river, and dumped us in it. As I woke up, I remember one of the Sherpas shaking his head at me in disgust, saying, "Sahibs like buffalo."'

After a continuous push of 13 days, the last of them without food or fuel, up the elegant and difficult East Pillar of the mountain, Scott and Bettembourg, Child and White climb (or in the case of the latter two, tumble) down the West Face and reach the descent path along the lateral moraines of the Meru Glacier:

> As we descend the final slopes . . . we see a figure waiting below, perched on a rock at the foot of the mountain. As we grow closer the figure takes on a familiar form – Whillans!
>
> Whillans the phrase-maker, the clairvoyant, the sage – the bringer of food! Thoughts of what he might have brought – chocolate, biscuits, sardines – squeeze a last burst of energy from our legs. I hallucinate the sweet aroma of tea wafting through the air. By the time I reach him Doug has told him the tale of our 13-day climb, including an account of the exploding tent and our tumble down the mountain. Whillans sits calmly, like the all-knowing Buddha . . . The merest hint of a smile cracks his parched lips.
>
> 'Well done, lads. You made it back,' he says.[29] Then, satisfied all is well, he trots off down the Meru Glacier, beginning the four-mile hike back to Tapovan.
>
> 'Did he bring anything to eat?' I ask.
>
> 'Yeah. But he got hungry while he was waiting and ate it,' Rick replies. 'But it's the thought that counts.'

---

[29] Doug's recollection of Don's response is that he commented, 'Yer did all right.'

So for Doug – the man for whom he had secured an invitation to Chomolungma nine years before, and insisted to Herrligkoffer that his own participation depended on it – there was yet another success, in the new style, technically outstanding, with a young team, to add to a portfolio that included the first ascent with Haston of the 'Everest South-West Face' climb in 1975. For Don, his team turned back by the wind from high on the West Face, it was 'the rankling emptiness of a missed summit', as Child expresses it; or to put it more prosaically, another expedition, another failure.

The magical peaks of Gangotri were not the only ones to which Don ventured in 1981. In October of that year he had been invited to be climbing leader on the British Autana Expedition, led by Peter McKenzie, who gave this account of the trip and its changing objectives, whilst making some generous and insightful comments about Don in passing:

Our objective was to climb Autana, a blunt sandstone spike in south-west Venezuela, and then go on to explore the summit of Kukenam, on the borders of Brazil, Venezuela and Guyana. Kukenam is the sister mountain to Roraima, which Don had climbed in 1973 from the Guyanese side by a route not likely to be repeated on a regular basis. Our plan was to ascend Kukenam from the Venezuelan side – an approach which had been used by myself and two other members of the expedition on previous occasions. The ascent of Autana was ruled out at the last moment by the Governor of that part of Venezuela. Even Don's arriving at the Governor's house in the modified pyjama trousers which he habitually wore in warm climates, and in a suitably aggressive mood, failed to obtain a change of mind. So we went on to Kukenam. The Autana climb would have exercised Don's skills, whereas Kukenam is basically an arduous scramble. I thought Don might have been disappointed by the loss of our prime objective, but he said he was 'not bothered'. He told me he was now more keen on moving in interesting landscapes. Roraima had been of interest because it was not just a sharp point; when you got to the top there were several square miles to explore, and Kukenam was the same.

You spend long hours lying in hammocks and talking on trips in tropical South America. Don's dry, perceptive humour was appreciated by all of us at these times. I worked for the tank-manufacturing division of Vickers, and on one occasion I mentioned a self-propelled howitzer – a well-known piece of military equipment. Don cackled with laughter at the term, and said that when he got home he would set about designing a self-propelled rucksack. On another of these hammock conversations, he acceded to our requests to tell us about when he saw a yeti, and left us in no doubt as to the creature's existence.

No one else on the trip had any significant climbing experience, so Don taught us rope-management from a tree in the garden of his house in Penmaenmawr. I recall his painstaking and meticulous approach, and realised that this attitude had been one factor in his long survival. A careful genius, I called him. We stayed in contact after the trip, and he often called to stay on his progresses around the country. He was a hard, self-centred man in many ways – another factor in his survival – but like so many street-wise, small men, he had a core of kindness in his spirit. My family and I stayed with Don and Audrey, and I recall one occasion when our six-year-old daughter made him toss a balloon between them for some considerable time. Don clearly enjoyed the game, but only let this show when he thought no one was looking. I also recall that both he and I had to renew our passports by calling in person at the Liverpool office because of a civil servants' strike. As we stood in the queue he said, 'I'm getting on a bit now – I expect this will be my last passport . . .'[30]

Don's own account of the British Autana Expedition amounts to two brief diary entries: '21 October. Killed fer-de-lance.' '22 October. On summit of Kukenam – went to Hobbit Garden.' Whether he found any 'fucking fairies!' there is not on record (see page 27, note 1), but the following April he was immersed – literally – in the fairy-tale world under the surface of the Red Sea. Jack

---

[30] Derek Walker: 'We always thought at this time that his attitudes were very old. For example, he would say to me, "You'd better get that early retirement deal as soon as you're 50, Derek, so that we can do some trips, 'cos when you're 60 you really are absolutely fucked.' Sad to compare him with what Joe and Chris and loads more have managed since passing 60 . . .'

Jackson, one of the 'London Sherpas' on the 1970 Annapurna Expedition, and now one of the world's most respected underwater photographers, explains:

When Don moved from Rossendale to Penmaenmawr he really started to develop his interest in tropical marine fishes. Whilst in Tobago in 1980, he tried taking a diving course, but the instructor took him down to 100 feet on his first dive, and not surprisingly this put him off. In the 1980s I was spending part of every year running a dive boat in the Sudan Red Sea, so in April 1982 he came out to give me a hand. The situation was perfect for him, based on an artificial island on a coral atoll 17 miles out to sea. It was a pure, self-contained expedition situation, with some of the world's best visibility and fish life. He soon learnt to dive, and was a great help to me running the boat, and lifting heavy anchors, compressors and diving cylinders. Don always showed his best side when conditions were difficult. We had one spell of very bad gales where he helped me keep the boat safely lashed to the jetty, through different wind changes, all through the night. He wanted to see sharks, but like any newcomer was afraid of them, so I would hide him behind the coral while I fed them.[31]

Another activity he pursued briefly at this time was sky-diving, in which he took a course in Florida.

Still – these diversions apart – he hankered after the Himalayas, and pestered Doug Scott, who was planning another of his loosely structured sorties to go to the Karakoram in 1983, for an invitation. 'I'm fancying another eight-thousander,' he had written to Doug, 'before I'm done.' The invitation came – albeit with an admonitory note that this time he had better shape up and start to take his share of the work if he were not to alienate the members of the new and dynamic young team who would be travelling out there. 'He still thought I owed him one, and thought it would be good,' said Scott, 'but he had no enthusiasm for getting fit.' And so – holding to his usual dictum that an approach march was training enough for a

---

[31] In the course of a year in which he travelled to the Sudan, Nepal and Iceland, Don got his own back on the sharks by catching two of them whilst deep-sea fishing off Cornwall.

major Himalayan climb, and with the intention of attempting Broad Peak – in April Don left Wales to spend the next three months, and his real fiftieth birthday, on his last trip to the Greater Ranges.

The stellar cast for this last act in the 26-year drama of Don's personal involvement with the Himalayas included Doug and Greg Child; young British stars Andy Parkin, Roger Baxter-Jones and Al Rouse; the Frenchman Jean Afanassief, a British climbing doctor, Pete Thexton, and the American Steve Sustad. After an arduous journey, they reached K2 base camp and paid the porters off: 'As they leave, Whillans watches them disappear into the rocky glacier. "That's the best sight in the Karakoram," he told Child, ". . . the backs of our porters, heading home."' Don wrote to Audrey to give her the news:

> Arrived at K2 base camp four days ago. Doug and four others stayed at Urdokas to try to climb a rock-peak[32] – they should arrive in about three days. The boys here have gone off to recce the ridge on K2 (eight hours away!!). I've just washed all my clothes and am sorting my gear for climbing, probably Hermann Buhl's route on Broad Peak (over 26,000 feet). We can see two Polish girls trying it through our glasses. It has been a tough slog to get here, but is an impressive area, a bit too rugged for trekking. Don't know what will happen about the climbs, or who does what, but this kind of team seems to lessen the sense of purpose. I haven't had any problems (apart from being slow) so far. The spot is at about 16,500 feet, and I'm not pushing myself any more than I have to. I won't start climbing for another four or five days, weather permitting, until I get acclimatised here. A good bath would be favourite, with a proper dinner second. I hear 'Maggie'[33] is in power again – Thank God! I expect I'll stay the full time, though if we climbed Broad Peak and the weather was lousy I might start trekking back. Four Spaniards arriving – might have to make a cup of tea. Cheerio for now. Don XXXX.

The background to the dissatisfaction expressed in the letter about 'this kind of team' is given by Greg Child: 'Doug . . . hoped

---

[32] The Lobsang Spire – climbed by Child, Thexton and Scott after an earlier attempt by Rouse and Parkin had failed because of bad weather.
[33] I.e. Margaret Thatcher.

to shed the traditional hierarchical structure of an expedition and for us to move about the mountains in pairs or groups, climbing with whoever we felt comfortable with, as one would in Yosemite or Chamonix.' Child goes on to comment that 'the plan was idealistic, perhaps demanding more flexibility from us than we were capable of giving'. There was dissent from early in the expedition:

'Well, Doug,' said Roger [Baxter-Jones], 'I'm afraid that your plan for us all to climb with each other simply isn't going to work. Teams have been formed and I doubt that they'll change. I personally have no intention of taking risks on big peaks with people whose experience in the Himalayas is limited, or who are too old. I mean, let's be realistic – alpining eight-thousanders is a bloody serious business.'

Roger spoke openly and honestly, so much so that Don got up and left the tent. But Roger was right. It was imperative that we have absolute faith in our partners for these ambitious climbs.[34]

Baxter-Jones became even more direct after Don had left the tent:

'What about Gohar – is he the tenth member?' he added pointedly. The issue of Gohar was a conundrum to us all. Though he'd been invaluable in organising the shuttle of loads up the Baltoro his presence as one of the climbing team wasn't welcomed by everyone.

'Well,' said Doug, 'Gohar has a lot of experience at 8000 metres, yet on all his expeditions management has cut him off before the summit. I thought it'd be a good gesture to give him a chance for the summit of Broad Peak. Not to mention the fact that he could team up with old Don.' Doug whispered the last sentence.

'Well I won't be roping up with Gohar or Don. Gohar is a high-altitude porter – all he's ever done is jumar ropes and carry loads. And Don is too old and slow. He won't even make a cup of tea,' said Roger.

---

[34] K2 alpine-style was one of the team's objectives.

And so, on his last expedition, Don was sidelined from the climbing strength of the team, regarded as the odd man out, and was paired off, as he complained bitterly in his letters to Audrey, with a black man, whilst the rest of the team were 'rushing around like blue-arsed flies' with 'no idea of the proper way to get the job done'. Even Doug was gradually withdrawing, distancing himself from Don, pursuing his own ambitions. Only the young Australian, Greg Child, was ready to lend an attentive and friendly ear to Don's complaints: ' ". . . bloody typical of this crew. Couldn't organise a fuck in a brothel," sneers Don.' And to his reminiscences and beliefs:

'Back in the fifties when I was a lad, it was a real event if you met another expedition in the mountains. Now all you do is fall over every other bugger and his dog. I remember meeting Buhl and his mates in Skardu – now there was a bunch of blokes worth meeting . . . all this alpine-style nonsense. In my day an expedition was an expedition. Everyone worked for the same thing. On this trip, I'm buggered if I know what we're working towards. All these jaunts here and there – we're all over the bloomin' place, up and down like a bride's nightie.'[35]

'It's a different philosophy, Don, a different time.'

'Aye. Then I'm glad it passed me by and I did my climbs when they counted for something.'

And because Child had the insight and patience to get through Don's habitual aggressions and criticisms and resentments, he began to get through to the better side of the man: 'Up until that point Don had been a caricature of the tales I had heard of him, speaking in a dialect of witticisms and wisecracks. Now that the numbers were pared down he began to talk more seriously . . .'

There was soon matter for him to be talking more seriously about. With Don and Gohar trailing in their wake, Child and Pete Thexton climbed up through the camps on Broad Peak, ascending

---

[35] A favourite late-period Whillans-ism, this, which I've come across in three different written sources as well as having heard Don himself use it. This degree of repetition does point up how rehearsed, or even jaded, the routines and the patter – the comic, defensive front – had become by the 1980s.

11,000 feet in the space of 60 hours. It was too much, too soon. After reaching the false summit at 26,382 feet on the final, lateral ridge, both had to retreat, Greg suffering from cerebral, Thexton from pulmonary oedema. A dreadful descent into the night, Thexton blind and increasingly incapable, brought them back to the two tents of the camp at 24,500 feet, at which Don and Gohar had arrived. Thexton was taken in with Don and Gohar, given hot drinks. 'I'll watch him, lad,' Don told Greg, who then went into the other tent to sleep. At dawn, with Gohar pressing liquid he had asked for to his lips, Thexton's eyes rolled back in his head. Greg was called, tried resuscitation, but to no avail. Thexton was gone.

'Notice that the wind has suddenly dropped?' asked Don. 'Not a breath. It's always the same when death is about, always a lot of noise and wind, but as soon as it gets what it's after it quietens down. I've seen it before and it's always the same.'

Greg, Gohar and Don zipped up the tent, leaving Thexton's body behind them, and descended to base camp, where the conversation, news of Thexton's death having been assimilated, was focused around the remaining teams' ambitions on K2. One of the team tried to engage Don in conversation: 'About your position on K2, Don . . .' 'I've got no position on K2,' he snapped back. Child describes how he responded next:

> Whillans . . . got up and went to his tent, returning with his still-nearly-full bottle of whisky. He opened it, tipped it back, took a gulp that made him gasp, then passed it around. After a nip from each of us he finished the contents in two or three mighty swigs. 'This is how I say goodbye to my mates,' he said, thumping the empty bottle on the crate in front of him. From the moment he had seen Pete, when we dragged him into the tent, he'd known nothing we could do would save him. He now sought to anaesthetise that memory. As the booze coursed through his veins he began to stagger and roar about the tent, his wildness driving all away . . .[36]

---

[36] Don made his views on how unnecessary, and how direct a result of fast alpine-style ascents, he felt Thexton's death to be at a joint Alpine Club/Alpine Climbing Group symposium on 'Lightweight Expeditions to the Greater Ranges' held in March 1984, when he compared Thexton's death to that of Bob Downes on Masherbrum in 1957, and to a hushed audience posed the question of how much, in a quarter-century, had mountaineers learnt?

The following morning Don and Child began the long walk out through Urdokas to Gilgit, to get news back to Thexton's parents in England. They parted company in Islamabad:

'Tooroo, youth, I'll be off now,' he said, casual as ever, bidding me goodbye at the gate of the residence we were staying in. 'Just a minute,' I called, and thrust my hand into his. 'At least a handshake after all this . . .' He clenched my hand firmly, perhaps thankfully, grinned, then disappeared into the hot night.

Greg's impressions[37] of Don, based on the 1981 and 1983 expeditions, are warm and judicious:

My sense of him is that he was a sheep in wolf's clothing; a guy who played with a hard exterior but who was really a soft-hearted person. I think, being a youngster, that I was the recipient of his kindness in a fatherly way – especially after the sadness on Broad Peak. He had very traditional British chauvinistic attitudes, particularly towards women, whom he regarded as bad additions to an expedition. He was conscious of the weight of his own legend, and seemed to regard his presence on a trip, or at times when we were recipients of the hospitality of British Embassy staff in Islamabad, as a privilege for those around him. Now this is often where Don wore out his welcome. I recall he blew their minds in Islamabad by guzzling their booze and eating them out of house and home. On the expeditions, he never lifted a domestic finger, expecting young lads like me to act as serfs and tend to him as his wife would. Still, it actually was a privilege to be privy to his tales of the past. Two slight incidents I remember particularly. At Skardu on the walk out after Pete Thexton's death, he was telling me the tale about his friend Bob Downes, who died of the same cause on Masherbrum 26 years before. Gradually it dawned on him that he couldn't be buried too far away from where we were, so we set off to search for the grave. I noticed that, as we wandered about quite aimlessly, he was getting more and

---

[37] From personal correspondence dated 27 December 1991.

more anxious about this search, and the usually aloof exterior was showing cracks; he really wanted to find his companion's grave, make contact with the past and his own prime, and when we didn't find it there was a moment of sadness and vulnerability in him, then very quickly he put on his tough exterior and we walked back to the K2 Hotel.

The other incident is more trivial and light-hearted. At an embassy party in Islamabad the hostess offered us a plate of hors d'oeuvres, on which were some sunflower seeds. I gobbled the seeds and noticed Don eyeing me as I did so. 'Have some, Don – they're good!' I said. 'No, youth, not me – they'll send you loopy,' he replied. It came out as we discussed this that he firmly believed sunflower seeds had psychedelic properties: 'I've seen Harris into those, and he got high as a kite.' I can only imagine that Harris had once conned Don into believing they were a drug.[38] The whole gathering of very straight embassy folk thought this all quite odd, being told by Don that they were drugging out on the seeds and being buffaloed by him into not touching them, as he carried on swilling the booze and getting belligerently drunk.

The last note to be sounded from the 1983 expedition comes from Doug Scott, and is one of regret:

I'm sorry, now, that I didn't get Don up the mountain, and he would have made it, with encouragement – he got up to close on 25,000 feet with no acclimatisation problems. OK, he was slow, and Gohar was quite legitimately complaining about the weight of the load he was carrying and the amount of trail-breaking he had to do when climbing with Don. But even so, Don would have made it if we'd been more supportive. But at that time we were all ambitious, had our own plans, and

---

[38] Almost certainly true – Harris used to enjoy winding people up, and Don's pugnacious response to the drugs which freely circulated at his parties was grist to his mill. I can remember a very drunk Whillans delivering a long and censorious lecture to the spliffing-up contingent in Harris's kitchen one night about the perils of cannabis. His one-man campaign didn't seem to find many followers, though it did provoke a certain degree of hilarity. On one occasion, with Don dead-drunk and asleep, propped in a corner of the sofa, Harris set up a photograph of him with a joint in his mouth – all good, innocent fun. I have no recollection of whether anyone ever dared show it to Don . . .

with Al [Rouse] being there an element of competition came in, so Don got marginalised and it didn't happen . . .

Having bade farewell, consciously or not, to the Himalayas, Don spent the British summer travelling around friends' houses and climbing club meets, often on one of the motorbikes he owned. He snorkelled in Cornwall and climbed a little. In Wales, too, he followed several rock-climbs – Creagh Dhu Wall at Tremadog, Pentathol and Dream of White Horses on the great Anglesey sea-cliffs of Craig Gogarth and North Stack – in a flurry of activity that was his concession to training for two television climbing programmes in which he had been invited to feature. He flew out to America in October, lectured, went wine-tasting in the Napa Valley and on a visit to Alcatraz, boated down the Grand Canyon of the Colorado River in a dory, climbed the East Face of Mount Whitney with Larry Giacomino and Buck Ravenscroft – his gear and food being carried up to the foot of the climb by Audrey – and spent a nostalgic and inactive week in Yosemite in the late fall, returning from America in time for the British Mountaineering Council's 1984 National Mountaineering Conference, then held in Buxton in March.[39] One of the guest speakers was Pat Ament, with whom he had climbed in Colorado nearly 20 years before:

> After my lecture I was in a room with a big mirror and those light bulbs around its edge. Whillans was suddenly standing behind me, staring silently at me in the mirror. I glanced up and saw him. He was the same old Whillans, with a little bigger stomach. When we were outside he heard a couple of younger climbers discussing the merits of mental versus physical strength, and interjected, 'What if you don't 'ave either?' I said to him, 'You look good.' He replied, 'I'm still alive,' and pointing up to the sky he chuckled, 'They don't want me up there. I'll go down there!' He pointed at the floor, then spoke of his new interest, scuba-diving, told me how easy it was to do a one-finger pull-up underwater. To read the programme for the conference, he donned a pair of octagonal

---

[39] Don had headed the bill at this event in 1982, when his talk on 'My Life and Hard Times' was interrupted by a streaker, about whom Don commented to his audience, 'Well I'll be buggered, and so will 'e be if I get 'old of 'im.' This should not be taken as proof of incipient homosexual tendencies on Don's part.

bi-focals that sat low on his nose. He participated in the conference as a member of a discussion panel, and his insights brought tumult: 'Don, how do you feel about climbing versus marriage – it's said that they don't mix?' Don, by this time drunk, responds, 'Is that a two-part question?' Later he took part in a fashion show where he and several other well-known British climbers were got up in drag and paraded on stage. He raised the back of his dress to the female judges to reveal solid, gnarly legs. He was awarded the beauty queen title, and sat on stage on a throne, hailed by the masses, drunk as a lord, a paper crown fastened to a climber's helmet on his head.

I remember Don at the Kendal Film Festival that year, taking part in a celebrity quiz. He was drunk again. He didn't need to say anything meaningful, because the instant he opened his mouth the clapping was immediate and deafening. There was little of the sharpness any more, the instantly responsive wit – just his presence was what was being applauded, and he accepted the compliment with a benign, slightly vacant smile. In April he travelled out to the Red Sea again to pursue his new interest as Jack and Babs Jackson wrote, 'this time bringing with him Audrey, and Derek Bromhall of Genesis Films, with a view to making an underwater film for Channel Four. He and Audrey[40] snorkelled more than they dived, but they saw just about every fish in the sea, including a couple of shark scares that had them "walking on water". They spent many hours each day round the reef, and we had trouble getting them out of the water to eat.'

The television programmes he was to record were to be filmed in August and October. He put in a minimum of physical preparation, following Variety Show, an HVS in the Great Zawn at Bosigran, behind Derek Walker, and experiencing a little difficulty in getting his paunch round an overhang on the top pitch. The television invitations had come from the two men with whom he had shared some of his best climbs. From Joe Brown, the proposal was that they do an ascent of Cemetery Gates together; from Chris Bonington, that they share one of the programmes in a Border Television series entitled *Lakeland Rock*. The idea for the

---

[40] 'Resplendent in eye-catching swimsuit, and a bathing hat ornamented with a psychedelic profusion of rubber flowers.' (Derek Bromhall)

latter was that Chris, using the gear available at the time of its first ascent,[41] would lead Don up Dovedale Grooves. It was filmed a day later than planned, to give Don a chance to recover from a monumental binge in the hotel on television expenses. Of the climb itself, he commented rather tortuously that:

> It was bloody hard, but the top part which many people regard as the hardest pitch, because it's an overhanging crack in a chimney, I can actually take quite a lot of my body weight off my arms. That's the type of climbing I used to do. I could reduce my body weight by getting my shoulder on the rock and leaning my backside on one wall. Other people I know find it very hard, that . . .

The programme with Joe was filmed on a damp early October day. Don arrived at Pont Cromlech on his Kawasaki, smoking a cigarette behind his helmet visor. 'Is that to protect your head, or keep your fag dry?' quipped Joe. The relationship between the two men came across as edgy, distant, but still with a residual respect. Don told of his training routine – three square meals a day, six pints of beer a night, the fags . . . He panted up to the foot of the cliff, clothes tight on him, eyes narrowed beneath the flat hat. Joe, at 54, led the climb in the wet conditions smoothly and easily, and the banter between them devolved around restoring Don's weight to the nine-stone mark by tension on the rope. I look back on it, and it seems to me one of the sadder pieces of television I have seen – the cult hero revelling in his own self-destruction; his humour coming across as laboured, trite; and his former companion – against whom, privately, he had vented so much spleen – reticent, watchful, caring, capable and skilled; and skilled Don too must have been to haul, with a little help from his friend, 14½ stone of blubber up one of the great climbs of his youth, his feet in their antiquated EB's imprecise in placement, his hands snatching for the holds.

That was Don's last completed climb. He plunged back into the social round. John Cleare remembers him descending on the Waterloo Hotel at Betws-y-Coed one night:

---

[41] A few line slings and a pair of plimsolls – very bold on Chris's part, particularly as the old frictional black rubber plimsolls he had worn in the early 1950s were no longer made, and the new ones he wore for the programme were very slippery.

He waddled in – really waddled. He was ashen-faced and obviously very unfit. He wore a Hawaiian shirt and a pair of khaki-drill pants, but someone had opened the top of the side seam on the pants and let in a wide triangular gusset of not-quite-matching material to accommodate his belly. The effect was bizarre. I introduced him all round and everyone had heard of him. After several pints they all went off to bed. I stopped drinking, but Don carried on relentlessly and I had to sit with him. After several more pints – all of them on my slate at the bar (Don knew that I was on expenses, of course) – I suggested I ought to go to bed, but no! he wanted one more. It must have been after 3 a.m. when the barman went on strike and Don had to leave. I shepherded him out – to his camper van. 'I don't drink and drive any more – I camp in the car park,' he said. He was gone in the morning by the time we got up.

His old mate from Torre Egger, Leo Dickinson, also ran into him at about this time, and gives the following impression of their parting:

He climbed into his motor-cycle leathers and pulled out a pair of spectacles:
    'I didn't know you wore glasses, Don?'
    'They were me dad's – pre-war – got me mam's as well.'
    'Do they work properly?'
    'They're almost alright, but I 'ave to keep taking 'em off for reading!'
    'You need bi-focals!'
    'Aye, but they're quite expensive.'
    'I'm sure you can get them on the National Health.'
    'Perhaps you can – if you're a member.'
    He kick started his bike, waved 'Tarra' and that was the last I saw of him.

The deaths of family and friends seemed to be tolling for his own mortality: Nikki Clough had died of cancer in 1983; his mother died at the beginning of February 1985; on 17 May that year, a new friend, but a man of whom he had long known by reputation and through his new climbs of the 1940s and early 1950s in Cumbria, died whilst he and Don were climbing together on Clogwyn Du'r Arddu. He had met Bill Peascod through the Border Television series, one of the programmes in which was devoted to Peascod leading Bonington up Eagle Front in Birkness Coombe above Buttermere – a climb of which Peascod had made the first ascent as a 20-year-old in 1940, and which is rightly regarded as one of the best of its grade in Britain. Whillans and the stocky, affable ex-miner-turned-painter from Maryport had established an instant rapport, and had been looking forward with excitement to sharing Peascod's first climb on the best of Welsh cliffs. With Ronnie Wathen, Bill Birkett, Jack and Babs Jackson, they walked up on a fine May morning, stopping for tea at Halfway House before scrambling beneath the West Buttress to the start of Colin Kirkus's bold exploratory journey of 1930, the Great Slab. With Don at the top of the crucial first pitch, having led it, Peascod started to climb, and almost immediately slumped on the rope, suffering from a massive heart attack. Jack Jackson spent nearly an hour trying to resuscitate him, Ronnie Wathen ran to Clogwyn station to alert Mountain Rescue and summon a helicopter, and Don abseiled down from his stance. As Babs Jackson helped him coil the ropes, he told her, 'It was a good way for Bill to go, doing what he loved doing best – and at least it was quick.' After the helicopter had taken Bill's body away, the five of them walked down, Don striding ahead, silent, alone with his thoughts.

I met him on a couple of occasions at this time, and the memories I have of them reflect very clearly the two sides of his personality – the abrasiveness on the one hand, the strange tenderness of which he was sometimes capable on the other. The first of them was a Climbers' Club dinner at Bamford's Marquis of Granby Hotel in Derbyshire. I was the main speaker after the dinner, and as I gave my speech I noticed Don and an old Climbers' Club member, Ivan Waller, with heads together glowering at me. My book *Menlove*[42] had just been published. I was standing around afterwards when I saw Don heading towards me, drunk and aggressive: 'What's all this yer bin writing, about J.M. Edwards bein' a fuckin' queer?' was his opening salvo, and he went on in that vein, making it quite

---

[42] The biography of John Menlove Edwards (Gollancz, 1985), greatest of pre-war climbing pioneers and a fascinating and tragic character, who was psychiatrist, adventurer, conscientious objector, homosexual and lover of Wilfrid Noyce, and the best of all writers about rock-climbing.

apparent that Ivan had been winding him up and expressing to him a degree of anger felt by several of the older generation of club members that Menlove's homosexuality should have been openly addressed. Over the preceding weeks I had had a bellyful of this, and now I lost my temper and rounded furiously on Don: why didn't he read the book for himself and make his own mind up instead of trotting out other people's opinions, and until he did so, why didn't he shut the fuck up? His eyes narrowed, he conceded the point. We sat down together, and I said I'd send him a copy or bring him one round (which I later did). We talked awhile, pleasantly, then a big Loughborough PE student came and sat opposite, challenged him to arm-wrestling, and that soon got out of hand, Don red-faced and livid as he strove to win.

A month or two later I walked into the Pen-y-Gwryd Hotel early one evening and Don was there alone. He took me by the arm, pulled me to the bar, and asked me what I was having. He bought the drinks, and we went to sit in the little room opposite, me wondering what this was about.

'I read yer book,' he started, fixing me with narrowed eyes, face breaking into a smile. 'I think there's one or two things in there that you might regret writing in twenty years' time, but yer did a good job.'

The generosity of it, the considered delivery, the graciousness of the implied apology, were utterly heart-warming. It was the last contact I was to have with him, and I am glad for the positive memory. Days later he was flying to Majorca, to spend a month in Deia at the house of Ronnie Wathen.

That was the month I lived alone with him, cooked for him ('Eh, what's that? Olive oil? Can't stand olive oil.' 'Eh, what's that? Garlic? Can't stand garlic'). One night we were preparing for a party and I had cleaned up, but there was a pile of unplaceable knick-knacks under a bench. Don saw them and attacked them with his boot. They offended his sense of order. He was, in his last years at any rate, a compulsive tidy-upper, though he never did any housework. He had arrived for a month with only a small rucksack. He spread his pens and paper neatly squared on a table. They remained like that. Yet in Chamonix as a youth, the forecourt of his tent had been a pig-sty. My wife Asta thought him a very dubious character, and other epithets bestowed on him in Deia were 'Mr Grumpy', 'a washup', etc. A fat, rich, young American woman who always had a drink and a fag in her hand stormed up to him one day and shrilled, 'Why are you smoking, and you a mountaineer?' Quick as a ricochet, he drawled back, 'I 'ave to give the mountain a chance.' The women might have disapproved, but there was a lot of male bonding about Don. You didn't rat on your mates, particularly if you were getting women on the side. I mentioned one on a postcard, and he said never do that, Audrey might read it. I think my favourite story must come from ✷✷✷✷✷✷, who was putting him up when he was over in Dublin to do a lecture once. At the party after this another woman, who appeared to be an old intimate of his, appeared and dragged him off home with her. 'Who was that?' asked a rather peeved ✷✷✷✷✷✷ when he returned next morning. 'Never seen her before – don't know her name,' said Don.

There is the Tebbit rottweiler brain to take into account, which is so hard to reconcile with his wisdom. ('Amnesty, eh? what's that?' 'Saving doctors and lawyers from torture.' 'Why?' 'Just to annoy you, Don. That's why I'm a member . . .') He spent his last hours in our house reading that Super-Rot Churchill[43] ('Gas the Iraqis!') and totally ignoring a noisy party of Deia drunks stampeding all around him. He was a Falklander, I was a Malvinas man. He didn't – outside the confines of an Imperial Expedition – travel well, and was scared of Europeans. His most frequently recounted story was of a mugging attempt in Barcelona. Barcelona is a notorious muggers' town, and the rule is, don't be seen carrying a suitcase there, so Don comes out of this well. But the point is his anxiety. He had Audrey's suitcase in his hand. They were standing outside a shop window. A youth blusters up, and says a bird has messed down the back of his jacket. It's white paint sprayed by a second member of the gang. Youth starts wiping it off. Third youth rugby-swerves past to gather up the suitcase Don should have put down, but hadn't – too bright to be caught like that! But the point is, it wouldn't have

---

[43] It's the war-time premier and patron saint of Little England to whom Wathen is referring here.

happened to me or you – he wasn't, in Europe, streetwise, and this came out of his Englishness,[44] his unwillingness or inability to learn from others.

Don's plans for the summer took him away from Deia early in July. He had arranged to meet his old friend from the Rock & Ice, Harry Smith, out in the Dolomites later that month: 'We want to do classic climbs, climbs of great character and a fair standard of difficulty. The modern climbs would be too hard for us, and wouldn't have the appeal.' He rode out to Alleghe on his Kawasaki.[45] Harry Smith didn't arrive. His old friend Derek Walker was there, preparing to climb the Philip-Flamm route on the Civetta. Don lent him and his partner a pair of waterproof trousers for the ascent. Another acquaintance at the campsite was Roger Salisbury: 'I had proposed to climb with him, but he was so hideously unfit that walking up to the hut was almost beyond him, so any climbing was totally out of the question. It was all very sad – he seemed to be adrift in time and space. It was good talking about bikes and the past, but there was nothing else.'

I have a snapshot of Don in his shorts entirely filling a folding chair under an awning on the campsite, a glass in his hand, dimpling fat obscuring the musculature of those mighty arms, breasts like a woman's and a billowing midriff. With nothing for him in Alleghe he turned for home, rode through Italy and France in the rain, and on reaching England decided to visit his Tunisian acquaintance Roy Hardcastle in Berkshire.

I was working for an American computer company and received a call saying a Mr Whillans was on the phone. He was on his way back from the Dolomites and invited himself on a visit to us for a few days. He walked in through the huge, open-plan office, a diminutive figure wearing a crash helmet and with a rucksack as big as he was strapped to his back. Dumping his rucksack on the floor and his crash-hat on my desk, he lit a fag (it was a non-smoking office, of course), and

---

[44] Ronnie Wathen was Irish; as a Welshman, it's a point with which I cannot help but agree.
[45] A GT550 – a light and compact bike with no weather protection, an upright riding position, good handling, and an unburstable four-cylinder engine.

said, 'D'yer fancy a pint?' The other 70-odd people in the office would have looked less surprised if a small Martian had walked in. He stayed with us for the next few days, cheerfully eating us out of house and home and working his way through my supply of Scotch. Most nights we went to my local, the White Hart in Eversley. On the Thursday night he felt unwell. A whisky 'all-in' seemed to do the trick, but he was under the weather. We had thought about going to the British Grand Prix on the Sunday, but the weather was lousy Friday and Saturday and I decided it wasn't worth the trip. Don decided to head up to Oxford on the Saturday afternoon. We stood in the drive to say goodbye as he mounted his bike. 'Ta-ra the noo and thanks for having us,' he said as he rode off. Louise looked at the six inches of bare leg between his boots and trousers (he didn't wear socks), and said sadly, 'He'll catch his death.' 'No,' I said, 'he's tough as old boots . . .'

Derek Bromhall takes up the story:

He arrived in Oxford tired, wet and chilled to the bone, and unwound over a jar or three of beer and a meal – chicken casserole, which he thought was so good that he asked Julia to write down the recipe for him to pass on to Audrey. After supper we packed him off to bed so that he would be in good shape for Silverstone next day. During the night an unusual sound awoke me, and I looked in on Don to see that he was all right. He seemed to be sleeping peacefully. In the morning he did not appear for breakfast but we decided to let him sleep on. Later, when he still had not appeared and we were concerned that he would be late for Silverstone, I went to wake him. He was lying as I had last seen him, but the colour had drained from his face and I realised that he was dead. During the night, in his sleep, his heart had stopped beating.

The cause of death was given as myocardial ischaemia; the date was 4 August 1985. He was 52 years old. His funeral service was held at Bangor crematorium in North Wales a few days later, hundreds gathering for it, attentive to every word of Dennis Gray's address, with its rehearsal of all the legends, its fondness, its apostrophising of this 'pocket Hercules'. Along with the sense of loss, of the passing of something titanic from the small world of mountaineers, there went too a sense of its timeliness. Ronnie Wathen again:

> Ah, Don, I'm afraid Chris was right: you died at just the right time. Any older and you'd have become a perfect pest to us. Walking down the Chomolungma Glacier minutes before I met an incoming party who gave me the news, I had been obsessed all morning with our forthcoming Mount Kenya trip together. I was going to disinvite you. And we would not have got to the summit with you along . . .

Hard recognition from a good old friend. Yet he was right. Don's summit had been reached 15 years before, and even then he had been on the way down. In his fifties some of the royalties and sponsorship were beginning to dwindle or dry up, the wit was slowing down, the stories becoming threadbare self-caricature, the lifestyle more than ever self-destructive. As to the end, 'at least it was quick' – and peaceful, which is not, I think, a quality that had distinguished and blessed much of Don's life. 'His eyes (ice-blue) would narrow with the look/Of a trapped ferret, he snarled as he spoke,' wrote Wathen in 'Don's Ode', before concluding, with an ambivalence that always hovers around recollections of the man, '. . . the greatest Climber of our age,/A man of supreme strength, supreme courage,/The supreme friend, if you could avoid his rage.'

Envoi

Chew Piece, Autumn Twilight

Now that my ladder's gone,
I must lie down where all the ladders start,
In the foul rag-and-bone shop of the heart.
                                    W. B. Yeats

On the lee side of Chew Piece Plantation, huddled among moss and boulders out of a bluster of west wind, shadows lengthening, I sit and look around at a landscape I have known since the last golden summer of the 1950s. For me then as a 12-year-old, as for Don at the beginning of that decade, this place was one to which I came time and again: a focal point, a magnet, a lode-star. I would catch the cream-coloured Oldham Transport double-decker at Stevenson Square for the 10-mile bus-ride from the centre of Manchester to Greenfield. All the way up from Oldham, excitement mounting, I could see the Pennine moors rising in front. From the end of the journey at the Clarence Inn I would walk alongside the dye-stained beck that flowed down past the mills, and find my way to Chew Piece to pitch my tent on one of the little greens above the Chew Brook, as Don had done less than 10 years before.

It was not then as it is now – the huge grass wall of the Dovestones Reservoir dam, completed in the late 1960s, has changed it. But in those days it was somewhere of peculiar magic. It was where I began both to walk wild, and to rock-climb. Time and again favourite circuits: up that enticing green track called the Chew Road on to Laddow Moss and Black Chew Head, then north along the rim of Crowden Great Brook to Red Ratcher and Grains Moss before westering across heather where mountain hares, white in winter, rear up to watch you passing and the golden plover's plaintive call choruses the spring, over Howels Head Flat for the head of Birchen Clough, and stumbling down past the waterfalls in the flagged stream under the Raven Stones to return by that mysterious, splashy waterworks tunnel between the Greenfield and Yeoman Hey Reservoirs below Bill o'Jacks. These names are poetry to me, and these too: Alphin Pike, Charnel Clough, Dishstones Moss, Hoarstone Edge; and this beginning is not so different from Don's own escape from the city. He would have known these ways, these names with all their redolence, northern British to the core, and delighted in the bleakness, and the space.

I saw the people on the crags here with their ropes, their skill, wanted that mastery. On Wimberry Rocks at 12 years old, an old hemp rope trailing behind me and my friend Ricky Richardson vaguely paying it out, I led the Sloping Crack and thus lost my sanity for decades: such intensity of thrill. Thereafter, every weekend, every holiday, rocks and moors; I was one of a generation of 'Greenfield Lads', among whom lingered a few survivors from those of Don's time. I remember my companions now as though they were benign elder brothers: Brian and Alan Ripley, Paul Fletcher, Jack MacCormack, Dave Featherstone. They taught so well and gave so much. I know too climbers of other generations who have left here the signs of their passing, the tokens of their accomplishment: Malcolm Baxter, Nick Plishko, Dougie Hall, John Allen, Chris Hardy. A glance up at Wimberry Rocks, finest of all the gritstone crags, and the features they climbed in the 1960s and beyond, the features Joe – the inveterate enthusiast, still active in his mid-seventies, still finding delight – climbed in the 1940s, are all there, ranged across the rim of the moor, instantly recognisable to me, the signatures now of quiet, modest, accomplished men.

By some strange conjuring trick, although none of the climbs here are his, Don himself is assimilated into the spirit of the place in a way no other from the history of climbing approaches. Gritstone is his rock, apotheosises his approach, slipping round his rejection of it to proclaim affinity: 'Even when we were doing those first climbs on grit, I was always thinking in terms of training for when we went to Skye in the summer.' Well, Don, that grit is now perceived as in your soul. What did you want out of climbing? Where were you making for – 'Everest', that should not even bear its Victorian Welsh country gentleman's name? Those who continue long in the practice of any discipline look beyond reward and acquisition to the nature of the thing, and its joy. What awareness of that truth did we have when we camped on these streamside greens, lit our fires, played boyish games and talked long into nights that knew nothing of lives to come?

At the edge of the old plantation I sit on moss, my back to a boulder, feet on a gritstone slab into which is stilled an eddying wave-pattern from aeons past. The sound of the stream drifts up to where I rest, its water peat-brown, a dipper working the pools. The unexpected loveliness of the place stills my breath, quietens me. Suddenly I am at peace in the presence of the trees. There are beech, birch, rowan, sessile oak, Scots pine, holly, an elegantly trailing larch, all gathered here, and the pink and umber hues and tints of the moor all around, the muted cast of landscape that expresses in greys, khakis, faint tinges of pale brown or washed-out yellow; and that cyclopean masonry of rock above on which you and I, Don, used to climb. What did we learn from it, other than that it could be overcome? Never mind what we did on the rock. What did the rock do to us – what lessons did we learn, in that unhuman sphere? What did we bring to it, and what did we take away? What choices did we make? Rancour, ego, resentment, aggression – or things more positive?

A dead tree twists and writhes, one brittle branch pointing like a finger up-valley, two more enclosing empty, heart-shaped space. Two mountain-bikers, brakes squealing, judder past on the Oldham Way; three young men wander among the boulders, dabbing chalk, pawing, essaying moves. One of them ascends, pale arms reaching out, an oddly vulnerable and imploring gesture against the dark cast of damp gritstone. I pick up a fallen leaf from among the beech-mast, and study remnant greens perfectly offset and balanced by purples, ochres, a flaring orange. It reminds me somehow of you, in your later years, musing quite softly on the beauty of the Royal Angelfish among the coral reefs of the Red Sea. I let the leaf drop, for the earthworms to draw it in, 'at night-time, noiselessly'. Were you a man who used to notice such things? I think you had that capacity, and towards the end were. On the moor-rim, rocks balance; the crags are seamed and riven; streams thread down; through and through, the same fault-lines, the same pattern, the same design, in the land, in our lives. Our fractal universe, faces and creatures in the rocks, monsters even, threatening; all's here, in our imagination, that we perceive or desire. In a beech tree two lovers have carved their initials; on a boulder too, bold lettering, the lichens softening, filling the incisions in like tissue does a scar. The western sky beyond the plantation is wild with sunset, a wind sweeping through, dark intersections of dead branches against the dancing leaves. Here in Chew Piece at autumn twilight, some healing power is at work; and I hope your spirit feels it too and finds rest:

If the place I want to arrive at could only be reached by a ladder, I would give up trying to arrive at it. For the place I really have to reach is where I must already be.

Ludwig Wittgenstein

Select Bibliography

Pat Ament, *High Endeavours* (Mountain 'n' Air, 1991). Beautiful essay-writing by one of American climbing's great literary stylists.

Adrian Bailey, *Lakeland Rock: Classic Climbs with Chris Bonington* (Border Television, 1985).

Chris Bonington, *Annapurna South Face* (Cassell, 1971); *I Chose to Climb* (Gollancz, 1966); *The Next Horizon* (Gollancz, 1966); *The Next Horizon* (Gollancz, 1973); *The Everest Years* (Hodder & Stoughton, 1986). Re-issued in one volume, *Boundless Horizons*, by Weidenfeld & Nicolson, these last three titles together constitute one of the most vivid and engaging – and consistently under-rated – climbing autobiographies ever written.

Joe Brown, *The Hard Years* (Gollancz, 1967). Honest and generous – interesting, too, where the ghost-writer allowed Joe to speak in his own voice.

Eric Byne and Geoff Sutton, *High Peak* (Secker & Warburg, 1966). A marvellously rich and stylish regional outdoor history, now a much-sought-after collector's item.

Greg Child, *Thin Air* (Patrick Stephens, 1988). The best account of a Himalayan novitiate ever written – indispensable!

R.W. Clark and E.C. Pyatt, *Mountaineering in Britain* (Phoenix House, 1957). Stately, if sketchy, history.

Jeff Connor, *Creagh Dhu Climber: The Life & Times of John Cunningham* (Ernest Press, 1999); *Dougal Haston: The Philosophy of Risk* (Canongate, 2002). The Cunningham book in particular is a fascinating and exhaustively researched biography.

Ingrid Cranfield, *The Challengers: British & Commonwealth Adventure Since 1945* (Weidenfeld & Nicolson, 1976).

Peter Crew, Jack Soper and Ken Wilson, *The Black Cliff* (Kaye & Ward, 1971).

Ken Crocket, *Ben Nevis: Britain's Highest Mountain* (Scottish Mountaineering Club, 1986).

Graham Desroy (ed.), *Yorkshire Gritstone* (Yorkshire

Mountaineering Club, 1989). This guide was also available bound in Lycra.

Dennis Gray, *Rope Boy* (Gollancz, 1970); *Mountain Lover* (Crowood, 1990); *Tight Rope* (Ernest Press, 1993); *Slack* (self-published, 1998). Dennis's multi-volume autobiographical project is the perfect counterpoint to the Bonington saga – Homer comes to Vaudeville, entrancing story-telling.

Chris Hardy and Carl Dawson, *Moorland Gritstone: Chew Valley* (British Mountaineering Council, 1988). The best-ever gritstone guide, utterly redolent of the Whillans persona and one of the keys to his character; and with Malcolm Baxter's crag diagrams to intensify the atmosphere even further.

Dougal Haston, *In High Places* (Cassell, 1972). An autobiography, of sorts.

Robert Macfarlane, *Mountains of the Mind* (Granta, 2003). A classic of modern mountain writing, unjustly dismissed in much of the outdoor press, this exquisitely written syncretic view of the history of mountain experience, produced from within a literary and allusive tradition, reworks familiar material in a subtle, wise and resonant way. I suspect its author was simply too young and too extravagantly gifted for most climbing reviewers to bear, and Kleinian envy came strongly into play in its negative reception.

Wilfrid Noyce, *To the Unknown Mountain* (Heinemann, 1962). A book considerably enlivened by the inclusion in an appendix of Whillans's account of his ride by motorbike from Rawalpindi to Rawtenstall.

Tom Patey, *One Man's Mountains* (Gollancz, 1971). Collected essays of the sublime Patey – climbing's finest humorist. Why has no one yet written his biography? I could voice a few suspicions . . .

Mirella Tenderini, *Gary Hemming: The Beatnik of the Alps* (Ernest Press, 1995). Perfectly captures the mood of 1960s alpinism.

Walt Unsworth, *Everest* (Allen Lane, 1981); *Savage Snows: The Story of Mont Blanc* (Hodder & Stoughton, 1986). Exemplary historical writing, scrupulously researched and dramatically related.

Don Whillans and Alick Ormerod, *Portrait of a Mountaineer* (Heinemann, 1971). Highly unreliable memoirs.

Ken Wilson (ed.), *Hard Rock* (Hart-Davis, MacGibbon, 1975); *The Games Climbers Play* (Diadem, 1978). The former is the first in a vastly influential series, in which Ken's formula of engaged writing and breathtaking photography revolutionised climbing publishing; the latter the best-ever climbing anthology, worth buying for Mike Thompson's 'Out With The Boys Again' alone.

Geoffrey Winthrop Young, Geoff Sutton and Wilfrid Noyce, *Snowdon Biography* (Dent, 1957). Sutton's account of rock-climbing in Wales from 1927 to 1957 remains the finest historical essay on rock-climbing ever written.

All that having been said, none of these bears comparison with A.J. Liebling's *The Sweet Science*, which will tell you more about Don Whillans than any plain and related facts ever can . . .

The author and publishers would like to thank the following for the use of previously published material: J. Allan Austin, 'Red Rose on Gritstone' from *The Climbers' Club Journal*, 1958; Adrian Bailey, *Lakeland Rock* (Border Television, 1985); Chris Bonington, *Annapurna South Face* (Cassell, 1971), *I Chose to Climb* (Gollancz, 1966), *The Everest Years* (Hodder & Stoughton, 1986); Joe Brown, *The Hard Years* (Gollancz, 1967); E. Byrne & G.J. Sutton, *High Peak* (Secker & Warburg, 1966); Greg Child, *Thin Air* (Patrick Stephens, 1998); R.W. Clark & E.C. Pyatt, *Mountaineering in Britain* (Phoenix House, 1957); Jeff Connor, *Creagh Dhu Climber: The Life and Times of John Cunningham* (Ernest Press, 1999); *Dougal Haston: The Philosophy of Risk* (Canongate, 2002); Dennis Gray, *Rope Boy* (Gollancz, 1970); *Tight Rope* (Ernest Press, 1993); Dougal Haston, *In High Places* (Cassell, 1972); Hamish MacInnes, *Climb to the Lost World* (Hodder & Stoughton, 1974); Colin Mortlock, 'Entity' from *The Climbers' Club Journal*, 1961; Tom Patey, 'A Short Walk with Whillans' from *One Man's Mountains* (Gollancz, 1971) Greg Rimmer & Mick Ryan, *Yorkshire Gritstone* (Yorkshire Mountaineering Club, 1989); Paul Ross Interview (*Leeds University Mountaineering Club Journal*, 1973); John Streetly, 'The Bloody Slab' (*Cambridge University Mountaineering Club*, 1953); Doug Scott, *Mountaineer* (Baton Wicks, 1998); Geoff Sutton, 'The Greased Pole' from *Snowdon Biography* by W. Noyce, G. Sutton & G. Young (Dent, 1957); Tom Waghorn, 'Confessions of a Yo-Yo' from *The Rucksack Club Journal*, 1961; Don Whillans & Alick Ormerod, *Portrait of a Mountaineer* (William Heinemann, 1971)

Index